D0530477

CYRIL C_____

'This excellent biography brings [Connolly] wonderfully to life.'
DIANA MOSLEY, *Evening Standard*

'Clive Fisher brings out [the] mesmeric aspect of Connolly's personality in his well-researched, sensitive and readable biography.'
PAUL JOHNSON, *Sunday Telegraph*

'Excellent . . . intelligent and sympathetic.'
CRESSIDA CONNOLLY, *Daily Mail*

'Sane and humorous.'
JOHN BAYLEY, *London Review of Books*

'A superb evocation of the lost era when gents ran literature and imperial Britain was beleaguered but still universal in its interests.'
ROBERT CARVER, *New Statesman*

'Just and well-balanced.'
PETER PARKER, *Times Literary Supplement*

'This excellent, intuitive account of Cyril Connolly's writing and life also goes far to explain why his friends were so attached to him and why his gifts and foibles are still so unfailing a theme.'
PATRICK LEIGH FERMOR

CLIVE FISHER is the editor of *Gielgud Stories* and the author of the acclaimed biography *Noël Coward*, which appeared in 1992. He has worked as a theatre, cinema, and literary critic, and his reviews have appeared in a variety of publications. He is thirty-four and lives in London.

CLIVE FISHER

CYRIL CONNOLLY

A Nostalgic Life

PAPERMAC

First published 1995 by Macmillan

This edition published 1996 by Papermac
an imprint of Macmillan Publishers Ltd
25 Eccleston Place, London SW1W 9NF
and Basingstoke

Associated companies throughout the world

ISBN 0 333 64965 6

1 3 5 7 9 8 6 4 2

A CIP catalogue record for this book is available from
the British Library.

Typeset by Parker Typesetting Service, Leicester
Printed and bound in Great Britain by
Mackays of Chatham plc, Chatham, Kent

For Alex and Charlotte di Carcaci

'What is there to say about someone who did nothing all his life but sit on his bottom and write reviews?'

Cyril Connolly to art critic John Russell[1]

CONTENTS

LIST OF ILLUSTRATIONS

SECTION ONE

INTRODUCTION

Even when he was alive Cyril Connolly's name was always invested with gossip and invention. To his contemporaries he was like Falstaff, a wit and a cause of wit in others, whilst today he animates the biographies of his famous friends as an episodic, almost comic figure who sometimes wrote great prose and often encouraged great achievement but who never fully justified the celebrity of his own cleverness. Far from combating these elaborations, Connolly encouraged them, proud of his fame and half aware of the paradox that the more he was discussed the harder he became to define. Anthony Powell considered him one of those figures who appear to have been sent into the world almost expressly to be talked about; inevitably – like Dr Johnson before him – he acquired a legend greater than the sum of his works, a legend, moreover, which has resisted oblivion and exemplified the enduring fascination of defeat: for all his claims of failure Connolly has become a part of our literary folklore, and as the centenary of his birth approaches his name is known even where his books are not.

He was alerted to the glamour of failure by his incorruptible romanticism, which also encouraged him to idealize the joys and miseries of the writer's solitude. Romantics are restless and the sanctuaries he acknowledged – the hard-won perfection of his prose and the tempting, intractable past – were remote and impalpable. Perfection was his ideology and nostalgia his instinct and it is that latter tendency which persists in Connolly's life and writing and which led him, like the proverbial sundial, to record only the golden hours in his autobiographical excursions. The following account offers a context and a complement to that documentation – of the self-proclaimed failure who will not go away – and places in his lawful limelight the supporting player of all the diaries and literary testimonies of his distracted age.

I
AN EDWARDIAN
BOYHOOD

CHAPTER ONE

CYRIL CONNOLLY believed that the first and most formative incongruity of his life established itself before his birth. He saw himself as the child of ill-assorted parents and would proclaim this misalliance to his friends and incorporate it into the scheme of facts and fiction which he constructed around the disappointments, imagined and otherwise, of his career. Genealogy, an interest he inherited from his father, complemented his nostalgia and his nervous self-regard and fortified convictions of hybrid status. On either side his forebears had been consistent, even predictable, but he alone, the hope of his father's line, seemed incongruous, pursuing an occupation rather than a profession and longing for an artist's fame instead of dull security. It was widely agreed among his adult friends that he would have made an ineffectual combatant, yet his father's family was proudly naval and military. His grandfather's grandfather, Matthew Connolly, who was born in 1740, ran away to sea and appears to have served with one of Anthony Powell's ancestors. He was known to have died at Southsea in 1790, but the rest of his life remained in obscurity. In 1960, determined to establish more about this man, after whom his grandfather and father were named, Connolly consulted Noël Blakiston, a life-long friend who worked at the Public Record Office. Blakiston resorted to ships' musters and discovered that the first Matthew Connolly had been Master Gunner of the *Britannia* and had had six sons, all of whom obtained commissions.

Connolly liked to develop extravagant theories about this ancestor: that he had run away to sea despairing of social advancement; that his tombstone had been disfigured because it had denied him his officer's rank; that he was illegitimate; that he had been the press-gang's captive. What is certain is that Matthew Connolly had at least one son who fought at Trafalgar and another, also called Matthew, who was born at Chatham, spent most of his life at sea and retired to Bath, where he died in 1853. This second Matthew's other career was of particular interest to Cyril Connolly: besides his naval activities, he was a social arbiter during the Regency and an impresario of fashion at Bath. Maritime heroism was all very well, but the vanished world of beaux and dandies held greater appeal and here was an ancestor who had witnessed the rites of the Assembly Rooms and may have glimpsed the innocent prototypes of Jane Austen's fiction as they patrolled the glorious crescents. He had taken his festive office seriously and duly accepted a chased silver claret jug inscribed with the gratitude 'To Captain Matthew Connolly late R.N. from the citizens of Bath in recognition of his invaluable services at the Winter Assembly 1831'. But it was his nephew, yet another Matthew, who perpetuated the naval tradition and the Connolly descent.

Born in 1816, he sailed the Mediterranean and the Pacific and never doubted the superiority over 'ironclads' of the wooden ships in which he learned his seamanship. Flamboyant and arresting, with tendencies towards despotism and profanity, he was also a charmer and said to be the best-looking man in the British Navy. He attained the rank of vice-admiral but his complex disposition could be put to other uses besides and in 1864, when the British Assembly convened at Bath, he met and amused Harriet Kemble, the daughter of a wealthy West Country family. In 1865 they were married at Bath Abbey and the city turned out in force to solemnize the alliance of two distinguished local families. The ceremony occurred on the bride's twentieth birthday; at forty-nine the groom was not only her senior, but also his father-in-law's. Nevertheless the wedding, as recorded in the diary of a youthful bridesmaid, went well:

> The church was so thronged I'm sure you could have walked on the people's heads. Mr Kemble performed the service alone and got through it pretty well. Old Mat looked very nice too. When the service was over we all went down into the vestry where all the kissing and congratulations flew from mouth to mouth in plenty.[1]

Harriet's father, Charles Kemble, was the Rector of Bath but he had little need of its stipend. The Kembles had amassed a fortune in the tea trade and augmented it through judicious marriages, so that Charles had not only inherited from his father but through his mother acquired the estate of Cowbridge House near Malmesbury. While still incumbent of his first living, St Michael's in Stockwell, he married a Miss Cattley, who enjoyed some family celebrity on account of an expedition she had made to Russia in 1839 and who was a kinswoman of the great botanist William Cattley who gave his name to the *Cattleya* genus of orchids, one species of which so obsessed Proust. Kemble earned praise for his pastoral diligence and with his huge legacies he turned to architecture on a cardinal scale. He built a Gothic church in Stockwell and when in 1859 he was appointed to the rectorship at Bath he rebuilt Cowbridge in the baroque manner. He lived at Bath in a substantial house called Vellore, later the Spa Hotel, and contributed £50,000 towards the restoration of the Abbey. However, his munificence went unanswered, tainted perhaps by his early association with a Broad Church brotherhood called the Clapham Sect, and if Kemble had episcopal ambitions, they were disappointed. By the time he died in 1874 his money was almost spent and besides his book, *Memorials of a Closed Ministry*, he left his hopeful heirs little besides the reflection that he was not the first prelate to have found a monument in profligacy.

Matthew and Harriet's first child died in infancy but Matthew, born in 1872, and Harriet, who followed in 1878, survived and grew up in Bath at 20 Marlborough Buildings, the Connollys' home from 1876 until the Vice-Admiral's death in 1901. Their childhoods remain in Victorian obscurity but by the time Matthew went to Haileybury he was a dedicated collector of minerals. In 1890, breaking with family tradition, he went to Sandhurst, where he passed in first. He passed out with honours and was commissioned as a Second Lieutenant of the King's Own Yorkshire Light Infantry. Postings followed in Guernsey, Sheffield and Pontefract. He was made a Lieutenant in 1892 and in Dublin in 1898 he was District Signalling Officer. He was stationed in York the following year and returned to Ireland with the rank of Captain in 1900. All his life he had an eye for pretty girls and even in old age would reminisce about the diversions an officer could enjoy in the Dublin of the late 1890s. He liked in particular to dwell on the beauties who graced both the grandest assemblies in the Georgian squares and the more subdued parties in the Wellington and Waterloo Roads, and to remember those fading families who were invited to the St Patrick's ball but never to the smartest evenings at Dublin Castle. Muriel Maud Vernon, whom he met in 1898, was the daughter of Edward Vernon of Clontarf Castle and probably had an *entrée* across the city.

It is impossible to say what articles of persuasion Matthew brought

to his courtship of Maud, whom he always knew as Mollie. He had a
respectable career and a modest private income but surviving photographs reveal a plain face with small eyes and the intrusive moustache
of the period. Extant correspondence suggests a man of desiccated
emotions and those few friends of Cyril Connolly's who met Matthew
remember a military archetype whose good manners were slightly
ponderous and whose humour could be leaden. It is possible, however,
that like his son he could be irresistibly charming to women. It is also
possible that Maud was eager for independence from the stultifying
climate of Victorian Dublin; moreover, the daughters of the Vernons
traditionally married Englishmen. The couple announced their engagement at Christmas 1899 and were married the following July at
Clontarf, the Vernons' home outside Dublin.

The family motto was *Vernon Semper Viret*, 'Vernon always flour-
ishes', but the dynasty's history was less ancient than that of Clontarf.
A church or monastery is thought to have occupied its site as early as
AD 550 and the occupying Normans built the first fortress there in
1172. The property later passed into the possession of the Knights
Hospitaller and in 1540 it was surrendered to the Crown. In 1649
Oliver Cromwell granted the estate to a parliamentary officer, John
Blackwell, and he in turn sold it to John Vernon, Quartermaster
General of Cromwell's army in Ireland. Clontarf changed hands for the
last time when John Vernon sold it to his cousin Colonel Edward
Vernon, a royalist, so that the family arrived in Ireland as Cromwellians
and not, as Cyril Connolly liked to believe, as servants of Charles II. It
was part of a larger romance: he liked to see his mother's family as 'a
fiery race, proud of their Anglo-Norman descent, their sixty-three
quarterings',[2] but the Vernons' historian, Dennis McIntyre, admitted
that they failed to produce 'any colourful geniuses in the course of their
long and unchequered family records'.[3] By the middle of the eighteenth
century Clontarf was a rambling conglomeration with a Gothic façade
and was illustrated by Beranger in 1772. In 1835 the entire structure
was found to be subsiding and the resident Vernon called on the Irish
architect William Vetruvius Morrison who razed the citadel and
replaced it with the Tudor, Gothic and Norman counterfeit, complete
with gimcrack tower, which survives to this day. The demolition seems
not to have affected the castle's ghost which, according to family
legend, first began its visitations in 1014 with attempts to warn Brian
Boru that he would be defeated by the Danes.

Edward Vernon was High Sheriff of the county and a member of the glamorous Kildare Street and Carlton clubs. He had eight children, of whom Maud was the youngest, but seems to have attached quite as much importance to his own pleasures as he did to his family's and could spend thirty pounds on a gun dog while begrudging his daughters their evening dresses. Anglo-Irish society was tightly knit and Maud's mother's, Jane Brinkley's, connections ramified across generations, so that Cyril Connolly was connected to the poet Robert Graves and the writer Elizabeth Bowen. The former would blandly assure him many years later that 'we are linked with most intelligent Anglo-Irish families since 1575, and especially with mathematicians, physicians, bishops and folklorists.'[4] Maud was also the niece of the Countess of Kingston, châtelaine of Mitchelstown in County Cork. Built in 1825, the castle was gutted by fire in 1921 and its masonry used by the Cistercians in the construction of Mount Melleray Abbey in Waterford: now engravings alone can testify to the extravagance of the Gothic vision of its architects, James and George Richard Pain. Although the Vernons were technically grander than the Connollys, any superiority was undermined by the ambiguity inherent in the Anglo-Irish condition. Brendan Behan defined the Anglo-Irishman as 'a Protestant on a horse' but behind this formula lay greater contradictions: the families of the Ascendancy may have seen themselves as more graceful than the English and more prosperous than the Irish, but they knew too that although they were unwanted by the native population they could not return to England without a loss of standing and a fall in income. Trapped in a backwater, they sustained themselves by an element of illusion while London beckoned irresistibly to hopeful Goldsmiths and Congreves.

Maud too now left, to transmit the ambiguities of her race to her son. Matthew was presently seconded as adjutant to the Second Battalion of the Royal Warwickshire Regiment and the newly married couple moved to Coventry in 1900. As military duties could send them far afield at short notice, there was little point in buying a house and they rented Whitley Villa, then just outside the city. No details of this period survive. Matthew had his career to consider and the company of fellow officers to enjoy, and his wife would later reflect that he 'never swerved in his wish to be a soldier', adding that he had 'the *wish* to command men – without the power'.[5] She herself was a soldier's daughter and may have been equipped for the life she now faced, that of regimental gossip and regimental wives; in any case, true to her age and upbringing, she would have seen it as her duty to adapt. The Connollys cannot have known each other very well when they married and even the most mundane evidence suggests that they were very different characters. While Matthew sent dry and detailed letters full of dates and times in his cursive yet immaculate copperplate, she wrote in an untidy hand of matters suggestive of a poetic disposition. She was responsive to the physical attributes of her surroundings and noted the earliest cuckoo or camellia or the wind and weather of her environment. She knew the habits of wild animals and was an enthusiastic gardener, later telling her son that years of watching plants grow had made it hard for her to believe in mere chance.

Romantics often have a practical and pragmatic side and Maud endured. In 1901, in the same year as his Queen, Matthew Connolly's father died, leaving Harriet a widow at fifty-six. The death left the Connollys better off but they were never prosperous and for all his love of exactitude Matthew had no mind for money. He worked hard, however, and was rewarded when in September 1903 the *Illustrated London News* reported on the progress of 'The Volunteers' since they had come under his jurisdiction:

> The rifle ranges are situated at Coventry, Rugby, and Stratford-on-Avon, and it speaks well for the interest taken in its shooting when one finds that in each of the last two years, 1901–2, it has come out first in figure of merit in the North-Western District, which comprises forty-seven Volunteer battalions. Much of the credit for this is due to its adjutant, Captain M. Connolly, Yorkshire Light Infantry, who has done much to stimulate interest in musketry throughout the corps.[6]

Whatever Matthew's pleasure at this recognition, Maud was honourably distracted: on 10 September 1903 the Connollys had their first, and last, baby.

The child was christened Cyril Vernon Connolly. His middle name was a straightforward acknowledgement of his mother's origins, while his Christian name was taken to honour Cattley the botanist. It was an appropriate patronymic for a man who grew to be obsessed both by Proust and by flowers and in an early draft of his autobiography Connolly proudly explained the derivation. Research brought disappointment, however, and the explanation was removed: Cattley had

been called 'William' and the boy and his christeners had been misin-
formed. That autobiography, *A Georgian Boyhood*, is based on the
romantic premise that childhood is a lost paradise, with intimations
more lovely than anything that follows. It is a stylish and readable
narrative rather than a faithful deposition but it remains significant as
one of the few sources of information for its author's first years. One
learns there that Connolly's earliest memory revealed a chemist's shop
in Bath and its traditional display of coloured bottles, an encounter
which must have occurred when he was only about two and a half years
old. Shortly afterwards, in February 1906, the family left for Gibraltar,
where Matthew had been appointed Commandant of the North Front.

In September they moved again, this time to South Africa; Matthew
was now Commandant of the School of Signalling in Pretoria and took
a house at Roberts Heights. The family returned to England via East
Africa in 1907 but in October 1908 they made the long journey back
and settled at Wynberg near Cape Town and the Cape of Good Hope.
Neither of these distractions seems to have impinged on the young Cyril
Connolly, who absorbed interests nearer home – all his life he remembered that the garden was full of squashed apricots and chameleons and
that there was an abundance of freesias, arum lilies, loquats and eucalyptus. Early expeditions to the sea at Cape Point confirmed a remoteness from England and left an indelible impression of hot light and
briny wind and an immensity of space. Early prejudices were forming:
in maturity, happiness for Connolly tended to imply a warm climate
and proximity to the sea. Companionship was limited. Besides Wups
the dog and One-Eye the cat he had only one playmate: Victor Hely-
Hutchinson, in later life Director of Music at the BBC, was two years
his senior and the son of Sir Walter Hely-Hutchinson, Governor and
Commander in Chief of Cape Colony. Unsurprisingly, Connolly's
recollections of this South African childhood were dominated by a
sense of solitude but he had no regrets: he enjoyed being alone and
delighted in the invention of the games of isolation. Later, he would
learn from his friend George Orwell that this condition was neither
unique nor damaging. The latter too was often alone in infancy: 'I had
the lonely child's habit of making up stories and holding conversations
with imaginary persons, and I think from the very start my literary
ambitions were mixed up with the feeling of being isolated and under-
valued.'[7]

Connolly found pleasure in other quarters thanks to a strong visual sense and a keen faculty of smell: swooning amidst the blossom and vegetation, he had already taught himself that life could – or should – be a series of 'ecstatic moments'.[8] Yet romantic though these exaltations sound, they occurred in a military context. The Boer War had ended only six years earlier and Matthew Connolly was merely another figure in the British presence stationed in South Africa after the hostilities. Cyril Connolly was a child of the British Empire and its ceremonies were pervasive: 'On Sundays the Regiment had church parades and there were smells of pine and eucalyptus paint blisters and hot tar.'[9] Matthew himself was now District Signalling Officer for Cape Colony; his duties took him out on to the veldt and there his interest in minerals led him to the observation of snails, which soon began to take precedence over his enthusiasms for philately, cookery and the pedigrees of race-horses. In 1908 he joined the Malacological Society and by 1912 he had published one of his earliest important papers, 'A revised reference list of South African non-marine Mollusca'. While at Wynberg he found and catalogued thirty different types of snail and eventually his African land and freshwater snail collection became the most important in the world, his activities in that sphere conferring greater fame than any he would win in uniform.

What remained of his time he gave to his wife and son and the latter recalled that he was brought up to respect patriotic maxims: 'An Englishman's home is his castle' or 'Nothing is more feared than a question in Parliament'. A deletion from *A Georgian Boyhood* reveals that Matthew was the only figure in the young boy's life who could instil fear: his nurse and the servants obeyed him, his mother indulged him and his father's brother officers tried to amuse him; Matthew alone embodied law. Nevertheless Maud was not negligent or lazy. She wrote a children's story for Cyril called 'Grass-Haired Peterkin' and there were picture-books and nursery fantasies embellished with her own variations on the Peter Pan verse of the 1900s:

> Rest my baby, God says you may
> Rest once you start on Life's weary way.[10]

She noticed eccentricities: her son would have his bed pulled to the window to watch the sunsets while a fear that he might develop a receding chin presently led him to sit with his underlip sticking out for prolonged periods. Although he liked caterpillars and fairies and certain types of succulent plants, which he called the 'bad families', he was not always cheerful. He developed a morbid fear of his birthday and used to mourn on the day preceding it for the time that could never come again.

The interludes at Wynberg were contrasted with life in Ireland, where his parents returned when on leave. They stayed at Clontarf and Mitchelstown – the tropic flora and fragrant fruit of the Cape gave way to soft wet weather and potato cakes, the uniforms of regimental life to footmen and horses. For the first time the boy glimpsed snow and remembered vividly the mystery of his first icicle. He also encountered some of his mother's relations: his grandfather, whom he found intimidating, and his mother's sister and brother-in-law, Mabel and Walter Summers. Maud had four sisters, Mab, Kathleen, Edith and Louisa. A quarrel led to lifelong estrangement with Louisa and one hears nothing of Kathleen and Edith. Mab, however, was close in age and affection and in 1896 she too had married into the military: Walter Summers was a wealthy officer and their son Noël could have become a sibling substitute for his cousin Cyril if their parents had not lived half a world apart. As it is, *A Georgian Boyhood* gives the impression that Connolly was a virtual orphan: not only are his parents largely absent from its pages, but his numerous cousins either did not impinge or else made no great or favourable impression.

Aunt Mab and Uncle Walter gave their nephew a watch and a steam train for Christmas and were soon agreeably associated with furs, presents, and the large and evocatively named houses which they inhabited at various times – Rochestown, Marlay, Loughananna and Bishopscourt. Although Grandfather Vernon seemed forbidding, he too had his charms, not the least of which was his possession of a two-handed sword which had supposedly armed Brian Boru and with which grandfather and great-uncle would pretend to decapitate the small boy. When he was a little older he was allowed to improvise a kind of cricket in the musicians' gallery of the Gothic hall at Clontarf and his grand-father tried to give him real fielding practice on the lawn. This second measure failed, but grandfather and grandson seem to have had contact of a sort and the latter came to understand that the former owned a shoot in Kerry and a thousand acres of suburban Dublin. The Easter Rising, which shook the stratified certainties of this world and signalled the implacability of Irish nationalism, was less than a decade away, but Connolly was too young to understand the implications of his grand-father's status, too young also to know why Fenians had invaded the

30,000 acres which surrounded Mitchelstown to besiege his great-aunt, Lady Kingston. Yet he did not take these mansions for granted and in later life insisted that it was this exposure to the faded grandeur of his Irish connections which had made him a snob.

In 1910, following promotion to the rank of Major, Matthew Connolly was transferred to Hong Kong but it was soon decided that Cyril should not accompany his parents to the Far East. The climate would prove unhealthy for a small boy: moreover, it was time he returned to England to begin his formal education. He was not even to sail back with them: Matthew and Maud remained at Wynberg to settle affairs while their son, aged six, went ahead with his nurse, Betty, to a country he did not know. During the voyage he developed East Coast fever but there were other afflictions besides. The separation was inevitably traumatic: he felt rejected and unloved and for years afterwards was convinced that the parting had lasted for much longer than it really did. Later he would understand that his new standing as an orphan of empire had literary precedents, but it was no consolation that Thackeray, Kipling, Orwell and Saki had undergone similar bereavement. Indeed Connolly insisted that the episode was formative and in a sense it was: it marked the beginning of his mythopoeic career, the career of the self-proclaimed failure who always had excuses to deflect competitiveness; the clever but neglected boy whose genius had been frosted by abandonment. In middle age, romantically convinced that an unhappy childhood was a prerequisite for artistic ambitions, he referred repeatedly to his apparent betrayal. Furthermore, the excuse could be extended: those who had been deprived of emotional stability could never hope to confer it and would be driven instead by 'an impulse to repeat the forlorn unconscious patterns of desertion, to flee the crowd and induce the accidents which recreate our ancient loneliness'.[11]

The migrants broke the journey at Corsica, where Matthew's mother and sister, Mrs Blake, had taken a house outside Ajaccio called the Villa des Orangers. The boy's subsiding fever was treated with orange-leaf tea and soon he was sailing prickly pear leaves in the garden tank and tentatively exploring the *maquis*. His autobiography records no details of his relations with his aunt and grandmother but one does learn that he experienced synaesthesia, seeing names, numbers, people, in notes of music or in colours – a faculty common among those in whom certain senses have been developed out of proportion to others. In childhood an entire career of love and mutual confidence can be compressed into a friendship of two weeks: Cyril Connolly met a Polish boy called Zenon who was nine and who introduced him to combat with cardboard swords and shields, and soon the young traveller was besotted. It was another formative experience, as he later recalled: 'From that moment I have seldom been heart-free and life without love for me has always seemed like an operation without an anaesthetic.'[12] From Corsica he and Betty progressed to Tangier and another infatuation, this time with a Moorish guide called Salem who gave him a drum.

It was an eventful year in which to return to England: Edward VII died and Asquith led the Liberals to victory in two general elections. The bewildered young boy was dressed in a dark blue cockade to signal his family's Tory allegiances and, absorbing family prejudices early, he retained a conviction that the dentist's son, child of Liberal parents, smelt oily. Other portents of change and danger intruded and his earliest memories of the outside world included Captain Scott's expedition to Antarctica, the return of Halley's Comet, the week of George V's coronation and, most vividly, the sinking of the *Titanic*. He had been placed in the charge of his grandmother, Harriet Connolly – now living in Bath in a terraced house at 17 The Vineyard – and it was under her jurisdiction that he underwent the greatest change so far: enrolment at St Christopher's in North Road. When not kept away by illness he appears to have had an enjoyable and typical early school career and was soon equipped with red cap, cricket bat and snake-buckled belt (which he kept under his pillow at night). He liked chess, collected stamps, pressed flowers in blotting paper, devoured sausages, kept caterpillars and could recite strange and sinister facts of nature or history. He participated in the erotic rehearsals of the dormitory (which were known, a deletion from *A Georgian Boyhood* reveals, as 'showing sights'), read comics like the *Magnet*, *Comic Cuts* and the *Gem* and found a first friend – never heard of again – called Hubert Fitzroy Foley.

Yet if St Christopher's saw Cyril Connolly as typically earthy and uncomplicated, he felt himself to be unusual in two particulars: indifferent at games, he courted popularity by trying to entertain his fellows; and he lived with a grandmother who indulged him to a degree his young friends could only envy. Harriet Connolly was lonely in widowhood and her grandchild was a lively receptacle for her affections and complaisance; he was also canny and ready to fall in with the patterns of devotion that were soon established. In exchange for performing

winsome acts such as sitting on her knee and drawing maps or going to
bed in his red cap and tie, he could exact large rewards. When he
hesitated with indecision before two toys in a shop she bought both.
Soon, he later declared, he was 'a vicious little golden-haired Caligula',
deploying laziness, impatience, ingratitude, cruelty and moodiness to
profitable effect.[13] She flattered him with notes addressed to the Duke
of Vernon KCMG signed by the Duchess of C., while her attempts at
sternness made misplaced appeals to maturity and idealism. She
reminded him that he could not become a gentleman of leisure: he must
think of palatable careers for the future. He should also address the
hereafter: as a rector's daughter she inevitably tried to steer him in the
paths of righteousness and many of her later letters to her grandson
quote St Thomas à Kempis and St Francis de Sales. To no avail,
however – she exaggerated the tendency to manipulative behaviour
which doting mother and nurse had already begun to foster and was
rewarded with blame by the child and his parents.

It was unfortunate that a series of illnesses – whooping cough,
measles, German measles, chicken pox – frequently kept him at home
and subject to his grandmother's blandishments throughout 1911. She
imposed a valetudinarian diet and left him with memories of (and
appetite for) the invalid's temptations: the pat of butter, tangerine,
cutlet and grape. Tea was a great ritual and its buttered fingers of toast
and boiled eggs were eagerly awaited: it became one of his most
celebrated admissions of indulgence that while the third egg was less
good than the first and the second it was no less inevitably consumed.
Such pleasures aside, this life was far removed from the ceremonies and
certainties of his other existences: old Mrs Connolly was living in
reduced circumstances and her grandson was both quick enough to
notice and straightforward enough to mind. Africa had been exotic
and sensuously gratifying, Ireland graceful and grand. England was
neither and his dislike of it began now. The difference also posed a
problem particularly acute in such a rigid and class-conscious time:
existence in England was middle-class, in Ireland it was patrician. But
where did Cyril Connolly belong?

His uncertainty was revived when he was reunited with Matthew and
Maud for a holiday in Ireland in the summer of 1912. Shortly
afterwards disaster struck: the Connollys' anxieties about Hong Kong's
debilitating climate seemed vindicated when Matthew succumbed to
rheumatic fever and was placed on half-pay in December. The

implications for his soldiering career were to prove serious and immediately plans were made for a return to England. The boy's schooling was not to be interrupted, however, and bulletins from St Christopher's suggested that all was well. In October 1912 Cyril wrote thanking his parents for their letters and told them of his progress in football and Friday dancing lessons. He added that he had bought a Swedish knife for 1s 9d. Two months later he asked for the correct spelling of 'Brian Boru', which was what he called himself in playground antics, and revealed that he wanted a box of conjuring tricks and Kipling's *Barrack-room Ballads* for Christmas. Maud nevertheless disapproved of St Christopher's: her son seemed always to be ill there and was perhaps too much under her mother-in-law's influence. The decision was taken to remove him and the headmaster, Carrick Trask, wrote a glowing valediction after the Easter term of 1914: 'We shall miss him most horribly ... He is of course a boy *quite* out of the ordinary with many most interesting and unusual traits, not at all the usual type of schoolboy. I should have loved to watch the maturing of all his character and we do regret losing him.'[14]

Connolly and his mother went to Ireland while she pondered where to send him next. He renewed his acquaintance with his grandfather and now took to the lawn for fielding practice. He decided he wanted to learn Gaelic and to cultivate his Irish inheritance; whilst he was alert to Anglo-Ireland's jokes about the English, he knew scarcely any Irish people beyond the servants. His moods were volatile and he developed an obsession with titles. He longed to charm, to amuse, to be liked, but his cousins considered him merely eccentric. By their standards he seems to have been clever and was soon reckoned to be the first 'intellectual' to stay at Clontarf since Handel, whose bedroom was thought to have occupied the area now taken by the boy's nursery. He returned with his mother to London to 18 Brompton Square, leased when it became clear that illness had terminated Matthew's itinerant career, and soon afterwards, with the death of Grandfather Vernon, his widow joined the new establishment.

The house had a vine growing over the drawing-room balcony and the rosewood furniture in its rooms came mostly from Cowbridge; the nursery ordained on the top floor was deemed a fitting resting place for Vice-Admiral Connolly's sea chest. For Matthew, who retired from the army in May 1914, the proximity of the Natural History Museum was exciting but mother and son discovered other enthusiasms. Besides

Hyde Park and the museums of South Kensington there was the famous Prince's skating rink, newly constructed on the site now occupied by Knightsbridge Barracks, and Maud and Cyril became regular visitors. One day he fell, badly hurting his snub nose but supplying himself with the heroic and school-proof excuse that it was broken rather than merely misshapen. Maud wrote later of the nightmares she used to have of losing him in the traffic half-way across the Brompton Road; simultaneously he dreamed of getting lost without her on the far side of that thoroughfare. She consulted a fortune-teller and was told that her son would find fame in America. Meanwhile he had progressed from comics and now enjoyed the complete work of Stephen Leacock, Mark Twain's *Library of Wit and Humour*, the stories of O. Henry, E. Nesbit, Ian Hay, Barry Pain and eventually E. F. Benson. The time had come for him to apply himself more seriously to his education. Maud had made her decision and soon her adored son, whom she dreaded losing in the Knightsbridge traffic, was despatched to a school which he helped to make notorious, though he at least disguised its real name, St Cyprian's.

CHAPTER TWO

THE *ST CYPRIAN'S CHRONICLE* was the work of the school's proprietors, Mr and Mrs L. C. Vaughan Wilkes, and was a publication typical of its kind, in which the complacent tones of officialdom assured old boys of continued academic and sporting triumph and conveyed a general sense of team spirit and duty well done. Again rather typically, it sought endorsement from the ancients and beneath its title carried a poignant Virgilian formula: *Forsan et haec olim meminisse juvabit* – 'Perhaps one day even these things will be pleasant to remember'. Preparatory schools seldom muster the impressive catalogues of alumni which are the pride of the great public schools but the Wilkeses' establishment was remarkable as the nursery of a small but gifted generation which never forgot its Cyprian initiation. However, Cyril Connolly, George Orwell, Cecil Beaton and Gavin Maxwell felt little nostalgia for its precepts and their adult recollections gave the Wilkeses' antique promise an unfortunate and lasting irony.

The school was founded in 1900 when its proprietors were in their mid-twenties. Its dozen masters and ninety or so boys were housed and taught at 71 Carlisle Road in the suburbs of the Regency and Victorian resort of Eastbourne in Sussex. In 1906, the establishment moved to a newly built premises, a tiled, gabled, many-windowed and redbrick edifice set in Summerdown Road and boasting a sunken playing-field, a cricket pavilion, a plunge pool, a gymnasium, a chapel, a carpenter's shop, a riding class and a rifle range, all disposed within five acres of grounds. It presented itself as a modern and well-equipped establishment at a time when the Connollys were wondering where to send their son. If he seemed bright, he had also had poor health; St Cyprian's proximity to the sea and the South Downs may have been decisive. Despite Matthew Connolly's retirement, with Maud's mother contributing towards the maintenance of Brompton Square, the fees, approximately £180 a year, seemed manageable, and the boy soon found himself donning his new uniform – corduroy trousers, a green and pale blue jersey, an emblem: on a field vert a Maltese Cross azure – in the summer term of 1914 and seeing his mother weep as they once again said goodbye.

As the last few weeks of the European peace ran their course, the new boy who had begun a career of charm and entertainment at St Christopher's could look around for susceptible spectators in his latest environment. If the numerous accounts of the school are accurate, it would have been immediately clear to him that life at St Cyprian's revolved around the Wilkeses and that Cicely Ellen Philadelphia Vaughan Wilkes in particular was its motor and embodiment. They were a hard-working and ambitious couple and not only fought to recruit the heirs of the peerage and send them on to Eton but struggled to do the same for their own sons.

Nobody could ever satisfactorily explain why throughout the school they were known by the innocent names of Sambo and Flip, although Gavin Maxwell has suggested that the latter title owed something to the motions of the headmistress's ample bosom. Officially she was known as 'Mum' and taught French, history and English. Sambo taught scholarship Latin and Greek, wooed the housemasters of the major public schools and was the ultimate dispenser of discipline, although his wife was capable of reducing boys to tears when she pulled their hair, slapped their faces or adopted the subtler reproofs of sarcasm. She was a woman who provoked intense feeling. George Orwell, whom she knew by his real name, Eric Blair, loathed her, and thirty years after he left her jurisdiction continued to denounce her for being a snob and a bully who taught her pupils nothing but the perpetuation of that snobbishness and a few sterile mnemonics which were intended to help them pass history exams. 'Such, Such Were The Joys' is one of his most famous essays and in it he reveals his two abiding memories of the school: that he was repeatedly thrashed for wetting his bed, and that both Sambo ('a round-shouldered, curiously oafish-looking man, not large but shambling in gait') and Flip (whose eyes 'never lost their anxious, accusing look') reminded him constantly that as a scholar he was 'living on their bounty', and was thus inferior to the richer pupils. St Cyprian's represented 'a world where it was *not possible*' for him to be good, a world where all the boys were undernourished, dirty, miserable and blue with beatings.[1]

Cecil Beaton, a contemporary of Orwell's, found his jeremiad admirable but exaggerated. Nevertheless he too hated the Wilkeses and 'the escape from Flip when at last we left St Cyprian's was one of the great milestones in my early career'.[2] David Ogilvy, later an advertising tycoon, was at the school on a scholarship a decade after Orwell and claimed to have experienced similar humiliations. He never forgot the way in which Flip, a 'satanic woman [who] carried the art of castration to extraordinary perfection', screamed at him in front of the whole school when he wanted to buy a peach: 'Your father is so poor that we are obliged to keep you here for almost nothing. What right has the son of a pauper to spend money on luxuries like peaches?'[3]

Nevertheless, Mrs Wilkes had her partisans. Henry Robert Foote, who won the Victoria Cross in North Africa and became a major-general, venerated her: 'I owe a great deal to her. She was a mother to me.' Charles Rivett-Carnac, who became Commissioner of the Royal Canadian Mounted Police in 1959, praised her in his autobiography, *Pursuit in the Wilderness*, for inculcating self-discipline: '[She] taught me much which stood me in good stead in later years, when, despite risks and consequences, I always had to go on.'[4] It might be specious to conclude that her teaching methods better suited those pupils who later found success in rigidly hierarchical careers rather than in the more wayward disciplines of literature, but it seems relevant that further endorsement of her behaviour came from another old boy who attained eminence in imperial service. Walter Christie was contemporary with Connolly and Orwell: he went to Eton as a King's Scholar and thence to King's College, Cambridge. His career in the Indian Civil Service culminated in his being made Joint Private Secretary to the Viceroy in 1947. He too was at the school on a scholarship, but in his memoir, *St Cyprian's Days*, he insisted that the Wilkeses never made any reference to his straitened status. Furthermore he applauded Flip's professionalism:

> Where [her] real genius emerged was in her talent for cultivating, wherever receptive ground could be found among her uncouth charges, the germs of literary taste, style and appreciation, within the limits of current orthodoxy. In this, although her methods were rough and ready, I believe she was in advance of her time ... She helped us to compile history notebooks; she supervised, and somewhat tyrannically guided our reading; she encouraged us to read and learn poetry by heart, and to try our hand at writing verse.[5]

Yet although he was an apologist, Christie conceded that she was
dangerously mercurial: 'No primitive farmers ever scanned the omens
of the sky more anxiously, to divine the mood of the Earth Mother,
than we watched for changes in the climate of Flip's grace and
geniality.'

The prevailing morality of the school was traditional: duty, discipline, character and service were the official preoccupations, and the
values of the Empire were never questioned. The imperial and military
presence was strong but not exclusive; Orwell characterized the boys as
being mostly 'the children of rich parents, but on the whole they were
the un-aristocratic rich, the sort of people who live in huge shrubberied
houses in Bournemouth or Richmond, and who have cars and butlers
but not country estates'.

Connolly was afraid of the dark when he started at the school and at
Brompton Square he always went to bed with the reassurance of a
night-light. For the first few weeks at St Cyprian's, however, he was too
overwhelmed with homesickness to feel afraid and had no memories of
his first term beyond those of the cold and misery of an unfamiliar
school. When he returned home for his first school holidays he learned
that Matthew had bought The Lock House, a substantial property in
turn-of-the-century Tudor situated in Surrey outside the village of
Frimley. Connolly listed the new property's dimensions, noting a drawing room, smoking room, dining room, parlour, cloakroom and six
bedrooms, along with stables, a garage, farm buildings, garden,
orchard and tennis court. Within The Lock House's secluding trees lay
the Basingstoke Canal; beyond were spreading conifers and the faint
reveilles of Aldershot and Camberley.

The terrain surrounding the house became a land of private fantasy
and eventually he had names and imagined episodes for every thicket,
clearing and subsidiary waterway. But if Matthew's aim in buying The
Lock House had been to provide his wife and son with a lasting home,
events overtook him, ensuring a continuation of the impermanency of
their surroundings. The family took a house briefly at Hythe in Kent,
and while they were there during the August heatwave the First World
War was declared. Connolly remembered crying in the skull-lined
crypt, his grief compounded by the death of his Grandmother Vernon.
Again there were worries about money: with her death, there was
nobody to share the costs of Brompton Square, and because of his
ill-timed resignation from the army earlier in the year, Matthew now

missed the rapid promotions which took place as hostilities began on the Western Front. No sooner had The Lock House been bought than there was talk of letting it.

With the war, Matthew at once volunteered 'to go anywhere in any capacity'.[6] Joining the Seventh Battalion of the King's Own Yorkshire Light Infantry for home service, he was posted to Woking in October. Meanwhile, with the fall of Liège and Namur, his son began buying a magazine called *War Illustrated* and on his return to school found St Cyprian's braced for austerity and grimmer self-sacrifice. Walter Christie recorded how the war 'pervaded and influenced almost everything we did or that was done to us' and remembered the manoeuvres of the Cadet Corps across the Downs on Field Day 'in extended order under covering fire, against the grey-uniformed veterans of the Volunteer Reserve'. Presently Summerdown Camp for convalescent soldiers was established near the boundaries of the school and – in exchange for regimental buttons and badges – the boys were encouraged to save their pocket money in order to buy sweets and cigarettes for the men, to grow vegetables for victory and to learn to knit soldiers' socks.

Austerity did not yet extend to birthdays: it was a school custom – and one the impoverished Orwell always claimed to have been denied – that whenever a boy had a birthday a cake was baked for him and then shared among the others. A letter written in September 1914 revealed that Connolly got his cake; he went on to tell his mother that he got up at 7.15 and had a cold bath with four other boys before proceeding to chapel and then breakfast. Either truthfully or tactfully (and it is significant that Flip inspected all letters home, ostensibly to eradicate poor spelling), he added that despite homesickness he liked the school very much. That December his report was encouraging: 'I am very pleased with your boy. I consider that he has made an admirable start in his new surroundings. I feel sure he will be a credit to us.' The following term Connolly wrote to tell his mother of the newest aristocratic admissions: His Highness Prince P. Chira of Siam, the grandson of the Earl of Chelmsford, another young lord and the nephew of the Bishop of London.

In March 1915 Matthew was transferred from Woking to Harrogate before being moved back to London as an army Record Officer. A bomb fell on the Territorial Record Office where he was working later in the year, its arrival suggesting that civilians too were in a firing line, while in foreign fields the carnage had already deprived numerous families of sons and brothers. The Connollys were affected when Maud's brother Granville Vernon lost his son, Charles, on his first day at Gallipoli. Financial problems were less dramatic but no less urgent and in an attempt to control them Matthew resolved to let Brompton Square as well as The Lock House. By the beginning of the summer he and Maud were installed at Gresham Cottage at Brentwood in Essex.

Shielded from these developments, Connolly had begun to feel his way at school, but if his successful adaptation pleased his parents, to their son it brought perilous confidence. *A Georgian Boyhood* reveals that Flip sometimes had to rebuke him publicly for courting cheap laughter and on one occasion she compared him before the whole school to the tribe of Reuben because 'unstable like water thou shalt not excel'. Happily there were various ways of recovering from disgrace and by the end of his first year Connolly knew the tricks. One might secure a visit from parents or cling shamelessly to boys whose favour was more sure. A reminder of good connections never hurt: a long period of disfavour ended when Lord Meath, founder of Empire Day and a friend of his parents, asked after him. The surest way of winning approval, however, was to be seen requesting library books which it was known Flip approved. Connolly remembered that these sacred texts included *Puck of Pook's Hill*, *Henry Esmond*, any novel by the prolific and forgotten Victorian novelist Charles Reade, or any solid historical fiction. He was diligent in charm, and it comes as no surprise to find that in July 1915 the *Chronicle* cites him as winning second prize for 'boys who read the best list of books during the term'.

Every year C. Grant Robinson, Fellow of All Souls and Senior Tutor in Modern History at Magdalen College, Oxford, delivered a report on academic progress at the school. Robinson's credentials were no doubt intended to impress parents, but the fact that a distinguished academic visited the establishment regularly was a tribute to the Wilkeses' commitment to excellence as well as a confirmation of their courtship of the ancient universities. His conclusions were published in the *Chronicle* and in July 1915 he had satisfactory cause to mention Connolly, who was by now in the scholarship class for Greek and Latin: 'Grotian, Blair and Connolly in their class have done very promising work, and they have a good prospect of obtaining next year distinction for themselves and their school.' Eric Blair had started at St Cyprian's in 1911 and was therefore Connolly's senior. It is not clear exactly when mutual sympathy was kindled but there were numerous reconciling parallels in their circumstances and they became each other's best friend in the school. Both had fathers involved in imperial service who came to seem emotionally remote; both were indifferent athletes; both were only children; both were seen as scholarship material; both were keen readers who relied on the printed word to transport them from the realities of solitude. Orwell recognized the similarities between them years later when he wrote: 'Of course you were in every way much more of a success at school than I, and my own position was complicated and in fact dominated by the fact that I had much less money than most of the people about me, but as far as externals go we had very much the same experiences from 1912 to 1921.'[7]

Eager to emphasize that St Cyprian's was a spartan hell with no mitigating friendships, Orwell excludes Connolly entirely from 'Such, Such Were The Joys'. Connolly, by contrast, describes his friend with care in *A Georgian Boyhood*: 'Tall, pale, with his flaccid cheeks, large spatulate fingers and supercilious voice, he was one of those boys who seem born old.' Orwell is also made precociously political: 'Of course, you realize, Connolly, that, whoever wins this war, we shall emerge a second-rate nation.'[8] They used to take regular walks across the Downs, stopping at outlying villages like Jevington, Westdean and Eastdean in order to buy sherbert cones and cherryade in the tiny village shops which Orwell liked not only because they were remote from St Cyprian's, but because they reminded him of the world of H. G. Wells. He was fascinated by sex and also, Connolly remembered, by melodramatic points of morality and conscience such as 'Would you drink a pint of blood to save your father?' Perhaps while together on these walks they encouraged each other in disapproval of the Wilkeses and even developed the evils of the school into a private fantasy world. More certainly, they discussed literature.

Orwell had been given *Gulliver's Travels* on his eighth birthday and studied it repeatedly. In later life he recalled reading various authors in happy competition with his friend: Swift, Thackeray, Kipling, Wodehouse and Wells – all of whom, Thackeray apart, were to become the subject of essays in his maturity. They both read *Sinister Street*, not understanding why it was proscribed and confiscated, and over twenty years later Orwell could still dwell on the tenderness of their rivalry when writing to Connolly:

Do you remember one or other of us getting hold of H. G. Wells's 'Country of the Blind' about 1914, at St Cyprian's, and being so enthralled with it that we were constantly pinching it off each other? It's a very vivid memory of mine, stealing along the corridor at about four o'clock on a midsummer morning into the dormitory where you slept and pinching the book from beside your bed.[9]

Connolly was more important to Orwell than he knew: the latter had only one other close childhood friend, Jacintha Buddicombe, and she was struck by his isolation. She remembered that while friends never came to visit him during the school holidays, 'he occasionally and appreciatively quoted the dicta of a friend whom he never named but referred to as "C.C."'[10]

Orwell proved to Connolly that an alternative to the Cyprian creed of character existed: intelligence. There was another, however – sensibility – and that was the lesson embodied by Cecil Beaton who, with his brother, Reggie, arrived at the school in September 1915. Beaton had already survived the precociously vindictive attentions of Evelyn Waugh at his previous school, Heath Mount, in Hampstead, but not even this initiation had sufficiently hardened him against the rigours of St Cyprian's. He could find no consolation in the society of Orwell, recalling later that 'there could hardly be two people further apart than Orwell and myself'.[11] Connolly, however, seems to have fascinated him. They ate gooseberries together in the kitchen gardens, mowed the lawns in partnership and polished the chapel brasses. Connolly found Beaton polite and curiously independent. Beaton found Connolly shockingly well informed:

He seemed so grown-up. Even his face was dotted with adult moles; and his long fingers ended with filbert nails ... I got a bit of a shock when I discovered how much he knew about life. A few of us vaguely realized that someone's parents were rich or titled, or had a large motor-car. But Cyril knew which of the masters had a financial interest in St Cyprian's, and which were only there on sufferance. He said it helped you to know how to behave towards them.

As the war progressed and rationing tightened, it became a point of patriotic honour and discipline that the boys should eat all their food, however unpalatable it sometimes was. If Beaton is to be believed (and the photographer never lies), Connolly was no traitor at table:

What made me tremble was that Cyril's greed seemed stronger than his sense of self-preservation. When it came to food, he did the most dangerous things ... after breakfast, during Flip's alarming scripture lesson to the assembled school, [he] seemed unable to resist continual nibblings at the bread and honey. By the end of the meal, it seemed as if a hundred snails had been travelling forwards and backwards between Cyril and the honey bowl. Astonishingly, I never remember Flip catching him in the act.[12]

One looks in vain for mention of Beaton in the *St Cyprian's Chronicle* but he seems to have disdained the trophies of the classroom and the gymnasium. It was on Saturday nights, when the school gathered in the hall for entertainment, that he warily took the spotlight and earned renown, at least according to *A Georgian Boyhood*, for his rendition of 'If you were the only girl in the world and I was the only boy', which he delivered in imitation of Beatrice Lillie or Violet Loraine in a voice 'small but true' and with unsettling persuasiveness. Beaton was considered an unwholesome influence on Connolly and when a correspondence was discovered between them, the latter was reprimanded and the letters were stopped.

The war, which created shortages in so many areas, created them also in the teaching profession, and many of the schoolmasters available at the time were either elderly, having been brought out of retirement, or young, inexperienced and awaiting conscription. Nevertheless St Cyprian's boasted a respectable complement of masters, remembered by Christie as being 'Dickensian in their variety', and most of them would have encountered Connolly and helped to shape him. Sergeant Barnes, a former army middle-weight boxing champion, supervised the gymnasium, the runs to Beachy Head, the morning's brutal immersion in the plunge-pool, and the boxing ring; Sergeant-Major Moody taught shooting; Mr Fielding took football and dancing lessons; Mr Ellis, whom Christie remembered as 'dry in appearance and speech', was a good maths master remembered by Connolly for explaining the mysteries of algebra and for praising the superior efficiency of the Germans.

The most important master after the Wilkeses, disguised in *A Georgian Boyhood* as 'Mr Potter', was Robert Sillar. He had taught at St Cyprian's since its foundation and seems to have been universally adored. Gavin Maxwell remembered him saying: 'No one can understand difficult things like their own lives and other people unless they understand simpler things like animals and birds first.'[13] He was a

passionate lepidopterist and not only organized netting expeditions on
the Downs but also enlivened the *Chronicle* with his bulletins for
fellow-enthusiasts: 'Specimens of Dark Green Fritillary have been taken
on the cricket field for the first time, as also Ligniperdi, the goat moth,
Sambrucaria and the Ghost Swift ... The White Admiral has been
plentiful in Abbotts Wood, but restricted train service has made it
impossible for anyone to go there without a bicycle.' It is hard to
imagine that the boy who wrote to his parents asking for a book called
Of the Wilderness and Jungle, and who watched the gardens of
Brompton Square for looper caterpillars and the privet moth, did not
look forward to these lessons and expeditions. Sillar was also prominent in school entertainments: he celebrated his birthday by treating the
boys to a rendition of *A Tale of Two Cities*; on the last Sunday of
Michaelmas term he would read from *A Christmas Carol*; and on Guy
Fawkes Day he was master of ceremonies.

The consensus of Connolly's masters was enthusiastic and in December 1915 Sambo was able to inform Major Connolly of satisfactory
progress. Holiday work was recommended, but with the glowing
affirmation that the boy was 'a willing worker – intelligent and has a
retentive memory – good assets for success'. In the summer term of
1916 he was nicknamed 'Tim' Connolly in reference to the recent
Easter Rising; the name was adopted by the Wilkeses and the other
boys, although not all of them accepted the accompanying change of
personality by which Connolly was now the Irish rebel. He himself
claimed to like the new identity and seems to have shown simultaneously an increased disregard for authority. Writing to Maud to inform
her that he intended to sit the Harrow History Prize, he added that he
had been put into a dormitory known as the 'naughty boys' room' as a
punishment for late appearances in the morning.

In May 1916 he wrote mentioning that he had been taken with a
party of boys to see *The Scarlet Pimpernel* and that he was reading a
book called *Folk of the Wild*. In June, Lord Kitchener drowned when
HMS *Hampshire* was mined off Orkney, and Flip instructed the boys
to compose an elegiac tribute. Connolly needed no persuasion and sent
a copy of his tribute to his mother. He had shown his effort to Orwell,
who was also composing obsequies, and the latter had praised it:
'*Dashed* good [over which Connolly wrote, "My dear Blair! I am both
surprised and shocked."] Slight repetition. Scansion excellent. Meaning
a little ambiguous in places. Epithets for the most part well selected.

The whole thing is neat, elegant and polished.'[14] Connolly must have liked his effort, as he preserved it:

> . . . Bury him not in an abbey's shrine
> Midst tablets of stone and coffins of pine
> But let him be where no light can shine
> And the north sea waves rush in.

It was Orwell's elegy, however, which was considered the finest and was subsequently published in the *Henley and South Oxfordshire Standard*. In July the laurels were Connolly's when he took the Harrow History Prize, hallowed object of Flip's untiring efforts in the class-room, beating Orwell into second place and a boy from another school, Steven Runciman, a future historian, into third.

The *Chronicle* described a royal visit to Summerdown, in which the school Corps played a part, and gave an account of the theatricals with which the Michaelmas term culminated and which contained a balanced and varied programme. The Wilkeses' daughter Marygold recited 'Great-Grandmother's Rhymes' and young Lord Pollington, 'La Cigale'. Whimsy and Continental culture were all very well in their place, but there were other, patriotic, dues and a group of boys per-formed 'The Kaiser's Visitors', illustrating 'the bad time the Potentate of Potsdam would have if ever these young sailors and soldiers got into Berlin'. There was a vignette from *HMS Pinafore* called 'Pinafore Potted' in which Cecil Beaton played the part of Little Buttercup, and for the finale, an adaptation of *The Pickwick Papers* called 'Mr Jingle's Wooing'. Marygold's sister Rosemary acted with various boys includ-ing Connolly and Orwell. The latter was commended as 'exceedingly good in [a] somewhat difficult part' but the *Chronicle* had no hesitation in identifying Connolly as 'an artist of most exceptional merit . . . as the much desired and quite undesirable mature spinster. His acting was of the highest quality and more than deserved the recognition it obtained; his entire performance was exquisite.'[15]

It was not only the theatrical honours that Connolly took that Christmas. In his customary report Grant Robinson singled out Con-nolly and Orwell repeatedly – in Greek, Latin, French, History, Divinity and the English Essay. But the rivalry between the prodigies ended there: Orwell left St Cyprian's to go briefly to Wellington, where he had won a scholarship, before opting for Eton instead. Connolly's progress continued unchecked through 1917, although that summer

Matthew and Maud were warned that their son was 'good on all branches requiring originality, thought and perception, rather than mere adherence to rule'. He too sat a scholarship examination for Wellington, a military establishment which Matthew might have approved but which his son disliked. He was not accepted but the failure was considered useful experience. A year later he travelled to Eton with Sambo and a group of other boys to sit the scholarship papers. As he later recalled in *A Georgian Boyhood*, he was captivated: there were Cyprian reunions amidst the luxuriant landscape of the Thames Valley while all around were the gaudy summer rituals of the world's most famous school. He took one more scholarship examination, this time at Charterhouse, in a cellar during an air raid, but it was an unnecessary precaution, as he soon learned that he had been placed thirteenth in that year's election of King's Scholars at Eton. Sambo wrote with congratulations: 'The examiners tell me that Cyril did a very fair Latin prose, very good Greek unseen, very poor Latin unseen, an excellent English paper and fair French.'[16] Flip also made enquiries and learned from a history master, Mr Martin, that Connolly's history paper had been 'phenomenal'.

His remaining time at St Cyprian's passed quickly and happily. The rigours of the school had transformed the sickly child of 1914 into something altogether more sturdy. Exhibitionism seemed now ingrained and again he was praised by the *Chronicle* for his part in the school play, which had been adapted from *Barnaby Rudge*: 'Connolly, as Miggs, made the most of a long and exceedingly difficult part. His subtle humour, mordant irony, rapid turns from sarcasm to reproach, and his mincing ways won much applause.' Academic praise now seemed almost predictable, though his report in April 1918 saw Sambo sound a note of caution: 'He can write good English but is a little inclined to write for effect ... He is rather apt to fly off at a tangent; and not finish one book before beginning another.' He was reading Dickens, Thackeray, Carlyle, Scott and John Buchan. He was also self-conscious: he hoped to mask his plain appearance by polished charm and to develop a rejoinder equal to every social contingency. In his last days at St Cyprian's that rejoinder was: 'Dear me, how very uninteresting!' The leavers were treated by Sambo to the inevitable homilies about schoolboy romance and the lecture was painfully reiterated by Matthew. He would need all his Cyprian virtue to make a success of his new school, a point Sambo made in his last letter to the

Major: 'It is a test of character as much as of brains for a boy to hold his own in College ... You will find the school a good financial investment – the fees being only £7 10s a term!'

As though to emphasize the imminence of great change, the end of his career at St Cyprian's anticipated the final convulsions of the war and the victory of the allies. If Connolly ever saw the school *Chronicle* of July 1918, he will have sensed that Sambo and Flip saw that victory as an endorsement of their school's stoic and martial aspirations, and will have seen the tribute paid by an anonymous 'Officer in the regular army' to the spirit of the schools:

> In days to come, somewhere on high ground in England, there should stand a monument which all should pass bare headed, and on it the simple phrase 'To the memory of the boys of England.' Simple, straight-forward, calm and utterly unselfish, they fulfil more than any in our life and history that old attribute of knightly character, '*Sans peur and sans reproche.*'

II
GRATEFUL
SCIENCE

CHAPTER THREE

THIS CHIVALRIC CREED was the legacy of Dr Arnold who had instigated a reformation of the public schools in the nineteenth century and whose educational convictions had permeated the quadrangles and common-rooms of numerous unruly Victorian academies. When one of his pupils, Thomas Hughes, wrote the most famous schoolboy novel, he reaffirmed Arnold's priorities and Squire Brown knew in sending Tom to Rugby that he most hoped for excellence outside the classroom: 'If he'll only turn out a brave, helpful, truth-telling Englishman, and a Christian, that's all I want.' This morality, which subordinated scholarship to leadership, was indispensable in the jungle and savannah of Empire and was invoked repeatedly throughout the First World War as the public schools surrendered their paladins and the roll of honour grew longer in Sunday Evening chapel. By the time the Armistice was signed, during Cyril Connolly's second term at Eton, that school alone could number 1157 old boys who had died in the conflict.

Yet there was an equivocation in the muscular Christianity of many of the schools and perhaps nowhere more so than at Eton. The diplomat Gladwyn Jebb arrived there five years before Connolly and sensed this ambivalence, reflecting that 'we still lived in an Homeric Age. We were brought up on the classics, and though we were nominally Christians, I think that the majority of us, consciously or unconsciously, were much more Stoic in outlook, if we were not, frankly, Epicurean.'[1] Eton dispensed Homer and Virgil in surroundings of unusually seductive beauty which predated the Empire across which its fame spread. It educated more wealthy and more aristocratic pupils than any other institution, its towers and crenellations guarded a greater complex of arcane lore and it was those rituals that Connolly had to learn when in the summer of 1918 he assumed his new identity.

Henry VI had founded Eton in 1440 as a preparatory establishment for King's College, Cambridge, and required one service of the seventy scholars of his charter: that once a week they prayed for his soul. By the time Connolly arrived to join these intercessions, Eton had grown enormously and the studious and indigent beneficiaries of the original scheme were outnumbered by approximately one thousand regular fee-payers who were housed in the town and known as 'Oppidans' or town-dwellers. The Scholars, however, inhabited the ancient precincts of the College itself and in their first year slept in a medieval dormitory divided into cubicles which was known as Long Chamber. Their head boy was always the Captain of the School, they appended the initials K.S. to their names and wore gowns over their uniforms. They were known, sometimes disparagingly, as 'Tugs', and fell under the nominal jurisdiction of the Master in College, then J. F. Crace. 'Janney' Crace was a product of the system he supervised: a Colleger, he had progressed to King's, Cambridge as an accomplished classicist before retracing his cloistered past to Eton. His family had moved in Pre-Raphaelite circles and he himself was sensitive and cultured, devoted to Browning and a timid paedophile who suffered the knowing pranks of his charges before finally marrying the sister of a Colleger younger than Connolly. He was remembered by one pupil, George 'Dadie' Rylands, as being 'sweet, ineffective, unassuming and not at all a martinet'.[2]

The prevailing constitution gave sweeping disciplinary powers to the ten boys of Sixth Form who constituted the senior leadership of College. Beyond this faction lay other arbiters, most notably the Eton Society, or Pop, the self-electing oligarchy of senior boys who were the admiration and envy of the entire school. The system was rigidly hierarchical and companionship across years or houses was made difficult, at least in the lower rungs of the community, by its elaborate and unyielding etiquette: Orwell, the one figure to whom Connolly could have turned for guidance in this new world, was inaccessible, being in a senior election, so Connolly would have to brave his new station alone. Sambo and Flip had assured him that there was a boy of 'character' who would look after him: Godfrey Meynell had not been at St Cyprian's, but he was in Connolly's election and another soldier's son. Unfortunately the assurance was premature. Meynell turned out to be a handsome bully who devised torments for those he considered suspicious, and *A Georgian Boyhood* describes how Meynell brandished a red-hot poker between Connolly's legs and forced him to admit that he was ugly and that 'Ugly' was really his name. Meynell was an enemy for the first two terms before his victim, disarming him with unexpected laughter, engineered a truce. By the time John Lehmann arrived in College two years later Meynell had developed into a handsome hero who captivated the younger boy completely. However, his destiny lay remote from Connolly's or Lehmann's: he had well imbibed the Homeric values and for his defence of the North West Frontier in 1935 he was awarded a posthumous Victoria Cross.

Bullying tended to occur within years, so Connolly was the same age as his demons. There were those, like Meynell, who thought that his face was his misfortune, and those who resented his renewed attempts to amuse, and Connolly remembered that they armed themselves prior to their visitations with siphons and bat handles. The new boys also had to endure the caprices of their fagmasters: failure to perform exactly the tasks with which they had been charged – whether delivering a message on the other side of the school or buying cakes in Eton – could easily result in a beating. Indeed corporal punishment was widespread – it was not restricted to the junior boys and there were often mass-thrashings. The worst of it seems to have been that there was no court of appeal. Not only was Crace powerless, he was also complicit, at least according to *A Georgian Boyhood*, and the terrible persecutions were regularly followed by 'the knowing inquiries of the vice-haunted virginal master in college, a Jesuit at these executions'.[3]

A notebook Connolly kept at the time described his first two terms at Eton: 'Period of complete nonentity. Chamber games – Armistice. Dim and bullied.'[4] He seems to have had only one friend, the top scholar in his election, Randall Delves Broughton; but like the friendship with Meynell, it was not an intimacy to outlast College. Athletes are never lonely at school, but Connolly could certainly not look for popularity on the playing-fields of Eton. Accounts of matches in *Chamber Book* reveal that he cut a dismal figure on winter afternoons. One account of a Field Game played on 8 October 1918 reveals that 'Connolly, Wayne, Christie and Delves Broughton were feeble', while on 22 October, he was again on the losing side and was thought to merit a dishonourable mention: 'Connolly's efficiency was impaired by a dip in Jordan's.' Practice did not make perfect: another game on 7 November brought further disgrace: 'Christie, Buckley, Connolly and Delves Broughton were *very feeble*, the last three narrowly escaping being reported.'

Connolly's academic work in these early weeks was not much more impressive, although his masters seemed to expect a future blossoming. Crace reported to the Connollys in December that the boy had enjoyed 'a fair, though not very startling, rise in all subjects but Science and French . . . I have had sometimes to send him out of pupil room to wash his hands or change a very dirty collar.' Connolly's excuse was that endemic savagery broke the spirit of the more fragile and that he himself was presented with several 'tickets' for poor work which had to be shown to a disapproving tutor. In the face of these oppressions, however, he still maintained a relatively equable disposition, at least in the eyes of his classics tutor, J. C. Butterwick:

> An extraordinary boy of great individuality and a way of looking at things at once quaint and amusing and unexpected. Had the division been placed on its feeling for good English or for any aesthetic qualities it possessed he would be near the top, as he is something of a writer himself, something of a humorist and a lover too of literary beauty. But as a writer of Greek and Latin prose, he is for a KS a perfect scandal . . . As a boy he is friendly to a degree, cheerful, good-tempered and amusing.[5]

He sought refuge from these tyrannies in School Library where he wallowed in a newly acquired love, the Celtic Twilight. At St Cyprian's he had learnt that poetry meant 'the romantic escape, the purple patch'. 'We were still in the full Tennysonian afterglow.' Tennyson was to be admired because he showed 'character' in a poem like *The Charge of the Light Brigade* and was also master of the seductive dying fall. (This education was very much of its age: where it was not an exhortation to duty, poetry was a procession of rhapsodic moments, a lyrical discipline, and its triumphs were enshrined in two popular anthologies which appeared at either end of a half-century, the *Oxford Book of English Verse* and *Other Men's Flowers*.) The schoolboy absorbed the connotations of this prevailing lyricism and took them to heart: 'Because poetry was associated with emotional excess, night and unhappiness, I felt disgusted with it by day as by a friend in whom when drunk one has unwisely confided.'[6] Poetry was a glorification of doomed love, lost contentment, remembered bliss; an almost codified nostalgia. To the poets he had been taught to admire at St Cyprian's – Milton, Gray or Keats at their most seductive and anthologized, as well as Kipling, celebrant of 'character' – he now added such early lyrics of Yeats as the *Lake Isle of Innisfree* and the easy enchantments of other Georgian poetry, including James Elroy Flecker's *Golden Journey to Samarcand*: 'We who with songs beguile your pilgrimage/And swear that Beauty lives though lilies die.'

Was Cyril Connolly already a romantic who found his sympathies fortified by the poetry he was encouraged to read, or a malleable disciple of the prevailing poetic anguish? The transference probably operated in both directions; but as an unquestionably romantic adult he had no doubt that romantic poetry offered a sanction for schoolboy passions which were as doomed and illicit as any the poets knew. At St Cyprian's he had conceived a love for a boy he calls Tony Watson in *Enemies of Promise*, a precocious swearer, smoker and fighter who was also good at boxing, running and diving. He was wiry, small, brown, and joined his admirer in the sort of ceremony schoolboys revere: they swore blood-brotherhood by incising crosses in their left hands and pressing the cuts together. Soon there were other gestures of allegiance: Watson tried to kiss him when they were alone together in the bath-room one night. Despite the fact that his advances were rebuffed (and Connolly reproached himself nightly for his loss of nerve), Watson would 'get into my bed where my innocence hung round my neck like an albatross'.[7] They continued to correspond when Connolly went to Eton, but inevitably Watson's place was soon usurped. Later Connolly would develop classifications into which he could group the types of boys who appealed to him while at school: the Faun, the Redhead, the Extreme Blond and the Dark Friend. Watson had been a first Faun and now there was another. In the best tradition, this boy was made unobtainable, even unapproachable, by school etiquette, being older and an Oppidan. *A Georgian Boyhood* calls him 'Wilfred' and records the trembling devotions, which were tolerated 'even as a beautiful orchid accepts the visits of some repulsive beetle'.[8] But love and desire were not to remain offices of self-denial.

At some stage in 1919 Connolly joined the Junior College Debating Society. A glance at its minutes reveals that Orwell's contemporary Bobbie Longden was as prominent in its activities as he was in the struggles of the Field Game and the Wall Game. He was an extrovert and at times a clown, and the solemn deliberations of the debating chamber provoked his self-confident mirth: 'Mr Longden, who was a visitor, rose and made many nonsensical and irrelevant remarks for the continuation of which he was ejected later on in the debate.' The Junior College Debating Society was an active caucus of controversy, and the records of a debate in October 1919 on 'Ancient and Modern Torture' suggest that Connolly took the proceedings quite seriously: 'Mr Connolly proposes the motion, Tortures, and when called upon to open the debate, suggests the torture of the Treacle and Ants, in which the victim was covered with treacle and pegged on an ants' nest and was gradually eaten.'

The contribution was hardly memorable but nor was his academic work. At the end of the Michaelmas term 1919 he was fourteenth out of fifteen in maths and 'his written work is intolerable'. He was confirmed in the College chapel on 6 December by Bishop Burge of Oxford, but Crace, unsure of the boy's religious devotion, was inadvertently perceptive: 'Of his confirmation I hardly know what to say . . . He has a keen and sincere mind but not one to which reverence comes very naturally . . . And he has not any very romantic ideals – intellectually, for instance, his point of view is more that of a journalist than of a scholar or scientist.'[9] By Easter 1920 the situation had not improved. He could tantalize some masters with gleams of promise (his English master, Hugh Macnaghten, quoted him as having written: 'It is really a disadvantage of Christianity that the arts, painting, music, poetry and sculpture, are given no place at all either in the Old or the New Testament'), but he still came bottom in some subjects by what Crace termed 'a too easy margin'.

> He is a boy who has thought for himself already a good deal further than many boys of his age have done. But he is in danger of achieving nothing more than a journalistic ability to write rather well about many things, if he is impatient of real study and thoroughness . . . I feel sometimes that a little more humility of mind would help him onwards more than anything else. Yet one real point about him always makes me respect him and that is his real candour.[10]

The Connollys were disappointed and Matthew threatened to stop his son's pocket-money if his work did not improve; only Crace's assurance, given in June, that such a step was unnecessary, averted the loss. Perhaps he did not know that his son received further support from his Grandmother Connolly. She wrote to 'Spratkins' in September 1920 to report that she had been unable to find the accessories he needed for his part in the OTC. By way of compensation she sent him a portable chess set which she hoped would be useful for practising for the Eton tournament, a new sponge bag and some nail scissors, and indicated that she was going to settle bills for books and shoes.

Meanwhile, what had happened to Orwell? Etiquette limited the amount of time he and his prep school friend could see of each other, and when encounters arose Connolly found that the scepticism fore-shadowed at St Cyprian's had become entrenched and that Orwell regularly and sardonically alluded to the crimes 'They' had committed, 'They', *A Georgian Boyhood* explained, being 'a Marxist–Shavian concept which included Masters, Old Collegers, the Church, and Senior reactionaries'.[11] Their literary tastes were now divergent. Orwell rejected the passivities of the Celtic Twilight: his sense of social injustice and the inevitability of political ferment led him to explore Samuel Butler, Jack London and George Bernard Shaw. In more resigned moments he admired Shelley and A. E. Housman. He knew *A Shropshire Lad* almost by heart and later declared an admiration for the poet's 'unvarying sexual pessimism (the girl always dies or marries somebody else) ... [which] seemed like wisdom to boys who were herded together in public schools and were half-inclined to think of women as something unobtainable'.[12]

Connolly too admired Housman (and may have met him when the poet went to Eton to deliver a lecture on Erasmus Darwin). Meanwhile, Orwell did not allow his friend's other literary loyalties to temper his affection. He was somehow untouchable, at least as Connolly later remembered him: 'no one could bully Orwell', he was seldom beaten, and although he was an indifferent athlete, he was not despised. Part of this invulnerability must have stemmed from his lack of fear, a characteristic Connolly would recall half a century later:

> I remember once after prayers walking down the corridor in College ... a hand reached out, yanked me into this room, and there were the bullies ... 'Connolly, what the hell do you mean by talking so much to the boys in the election above, you're sucking up to them ... you spend all your time bleating poetry to Rylands' and so they proceeded to start hitting me.[13]

Happily, he had been discussing Samuel Butler with Orwell who followed him, attacked the bigger of the bullies, rescued his friend and continued the conversation. Steven Runciman, whom Connolly had beaten to the Harrow History Prize a few years before, was also a Colleger now and thought it inevitable that they should form an alliance: 'Blair was not gregarious, not really interested in people, more interested in ideas. Theirs was therefore a friendship of ideas, that of two very clever boys. Also, Connolly could be very amusing and Blair was certainly not immune to such charms.'[14]

*

In July 1920 Connolly obtained his School Certificate. He passed with credit in Elementary Mathematics, Latin, History and Scripture Knowledge (Greek Text) and satisfied examiners in the English Essay. Perhaps the paternal threat of financial penalties in the event of more bad work had had some effect. He was now free to study more selectively and in September Crace informed his parents that their son had dropped maths and would aim for a history scholarship at Oxford. 'There is no doubt that Cyril has the capacity to develop into a good writer of English – at present he is over critical about everything perhaps.' Matthew, however, was not convinced and plagued himself and his family with patriarchal misgivings. What professional application lay beyond an Oxford history degree? And what of the military and naval tradition of the Connollys? Crace knew his charge better than his father did and defended the chosen course in December 1920: 'I think it would be a very great pity, and a mistake too, to press [Cyril] to go into the army when that career is so entirely against his present inclinations and convictions.'

If Crace was accurate in his assessment of his pupil's probable aversion to a regimented life, he may at the same time have been surprised to see how he reacted to the new freedom of his academic syllabus. Connolly had the sort of disposition which chafed under obligation, a condition often and incorrectly equated with laziness. The moment the appreciation of the classics had ceased to be a duty it became a pleasure, and now he threw himself into the extra-curricular study of the Roman poets. This conversion coincided with the appearance of the Loeb Classical Library, which printed an accurate prose rendering side by side with the original. Now he could read without hindrance or censorship that Ovid saw the dealings of the sexes as the material of comedy; that Horace counselled the young to drink and make love, since afterwards oblivion overtook the virtuous and the profane alike. In an act of flamboyant and widely remarked defiance, he had a volume of Propertius bound to resemble a psalter and was thus free to read every morning how that poet mocked his own infatuations. Fresh vistas opened on his middle adolescence: his chosen reading told him that gossip and gratification were the ends of existence and tempted him to be unshockable. These new literary loyalties inevitably entailed a rejection of the writers his parents admired: Matthew's hero, Kipling, was the first to suffer reappraisal and the shift was symptomatic of his alienation from his parents' values.

By the summer of 1920 Connolly had a room of his own and had settled into Etonian life. He had a group of friends – Charles Milligan, Kit Minns and Jackie O'Dwyer – but his increasing sophistication and security led him to form alliances with some of the older boys in College – Steven Runciman, Dadie Rylands, Roger Mynors and Robert Longden among them. Runciman, to begin with, had not greatly cared for Connolly, finding him 'inclined to show off somewhat' and 'quite the ugliest schoolboy I've ever seen', but with time came acceptance and in later years Connolly remembered Runciman fondly as a 'tall, quiet boy, so generous with bananas and cream' and one 'in whose small high room some of my most enlightening moments were spent'.[15] Rylands had not cared for Connolly either. 'He was so very plain and I remember him looking like a little convict; one felt that he should have had arrows all over his clothes.'[16] Now the two became friends, united by an admiration for the same English poets, and were both members of a literary society run by an English master called George Lyttelton. Connolly was the youngest member of the group, which met on an occasional basis to read poems and plays, but to Rylands he was the most sophisticated and adventurous in his literary tastes. It was he, along with his friend Terence Beddard, who invented a Georgian poet called Percy Beauregard Biles to show that while he was familiar with the poetic conventions prevalent in these years before T. S. Eliot's spectacular advent, he was also capable of satirizing them. He was already exploring Baudelaire and Petronius, and Rylands, engrossed in the novels of George Eliot, felt himself 'backward and callow' by comparison.

In 1920 Connolly felt able to congratulate himself on his career: 'I am becoming quite a Socrates in the Lower Half of College, I do want People to like talking religion and morals, to read good books, like poetry and pictures, and think for themselves ... I used to think Perfection the aim of Life, now I think it is Perfection in Happiness.'[17] That year the OTC camp took place in Surrey conveniently near to The Lock House, where Matthew and Maud had installed themselves the previous year. Connolly was able to invite his friends there for dinner and thus to attain a new prominence in their circle. Dadie Rylands remembered that a group of them went for a walk one day and sat outside a country pub getting drunk on homemade cider. It was very hot and Connolly recited Housman. Denys King-Farlow, another close friend of Orwell and a fellow history specialist of Connolly's, described him as the group's 'self-appointed jester, whom we had, disregarding a strict College custom, taken up from our junior election year'. He indicated that although the precocious and self-conscious aesthete set out to entertain, some of his audience occasionally laughed at him as well as with him. '[Orwell], knowing Connolly from preparatory school ... warned we could expect to hear plenty about a "Connolly's (probably no family connection) marrying in 1758 the second Duke of Richmond's third daughter." We did.'[18] Generally, however, the youngest member of this clever circle was esteemed more than derided. In the words of Dadie Rylands, who left Eton at the end of 1920: 'We all recognized that he was a peacock among fowls.'

CHAPTER FOUR

CONNOLLY WAS BECOMING an Eton figure. Anthony Powell, arriving at the school a year after him, had no dealings with him then but certainly knew who he was. 'It was impossible not to notice [him] as he passed in the street, or loitered in School Yard. He looked like no one else.'[1] John Lehmann, also his junior, but a fellow King's Scholar, observed him from horrified proximity. He now occupied an 'isolated' room on the other side of the corridor from Lehmann's own first room:

> It was notorious amongst us, dangerous, shocking and exciting at the same time . . . Cyril was already high in the school, and under the tolerant regime of the time did more or less as he liked: one of the things he liked was to invite one or two boys from my Election to come to his study and join the privileged circle of his friends in emancipation. I was appalled by this; I felt responsible for the boys . . . I was convinced they were being corrupted by an evilly cynical worldliness, a tone one associated with the faster and more disreputable Oppidans, only worse because much more intellectually sophisticated.

Again protocol was involved, but now it served Connolly and Lehmann was powerless to intervene in what he considered these unwholesome cabals. Worse still, his frustration and disapprobation were not lost on his neighbour, who was 'much amused at my studied disapproval'.

> He would stand at the door of his room, slim, self-assured, smartly-attired, with a teasing look on his puggish face, and when I passed would say, in a tone which made the simple greeting heavy with malice and mockery, 'Well, Johnny Lehmann, how are *you* this afternoon?'[2]

Lehmann's fears may well have been unfounded and it is possible that he was witnessing the assembling of a court rather than the attendances of a harem. But it is clear what underlay his suspicions. Sport and the chaplain's exhortations were unequal to the channelling and cooling of adolescent blood and the consequences, as remembered by Anthony Powell, were inevitable: 'Romantic passions were much discussed, but – on the romantic level – I should have thought physical contacts were rare, though contemporaries indulged at times in more knockabout performances together.' The frequency of these entanglements seems to have varied, subject always to the yearnings of the boys and the indivi-dual command of their housemasters. But if some houses were licentious, College, at least in Dadie Rylands's recollection, was 'rather pure'. Perhaps on account of his appearance, Connolly seems to have been spared the predatory attentions of his seniors when he first arrived at Eton. Now – reassured by the easy morality of the ancients – he was old enough to hunt himself. It is certain he did so and Orwell supplies the evidence. Although he had no homosexual interest in later life, in youth Orwell seems to have been an erotic pragmatist and took what was available. He developed an interest in a boy in Connolly's year but, knowing that his old friend could be irresistibly charming and fearing that he might be tempted to poach, Orwell incautiously wrote to his rival, begging him not to interfere. The entreaty is now lost; but Connolly copied part of it in a letter to a mutual friend, Terence Beddard. Orwell's tone is not quite supplicating, but nor is it casual. Connolly had obviously become a force to be reckoned with in Eton's lists of love:

> I am afraid I am gone on Eastwood . . . I think you are too . . . If I had not written to you [until] 3 weeks into next half you would notice how things stood, your proprietory instincts would have been aroused, and having a lot of influence over Eastwood you would probably have put him against me somehow, perhaps even warned him off me. Please don't do this I implore you. Of course I don't ask you to resign your share in him only don't say spiteful things.

Connolly could show Orwell no sympathy; and with an urbane callousness suggestive of the rakes of Restoration comedy, he told Beddard of his determination to steal the quiescent Eastwood: 'When gone on someone you do not ask for a half share from the person you think owns the mine.'[3] He had been busy in the meantime pursuing another idol, Noël Blakiston, referred to in *A Georgian Boyhood* as 'Nigel'. Blakiston was his junior and another member of the romantic genera of Fauns. 'My God he has lovely teeth and lips,' the enamoured – laying his plans – told Beddard. However, although Connolly later remembered 'evening chapel and looking at you through my fingers in the sevenfold Amen',[4] although he circulated verses among his friends during the holidays anticipating the pleasures of the new term, 'To love the curve of Milligan's hips/And Noël Blakiston's proud lips/And Freddy Harmer's hair', he seems to have found it difficult to provoke much beyond a grudging friendship.

The most significant of Connolly's attachments, however, was more successful and the beginning of a long intimacy. Everybody seems to have liked Bobbie Longden. Dadie Rylands remembered him as 'a sort of public school golden boy' and in *A Georgian Boyhood* Connolly later evoked him as 'one of those angel-faced Athenians whom the school delighted to honour'.[5] Steven Runciman saw him as 'red-haired and freckled, attractive rather than good-looking, sweet, quite vague and charming'. His charms were certainly not lost on Connolly, whose interest in Longden was common knowledge among the monastic Scholars. Runciman said it was 'generally assumed' that he and Connolly enjoyed carnal relations at Eton. They certainly did afterwards, bound together perhaps by complementary characters and similar backgrounds. Longden, the son of Vice-Admiral H. W. Longden, had no means but he was intelligent, hard-working and accomplished. He won the prestigious Newcastle medal and was Keeper of College Field; and beyond his gregarious and open charm lay a determination which would soon win him membership of Pop, the Eton Society, as well as early success in adult life. Perhaps his greatest asset was his ability to establish cordial terms with a wide variety of people: a clever and insecure outsider like Cyril Connolly would have presented no challenge to his charm.

In April 1921 Crace wrote to the Connollys indicating that their son's academic work had not suffered under amorous distraction: 'I should judge that he might have a reasonable chance [of a scholarship]: he has *some* classical knowledge, though it is of a rather vague kind: and he can write English well ... I do not think he has ever worked hard at Eton.' That summer, however, Connolly began to apply himself. He came eleventh out of the entire school in the specialists' examination, the 'Grand July', and was engrossed in sophisticated, deliberately difficult reading: Gibbon, Verlaine, Villon, Horace, La Rochefoucauld, Voltaire. He was rebuked for reading *Tristram Shandy* because Sterne 'talks smut against his own mother'.[6] Lighter reading was available in the shape of *The Loom of Youth*, a novel published to sensation and scandal in 1917. Its treatment of the romantic friendships which the public schools fostered and the worship of athletes which they encouraged made its author, Alec Waugh, notorious in the common-rooms and a hero to self-conscious schoolboy rebels.

If contemporary iconoclasm palled, there was also the exquisite legacy of a renowned Etonian circle. Connolly became fascinated by the friendship of Horace Walpole and Thomas Gray, begun when the two men had been at Eton in the early 1730s. Walpole had become the most elegant man of letters of his age and in his huge correspondence had left behind a testimony to his particular creed of friendship which was alternately spiteful, gossiping, good-natured and unshockable. It seemed to Connolly the essence of the sophisticated eighteenth century and it was a manner of correspondence which influenced his own extensive adolescent letter-writing. Presently, like Walpole, he would ask his correspondents to return his letters. Gray, by contrast, progressed to a cloistered life. His muse was more hesitant and the few poems he produced, grounded in the classical education which also shaped Connolly, were distillations of nostalgia and regret. One of the most famous, 'Ode on a Distant Prospect of Eton College', may have suggested to the schoolboy the idea that Eton was a paradise which its votaries should cherish before their expulsion into the outer world of expectation and appointments:

> Ye distant spires, ye antique towers,
> That crown the watry glade,
> Where grateful Science still adores
> Her HENRY'S holy Shade.

His imagination and romanticism wandered: it was more appealing to think of the ancient community he inhabited as a sort of eighteenth-century club where urbane figures like Walpole could flourish, rather than as a monastic seminary. He liked also to consider the parallels with another unreal community, that of Versailles – College, too, was hermetic, riddled with intrigue, blissfully obsessed with its own protocol. Both worlds denied privacy and secrecy; both revolved around custom and ceremony; both were slow to forgive breaches of unspoken rules; and later he would recall that it was unthinkable to be casual about matters like the exchanging of photographs, the acceptance of Christian-name intimacy, the apparently trivial matter of where, and with whom, to drink tea. His character blossomed and assumed a precocious authority. His friend William Le Fanu, the Walter Le Strange of *A Georgian Boyhood*, noted: 'Even people one wd: never suspect of it seem afraid of Cyril speaking of him only in hushed whispers.'[7]

When Connolly looked back at Eton fifteen years later his career there seemed in a way dream-like: some of its realities had been suppressed while others were heightened, its course seemed at once fleeting and unending, its distant truths still appeared to beckon. The tricks of time were responsible for one of the more famous lapidaria of his maturity – 'Boys do not grow up gradually. They move forward in spurts like the hands of clocks in railway stations'[8] – and by the summer of 1921 preparations were already afoot for the next stage in his education. His candidacy for Oxford was now more or less assumed and although Crace had to report one master's misgivings about the boy's 'inclination to try to mask the want of thoroughness by showy phrases', a quiet confidence seems to have followed his general progress. In February 1922 he won the Rosebery History Prize, beating into second place another history specialist, Lord Knebworth, and securing the bounty of £20 worth of books. By special dispensation he was allowed to buy Medici prints instead, but as he hung *The Man with the Glove*, *Beatrice d'Este* and *The Duke of Cleves*, he knew that it was time to select an Oxford college.

As an exceptional pupil Connolly was an automatic recipient of the inner culture of Etonian teaching. This teaching was only dispensed at the top of the school and then selectively, the province of the 'five real teachers' named in *A Georgian Boyhood*: C. M. Wells, C. H. K. Marten (a future Provost of the school and tutor at Windsor to the royal children), Hugh Macnaghten, G. W. 'Tuppy' Headlam and the Headmaster, C. A. Alington. They perpetuated what Connolly later recognized as the 'pure eighteenth-century Etonian tradition of classical humanism', a tradition he was able to imbibe when he ate with the Provost or the Headmaster or when some of the masters he knew better came to tea. There was also a cross-pollinating Pre-Raphaelite presence in this Etonian formula which gave it a strongly romantic quality. If the boys were exposed to Homer, Virgil, Plato and Socrates they were exposed inevitably to their subversive morality. Nervous of homosexuality, Eton tried to diffuse the problem: the officially sanctioned translations of Homer and Virgil were rosy and Pre-Raphaelite in tone and Greek homosexuality came to be seen as a form of heroic comradeship, a prototype of the brotherhood of the trenches or the football teams.

Connolly found this tension particularly apparent in the teaching of Macnaghten, who denounced romantic friendships yet ordered his pupils to put into Latin a sentimental verse addressed to a former Captain of the Eleven. 'Muggins' Macnaghten loved purple patches and taught all his boys to admire them, although 'jolly' was a favourite word and he thought 'little' the most beautiful word in the language. His poetic loyalties were lyrical; he liked Tennyson and Keats and first showed Connolly the way to admiring Milton, the poet who most preoccupied him for the next few years. Macnaghten's wisdom seems to have been steeped in the twilight aestheticism of the late nineteenth century, his sympathies to lie with a love of beauty which was either dead or unobtainable. He appeared synonymous to Connolly with what he christened 'the background of the lilies', a literary culture which, committed to the exquisite, estranged from reality and indebted above all to dead tongues, was inevitably sterile. It was also a literary culture which some found more provocative than others: 'The potentially homosexual boy was the one who benefited, whose love of beauty was stimulated, whose appreciation was widened, and whose critical powers were developed.'[9]

Literary beauty was an obsession also of his French master in his later Eton career, Mr de Satgé, whom he remembered being 'carried away by the "Sonnet d'Arvers", or Gauthier's "Symphony in White", a light foam on his lips, reciting through the summer dustbeam in the empty classroom while I chimed in with my ineradicable accent, Parisian as a pint of draught Bass'.[10] The literature Satgé taught Connolly to love, besides fragments of Ronsard and Racine and all of *Candide* and *Manon Lescaut*, was nineteenth- and early twentieth-century: Flaubert and Baudelaire, Verlaine, Hérédia and Mallarmé. Connolly had a taste for the dark and the ornate: the prose of Sir Thomas Browne, the conundrums of the Metaphysicals, the revenges of Webster, the dilemma of Hamlet. He disliked the Romantics and still knew nothing of the Augustans. His favourite Latin prose writer was Petronius. In Greek he knew all the sceptical epigrams by heart.

The history masters Marten and Wells were the men with whom he came into closest contact in his last year but Headlam was more influential still. An ironist and an admirer of Horace, he presented leavers with *Boswell's Life of Johnson* and encouraged his charges to

believe that while the only thing that mattered was Success, it was also
worth remembering that there was no justice in the world. He was a
Tory, he disliked laziness and seemed to Connolly to be an embodiment
of the eighteenth century. He had been to Balliol and it was out of
admiration for him that the self-conscious sceptic and aesthete chose to
apply to read history there at the beginning of 1922. It was a flamboyant gesture, since Balliol was known to be difficult, and he compounded
it by specializing in medieval history, when most of the work he had
done so far had followed from the Renaissance.

Connolly went to Oxford with Denis Dannreuther and Roger
Mynors, who had also applied to Balliol, and Bobbie Longden, who
hoped to read Classics at neighbouring Trinity. The candidates stayed
in their colleges and wrote two three-hour papers a day. Balliol
depressed Connolly: it seemed ugly after Eton and because the sheets
had not been aired in his bedroom he got rheumatism in the shoulder.
But when the results of the examinations were published in the *Eton
College Chronicle* of 30 March 1922 it was revealed that all applicants
had secured scholarships, and that Connolly had won the Brackenbury,
the most prestigious of all. His triumph won the whole school a
holiday. Headlam was complacent: 'I was not at all surprised . . . he has
acquired early the power of reading and digesting what he reads.' The
Headmaster was equally serene: 'He has a very alert mind, and I think
he is one of those people for whom intellectual success will be good.'
King-Farlow, now at Cambridge, was less pro-consular in praise: 'This
must be a proud moment indeed for the young boy. Sorry your character is thought meanly of by your preceptors . . . May I voice the
thoughts of your many well-wishers, don't bring disaster on yourself
and disgrace on the Old Coll.'[11] All was triumph; the need to work had
receded, to return at a later date in other cloisters. Today briefly was for
pleasure.

Connolly's ambition to become a member of Pop was at least as
extravagant as any hopes he had nurtured for Balliol. The Eton Society
was the most glamorous body in the school: members could wear florid
waistcoats and buttonholes, walk arm-in-arm, defy minor rules, levy
fines for indiscipline, use their own engraved stationery. Election was
the school's final accolade, the mark of a sublime popularity which was
uniquely Etonian. Pondering his campaign, however, Connolly knew
that while every boy at the school yearned for that popularity, only a
handful could hope to win it, and they were almost exclusively rich and

well connected or else the heroes of the playing-field and palaestra. Nobody was elevated merely in recognition of academic prowess: indeed, to be good at work was almost a stigma; beyond his wit and charm, however, he could offer no other credentials.

But his education had imparted early the lesson that life is not only about credentials but about connections. One of the demi-gods of the school was Lord Knebworth, who had been staying in the same hotel as Connolly and his mother when they went to Switzerland for Christmas 1921. The boys became friends, and because they were in the same divisions for history and English they maintained that friendship. Proposed by Knebworth, Connolly was accepted in the elections which fell just before the Easter holidays of 1922. The news caused an Etonian sensation. The other members themselves were pleased. In Connolly's words: '[The election] made them feel that they appreciated intellectual worth and could not be accused of athleticism; they felt like the Viceroy after entertaining Gandhi.'[12] There was incredulity at Cambridge, as Dadie Rylands remembered: 'That someone so plain, unathletic and unaristocratic could get into Pop amazed and delighted us all.' Anthony Powell recollected his House Captain, hearing of Connolly's elevation, wonder: 'Is that the tug who's been kicked in the face by a mule?' Even Jessel, complicit in this triumph, wondered about its implications: 'You've got a Balliol scholarship and you've got into Pop – you know I shouldn't be surprised if you never did anything else the rest of your life.'[13]

During the Easter holidays Connolly went to France with Charles Milligan and they stayed in Paris before adjourning to the south. It was the beginning of a lifelong infatuation: Avignon, the Greek theatre at Arles, St Rémy, Les Baux. 'There is the first time we go abroad,' he remembered, 'and there is the first time we set eyes on Provence.' Returning to Eton for his last term, he adopted the motto of Leo X: 'Since God has given us the Papacy let us enjoy it.' He surrendered himself to affectation and took to wearing a dinner jacket with grey flannels and a panama hat. Anthony Powell remembered that 'in this guise I first took him in as a formidable entity', although 'I felt conventional misgiving at the dinner-jacket as an innovation in school dress.'[14] Connolly played Mrs Hardcastle in a College production of *She Stoops to Conquer*, given 'under the patronage of HRH Princess Mary, Viscountess Lascelles' in aid of the Eton Mission for infant welfare work, and scored a success. But even as he savoured these last moments – savoured them because he knew they must end – he was made aware of an intimation of life beyond Eton's little world.

In March a magazine without parentage or posterity had enlivened the Etonian spring. The *Eton Candle* was the work of two contemporaries, the sophisticated Anglo-American Oppidans Brian Howard and Harold Acton. Both boys were members of the Eton Society of Arts, a constellation to which Oliver Messel, Robert Byron, Alan Clutton-Brock, Henry Green and Anthony Powell also belonged, and both were self-conscious crusaders. They resented what they considered their school's confident philistinism and Acton deplored the apathy and caution which even the brightest boys revealed when asked to help with the venture: 'In those days literary activity at school was still regarded with disfavour. Even Cyril Connolly hung back.'[15] Although Acton saw the inspiration behind the production as owing something to Max Beerbohm and to the 1890s, its loyalties were defiantly modernist. Both editors were eager to champion *vers libre*, and the *Candle*, or 'Eton Scandal', as it was soon known, opened with an essay by Howard on 'The New Poetry' which contained genuflexions towards Walt Whitman, Apollinaire, Verhaeren and Ezra Pound. The *Eton College Chronicle* had reservations and praised Howard in rather glum terms: 'If we hoped for something more new and exciting it was scarcely to be expected when nothing like it had ever before been done at Eton.'

However, if the school was slightly sour, the outside world was curious. With its shocking pink covers and gold lettering the production was not destined for obscurity; indeed its editors were making a deliberate bid for the attentions of the Sitwells, now emerging as figureheads for the youthful avant-garde, and even the *Times Literary Supplement* was forced to pay benign attention: 'Here we have the voice of the young persuaded as the new generation have always been that a new dawn of literature is at hand.'[16] For a boy as competitive as Connolly, the episode must have given food for thought. Although, like the rest of Eton, he might be generally ignorant about the modernist experiments then sweeping the rest of Europe, he had at least begun to explore beyond the culture of the lilies, borrowing de Satgé's copies of Huxley's *Crome Yellow* and *Limbo*. It was all very well parading in his Pop finery, but he was not the son of an aristocrat or millionaire and although it was amusing to pretend, he was fretted by suspicions that he had taken the wrong course. He would soon have to make his way in the outside world and his College friends assumed that he would follow some sort of literary path. Participation in the *Eton Candle* would have been a beginning. As it was he felt too unsure of his standing even to befriend Brian Howard who, perhaps snobbishly eager to have a Pop to tea, perhaps eager also to recruit a bright boy for the modernist cause, made hospitable overtures which only unnerved their recipient: 'I bolted down my tea like a lady who is offered a swig by a madman in a railway tunnel and bolted.'[17]

He gave a farewell tea where Debussy was played on the gramophone: 'Everyone was paired ... 6 couples, all musical and all gone on each other,' he wrote to Denis Dannreuther. He joined his final OTC camp, which took place on Salisbury Plain, and slept with Jackie O'Dwyer, though he reassured Noël Blakiston that 'I was not gone on him but in the dark one face is very much like another and it was the perfect understanding which arose out of such close embrace that I valued so much.'[18]

Later in the summer, in an ill-conceived gesture of unity, the Connollys took a holiday on the Continent. During their son's long absences at school Matthew and Maud had missed his cohesive presence and their marriage had begun to decline. They had played little part in his Eton career or in its intervals; indeed Maud often had occasion to write with regrets for her absence from the Fourth of June or some other school holiday, sending him instead rapturous accounts of her travels in Nyasaland or Zanzibar, and of the flora and fauna she encountered there. She travelled with her sister Mab and spent ever longer periods apart from her husband. Whilst she was restless and disillusioned, Matthew was crusty and emotionally inarticulate, and later Maud would try to explain to her son that his childhood had not been as she had wished and to concede that it had had its deprivations: 'There were so many longings I had for you at The Lock House – to let you have a pony – to let you have a dog ... the lemur you wanted, and it was all made so impossible – for nothing – I don't think Matt ever *lived* one day of his life.'[19]

Her husband in turn trusted to obscurer passions. During his war work at the Record Office he had befriended E. A. Smith, who as a civilian was Keeper of Mollusca at the Natural History Museum and who had recognized in the Major a passionate conchologist. In 1918 Matthew became an honorary worker in that department at the

Museum and was to remain there until his death. However, early promotions aside, he had failed as a soldier, and when his wife saw him she might have glimpsed indications of a subterranean unhappiness, not least in his heavy drinking. Their son inevitably registered Matthew's condition and remembered its humiliations: '[My father] remained a gentleman: I never heard him abuse my mother or saw him pass out delirious or covered with blood ... I soon found my "hate" of him infiltrated with compassion, that lethal engenderer of irresolution, and when my friends sympathized with me I felt uneasy.'[20]

The Connollys always maintained an amicable correspondence (she was his 'dear little Mollie') but now they began to lead separate lives. Their class and upbringing dictated a severance conducted with decorum, but the change seems to have been brought about almost affectionately and Maud presently moved into a flat of her own at 80 St George's Square in Pimlico.

She had found other havens besides. Travelling with the Connollys in 1922, along with Maud's sister and niece, was Brigadier-General Christopher 'Smiler' Brooke, at fifty-three a former Colonel of the King's Own Yorkshire Light Infantry and a decorated hero of the Boer War. Brooke was a popular and friendly man whose nickname spoke for itself; the sudden resignation of his commission in 1920 remained more mysterious, although Connolly later ascribed it to his embarrassing interest in a brother officer's wife. With no extant correspondence it is impossible to put a date on the beginning of Brooke's liaison with Maud. It is certain, however, that in 1924 he began a five-year career as MP for Pontefract and that in 1925 his wife died. In a mild way he was a dashing public figure: a diligent parliamentarian who was ever ready to give his presence to any event designed to raise money for charity, and if there is no evidence to suggest that Connolly sanctioned his mother's behaviour, equally none exists to reveal that he condemned it.

However genial Brooke's disposition, it seems to have done little to lighten the general mood in the summer holiday of 1922. Connolly's letters to friends speak of arguments and tensions and things did not improve when he continued with his parents alone to the Black Forest. At least with the collapse of the German currency everything was cheap and five shillings constituted a handsome daily allowance, but he felt awkward and estranged with two people he seems never to have known very well and who now lacked his education and sophistication. He sent his friends details of sulkings and confrontation and of how he had set his parents holiday reading: the *Odyssey* for his mother and for his father the Greek lyric poets. It must have been a relief when he set off alone to explore Oberammergau, Munich and Salzburg and then Budapest and Lake Balaton. (At the Hungarian border he declared that his numerous letters from school friends were 'lieber briefs'.) He returned to London on 12 October, saw his parents separately, and on 14 October set out for Paddington and the journey to Oxford.

CHAPTER FIVE

THE UNIVERSITY of the early 1920s, now embalmed in nostalgic fiction or the indulgent reminiscence of its alumni, was in a period of transition. The upheavals unleashed by the First World War threatened to rouse Matthew Arnold's Dreaming Spires and there were former soldiers in most of the colleges who spoke of eating in Hall as 'messing' and who, unable to forget their unimaginable initiation, misprised the discipline of the dons. The other great transforming forces ultimately entailed by the war – of egalitarianism and co-education – still lay some years distant: the women's colleges were set apart while the men's were largely occupied by the products of the public schools, so that the freshmen of 1922 discovered a new world nodding with the familiarities of the old.

Connolly arrived at Oxford to find it thronging with Old Etonians and in Balliol itself there were several former King's Scholars. He had also entered a world of emotional manners which cannot have surprised him as much as it seems to have struck the innocent Peter Quennell, who matriculated a year later: 'Many of my contemporaries ... were inclined to adopt the *mores* of an Hellenic city-state ... Plato paid his court to Agathon, and Socrates and Alcibiades strolled arm-in-arm.'[1] Yet far from being reassured by these displays and far from being stimulated by the new challenges of Oxford, Connolly was unhappy. On 18 October, after only four days at Balliol, he thought of returning to Eton and when he could not, cried for the whole evening 'but got better after a visit to [Hubert] Duggan who usually has a crew of queer oppidans ... and unlimited drink'.[2] In his first few weeks he widely advertised his disillusion in letters to friends still at Eton. To Freddie Harmer he complained that Balliol was tedious and that he was on hunger strike and lived on biscuits and oranges rather than enduring meals in Hall. To William Le Fanu, deploring the fact that the college was not more monastic, he wrote that Balliol 'bristles with acquaintances, bridge, tea-parties, debts and people ... who ask Bobbie to lunch and dinner and bridge'.[3] Other communications to Eton seem to have been of a less innocent nature. The mother of one boy still there recognized the subversive side of schoolboy aestheticism and took the dramatic step of writing to Connolly and asking him to leave her son alone: 'Keep him from those things which though beautiful might bring him to evil thoughts.' As late as June 1923 Headlam had to write to his former charge tactfully asking him to stay away.[4]

In later years Connolly complained that after school university was too large and too noisy, but that hardly explains the accidie and discontent which engulfed him. Friends soon learned of the aspects he most disliked: Oxford's Sundays, its weather, the incessant ringing of its bells, all of which suggested an entrapping and stagnant place of penance rather than the antechamber to worldly prosperity. At least part of the problem lay in the fact that whereas at school he was conspicuous in cleverness and social success, at Oxford he was thrown together with scores of others who had been similarly garlanded. And whilst at Eton the objects of ambition had been obvious, in a much larger environment like Oxford they were not only more keenly challenged but also more numerous. Where to begin, and whether to begin at all? To compound his disillusion, he found himself in a college selected without much thought. There were no Oxonians in his family to tell him what Steven Runciman remembered thinking, that he would probably have been much happier at one of the more expansive and colonnaded establishments such as Christ Church or Magdalen. Balliol remains one of the least architecturally distinguished institutions in Oxford, and the romantic freshman, acutely sensitive to his surroundings, remembered the glories of Eton and, in a notebook kept at the time he was preparing *A Georgian Boyhood*, was still inclined to draw resentful comparisons: 'Place of Education: Red brick, with huge stale elms, an old school – saturated in pagan splendour, effete with all the alluvial vices. Place of Atonement: A thin quadrangle faced with neo-gothic hutches, where everything tastes of tepid anchovy toast and guilt mounts up at compound interest.'[5]

With such apparent deprivations it mattered little that the college had played a prominent part in Victorian domestic and imperial history, or that the shadow of the great Jowett, Master for the last quarter of the nineteenth century, still lingered to lend endorsement to the Balliol ethos of worldly ambition tempered by scholarly achievement. Under A. L.

Smith, Master until his death in 1924, and under his successor, A. D. Lindsay, scholars, including Brackenburys, were supposed to work and get firsts: further education in beauty could wait. It was all a rather forbidding prospect but an ally was happily at hand. Francis Fortesque Urquhart always signed himself 'F.F.U.', but he was universally known as 'Sligger', a corruption of 'the sleek one', a reference in turn to his smooth features. Despite a manner which seems to have been discreet if not timid, he was an important figure on the Oxford stage and now became a major presence in Connolly's life. As an undergraduate he had caught the eye of Walter Pater, then a Fellow of Brasenose, who made him the model for the eponymous character in his novel *Emerald Uthwart*. When he became a Fellow of Balliol he was the first Roman Catholic in modern times to be so dignified and this distinction was followed in 1916 by his installation as Dean, in which capacity his duties were as much pastoral as academic. He was unequivocally snobbish but seems to have been capable of inspiring loyalty and affection, and it was his proud boast that even in the Cabinet there had been affectionate talk of 'Sligger'.

Urquhart's pastoral care was dispensed both in his set at Balliol and in the reading parties he took every summer to the chalet his father had built near St-Gervais in the Savoy Alps. These latter supervisions were frequently photographed and Balliol retains albums full of sepia tableaux of reading figures, simpering couples, naked Alpine bathing and never a girl in sight. The former occasions were also recorded by at least one *habitué*, Kenneth Clark, who was now Longden's contemporary at Trinity, and through whom he met Connolly. Sligger's set was above the West Gate of Balliol and to Clark it seemed

> an authentic relic of Victorian Oxford, filled with threadbare settees and lined with dowdy-looking books ... which absorbed whatever light entered through the gothic window ... Into this room drifted every evening a very mixed assortment of undergraduates – earnest young scholars, minor royalty, priests, budding poets, and a few lonely nonentities ... Of course there was no drink, which kept out the more spirited undergraduates, but it was a reservoir of kindness and tolerance ... Sligger (although he would not have relished the comparison) was the perfect hostess. He himself never said anything of interest, but he encouraged others to show off.[6]

Dadie Rylands, who visited Oxford intermittently, cast a less enamoured eye on these gatherings and thought the Dean 'a prim maiden aunt' who won popularity among the undergraduates he sponsored because he encouraged them to be men of the world rather than scholars. Now Connolly formed such a close alliance with Sligger that Anthony Powell, arriving at Balliol a year later, sensed that he had 'a strangle-hold' on the don.

Kenneth Clark, known always as 'K', was well-qualified for undergraduate popularity, as Connolly remembered. He was extremely good-looking, 'a polished hawk-god in obsidian', as well as being the owner of a car and a gramophone. Clark was equally impressed by Connolly whom he remembered as being 'without doubt the most gifted undergraduate of his generation', one who 'arrived at Oxford with the millstone of promise already hung around his neck'. He found him conversant with Silver Latin, much French poetry and criticism, particularly of the nineteenth century, and the writings of the Church Fathers. 'All this learning was almost entirely invisible below a surface of wit and intellectual curiosity.' Clark was interested to see that the prodigy disdained to woo or sparkle, even though his gifts, especially as a parodist, were already famous.

Trinity supplied another close friend, Patrick Balfour, who also found Connolly precociously sophisticated and was later to thank him for revealing 'a new world of living people, uninhibited in mind and in feeling, where human values and friendships counted above all things'.[7] This coterie was that of the King's Scholars at Balliol, among them Denis Dannreuther and Roger Mynors; and Balfour became a regular guest at the lunches they held in one another's rooms. Connolly saw little of Etonians in other colleges.

Balliol was not without its decorative presences, and the most conspicuous of these, with looks suggestive, Connolly later thought, of a 'Rosetti angel with a touch of Mick Jagger', had been at school with Patrick Balfour.[8] His name was Richard Pares, a gentle blond history scholar who attracted widespread attention, not least from Sligger and Connolly; at the end of his second term the latter admitted that Pares 'produced my most dog-like devotion and infantile mood'. Urquhart almost certainly had his suspicions about the intensity of feeling one of his charges felt for the other but did nothing to interfere. But he did act when he saw promise jeopardized: Pares had succumbed to the more turbulent charms of an obscure freshman at Hertford who was soon to emerge as the immortalizer and embodiment of that Oxford and the brightest light of his literary generation, Evelyn Waugh.

Waugh and Pares had become friendly at the Hypocrites Club, which had begun as a beery resort for those eager for an alternative to the relative decorum of the Union or the Carlton. (Its Hypocrisy lay in its motto, 'Water is best'.) Soon after Connolly's arrival its character changed and it became a smart club under the guidance of his contemporaries from school, Harold Acton and Robert Byron (with Oliver Messel supervising from the Slade). He stood aloof from this society, just as he did from other undergraduate associations, and therefore knew nothing either of Evelyn Waugh or of his interest in Richard Pares (also befriended by another contemporary, the future historian A. L. Rowse). Urquhart, deploring Waugh's bibulous influence on one of his brightest hopes, set about proscribing the Hypocrites, determined that a boy of Pares's intelligence should not go a stumbling way to mediocrity. He was successful in both aims: the Hypocrites was closed down and Pares continued a brilliant academic career which led him to a Fellowship at All Souls and the Professorship of History at Edinburgh. Waugh, meanwhile, promulgated the story, 'I was cuckolded by Connolly', and was no less explicit in the revenge he took on Urquhart. He entered Balliol late at night and to the tune of 'Nuts in May' roared 'The Dean of Balliol sleeps with men, sleeps with men, sleeps with men.' When Waugh and Connolly finally encountered each other it was again late at night and again Waugh was drunk and rowdy. But when Connolly asked him why he made such a noise, Waugh unwittingly gave an intelligible answer to a sympathetic audience: 'Because I'm poor.'

Patrick Balfour has recorded that poverty was one of Connolly's pressing undergraduate concerns and remembered receiving a note in which his friend offered to sell his blue overcoat for one guinea. Although most of the undergraduates of Connolly's time came from the same schools, there were stark disparities in wealth and few of the university's more flamboyant members made claims to egalitarianism. Money and connections mattered in the Oxford of the early 1920s and those without either – such as Connolly – never forgot it: 'When I was younger I minded very much about birth and whether people were well-born or not. That was a fault of my whole generation at Oxford. We were all terrific snobs ... all very sensitive, perhaps because our mothers were better families than our fathers.'⁹ He was speaking for himself when he mentioned having a better-born mother; but it is true that a number of his university contemporaries experienced something approaching alienation from at least one of their parents. Waugh felt neglected by both, while John Betjeman and Henry Green admitted to strained relations with their fathers. Looking back, Connolly gathered these distresses into psychological observations:

> To be accepted by the upper class, then in possession of money and authority and even glamour, was a natural ambition. Just as the following generation was to try and join the working classes and become communists to get away from their parents, we tried to escape from middle class homes by rising above them. This explains such meteorites as John Betjeman and Evelyn Waugh.[10]

Dadie Rylands, again visiting Oxford, witnessed one of these attempts to overcome bourgeois respectability. He went to a breakfast party at Christ Church with Cyril Connolly a reveller and was astonished to see the company drinking champagne, 'when we never set eyes on champagne at Cambridge'.[11] Nor was this worldliness restricted to undergraduates, as Connolly himself discovered when Kenneth Clark and Patrick Balfour took him to meet the most famous don of his day. Maurice Bowra, who was only five years older than Connolly, had been made a Fellow of Wadham in 1922 and in his long academic career, which made him Warden of Wadham and Vice-Chancellor of the University of Oxford, was a commanding figure in British intellectual life. He was a fine scholar and throughout his life published books on the classics but he exerted a wisdom at least as potent and enduring in the transformation he signalled in the lives of successive generations of undergraduates. Like Sligger he entertained, but his hospitality of oysters and champagne was more stylish. While Sligger's *salons* welcomed all comers, particularly the handsome, Bowra never suffered fools. And while the latter was familiar with literary modernism, Sligger had been scandalized by the publication of Lytton Strachey's *Eminent Victorians*.

So much has been written about Bowra that even to attempt his description is to risk repetition and it seems wisest to reiterate Noël Annan's encapsulation:

> He embodied the spirit of those who wanted to be done with the war and good form. Pleasure, vitality and spontaneity were his delight; caginess, philistinism, pretentiousness and pomposity his prey. He distrusted the Establishment, was the friend of freedom and the young, the enemy of

drabness and the *bien pensants* ... The power of his personality, his overwhelming voice and his lightning play with words dominated those who gathered in his rooms.[12]

Yet however strong his personality, nothing survives of it now except in reminiscence. He gave it full reign in his behaviour but in the interests of scholarship suppressed it in his books, causing Connolly to remark many years later: 'The device of his prose is "No flowers by request."'[13] Bowra never cared greatly for Waugh, although as Mr Samgrass in *Brideshead Revisited* he was to find his way into the ambivalent aspic of his fiction. Connolly, however, he liked at once; and although theirs was to be a friendship of interludes and disagreements, they were largely affectionate and admiring of each other. He noticed almost at once his guest's 'eager, questing eyes, a face that registered every change of feeling, and a soft hypnotizing voice'. He was quick to detect beneath Connolly's aloof posturings a winning insecurity and saw that he 'needed affection' and that 'he had lost his old stance and was looking for another'. If he sensed the young man's need to escape 'the inhibiting routine of home' he also found him 'excellent company' and 'very quick to take a point and enrich it'. 'I have never known anyone of his age who was in so many ways mature and yet kept the freshness, both sad and glad, of youth.'[14] Connolly was no less perceptive and glimpsed the romanticism beneath Bowra's bravado. At their first meeting the don told his young guest 'about the tigers swimming over to Formosa from the mainland, which set them above all other tigers'. By extension, human life was tragic and incomprehensible and only the great poets he admired had the courage to face great obstacles in trying to explain it.

Anthony Powell recorded that Bowra accepted 'as absolutely natural open snobbishness, success worship, personal vendettas, unprovoked malice, disloyalty to friends, reading other people's letters'. He also 'always talked as if homosexuality was the natural condition of an intelligent man' and adored intrigue.[15] Connolly must have seemed a Godsend: his Eton career indicated a love of success and a definite snobbishness and now he was starrily in love with Bobbie Longden and Richard Pares. Bowra warned his new protégé that Bobbie knew 'too many people' but seemed prepared to foster the friendship and jokingly promised to make Connolly and Longden Fellows of Wadham. He might play on more than Connolly's promise when he introduced him to his friends: 'This is Connolly. Coming man. Hasn't come yet', but he was an invaluable mentor, and under his instruction the history under-graduate began to read modern literature – the later lyrics of Yeats, the poetry of Hardy, Pound and Eliot – and to learn of important European modernists like Valéry and Cavafy. *The Waste Land* had appeared in 1922 and Connolly soon wrote to William Le Fanu: 'It is quite short and has most marvellous things in it – though the Message is quite unintelligible and it is a very Alexandrian poem – sterility disguised by superb use of quotation and obscure symbolism . . . it will ruin your style.'[16] He read some Sigmund Freud, which gave him ideas about his ill-matched parents, and turned to other reading hoping, as he explained to Balfour, for further glimpses of himself: 'I read almost entirely to catch reflections of myself in other countries and dead generations and so be able to express myself better in beautiful words no less sincere than the unsatisfactory excretions of most people's emotions.'[17]

If new intimacies were forged during term-time, the holidays were a potential ordeal. Although his parents never divorced, and although there is nothing to indicate that his relations with Christopher Brooke were anything other than friendly, Connolly found himself with nowhere to go from Oxford except The Lock House. Perhaps it was because of this problem that he instigated a society of five (his closest friends) called the Cicada Club, which imposed one binding code upon its members: each should spend every summer in the Mediterranean. In his first Oxford year southern excursions began earlier: straight after a Christmas with Matthew in Surrey he had joined a party of Sligger's satellites which included Bobbie Longden, Denis Dannreuther and Roger Mynors on a tour from Rome down to Naples, Amalfi and Sicily. For his first long vacation in the summer of 1923 he went alone to Spain where he travelled twenty miles a day on foot and with a haversack, walking between eight and lunchtime. Writing to Longden he announced that he looked 'very sleuth-like . . . lantern-jawed and lean-limbed . . . cheek bones a little prominent'.[18]

They were reunited at Avignon and together went to Sligger's house, the Chalet des Mélèzes, where the annual reading party was in progress. Their host thoughtfully gave them an attic and sitting room to themselves but Longden had to leave early and Connolly was desolate without him. On the eve of his own departure, just after he had turned twenty, he stowed a cache of 20-centime pieces in the hollow of a tree which marked the spot where the two had often read. The envelope containing the money was marked with a romantic flourish: 'CVC In Mem RPL Sept 13th 1923'. He and Sligger drove around France together. Connolly wrote to Longden that he liked the don more than anybody else he had met at the university, although their holiday together seems to have tried his patience: wherever they went they seemed always to end up sharing a room.

In later life Connolly regularly joked that the only exercise he took while at Oxford was the running up of bills and now in his second year he had a set which bore witness to his acquisitiveness and profligacy. It was small and painted a yellow-orange. Its contents, described to William Le Fanu, were eclectic: there was a sixteenth-century angel bought in Italy and six black-framed pictures of fifteenth-century young men. The packed bookcase was illuminated by a Florentine candlestick wired for electricity. The windows faced south; the fireplace was painted white. A New Columbia Grafenlas gramophone stood on a corner table and beneath it were five volumes of records and thirty or so loose ones, although he claimed only to listen to Ravel. His tea-service was Cantonese and the slippers he wore to take tea were bespoke. At Oxford, 'clothes were an intoxication' and Hall Brothers, who had dressed the undergraduate Prince of Wales, gave generous credit.[19] By the summer of 1924 Connolly had debts of £60; Matthew, ominously, could only be counted on for the provision of £40. Clothes were nothing without grooming and a bill survives amongst Connolly's papers from Germer's in King Edward Street, the university barbers where in *Brideshead Revisited* Evelyn Waugh sent Sebastian Flyte to buy a hairbrush to spank his bear, Aloysius – a bill for £3 10s 9d for soap, cold cream, cigars, cigarettes, a comb and bath salts.

Extravagance notwithstanding, Connolly had begun to address himself to the matter of work after Oxford. While a vaguely literary career remained the ideal, other more definite plans could do no harm. His school-friend Terence Beddard had gone into the Foreign Office, and perhaps to appease Matthew he wrote asking for advice about how to be recruited. A disillusioned Beddard replied that 'the Diplomatic Service is useless unless one has money.'[20] However, it was a career that could satisfy parental ambitions while at the same time allowing for travel, now Connolly's greatest passion, and he discovered that The Queen's College dispensed Laming Fellowships, which were intended to promote the study of foreign languages and were specifically aimed at hopeful diplomats. They were open to undergraduates from any college, the only provisos being a second class degree and unmarried status for the two years' duration of the fellowship. Successful applicants received £250 per annum to learn a language abroad and encouragement to enter the Diplomatic Service.

Oxford has always distorted time because the real world beyond its walls seems so remote yet so imminent to its undergraduate inhabitants. For Connolly, the unreality was heightened owing to the permeating vividness of his schooldays, which he perpetuated in Etonian company and which lent him the sensation he described to Noël Blakiston: 'This sense of living in a sequel tends to be the canker gnawing at the heart of undergraduacy and to make one feel so old at times.'[21] Peter Quennell, arriving at Balliol in the Michaelmas term of 1923, found this nostalgia pronounced and thought that Connolly 'was in one sense like Lord Byron, who liked to look back to a romantic past'. The two quickly became close friends and Quennell, besides discovering that Oxford, 'seen through his sharp eyes developed unexpected beauties', found Connolly 'protean'. 'Nobody had a livelier wit or, if annoyed, a sharper tongue. His cynical *bons mots* were apt to stick like burrs. Yet his pensive romanticism was just as conspicuous as his cynicism; and, besides his passionate devotion to Nature, he exhibited many of the other traits of an eighteenth-century Man of Feeling.'[22] What Quennell failed to notice was that Connolly was fully aware of his remarkable character. As the latter told Noël Blakiston: 'I am not a normal person, I can be normal at a pinch but have always been accepted as rather a phenomenon.'[23]

At Christmas 1923 he accompanied Matthew to Alassio, and because travel was now a 'consuming passion' which, allied to his feelings for Longden, 'is the basis of my existence', there was no question of returning to England before the Oxford term necessitated it.[24] He continued alone, travelling third class to get as far as possible, to Sicily and thence Tunisia. On the ferry, he wrote to Longden, 'I started a great argument by saying that I did not want to marry, that I wanted to go to South America with a friend of mine and when I had made money we would be explorers.'[25] In the letter he enclosed a poem in the manner of *The Waste Land*. In the spring of 1924 during the Hilary vacation he returned to Spain and found enchantment at Elche: 'The station is like a forgotten outpost in a tropical forest, in all directions under the palms grow orchards of pomegranates with fresh pink leaves, or figs or buttercups or clover ... I heard the water in the runnels and the frogs croaking and the wind stirring the palm branches, with their faint strange smell.'[26]

Somehow mustering funds again to fulfil the conditions of the Cicada, he took his first trip to Greece in the summer of 1924. The Parthenon was 'the most marvellous thing I have ever seen and more religious than any Gothic'.[27] He secured a letter of introduction to Sir Arthur Evans, then excavating at Knossos, and moved on to Crete: 'Candia is like a south-Spanish town, white or blue houses with flat roofs, clean winding streets, and the fronds of bananas showing above the garden walls.'[28] He saw the newly revealed Minoan frescoes but was disappointed. Now his passion was to be an archaeologist and he crusaded for the superiority over the Classical of the Greek Archaic.

He celebrated his twenty-first birthday at Sligger's chalet and the classical world stole over the surrounding Alpine scenery as he began his first attempt at fiction, a historical novel set in 500 BC and culminating in the battle of Marathon. Extant pages suggest that his characters, Gorgias and Tamanis, owe something to Longden and himself.

As a concession to the impending gloom of Finals, he decided not to travel for the Christmas of 1924 but to spend it with his father at The Lock House. By now it had been decided that the property would be sold, as Mrs Connolly had made it clear that she would never live with her husband again. Connolly's time with his father was not a success, though it might have been less appalling than the accounts sent to friends suggest. Complaining about Matthew was more amusing than revising for Finals and he gleefully laid on the horrors: there were no servants and nobody to talk to; the house was damp; Matthew got drunk every evening and had terrible table manners; he liked the wrong music and the wrong politics; he defended fox-hunting; he was mean. Connolly was also convinced that his father would read his letters if given the opportunity: the use of Greek in letters to Longden was therefore a protection as much as an undergraduate affectation: 'I always want to sleep with you more than anything but it is not very practicable at Oxford and the way we manage keeps me quiet (put on its lowest footing). I get awful ποθος ['desire'] here.'[29] After Christmas he escaped to yet another of Sligger's reading parties, held this time at Minehead: Bowra was also present and Connolly seems to have been engrossed in Milton, Plato, Yeats and Proust – in anything other than history. The discovery of Proust was as important as that of Eliot. Bowra remembered that Connolly became obsessed by the world of *A la Recherche du Temps Perdu* and found parallels between Proust's characters and his own acquaintances: he himself was Swann, Sligger was Françoise, the Morrells were the Verdurins and David Cecil was the Duchesse de Guermantes. For several years afterwards Connolly said that he tried to think, talk and write like Proust.

The determination to stay and work rather than travel was short-lived and in his final Easter vacation he made once more for Spain where at Granada he encountered the Sitwells, now idols of avant-garde artistry to his fashionable contemporaries at Oxford. Connolly was depressed: he had no money and his luggage had been stolen; but now he came face to face with these self-proclaimed arbiters, clad in black capes and black Andalusian hats. They fell into conversation and he praised Edith Sitwell's poem 'The Sleeping Beauty' as well as telling her how much he admired *The Waste Land*. She promised to tell Eliot and presently sent Connolly an invitation to one of her 'Saturdays' at Moscow Road. Pressed by debt and daunted by Finals, he stayed away and Harold Acton, who did go, brought back report: 'What an extremely rude young man Connolly appeared to be.'[30] In fact he was already ambivalent about the famous siblings and presently informed Blakiston that 'none are really our style'.

Conspicuously, as though to indicate that success measured in Oxford degrees was unimportant, he disported himself publicly in his last university term. He went punting and canoeing with Peter Quennell and paid frequent visits to the cinema. He had lunch with Sambo and Flip when they visited Oxford. He absorbed himself in Margaret Kennedy's best-selling romance *The Constant Nymph* and complained to Blakiston, when nemesis finally overtook him, that his ignorance of his history syllabus was 'colossal'. Later that summer Patrick Balfour met the Provost of Queen's and tried to put in a good word for his friend but Connolly was summoned for what he told Balfour was 'an acid viva' and learned that he had got a Third.[31] So much for diplomacy: both Balfour's intercession and Connolly's hope of a Laming Fellowship had come to nothing. Years later he would tell a friend in the diplomatic service – Donald Maclean – that he had always maintained a wistfulness for that career. But Connolly could be an exquisite casuist and he came to persuade himself – august exceptions notwithstanding – that diplomats rarely made fine writers: 'The typical slightly blasé men-may-come and men-may-go attitude of so many diplomats blunts their appreciation of character. They are unable to regard with wonder another human being, and since it is their business to be in the know they can seldom surrender to a work of art.'[32]

Putting on a brave face, he went to the Continent and found refuge at the Chalet des Mélèzes. Explanations and consolations began. He wrote to William Le Fanu saying that he was indifferent to his third because he had long since decided to make himself an educated man rather than let Oxford make him a historian. Maurice Bowra, who had always felt that Balliol should have admitted Connolly as a classicist or modern linguist, was understanding: 'It doesn't matter a bit, as no one ever thought you cared for history or for technical success in it.'[33] Sligger too was supportive and suggested that Connolly should consider journalism but the latter gloomily told Blakiston he thought that career degrading and precarious. Urquhart, however, wrote to Connolly on his twenty-second birthday to promise that all forces of support and initiative would be mobilized to help him. He wrote to contacts at the *Observer* and the *Manchester Guardian* and completed a testimonial: 'His failure to get a good Honours Class at Oxford was due merely to the fact that he worked at things which interested him rather than at the subjects of the examination ... I need hardly say that Mr Connolly is a gentleman of high character and perfectly trustworthy.'[34] It was typical of him to send Connolly money, now and in future need, in the interests, as he put it, of 'the republic of letters'.

Matthew, however, was less sympathetic. Suggestions were put forward that Connolly might try to get a job as a clerk in the House of Commons or Lords. With a literary career in mind, a meeting was arranged with John Buchan, whom Matthew and Maud knew and hoped might employ their son as a secretary. Buchan was sympathetic but suggested instead that the forlorn applicant might apply to *The Times* with some articles based on his recent travels in Spain. To his father's distress, nothing came of these ideas and to make matters worse the young man was seriously overdrawn. His grandmother wrote undertaking to discharge his debt with Mr Spence, a tailor, and took the opportunity to give him a gentle homily about living on credit. Soon, however, lawyers acting on another tailor's behalf were plaguing Matthew for settlement of a further bill of £54. Matthew had already testily announced that he did not propose to support his son indefinitely and that he must find work. A sterner lecture followed presently: 'I am sorry to say that I am more than disappointed with your behaviour during the past year ... Knowing that you had these huge bills you should have saved up every possible farthing.'[35]

There was no alternative. Following a course at other times adopted by John Betjeman, W. H. Auden, Christopher Isherwood and numerous other writers, he enrolled himself on the books of the scholastic agency Gabbitas and Thring and at the end of October was advised of a post which paid £3 a week plus expenses and would involve teaching a thirteen-year-old boy removed from Marlborough after a rugby accident. He was called Charles D'Costa and he lived in Jamaica. The opportunity promised escape with a vengeance – from his homelessness, from creditors, from Matthew, from his third – an escape almost as absolute as banishment. Longden, with a first and a fellowship almost inevitable, had advised work overseas; now his wisdom could be tested. Connolly accepted the post and Matthew assented, urging his son to investigate more permanent business possibilities in the West Indies. His passage was booked for 2 November on the SS *Patuca* of the Royal Mail Steam and Packet Company and it was arranged that he would meet his employer and her son on the ship. By then, embarked on a journey of 5000 miles which would take him to the palm-fringed Spanish Main, it would be too late to know whether he liked them, but Oxford, 'the cloakroom where I left my youth', would at least be far behind.[36]

III
MANDARINS ON
THE THAMES AT
CHELSEA

CHAPTER SIX

CONNOLLY'S FIRST DAYS at sea were miserable. The waters were high and fears of homesickness and rejection were compounded by a gnawing sense that he had failed, that after the triumphs of Eton and the defiance of Oxford he was nothing but an ill-paid usher. But with the Azores the oceans settled and the *Patuca*'s voyage across the Sargasso Sea culminated in tropical intimations: the flying fish, hotter nights, bluer waters and brighter stars delighted him; and when the young tutor first saw his temporary home, with green mountains and green lagoons distantly visible, he cabled Blakiston of his arrival in 'Eden'.

This temporary elation was coupled with other emotions, however, not least the apprehension induced by any first job and the sense of unreality which must have stemmed from the suddenness of it all. When he arrived on 29 November 1925 he found himself in an environment for which nothing in his classical education and romantic, literary ambition had prepared him. The D'Costas, whose forebears had migrated to Jamaica in the seventeenth century, were Portuguese Jews inhabiting an affluent suburb of Kingston. They were among the most important families on the island and by repute the richest. Alfred D'Costa had begun his career as a solicitor and had married another member of Jamaica's plutocracy, Ethel DeMercado. He was instrumental in the development of Jamaica's bauxite industry and was knighted in 1937.

Charles was the youngest member of the family and had sisters called Violette and Nell. His new tutor soon found him conceited, greedy and selfish, suspiciously interested in bridge and cars and almost certainly a future lawyer or businessman. He was difficult to control, 'quite humorous and quite affectionate . . . an *esprit moderne*,' Connolly told Blakiston.[1] Charles's son David D'Costa remembered that the other members of the family could be no less restless:

The D'Costa household existed between two poles: Alfred concealed himself behind carefully constructed walls of rectitude and reticence, and Ethel made no attempt to conceal her boredom with a colonial backwater and her dissatisfaction with a family fated never to fulfil her changing expectations of them. The three children divided their time between competing for parental love and attempting to escape its consequences. Connolly would have discovered himself in the midst of a *very* strange milieu.[2]

Letters soon reached London describing violent family scenes in which the combatants each tried to enlist Connolly's support. Blakiston had sent him a copy of *King Lear* and soon the tutor saw parallels between Violette and Nell and Goneril and Regan. (There were other literary analogies. Writing to Patrick Balfour, and reassuring him that 'black boys are overrated', he likened the D'Costas not only to the characters in *The Constant Nymph* but also to the quarrelling Bliss family in Noël Coward's *Hay Fever*.) Nell liked the new addition to the household and when she was living in England during the war and married to an army officer she happily passed on supplies of coffee to Connolly which had been sent from Jamaica. Violette, who was two years older than her brother's tutor, was less indulgent. David D'Costa remembered that for years afterwards she referred to him as '*such* a scruffy young man' and 'deeply resented [his] incursions into the supply of cigarettes kept on hand for guests and Connolly retaliated by leaving scraps of verse in the empty box that would begin in English "O Vi! The cigarettes hidden again?" and continue in Greek, knowing that she would understand not a word but suspect only the worst'.

Alfred D'Costa seems to have impinged very little on his employee's time and company; Ethel, however, became a friend and ally and Connolly suspected that Violette resented him because her mother had taken the young man into her confidence. All his life he showed an affinity with women, an ability to charm them and provoke a protective response, and that ability was already developed in Jamaica. He found Mrs D'Costa amusing and intelligent yet at the same time relaxing. There was somehow no necessity to talk in her presence; and soon he intimated to Blakiston that she had replaced Sligger as a reassuring and parental figure. When a fall from a horse on to some tram-lines left him cut, bruised and with water on the knee she was maternal; when he had a cold she was attentive. She encouraged him to go out in the evenings and her extravagance was disarming. His feelings for his pupil continued to fluctuate, however. In one letter to Blakiston he was dismissed as 'bone-idle, conceited and prosaic',[3] while in another Connolly mentioned appreciatively that Charles was not only amusing, interesting and intelligent but that he had a strong character, knew how to tease his tutor and could not be kept in ignorance of anything. It is significant that they maintained contact through a loose connection of mutual acquaintances for the rest of their lives and Charles D'Costa always ascribed his literary tastes to Connolly's influence.

The regime was less than exacting. They worked from eleven until one and then read or slept until four. Afterwards there was tennis or swimming and in the evening parties, dinners or expeditions to open-air cinemas bright with fireflies. Christmas 1925 was spent on the other side of the island: Connolly saw sugar estates and coconut plantations as they drove to Montego Bay and when they swam in the coral lagoons its fish lit up with the dusk. In no time, he was 'brown from head to foot' and aware that if island life was constricting there was much to be said for the servants, luxury and expansiveness of the colonial condition.[4] The skinny schoolboy and undergraduate disappeared, to be replaced by the plump young man who had a lifetime of rotundity ahead of him. He continued to take delight in the exotic vegetation and beautiful landscape but was haunted at the same time by the half-recognized suspicion that its pagan romance was muted by its colonial status. He noted 'the curious English sweetness of its tropics, like Christmas carols played on a Hawaian guitar' – a parallel which pleased him since it recurs in several letters.[5] Yet however great these delights, they failed to seduce him entirely: Connolly always missed what he did not have, was always ready to consider himself disseized: and now that tendency took the form of a nostalgia for London's winters when at home he would have pined for the heat:

> Rum punch and rocking chairs whose every tilt saps with the regularity of a pendulum, and the spicy and interminable summer, do for the White man what hookworm and sleeping sickness perform for the black ... Jamaican voices, which in some of their deep modulations promise so much, seem only fit to propose the most ignorant and fatuous topics.[6]

The English community he considered particularly depressing: almost all the men were preoccupied by thoughts of polo and bridge and he complained that he had met only one officer who read Proust. He found himself seeking out female company for the first time in his

life. As he explained to Blakiston, 'Girls are important in a country
where no man has been educated enough to be individual because they
at least are decorative and gentle.'[7] Again, like Jamaica itself, it was a
condition for which nothing in his education or career had prepared
him, and the novelty was slightly unsettling. He could claim in his
letters that he had to force himself to ignore the attractive mulatto
youths. He could insist, at least as a Hellenist, that male loves alone
brought forth masterpieces. He could even claim that the heat had
suppressed all sexual feeling. But there was a lot of dancing in the
moonlit tropical evenings, and although he could write telling Longden
that 'you seem so god-like from here', a slow change had begun. On the
passage from England he had befriended a girl called Dorothy Brandon.
The French he used in a letter he sent her may have been superfluous
and affected but it concealed also the emotional awkwardness of the
early twentieth-century English male: 'Je vous aime, pas passionement,
ni même à la folie, mais assurement je vous aime.'[8]

Despite these promptings, much of his time on the island was spent in
isolation. He devoted himself to literature, asking friends to send him
additional texts when the books he had brought were finished. He
pondered old enthusiasms – *A Shropshire Lad*, Walpole and Gray,
Proust, above all Milton, continuing to insist that 'I confess to finding in
the Paradise Lost all that my inclinations desire'[9] – but when he
immersed himself in unfamiliar writers he consistently turned to the
French for inspiration. Racine, Chénier, La Fontaine and Rimbaud
were the new arbiters, while his letters to Blakiston continued to
indicate only scant acquaintance with Shakespeare, Jane Austen, Keats,
Hardy or Dickens. He sent his friends alexandrines, told Blakiston that
lyric poetry 'consists of setting words to their own music' and filled his
notebook with reflections on the nature of solitude and its implications
for his own writing. Although he suspected that Jamaica was a denial of
personality, rather than an expression of it, the island had at least
taught him once more to talk to himself, and he felt sure that the next
step would be to write for himself and to abandon the clever parodies of
Eliot and Housman with which he delighted his friends.

He returned to England with Mrs D'Costa when his contract expired,
arriving at Avonmouth on 18 April 1926 to discover that those friends
had begun inevitable transformations into professional adults. Kenneth
Clark was now serving an apprenticeship under Bernard Berenson.

Patrick Balfour, with his sights on Fleet Street, had resigned himself to a journalistic training in Glasgow. Bobbie Longden had been appointed to a Research Fellowship at Magdalen College, Oxford, which would soon take him to the British School in Rome and thence to a studentship at Christ Church. Things had changed between them: 'our old friendship is of the past', Connolly informed Blakiston. The latter at least was still at Cambridge and the romantic friendship, conducted largely by letter, which he and Connolly had been pursuing for over three years, quickened in intensity. In the next twelve months Blakiston would be the main repository of his news, prejudices and opinions, but more than a desire to inform lay behind this faithful correspondence. Connolly was lonely. Formerly the most promising of them all, he was now directionless. Although he had begun to be aware of women as sexual presences, he was still committed to a world of masculine affections because that was the world he knew. Insecure, he turned instinctively to the Etonian past which Blakiston embodied and when he wrote 'Dere Noel I like you soe' he was disguising a complex declaration.

The country was in the grip of the General Strike. Most of the undergraduates and other young men who kept the trams and buses on the streets during the crisis thought the emergency an exhilarating lark. Connolly, who found a temporary solution to his problems as a special constable, could not agree, and complained to Blakiston that he considered his duties very dull. Matthew and the Oxford Appointments Board continued to make depressing suggestions about work in the colonies. Sligger meant well when he told Connolly, 'You must force yourself to write', but what should he write? He needed to be told. Then salvation arrived. Kenneth Clark had heard rumours about his friend's continued exile overseas and wrote to dissuade him. His employer had a brother-in-law named Logan Pearsall Smith who now proposed to follow Berenson in recruiting a young Oxonian with literary aspirations. Clark envisaged an unintimidating contract:

[Pearsall Smith], though a worldly old gossip, is not disreputable and goatish ... He wants a secretary, or rather he wants to keep some young man from journalism, and in return the young man is to do various odd jobs of scholarship – look up passages in C17 and C18 authors, mainly in quest of philological quarries ... you would find him a trifle pedantic, and very much the slave of polite civilization.[10]

Logan Pearsall Smith, one of the most important influences in Connolly's life, was an expatriate American living with a prospect of Wren's Royal Hospital at 11 St Leonard's Terrace in Chelsea. He had been born in 1865, the son of orthodox Quakers from Philadelphia with substantial interests in glass manufacture. Both Hannah and Robert Pearsall Smith became famous Evangelists, travelling and preaching throughout Europe. They finally settled in London in 1888, but Logan's father was disgraced after revelations that his endeavours on behalf of a female disciple had involved a rather free interpretation of the doctrine of Holy Love. Logan went to Harvard and thence to Oxford, where Pater's influence was supreme. He read Greats at Jowett's Balliol and was friendly with Philip Morrell, who married Lady Ottoline Cavendish-Bentinck, although that friendship ended when Ottoline became involved with Bertrand Russell, who had married Logan's sister Alys. His other sister, Mary, was married to Bernard Berenson; and after she and her husband had equipped I Tatti, their celebrated villa in Tuscany, Logan went regularly to stay.

From an early age he had nursed literary aspirations and his first loyalties lay with Walt Whitman, a family friend, and Henry James; unfortunately, the latter felt obliged to be discouraging when shown the disciple's first attempt at fiction. Pearsall Smith's admirations evolved, however, and gradually his ambitions. He became a great admirer of Baudelaire but grew also to appreciate the literary endeavour which was small in scale but exquisite in form. English baroque prose moved him, and he became an authority on the purple devotions of the Caroline divines, especially Jeremy Taylor, the chaplain to Charles I. The form of self-expression which he most refined, however, was that of the epigram or perfectly balanced paragraph, and the unimpeachably deployed adverb was a morning's work. However, if he was an exceptionally well-read man who could rely on his private income to allow him to devote his time to literature, he was far from being a timid scholar. He declared that 'friendly malice is to my mind the most delicious and enduring of all ties' and projected an intimidating persona.

Nor was he without awareness of the effect he produced. The factotum who succeeded Cyril Connolly in his employment, Robert Gathorne-Hardy, found him acutely self-conscious: 'The character he wished the world to appreciate was as carefully contrived as his prose.' His ecstasies were impersonal: 'Among the qualities of his character which had most impressed and bewitched me, was an unparalleled aesthetic sensibility . . . His enjoyment of any beauty – of countryside or picture or building or a concatenation of words – was like a delphic inspiration.'[11] Bertrand Russell noted: 'He has a passion to be first-rate and says other people's good work makes him miserable.'[12] Beatrice Webb concurred, noting 'a deep-seated melancholy, due to a long record of self-conscious failure to become an artist in words'. Pearsall Smith had no need of their analyses; he knew all about the enemies of promise:

> There are of course many lions (& lionesses) in the path . . . But the worst lion in the path is one that I happily escaped – the lion of an early and premature success, which makes one satisfied with one's facile and acceptable writing, & keeps one back from the lonely & difficult path which alone leads to excellence.[13]

Not everybody found this proud and difficult presence winning. Virginia Woolf detested him: 'What a bore: a dogmatic cultivated American bore; no truth in him; but an uneasy worm squirming for compliments.'[14] He was certainly strange to behold. Clark described him as having a 'tall frame, hunched up, with head thrust forward like a bird . . . balanced unsteadily on vestigial legs which seemed to have lost their sense of direction through long disuse'.[15] However, if Pearsall Smith was a pedant, he was not an untalented one, nor did he languish in obscurity. In 1903, as Anthony Woodhouse, he had published his first belletrist offering, *Trivia*. When the book was reissued in 1918, it appeared under its author's name and Pearsall Smith found himself discreetly famous. Meanwhile, he had adopted British citizenship in 1913 and opened a second establishment, a Tudor farmhouse on the Solent called Big Chilling, in 1915. Further volumes of aphorisms and paragraphs followed, some of them very revealing – 'An improper mind is a perpetual feast'. Yet for all its spite and euphony, Pearsall Smith's writing is unintentionally poignant: his immaculately tailored reflections are so much wishful thinking, so much lonely contemplation of the exigencies of love, life, passion and endeavour, so much repression of the dark moods which eventually engulfed him.

Negotiations began between Pearsall Smith, Urquhart, Matthew and Maud. The aphorist always asked the same questions of his intendant secretaries. Did the candidate for his employment carry a notebook in which to record striking speech? Did he mark and index the reading

that inspired him? Did he read the dictionary? There were always two
further stipulations: the factotum was not to try to write for money and
was not to marry. Connolly fielded the enquiries satisfactorily and was
offered the job at £8 a week. His grandmother was delighted and wrote
enthusiastically, convinced that a foothold had at last been secured in
the mysterious world of letters. Matthew was more controlled in his
congratulation: he offered to supervise his son's income in order to
prevent renewed insolvency and advised him to buy clothes only when
he needed them. He was pleased to hear that Pearsall Smith played
chess 'as it will be an additional inducement for him to keep you'.[16]

It was decided that the new protégé should have a holiday before
taking up his post and Connolly accordingly went to Urquhart's chalet
in June. He found a new guest staying there, John Sparrow, who
seemed 'as intelligent as one could wish'.[17] By July he was back in
England and despatching reassuring bulletins to his friends from Big
Chilling: Pearsall Smith was benevolent, witty, tolerant, and the regime
he imposed was undaunting. Proof of this latter claim lay with the fact
that in September Connolly left England again, travelling this time to
Austria and Turkey with his schoolfriend Freddie Harmer. Their plan
was to write a guidebook to the Balkans: the itinerary was extensive,
and in Constantinople a letter from his new employer awaited Connolly
saying how much he was missed. Some work seems to have been done
on the text but the manuscript was lost. However, Connolly certainly
got as far as asking Cecil Beaton to design a cover for what the latter
then understood to be a 'psychological' travel book. The two prep
school friends were reunited in November when they met to discuss the
project. Beaton still found Connolly 'devilishly amusing' but thought
it 'odd that a person so devastatingly intellectual should give the
impression of so little aesthetic sense'.[18]

Pearsall Smith knew nothing of Beaton's disenchantment. Having
missed his pupil while he was in Turkey, he was prepared to indulge
him to almost any degree if the pampering resulted in the unstopping of
the literary powers he was sure Connolly possessed. In November he
wrote stressing that he asked for nothing from his young friend beyond
a determined application to his writing ambitions and that he believed
in 'the long delays of art'.[19] Six months later he felt he knew Connolly's
character well enough to be sure that he was right to have employed
him: 'Yours is a life of dizzy heights and deep abysses – I envy it in a
way, for it is a life of that poignant reality which is the stuff of art.'[20]

For most of November and December, servants apart, Connolly was alone at the Hampshire farmhouse. Pearsall Smith encouraged him to invite friends down to stay and himself went there at weekends. When it was fine they sailed, when it rained they played chess or read. Connolly liked to complain to friends that he felt isolated during the week but Big Chilling was not a disagreeable prison. Dora Carrington had stayed there and was enchanted by it, describing it to her brother Noël as being 'quite the decentest place you ever saw . . . It's quite in the country miles from any village or houses. A very old Elizabethan . . . black-timbered house – with a huge garden and orchard behind and only two wheat-fields separate it from the sea and marvellous little woods full of primroses and bluebells.'[21]

Connolly kept a notebook, obedient to his employer's dictates and his own sense of literary propriety, and its entries show him perfecting the art of the stylish sentence and the aphorism – 'Youth feels every-where the presence of mortality and never the reality of death.' But its graffiti suggest also that if he did indeed have a literary aptitude it failed to blossom in rural isolation and hungered only for self-description: 'Day by day the office and the altar loom nearer and diminish the stature of my friends while I cower beneath the Tudor eaves, glance over the puddled fields.'[22] In various letters from master to pupil there are recommendations of Gibbon, Saint-Simon, the later Henry James, the inevitable Jeremy Taylor and his French counterpart, St François de Sales. In the spring of 1927 they were both re-reading Virgil; by way of digression, Connolly maintained his passion for Milton, and Pearsall Smith developed an admiration for Tennyson.

There were also projects to be completed and lessons to be learnt. Later Connolly looked back on these instructions as though they were arduous, despite half sensing that for the time being he had fallen on his feet. Pearsall Smith was currently compiling his *Treasury of English Aphorisms* and his disciple sometimes found the research tedious. He noted how the older man 'worked so hard, and so successfully, to give his own aphorisms an air of negligence' but despite his encroaching boredom he became an indispensable adviser. One of Pearsall Smith's enduring *bons mots* was crucially changed by Connolly. Originally the assertion had been: 'The young know what they want; the old are sad and bewildered.' It was as much a reflection of the younger man's condition at the time as his sympathy for verbal music that he per-suaded his mentor to adopt the enduring formula: 'The old know what they want, the young are sad and bewildered.'²³ Under the mandarin's influence, however, the apprentice shed some of his own confusion. He could now see the fabled literary life at close quarters, unaware that Pearsall Smith's was exceptional, and instead of realizing that it was an existence of financial anxiety, lived between overdraft and advance, saw it as bringing two houses, travel and a yacht. And his mentor's belief in the sovereignty of art over life fortified an inner perfectionism and a romantic suspicion that artists were a breed apart, vulnerable to different enemies and prone to finer joys.

Although a difficult man, Pearsall Smith was by no means reclusive and knew a respectable number of figures from literary and artistic London whom his amanuensis was either to meet or hear discussed. Most were Edwardians, survivors from before the flood, but he liked Osbert and Sacheverell Sitwell, who rebelled against tradition from their house in nearby Carlyle Square. Maurice Baring was another Chelsea writer liked by Pearsall Smith and with his wealth, his Etonian pedigree, his aristocratic connections, his classical learning, his linguistic skills and his standing as a Roman Catholic convert, he represented another glamorous embodiment of an unreal literary life. Connolly was romantically impressed and wrote to Balfour that he was 'very much nicer than his novels and nothing of the John Buchan'.²⁴ There was the Poet Laureate, Robert Bridges, the hostess Lady Colefax, the painter Ethel Sands and Evelyn Waugh's kinsman and the literary critic of the *Sunday Times*, Sir Edmund Gosse. Connolly 'listened to much half-hearted abuse [of Bertrand Russell] ... from Logan who could never conceal altogether an underlying admiration, if only for his croquet'.²⁵ He also claimed to have been indoctrinated against Ottoline Morrell, but the indoctrination cannot have been that effective since he certainly went to Garsington on at least one occasion, where he coincided with Walter de la Mare. Frances Partridge, who in 1928 began working at a bookshop in Gerrard Street run by Francis Birrell and David Garnett, remembered that mentor and apprentice used to come and browse and that the older man had prostate trouble and had to rush regularly to the lavatory in the back yard. Book shops were not the perfectionists' only terrain: Peter Quennell knew that on Sunday mornings they would explore Chelsea together and that Pearsall Smith would indicate to Connolly which houses he owned and how after his death they would devolve on his companion.

*

The nearest of the American's neighbours and the closest of his literary friends was an ambassador of Bloomsbury living in Wellington Square. Like Connolly, Desmond MacCarthy was an Old Etonian of Anglo-Irish ancestry. As an undergraduate at Trinity College, Cambridge, in the late 1890s he had been elected to the university's famous yet clandestine society, The Apostles, and membership had brought him into contact not only with the philosopher G. E. Moore but also with Leonard Woolf, Lytton Strachey and Thoby Stephen and later Stephen's sisters Virginia and Vanessa. By circumstance, though not by temperament or aptitude, MacCarthy could have become a founding father of the Bloomsbury Group. In 1919 he had been appointed literary editor of the *New Statesman* and in 1928, on the death of Edmund Gosse, he became senior literary critic at the *Sunday Times*, a post he was to occupy with distinction until his death in 1952. Bloomsbury, however, had hoped for more – the brilliant novel, the unanswerable biography – and disapproved of his literary journalism, despite its range, its informing acumen and its generosity. Like so many other writers he seems to have been beset by the compound frailties of perfectionism and laziness but amongst the Woolfs and their satellites the suspicion formed that he had merely dissipated his genius in grand society and the prodigality of talk. But what talk it was! Quentin Bell wondered 'how few plays have ever enchanted one half so much as Desmond's small talk'.[26] If Bloomsbury thought him a failure, it still recognized the grandeur of his disappointments and Virginia Woolf gave them wistful expression: 'Desmond was the most gifted of us all. But why did he never do anything?'[27]

Nobody doubted his sweetness and charm, however, and it was those qualities which allowed him to move freely between the envious literary circles of Chelsea and Bloomsbury. MacCarthy had a particular sympathy for the young and it was with this affinity in mind that Pearsall Smith introduced him to his clever but rudderless protégé in August 1926. Yet if he was directionless, Connolly was without complacency, and when he met his first editor and another of his life's great influences, he was already at work on other ventures. Pearsall Smith and Kenneth Clark, aware of his interest in the eighteenth century and his responsiveness to nature, were trying to encourage him to write a biography of the Scottish poet James Thomson, author of *The Seasons*. Besides the project on the Balkans, he had written two stories, one about the Bloomsbury prodigy Julia Strachey, whom he had never met, and the other a more ambitious effort which he called 'Dies Irae'. The latter story was set on the Day of Judgment and took the form of a dialogue between Ecclesiastes, Aristippus and Po Chui which developed over lunch in the house of an expatriate American and culminated in their dismayed discovery of eternal life. Pearsall Smith read the story and made suggestions, and both works, more in hope than expectation, were sent to America's modernist literary journal, *The Dial*.

Connolly's other literary focus lay with a magazine he intended to instigate and which he proposed to call 'The Athanasian'. It was the emergence of a long-standing ambition and remained to haunt him even after Pearsall Smith's remark a few months later that everybody had to survive three illusions: falling in love, starting a magazine and thinking they could make money out of keeping chickens. The idea behind 'The Athanasian', as described to Blakiston, was that 'this publication is to perpetuate the views of the editors for their own convenience.'[28] It seems to have been intended only for Old Etonian circulation and was to offer a diet of quotations, epigrams, essays on art by Clark and Longden, other appraisals of literature and travel. Now, in an astonishing gesture of self-absorption, Connolly contemplated collecting the letters to and from his friends and binding them, with notes and cross-references, into a huge work, 'so that one might at least be reminded what adolescence was really like and also preserve a fairly adequate likeness of a lost society'.[29] Neither idea came to anything, but the underlying sentiment, described to Blakiston at the time, remained: 'Surely we are the slaves of our memories.'

The meeting in August went well and Connolly wrote to Blakiston praising MacCarthy's humour, wisdom and kindliness. For his part, the latter must have been impressed by the restless intelligence he encountered because he apparently encouraged Connolly to give thought to the idea of writing another travel book and suggested that as a reader at Heinemann he would be in a strong position to persuade that house to publish it. Every competent editor is always hoping to discover talent to enliven his pages and it was inevitable that the matter should be raised of Connolly's doing some work on the *New Statesman*. Pearsall Smith must have been ambivalent; the employment could have violated his strictures against writing for money. Equally he was keen to advance the interests of both his friends, and if editor and struggling writer got on well, as they appeared to do, there could be no harm in it. Nothing was decided immediately but in the spring of 1927 MacCarthy took

Connolly on at the journal to proof-read and to write short, unsigned reviews. The work was another encouraging advance in activity, besides paying £5 a day.

One of MacCarthy's attractions beyond his generosity lay with the fact that he had a family. Connolly's parents are conspicuous by their absence from the letters he wrote to Blakiston at this time. The domestic focus of his life centred around donnish Big Chilling or else St Leonard's Terrace when he had to be in London. Blakiston offered secondary refuges at Cambridge and his parental home in Lincolnshire but Connolly had nowhere else to go unless it was to see Matthew and Maud and to be reminded that his father complained and that his mother made unwelcome emotional demands. In MacCarthy's wife Molly, however, he seemed to have found a literary mother. She was the daughter of Francis Warre-Cornish, the distinguished Vice-Provost of Eton, and could thus claim distant kinship with Thackeray and the Stephen sisters, Virginia and Vanessa. She was original, unconventional and with a sympathetic intelligence, and the appeal her character made to her husband's young friend was as powerful as it was immediate.

Soon Blakiston was being told of a pact between Connolly and Molly which apparently had as its cohesive force an admiration of the same aspects of the nineteenth and eighteenth centuries. He praised her freedom from convention and her 'vein of divine madness' and by the end of 1926 she featured in almost every letter he wrote to his friend.[30] There was talk of a collaborative novel, with siblings of the 1780s based on himself and her, and an assertion that when the MacCarthys and their close friend Maurice Baring left London his spirits declined. It also seemed that there was almost nothing they could not discuss: 'We have great arguments about women though she agrees really that they aren't very nice. I said they were just unnecessary – though really I have no use for them at all.'[31]

The remark was unfortunate and the assumptions it provoked revealed that there had been less mutual understanding between them than he had liked to imagine. Molly seems to have taken it as an admission of homosexuality and later blandly told her sister Cecilia Fisher that the young man was 'upside-down'. Of course it was based in part on a homosexual fact – until that time he had had no 'use' for women – but it was also made in a spirit of bravado and in an attempt to appear more of a man of the world than he really was at twenty-three. Even before he had made the comment, however, he had become friendly with the MacCarthys' daughter, Rachel, and although she was six years his junior more than mere friendship lay in his attentions. In November 1926 he recorded a midnight supper in which they discussed love, and the conclusion of that discussion, that discretion in courtship was vital. Eyebrows were raised when they started having dinner together – and she had to pay. (She told Frances Partridge that she would not have minded, except that Connolly tended to order either the most expensive dishes or those which were out of season.[32]) Whatever Molly's opinions of these encounters, her benign husband decided on intervention and told his young friend that he should strive for independence, thus avoiding bad habits and censorious gossip. But MacCarthy hated to rebuke anyone; and knowing how vulnerable Connolly was, he qualified his lecture with reassurance: 'I believe in you, & I don't readily believe in people's gifts.'[33]

CHAPTER SEVEN

CYRIL CONNOLLY'S first expeditions to Paris, undertaken with timid Etonians or a restless father, had been unmemorable or unsatisfactory, but in February 1927, returning with Pearsall Smith, he saw the café life and Haussmann's panoramas with new eyes: indeed, as he and his guide competed to number the literary ghosts which throng the banks of the Seine, he thought for the first time of moving to the city. They had arrived on the Golden Arrow; Connolly was in charge of making arrangements but Pearsall Smith paid, and for once the younger man found himself travelling as an affluent tourist with every comfort available. Presently they caught the Sud Express, stopping at Bordeaux to visit the Chapon Fin hotel and to inspect Montaigne's château before continuing to Spain. The detailed and rhapsodic letters Connolly sent to Blakiston, who may have envied the accounts of large cigars and larger hotels which found their way to Cambridge, testified once more to his responsiveness to southern life. They progressed through Avila, Madrid, Toledo, Cordoba, Cadiz, Seville and Granada, with Connolly growing more certain that Italy was eclipsed by Spain as a whole and by the south in particular. At Almuñecar they found a cottage for sale at £700. The price was high but twenty different fruits grew in its garden and its views were unspoilt. Escapist longings, never far distant, overwhelmed him. Pearsall Smith offered to buy the cottage and for an instant, when he wrote to Blakiston for advice, a southern exile shimmered before his eyes, only to disperse when Pearsall Smith said he would resent it if the cottage was left uninhabited for long periods. In March the travellers parted company: the older man stayed in Spain while the younger returned to Morocco, pleased to escape his garrulous companion. Tangier was as cosmopolitan as ever; the English abroad embarrassed him but 'Americans are the cure for Anglophobia.'[1] Returning to Spain, he was reunited with Pearsall Smith and together they caught the boat to Naples. Connolly went to visit Longden at the

British School in Rome before accompanying his mentor to Florence. There he and Longden stayed with Kenneth Clark and his wife, Jane, at their house, Chiostro di San Martino, while Pearsall Smith installed himself nearby with his brother-in-law and Clark's employer, Bernard Berenson.

Connolly tinkered with the Balkans guide while under the Clarks' roof but no doubt had more than one eye on the gathering at I Tatti – not least because of Pearsall Smith's assurance that had he been able to write Berenson would have been a true polymath. Inevitably the Clarks' party was invited to I Tatti for lunches and dinners and when Pearsall Smith proudly introduced his protégé, the latter was intrigued by 'B.B.' and found his mind 'purely feminine'. They disagreed over T. S. Eliot but the visitor was able to impress and ingratiate by correcting his host as to the birthplace of Juvenal. Berenson's talk seems to have been incessant and while Connolly resented some of its assertions, he never doubted its quality or the arrogance and lustre of the personality behind it. He liked Mary Berenson, finding her maternal and comforting, and she and her husband were in turn impressed by the young writer. They invited him to move into I Tatti and Connolly was happy to do so, since the Clarks were expecting John Sparrow and Maurice Bowra and the latter for some reason was a temporary enemy. Blakiston arrived in Italy for his Easter vacation and he and Connolly went to Sicily, the latter finally returning home in April via Vienna, Prague and Dresden.

He reached London with slightly more purpose than before. He began work with MacCarthy and stayed with him intermittently in Wellington Square as well as at St Leonard's Terrace and at Matthew's Naval and Military Hotel. There was talk of him being taken on as an all-purpose assistant to help his new friend with every aspect of the literary pages of the magazine. Nothing seems to have come of this idea, but soon MacCarthy had sufficient confidence in his protégé to entrust him with a challenging review and his own by-line. By now Connolly was familiar with his editor's cardinal rules of reviewing: the word 'I' was to be avoided at all cost and the various books under consideration should be linked by some common denominator. Raymond Mortimer, who also began his critical career writing reviews at the *New States-man*, remembered that MacCarthy took great pains with his inexperienced contributors and would go through their typescripts 'as if he were giving an undergraduate a tutorial'.[2]

Entrusted with a new seven-volume edition of the complete works of

Laurence Sterne, Connolly concentrated on *Tristram Shandy* and *The Sentimental Journey*. Scrupulously he avoided mentioning himself and invoked the critical pantheon of the eighteenth century as a concession to MacCarthy's love of range and learning. With poise and authority he identified the salient features of *Tristram Shandy* – Sterne's consumptive's fear of time, his particular sympathy for dreamers and solitaries and the benign incomprehension that reigns between them. Suspecting that the pace of the novel 'must be the slowest of any book on record', he remarked that it 'reminds one at times of the youthful occupation of seeing how slowly one can ride a bicycle without falling off; yet such is Sterne's mastery, his ease and grace, that one is always upheld by a verbal expectancy . . . and soon there will follow a perfect flow of words that may end with a phrase that rings like a pebble on a frozen pond'.[3] The review appeared in the *New Statesman* at the end of June 1927. He was only twenty-three when he produced this assured bouquet and sensed the pleasure of his allies: this was 'the first reassurance my donnish supporters had that they had not backed a non-starter'.[4]

It takes more than one published review to establish a literary panjandrum and after this debut he languished, reading *Dusty Answer* one day, *To The Lighthouse* another, and finally *Jude The Obscure*. He was restless; and it was a relief to travel once more in July to stay at Urquhart's chalet and become enamoured of a girl he met on the train. She was English, a friend of Jane Clark, and was called Alex, but there was nothing serious in his fascination. After returning from the Chalet des Mélèzes he went to stay with Desmond and Molly in Surrey. Besides the MacCarthys' children, he found Molly's niece Horatia Fisher staying at the house and surrendered himself to sweet obsession.

'Racy' was the daughter of Sir William Fisher, then at the Admiralty, and niece of the historian H. A. L. Fisher. She was seventeen and likely to be impressed by someone older and cleverer who was still too insecure to approach his contemporaries. He found her 'slim, golden, slant-eyed, in her boy's felt hat and brown jumper'.[5] Having witnessed his attentions to her own daughter, and being in any case convinced that Connolly was 'upside-down', Molly MacCarthy watched the courtship sourly. She had already begun to suspect that her husband's young writer was 'mean with his own money and perpetually extravagant with everyone else's' and confided her suspicions to her sister Cecilia who made tactful but ominous remarks to Connolly about the importance of money in marriage. He seems not to have decoded these comments and soon had to be forbidden to call at the Fishers' house in Chelsea or to send Racy letters.

He turned to Molly for support, but found her implacable. She had abandoned him for good and ten years later was still adamant: 'The odd thing is that the only person I have ever met in the large and varied community to which we belong whom I consider crude enough to be described as Bogus is Cyril Connolly.'[6] She was harsh. The amorous explorations of youth are often ill-conceived and if she was at least traditional in censuring his ability to make others pay for him, an ability often condemned by those who lack it, she had never encountered Noël Blakiston, who could have told a very different story of his friend's generosity. Meanwhile, 'Racyitis' took hold: what was forbidden or inaccessible achieved its usual potency for him and he was able to tell Frances Partridge years later that he had been 'mad about' Racy.

MacCarthy stayed aside from the drama, at least temporarily. By nature easy-going, he was also fair-minded, striving to balance his wife's annoyance with his own impressions and his hopes for Connolly's future; resolutely he asked his disciple to join the panel of regular reviewers at the *New Statesman* and to deliver an article once a fortnight at four guineas a time. The high-minded organ of the Webbs was then fourteen years old and still under the jurisdiction of its most famous editor, Clifford Sharp. A son-in-law of E. Nesbit and a lifelong friend of MacCarthy, Sharp was truculent and tyrannical with his freelance contributors but to his staff colleagues he seemed an editor of genius. He was a Fabian and a friend to all the Asquith Set; but he was also a heavy drinker, and when in 1930 the board of the periodical decided reluctantly that he could no longer continue in the job, it was to the America of the Prohibition that their consciences exiled him on a year's sabbatical. Connolly's opinions fluctuated. He thought him clear-sighted and enterprising but also found him intimidating, despite regularly attending the informal editorial meetings Sharp liked to convene in a nearby pub: 'I remember the terror of being sent for by him and entering his room to find his angry handsome bleary philistine face thrust at one. "Look here, Connolly, what the hell does this mean? 'Valéry says.' Who the bloody hell is Valéry? How much do you think our readers can stand?"'[7]

Connolly's appointment came as a surprise to Peter Quennell, who had left Balliol early without a degree and joined his friend in the precarious world of letters. As early as July, Connolly had written to

Patrick Balfour to tell him of MacCarthy's appointment and mentioned Quennell's confident expectation that he himself would be offered the field of new fiction, but would happily recommend Connolly as his substitute if he decided to turn it down. Now he was given poetry to review instead and the two friends would continue in a friendly rivalry on MacCarthy's pages, Connolly saying at one period that 'five minutes with Quennell turns the world like cream in a thunderstorm' and at another that he had an acute sensibility which, drug-like, soon became indispensable and unforgettable.[8] Meanwhile, between September 1927 and October 1929 in his fortnightly pieces Connolly's own critical technique began to emerge and his literary voice, always confident, began not only to be heard but to be listened for.

The junior reviewer accepts the lot of first fiction knowing that he must contend with a lot of rubbish and suspecting that however well he writes about it, readers might overlook his column in favour of more important appreciations. Connolly, however, rose to this problem equipped with two advantages: the Twenties and Thirties were a fertile literary interval and new and interesting writers emerged with a frequency that now lends the period the aspect of a golden age. Furthermore there was the particular complexity of his critical apparatus: alerted by Bowra to modernist experiment, prejudiced by Pearsall Smith against mediocrity, inclined by education to measure new writing against the unfading splendour of classical literature, he was also a stylist, a trained aphorist, an instinctive self-portraitist and, like all born entertainers, a petitioner for attention and applause. Eventually this disposition would prove too large for the narrow dispensation of self-effacing appraisal but in his first months he attacked his job with relish.

In Elizabeth Bowen's first novel, *The Hotel*, he found a promising narrative gift and a maxim which he first mentioned in a letter to Balfour also found its way into the review: 'Though nothing is so rich as life, like all the very rich it is very mean'.[9] In his next piece he indicated that even when required to write about novels long since as dead as their authors he would always try to entertain his readers, if only with pungent definitions: 'The mind is the patient taxidermist which stuffs and preserves the mauled experience laid before it by the senses.'[10] There were new and heart-felt cautions: 'To write an autobiographical novel is to live on capital, hence only permissible when, like Proust, you know you will not live to write about anything else.'[11] He praised the still little-known Ernest Hemingway for his 'consummate dialogue' and saw him as a significant harbinger. He recognized that the First World War had instituted an American dominion in European and particularly English culture and prophesied that figures like Huxley and Eliot would relapse into more conventional forms and less provocative opinions after their early work. He was bored by Radcliffe Hall's lesbian novel *The Well of Loneliness* and testy with its assumptions: 'The world is perfectly prepared to tolerate the invert, if the invert will only make concessions to the world. Most of us are resigned to the doctrines of homosexuals, that they alone possess all the greatest heroes and all the finer feelings, but it is surely preposterous that they should claim a right, not only to the mark of Cain, but to the martyr's crown.'[12] The Edwardian best-sellers seemed out-dated and equally annoying: 'Mr Galsworthy and Mr Walpole are borne down the stream of time, humped anxiously on slabs of property like Eskimo dogs marooned by the thaw on crumbling pack-ice.'[13]

Urquhart was delighted with his friend's success. Having written at the beginning of the year that 'I feel that I have watched over you at times like an old hen – hoping that the chick was really a young eagle', he now wrote promising to subscribe to the *New Statesman*.[14] At twenty-four Connolly's name became known and he later remembered that people would come up to him and ask whether he was the son of the reviewer. Sharp was impressed, recognizing a talented iconoclast and somebody whose style and standards he could trust. He began to charge Connolly with special commissions: 'I talked of the difficulty of putting Galsworthy in his proper place. Bennet agreed, but insisted that it was a thing that really ought to be done by somebody, because we could not allow the world to think that we really regard Galsworthy as one of our greater writers . . . I wonder whether the idea appeals to you?'[15] It did, but whatever his editors thought of *Swan Song*, the newly published conclusion to *The Forsyte Saga*, it would never have appealed to Connolly. It is easy to demolish, of course, but nobody now would disagree with his verdict: 'To read *Swan Song* is to enter a world in which move people who must once, one gathers from their chance allusions, have been human beings. Like paintings on Sicilian carts, like marionettes, the characters recall some buried legend of men's doings.'[16] Yet even as this early success took hold, Connolly felt restless. He complained to Balfour that the 'average book reviewer is an educated low brow, perpetually shocked by independence and hoping that by performing the acts of faith faith will eventually be given.'[17]

*

With his professional life at last beginning to take shape, Connolly turned to address the other major uncertainty which had dogged him since Oxford: his homelessness. His former nurse had just left him a cottage at Box near Bath but although the bequest was an agreeable surprise it could not satisfy his domestic needs: he had to have independence from parents and surrogate parents alike and that independence had to exist in London. Patrick Balfour, who had recently moved to London, was also in need of somewhere to live and they decided to share a flat. With his travels, his obsession with Racy Fisher and his nervous aversion to practical problems, Connolly himself could do nothing to find a property. The duty fell on Balfour and in July he sent good news of an exciting discovery in a letter addressed to the Chalet, forwarded to St Leonard's Terrace and forwarded again to Big Chilling. He had found a flat at 26a Yeoman's Row in Knightsbridge: 'It is very beautiful, furnished by an antique dealer in Italian and such-like furniture. A large sort of hall-studio downstairs which could be my room and sort of general drinking and sitting room and upstairs a sitting room, looking onto gardens, with lots of sun, which you could have as your own.'[18] There were only two bedrooms, but he was sure Connolly would like it. The total rent was £6 6s a week and in order to secure the lease he wanted to move quickly. He proposed also that they hire a maid. His friend, initially unenthusiastic, wanted to add a Persian cat to the ménage; the pet never materialized but Connolly reconciled himself: better Mayfair or Belgravia or the 'leafy tranquil cultivated *spielraum* of Chelsea',[19] but Knightsbridge was near to all three and he had once lived nearby in Brompton Square.

The property was secured, Connolly moved in at the beginning of September 1927 and Pearsall Smith gave his approval. Balfour found a maid and kitchen-help called, appropriately, Mrs Eggs, but did not propose to spend much time at home. He was now a gossip columnist for the Rothermere Press and warned his cohabitant that he might be 'slightly society'.[20] He also proposed a pact – 'no apologies for our guests . . . no mutual resentments if we lead fairly independent lives.'[21] His warnings proved no less than fair: his relentless socializing led Evelyn Waugh to re-create him as the Earl of Balcairn, gossip columnist for the *Daily Excess*, in *Vile Bodies*, but the parties at Yeoman's Row had begun long before then.

It was as a débutante that Georgiana Russell, later Mrs Noël Blakiston, met Patrick Balfour, and she often found herself at Yeoman's Row

either for a large party or for quieter evenings with Balfour and his
flat-mate, whom she now befriended. She remembered that the parties
were 'incessant', that the two friends were competitive about their
amours, and that Connolly used to pretend to despise Balfour for being
a hack and would call from his upper sitting room: 'We're having an
intellectual discussion up here but you can still join us if you want.'[22]
Another guest was Mary Lutyens, the daughter of the architect, who
also associated Yeoman's Row with 'huge and noisy' parties. She
remembered that whereas Connolly talked a great deal about his career
at Eton, Balfour, an Old Wykehamist who had been badly bullied at
school, seldom raised the subject. Money was a constant problem and
she sensed that nobody would have thought twice about selling Balfour
a morsel of gossip for £10. His friends suspected that he resorted to
other means to secure information to furnish his pages and played on
his journalist's prurience: Connolly used to leave his diary lying around
in the knowledge that Balfour was liable to read it. John Betjeman, who
named the house 'The Yeo' and who eventually succeeded Connolly as
an inhabitant, called it 'that almshouse for all exiled Oxford aesthetes',
indicating that an Oxonian presence pervaded it.[23] When self-
absorption, disguised as the muse of fiction, visited Connolly in 1927 or
1928, he began a story, 'The English Malady', about the cohabitation
of two Oxford friends called Miles and Hugo:

> [Miles] was short and ugly ... Hugo was tall and could telephone for
> ever. Both at first wore the stigma of their university, a facile, slightly
> shabby charm, a rather unscrupulous careerism, and an opportune belief
> that there existed a short cut to every worthwhile experience which only
> they knew how to take.[24]

The fragment continued with Miles deciding to write a novel and
exploring low-life London in order to escape Hugo's relentless
socializing but invention flagged and Connolly abandoned the project.
The late Twenties were a golden age of outrageous parties, with the
press delighting in the antics of the so-called Bright Young People, and
although Connolly's instinct told him there was comedy in the subject
he could only sustain insight and satire when lost in self-contemplation.
He lacked Evelyn Waugh's invention and abandon and it took the latter
to document the trend in a fiction of enduring worth, *Vile Bodies*.

All his life Connolly loved parties (although more as a host than a
guest) and his social career began at Yeoman's Row. But he combined

minor participation in Balfour's more philistine and patrician world with appearances at the literary parties of the day and saw many of the leading artistic figures of the time at play. There was that embodiment of the Twenties, Michael Arlen, 'double-breasted at the Ritz in London or Paris, in dark blue shirt and grey flannel trousers (Cannes) and sometimes late at night at the cabmen's shelter at Hyde Park Corner (White Tie)'.[25] There was Arnold Bennett, 'avuncular to the Sitwells and Aldous Huxley, a talent-spotter and friend to the young. . . . To meet him was an excitement, leaving one reassured by the prestige of letters and with an intimation of favours to come.'[26] There were encounters with the painter Pavel Tchelitchew, the private views of Cecil Beaton, Garsington, and 'the incredible stupid air of luxurious abandon on Lady Cunard's face as she danced with the Prince of Wales'.[27] The Berensons came to London and stayed with Lady Horner. They wanted to see their young friend and he went to dinner there on at least one occasion in October 1927. Over soup, fish, partridge, ices, champagne and port, Berenson was digressive and didactic, and spoke about the nature of rebellion, the significance of Bloomsbury, and the decadence or otherwise of England before reassuring Connolly: 'Ideas will come but youth will go.'[28]

'B.B.' was right – ideas were coming and Connolly confided to his diary that he felt creativity surging like sap through his system. He was working on a story he proposed to call 'Green Ending' and wrote to describe its plot to Blakiston: it began at Gabbitas and Thring, where the hero, sent down from Oxford, reports for an interview before being sent off to the Colonies and murdering someone. Sending a hopeful bulletin to Molly MacCarthy, he said that the novel was not autobiographical and that he hoped to invent all the characters apart from one drawn from Maurice Bowra.

His school contemporaries Brian Howard and Robert Byron were planning a magazine which they had decided to call 'Venture'. They had already established contributions from Evelyn Waugh, Peter Quennell, Henry Green, the Acton brothers and Tom Driberg, and had no doubts that Connolly belonged in this precocious company. They hoped he would write a story to be called 'The Red Earth of the South' and Howard assured him: 'Only a southern setting can produce that pagan atmosphere, with which I feel you will infect this section.'[29] Sadly, the venture collapsed before the piece could be written. Connolly had kept a Commonplace Book which he showed to Anthony Powell, who was then working for the publishers Duckworth. Nothing came of the idea, but Powell never forgot his friend's characteristic indemnity: 'If your firm doesn't like it, make some excuse when you give it back to me. Say the Autumn List is already full, or something like that. Not just that they don't think it good enough to publish.'[30] Powell had also been shown the book about the Balkans but Duckworth found its 25,000 words an inconvenient length and Connolly encountered more enthusiasm from David Garnett at the Nonesuch Press. He was 'delighted' with it and suggested that an American publisher, perhaps Viking, should be approached. He then asked for changes to avoid libel action: 'To be ruined by Thomas Cook and Son, or even by a motor-car proprietor in a Greek village, would be an awful fate.'[31] Connolly presumably made the necessary alterations and may have tried to interest Garnett in 'Green Ending' because a year later in February 1929 the latter wrote that the guide would sell better if published after a well-received novel. Connolly received an advance of £30 on either the guide or the novel, whichever was completed first. But the novel was abandoned and the guide lost by the publishers, and one is left to ponder Anthony Powell's letter, which praised the passages in the guide on 'sulking, traveller's loneliness, friendship' and suggested that Connolly should definitely consider bringing out a volume of his selected reviews.[32]

In the spring of 1928 Connolly went to the Continent once again: Paris first, which he liked even more, and then to I Tatti, from where he wrote in May to complain to Blakiston of the cheerless luxury of the life there and the boredom of the rich. Distraction came from the occupants of another villa nearby, L'Ombrellino, briefly the home of Galileo and now the property of George Keppel, the complaisant husband of Edward VII's last mistress, Alice Keppel. Their daughter, Violet Trefusis, whose affair with Vita Sackville-West had scandalized London a decade before, was staying at the villa when Connolly was a guest of the Berensons and now he got to know the famous beauty. He wrote to Balfour that she suggested the 'Queen of Gomorrah', attractive, 'vicious looking' and somehow the only person in the party who seemed 'modern'.[33]

By coincidence he went from Italy to Berlin to stay with Longden as a guest of Vita Sackville-West's husband Harold Nicolson, then councillor at the British Embassy. Gladwyn Jebb was present along with Raymond Mortimer; Ivor Novello, the famous singer and composer, appeared, as well as Lord Berners, the eccentric peer. Connolly was impressed by Nicolson: he envied his apparently perfectly arranged life, with its offices of husband, writer, father, friend, man of action and gentleman, and in spite of perhaps too much diplomatic polish and suave inscrutability, decided he liked him more than anybody he had met in London apart from MacCarthy and Maurice Baring. Nicolson seems not to have known what to make of Connolly, describing him in a letter to his wife as being like 'the young Beethoven with spots . . . He flattered your husband. He sat there toying with a fork and my vanity, turning them over in his stubby little hands. He tells fortunes. Palmistry.'[34] On the evening of Longden's departure, Nicolson, Mortimer and Connolly discussed their youth, a time which Connolly said should be enjoyed as 'a period of misadventure'. Novello appears to have played no part in any intellectual discussions but Connolly thought him sweet-natured and decided that his homosexuality was of the sort that seemed as though it had been picked up 'as part of a gentleman's education'.[35]

Gladwyn Jebb appears not to have cared for Novello, but he was delighted to accept Connolly's companionship on a tour of Dresden, Prague, Bavaria and the Rhineland. In Prague they were inspired by the Jewish cemetery and visited what Jebb called a *nachtlokale* where Connolly seems to have had an encounter with a prostitute. They played one of Connolly's favourite parlour games, the compiling and answering of questionnaires about each other's pet vices, favourite places and so on. On the subject of 'ambition', Connolly said he wanted to 'create a work of art'.[36] By the time the travellers parted company in Dusseldorf, they were contemplating the possibility of sharing a flat together at a later date. Connolly returned to England to be confronted by depression, particularly when he compared his own rootless existence with Nicolson's. He found England 'still fussing about the prayer book . . . Americanized without America's vitality', and he thought it significant that Joyce, now an obsession, had fled the British Isles – perhaps it was what artists had to do.[37] He went to stay at Long Barn in Kent as a guest of Harold and Vita Nicolson but although he enjoyed himself there, the interlude did nothing to lift his spirits. He had no money and no erotic life, although convinced that that interest now lay with women. There seemed nothing in prospect but an endless career of reviewing other people's books, some of which were good, some of which should never have been written, some by writers of his own age, some by writers he knew.

This last contingency was inevitable: every Oxford generation produces its crop of hopeful novelists and now, three years after Connolly's
graduation, the race for fame was underway. With 'Green Ending' and
'The English Malady' languishing in notebooks, the young critic
watched for familiar contenders. He was by nature competitive; his
character was prickly but never smug and like every successful examinee
he had learnt to glance over his shoulder at the challenger approaching
from behind. Whereas Noël Blakiston, about to join the Civil Service, an
institution where Connolly would have had neither competence nor
interest, could be viewed with unequivocal affection, Peter Quennell, a
fellow writer, could not. The man most tipped for fame and success
amongst Connolly's university generation had been Harold Acton, its
undisputed leader of style, fashion and literary precocity. So when
Connolly received his first novel, *Humdrum*, to review, he cannot have
been altogether surprised; but astonishment lay in the other book which
appeared simultaneously, Evelyn Waugh's *Decline and Fall*. Acton later
claimed that Connolly knew both novelists well when he came to
compare their books but that was not the case. He himself had half
avoided the future critic at Eton, where he seemed 'dictatorial' and 'a
bully', while Waugh, following their slight acquaintance at Oxford, had
disappeared to teach in remote parts. From that exile, however, had
come the material for his remarkable fictional début.

The novel had already been favourably received by Raymond Mortimer and also by Arnold Bennett in his important column in the
Evening Standard but Mortimer was not an aspiring novelist while
Bennett had been a well-established one for twenty years. Connolly still
had hopes of writing a comic novel but it was not the least of his critical
qualities that his literary acumen exceeded his capacity for destructive
envy. It was perhaps tactless to compare Waugh's work with Acton's,
especially as *Decline and Fall* was dedicated to Acton, but in some ways
it was almost inevitable. Both purported to be modern comedies but in
Connolly's assessment, only one was either modern or comic: '*Humdrum* falls rather flat ... [and] reads like a painstaking attempt to
satirize modern life by a Chinaman who has been reading *Punch*.' In
Waugh's novel, by contrast, 'the humour throughout is of that subtle
metallic kind which, more than anything else, seems a product of this
generation ... A reviewer has few epithets of praise at his command,
owing to the high mortality in the vocabulary of appreciation, but of
Decline and Fall he can say that though not a great book, it is a funny

book, and the only one that, professionally, he has ever read twice.'[38]

Acton was inevitably upset by Connolly's frankness and although his account of the episode in his autobiography, *Memoirs of an Aesthete*, is wearily philosophical – 'such was the treatment I had learnt to expect from literary friends' – he privately decided that the critic was 'a treacherous Irishman'.[39] Connolly, too, had reached a conclusion. Beside Waugh's début, 'Green Ending' seemed hollow and lame: his own account of the mishaps of a young man lately down from Oxford needed radical surgery and he destroyed six chapters. Soon he would abandon the project altogether. Waugh meanwhile was delighted and pressed the critic to lunch with him and his first wife at their home in Islington. Connolly recalled that the lunch lasted all day: there was a varnished map of London for a table-cloth; the house was tiny and immaculate; Mrs Waugh seemed to her guest like 'a very, very pretty little china doll' and they discussed Arnold Bennett, who had come to dinner the night before.[40] It was a reacquaintance between the two writers which was to last, with wary amity, until Waugh's death.

CHAPTER EIGHT

LITERARY LONDON saw another beginning that year. In June 1928 Desmond MacCarthy started his magazine *Life and Letters* and sought contributions from Connolly, who duly supplied an appreciation of Joyce which appeared early in 1929. Privately, however, he was disappointed with MacCarthy's new vehicle, which he found 'august and readable as any late Victorian arsewiper, and as daring and original as a new kind of Barley water'.[1] The existing literary journals, *The Criterion* and *The Mercury*, seemed to him to devote themselves to what was outdated and mediocre and now his trusted and admired mentor had launched a publication which, despite generous subsidies, trusted to caution and seemed reluctant to experiment and happy to ignore the immense experiments which were taking place on the Continent. Nevertheless his attempt to introduce Joyce to its readers was welcomed by MacCarthy who published the appraisal intact and expressed a possible interest in publishing Connolly's journal.

Suddenly, however, good relations between editor and apprentice temporarily soured. In August MacCarthy went to the *Sunday Times* and his post at the *New Statesman* fell to Raymond Mortimer, whose relations with Connolly were always happy and who remembered him as being 'grateful for advice, in contrast to some less talented contributors'.[2] MacCarthy, by contrast, was irritated. Finally succumbing to Molly's views, perhaps, and taking as vindication the fact that Connolly still claimed his stipend from Pearsall Smith without doing much to earn it, he wrote to his protégé accusing him of being opportunistic and exploitative. His generosity was such, however, that he wrote a second letter soon afterwards stressing that he still admired Connolly and pointing out that the younger man should strive for independence in order to avoid the gossip and censure of others. 'I believe in you and I don't readily believe in people's gifts.'[3] The attack still hurt and prompted an explanation from its victim which was

unsparing yet disarming: smart Bohemia daunted him and since the
difficulties with Racy Fisher a year ago he had felt like a pariah. He
admitted that he was vulnerable to all slights, real or imagined, and was
capable of trying to inflict injury on others. The brisker patterns of
London friendship bewildered him and he was only now relinquishing
the conviction that all women were either tarts or angels. His confession was fair as far as it went and appeased MacCarthy, since the rift
soon mended. What his mentor did not learn was that Connolly sought
distraction from his various insecurities in the consolations of a prostitute introduced to him by Gerald Brenan. She was called Lily – her
married name, intriguingly, was 'Connolly' – and although she could
find no lasting place in her young client's affections Brenan lent her
immortality of a sort when he put her in his pseudonymous picaresque
novel, *Jack Robinson*, as 'a lusty female with red cheeks and saucy
black eyes'.[4]

Meanwhile Connolly felt an increasing disillusion with the *New
Statesman*, despite his friendly relations with Raymond Mortimer. In
the occasional journal he was keeping at the time he confided his
irritation: Sharp was a bully, the secretary teased him for taking so
many holidays, nobody in the office approved of what he wrote. To
MacCarthy he developed his disquiet, and told the former editor that
his magazine now seemed little better than the worst of Fleet Street and
that like all other English journalism it was xenophobic and outdated.
The publisher G. Bell contacted him, wondering whether he would like
to write a book about the contemporary novel, on the strength of his
holding 'the chair of Novel Criticism at the *New Statesman*' but the
offer did nothing to dispel feelings of futility.[5] Europe beckoned. He
became increasingly and romantically convinced that life in England
was untenable for artists and writers and much of his journal in the
autumn of 1928 is dedicated to angry or lyrical wanderlust: London
was a city for middle-class families and rich bachelors but not for the
unattached and itinerant poor; Paris alone had café life and all that it
implied.

No doubt part of the problem was the fact that his salary at the *New
Statesman* did not cover his extravagance, despite the increment supplied by Pearsall Smith. Whatever Molly MacCarthy thought, Connolly
had a very generous streak and loved to take his friends to dinner at the
Ivy or Boulestin, or in Blakiston's case to supply numerous books. He
never had enough money and inevitably began to fall into arrears with

his share of the rent on Yeoman's Row. There seemed nothing to hold him in England apart from his new fiction column at the newspaper. A sudden expedition to Paris that autumn produced little but irritation, however. He encountered William Walton, Constant Lambert and Philip Heseltine and the evening turned into a long carousal in bars and then unseemly brawling: drunkenly, the others began to taunt Connolly as 'Desmond MacCarthy's bum-boy'. Connolly retorted that he was no more MacCarthy's 'bum-boy' than William Walton was Osbert Sitwell's. The incident inevitably reached Sitwell who promptly contacted his solicitors and a letter demanding retractions caught up with Connolly in Berlin in 1929. Peter Quennell rebuked his impetuosity: 'I must say Cyril dear it was scarcely tactful to attack the Sitwells to little Willie of all people . . . It must have been a very diverting evening.'[6]

He returned to England for Christmas and stayed at Sledmere in Yorkshire with the wealthy Sykes family. Anglophobia lifted in this opulent company – 'O the joy of lingering over port and brandy with men in red coats telling dirty stories while it snows outside' – and the well-staffed splendour of the establishment took his imagination back to 'the grim rich game-pie England of 18th century squires'.[7] He accompanied Richard Sykes back to Paris a few days afterwards and stayed on after his friend returned. He explored Montparnasse, developed a cold, saw Violet Trefusis. He also met two American girls, Mara Andrews and Jean Bakewell, and one day, after the three had had lunch at the Crémaillière, Mara slipped away leaving her friend and the young Englishman alone and 'Jean and I supped at the Vikings and fell for each other.'[8]

He had nobody to advise him and was uncertain whether to stay or leave. His parents were in every sense distant, Molly was inaccessible, Longden in Rome, Pearsall Smith unworldly and misogynist and Balfour torn between the pleasures of boys and the legitimacy of women. He came back to London and hated it, pining for Jean and resenting more than ever the rain and the cocktail parties. He went to stay with Julia Strachey and her husband, the sculptor Stephen Tomlin, and they convinced themselves that expatriation alone brought freedom. Jean cabled him in February and this time he was not uncertain. He resolved to go back to Paris at once, packed a large suitcase and left Balfour a note explaining that ever since his return he had been miserable. He had an empty carriage in the train to Tilbury and played slow foxtrots on his portable gramophone, feeling 'that at last I had become an interesting person again'.⁹ This was the romantic life, even though the passage was rough and sleepless and Dunkirk bitterly cold; and although nobody met his train when he arrived in Paris, dirty and unshaven, at ten on Sunday morning, Jean was waiting at home for him and it was a complacent and happy reflection that twenty-four hours after leaving London he was dancing to jazz in the Bal Nègre.

He took her to the places where he had been beguiled in Spain and they returned to Paris to explore its literary and cultural life in earnest. Besides jazz there was the cinema, and they hastened to see *Un Chien Andalou*, the collaboration between Salvador Dali and Luis Buñuel which shocked audiences everywhere and marked Connolly's introduction to Surrealism: 'With the impression of having witnessed some infinitely ancient horror, Saturn swallowing his sons, we made our way out into the cold of February 1929.'¹⁰ Above all, there was modernist literature. He already knew Sylvia Beach, the expatriate American who had published *Ulysses* and who ran the celebrated bookshop Shakespeare and Company at 12 Rue de l'Odéon. In March she had written saying she was looking forward to reading his essay on Joyce in *Life and Letters* and to assure him that he would get on with another wandering writer: 'The bulls will be a great bond between you and Hemingway if he is back here by the time you come to Paris.'¹¹ Having arranged that Pearsall Smith's unfailing stipend be sent to him at the bookshop, Connolly inevitably became a regular visitor and duly met Hemingway; presently they had dinner and established an enduring if unlikely friendship.

Sylvia Beach was happy to introduce her young friend to her most radical writer and Connolly met Joyce at his apartment in the Rue de Grenelle. The wandering dandy received him dressed in white cricketing blazer and blue trousers and talked about the scattered cricketing families of Ireland. He liked Connolly's comparisons between himself and Wyndham Lewis which had appeared in the *New Statesman* the previous July but steered the conversation away from literature to Ireland, the Vernons, Brian Boru's sword. In another introduction Connolly discovered that André Gide was no less remarkable: behind his clerical manner there was a suggestion of Bloomsbury in the black hat he wore and of the monoliths of Easter Island in his distinguished, stony features. Unlike Joyce, he was prepared to discuss literature: he asked the young Englishman his views of Huxley's latest novel, *Point Counter Point*, and they both laughed when Connolly said 'mais c'est un faux *Faux-monnayeurs*'.[12] Even without such august encounters there was Parisian bohemia, then at its most self-conscious apogee, and Jean and Mara knew many of its inhabitants, some domiciled, some transients, a few talented. Gregor Michonze was a young Rumanian Surrealist painter who had fought in the Russian Revolution before struggling to distil his vision in the mandatory Left Bank garret. Later he painted Connolly and Jean; later still he found his way into Connolly's only completed novel, *The Rock Pool*. Ford Madox Ford came and went, while Henry Miller and the photographer Brassai were friendly with Alfred Perles, who was then surviving on contributions to the Paris edition of the *Chicago Tribune*. Stern Orwell, simultaneously in Paris, avoided the carousel and Connolly had no notion of his presence in the city. Had they met, however, even Orwell might have accepted his schoolfriend's hope that here, surely, where people seemed to live for their art and subsist cheaply on the threshold of creative experiment, Connolly's own originality would rouse and stretch itself to permanent expression.

At Easter Connolly and Jean joined Peter Quennell and his first wife, Nancy Stallybrass, in Corsica. Quennell found the young American a 'sulky little girl, swarthy, not awfully *soignée*',[13] but nevertheless liked her personality. In May Jean returned to America, but even before her ship weighed anchor at Le Havre she and Connolly had made plans to live together in Paris in the autumn. In the meantime they would write. He returned to Berlin to see Harold Nicolson, but his time there went badly. James Lees Milne, also staying, complained that Connolly was 'not an ideal guest' and that he arrived without matches, stamps, soap or cigarettes. Perhaps in a bid to ingratiate himself with Nicolson he wrote playlets which were performed in the latter's apartment, sometimes in the presence of the ambassador, Sir Horace Rumbold. David Herbert, another guest, recalled that Connolly always returned to the same theme: 'Cyril was the pimp, Christopher [Sykes] the carpet-seller and I was the slave girl.'[14] Harold Nicolson wrote to Connolly in July: 'I tried to make myself think that what annoyed me was your having so much time on your hands, such liberty etc., and then gibing at me for my "work fetish" ... I was jealous, I suppose, of your being young and free and so bloody clever ... You fiddle with what I really believe is genius.'[15]

Connolly went back to Paris for a week before returning to England. Landing at Newhaven, he went to Rottingdean to stay with Enid

Bagnold, who was at once a successful novelist and Lady Jones, wife of Sir Roderick Jones, the head of Reuters. She was a friend to Desmond MacCarthy, Logan Pearsall Smith and Gladwyn Jebb and had already heard a lot about Connolly when she met him. Not the least of the rumours to have reached her was that he had been a poor guest in Berlin, and she approached a mutual friend, Leigh Ashton, Keeper of the Department of Textiles at the Victoria and Albert Museum, for clarification of other stories: 'Does he like men or women?'[16] In the event she took to her guest; they became quite close friends in the early Thirties and were on affectionate terms for the rest of their lives. Rumours from Berlin were corroborated when Connolly stayed and stayed, finally admitting that he was too poor to buy a ticket back to London. She lent him the money and he reimbursed her. Meanwhile Leigh Ashton relayed her curiosity and Connolly, staying with Pearsall Smith and Mrs Berenson, was stung into a lengthy letter of reproach and self-analysis which he despatched from Big Chilling. He admitted that he had stayed too long in Berlin and wished, although he had been warned against confiding in her, that she had asked him about his sex life instead of Ashton. It was typical of him to admit to his insecurity, and to confess that he had been worried to discover that, initially at least, he had liked her more than she had liked him. But it was part of his charm and his self-protection to plead guilty and hope for leniency: 'I have enough courage to acknowledge my misdeeds but only half enough to find them out.'[17] He mentioned that he had written an article which he thought might amuse her; an article which appeared in the *New Statesman* in August 1929 and was entitled 'Ninety Years of Novel Reviewing'. Completed only two years after MacCarthy had tried to recruit him as a journalist of objectivity and sober disquisition, it revealed how far Connolly had come. It was defiantly frank – for a romantic who had been taught to see literature as a cultivation of the exquisite and enduring, it was hell having to think of pungent responses month in month out to novels which should never have been written and he said so. But it was also defiantly individual: a brilliant style was harnessed to writing which was at once a defence of the best and a lifelong portrait of the critic as failure:

> The reviewing of novels is the white man's grave of journalism; it corresponds, in letters, to building bridges in some impossible tropical climate. The work is gruelling, unhealthy, and ill-paid, and for each scant

clearing made wearily among the springing vegetation the jungle overnight encroaches twice as far . . . Remember that the object of the critic is
to revenge himself on the creator . . . He stands behind the ticket-queue of
fame, banging his rivals on the head as they bend low before the guichet.
When he has laid out enough he becomes an authority, which is more
than they will.[18]

It was a valediction as well as an affirmation of strength of purpose.
It would in a sense have been easier to stay in London but Connolly
despised easy options and despised himself when he took them. Pearsall
Smith encouraged the idea of a Parisian life and the malcontent felt
wanted there. Sylvia Beach endorsed the move; Violet Trefusis, writing
to him on 20 September 1929, was enthusiastic: 'I am so glad you are
coming to spend the winter in Paris. I long to talk to you about this and
many other things – your letter was perhaps the most intelligent one I
received about my book excepting one from Colette.'[19] Above all, there
was Jean, now languishing in Baltimore but also believing that expatriation alone brought freedom.

Frances Jean Bakewell was eighteen and at an art school in Paris when
she first enchanted Connolly. Just as Paris was itself alien, full of artistic
innovation and freer morals, so Jean was an alien with it, separated
from everything familiar to him by her sex and by her upbringing,
which was modern American rather than Edwardian and English. She
had been born in 1910 in Pittsburgh into an affluent family responsible
for that city's first skyscraper and also for the construction of the first
glass factory in the United States. In 1918 her parents had divorced and
Jean, her sister Annie and brother Tom accompanied their mother to
California before returning two years later to the East Coast. Mrs
Bakewell married again, this time to Daniel List Warner, a businessman
from Baltimore, and the couple settled in Maryland. Mrs Warner had
been a suffragette in what Jean later called 'a giggling sort of way'; she
had Quaker connections and claimed distant kinship with Pearsall
Smith. Jean's father devoted his enthusiasms to golf and fast cars. He
died in 1932 but boasted forebears who had emigrated from Derbyshire
to Pennsylvania in the 1700s and suggested a tenuous cousinship not
only with the Vernons of Sudbury and Bakewell but with their cadet
branch at Clontarf.

In the 'Alpdodger' story, another fragment which revealed his attempts to turn experience into fiction, Connolly said that the American girls studying in Paris in the Twenties had an 'incalculable' effect on the young European men they encountered. Certainly Jean herself was to prove one of the greatest liberating forces in his life. Although she was younger than him, perhaps less intelligent and less remarkable and certainly the product of a less refined educational process, she was in some ways more sophisticated, more assured and more finished. He never forgot that when they first met she was reading the novels of Ronald Firbank. She too was abreast of modern writing but that particular taste suggested other interests; it was Firbankian of her to pretend that she was the lesbian lover of her friend Mara Andrews, with whom she shared a flat in the Rue de Vaugirard, more Firbankian still that in her earliest surviving letter to him she should admit: 'I should like to try flagellation but I am dreadfully afraid one of us would giggle. I shouldn't like to be beaten myself but I would enjoy being tied I think.'[20] Her sexuality was potent and uninhibited, especially compared to Connolly's. Lily aside, he had never slept with a young girl before, and he found something pagan about Jean, 'with her youth, her passive and natural pleasure, her lovely boy's body', which suggested the world of Tibullus and the Greek anthology.[21] She seemed an uncomplicated hedonist, independent, adventurous, a celebrant of the moment – everything which his profane and sophisticated education would have vouchsafed him had he not also been overwhelmed by self-doubt and introspection. Besides being liberating, she was an attractive personality: warm, sympathetic, generous, witty and approachable, and in her earliest days at least there was a sultry distinction in her high cheekbones and broad, strong features which apparently confirmed stories of some Red Indian forebear.

Yet there was a melancholy side to her adventures. She had had two affairs by the time she met Connolly and by the second of those lovers she was pregnant, the Frenchman involved having tricked her with a damaged contraceptive to force her into marriage and, as he hoped, into sharing her allowance. For Jean was rich, although Connolly claimed that he was ignorant of this good fortune when he first knew her and undecided as to the influence an eventual £15,000 a year had on her attractiveness. There was no difficulty at least in finding 500 francs for her illicit abortion but the operation was not without risk. She missed the post-operative consultation and the complications of this negligence were to have miserable and far-reaching implications.

But Jean was cavalier and succumbed easily to distractions. Meeting her a couple of years later the writer Sybille Bedford noted that something in Jean suggested a 'Daisy Miller of the Jazz Age'. She remembered her 'Toulouse Lautrec, sulky, erotic looks' but also noted, diplomatically, that she 'bore the marks of American Prohibition'.[22] She was not alone in her observations. Connolly proudly introduced Jean to his school-friend Terence Beddard but may have been surprised by the latter's reaction. Allowing that he found her 'a delightful companion and very attractive', Beddard was also convinced that 'she seems almost more unsuited to matrimony than you are'. He explained his misgivings: 'I should seriously attempt to cure Jeannie of cocktails ... A girl of 18 can go on drinking four or five before meals for a pretty considerable period without it upsetting her seriously, but she can't keep it up ... she seemed so very independent and yet really so very much in need of someone to control and look after her.'[23]

Beddard was perceptive – Jean proved more vulnerable and less resilient than she seemed in the spring of 1929 – but the letters she sent to her besotted Englishman gave little indication of inner frailties. In July, writing to placate his jealousy, she assured him that her previous affairs meant nothing to her now but left him in no doubt that she guarded her emotional autonomy: 'I am not ashamed of anything I've done though I may have regrets at times ... I feel though perhaps wrongly that I have as much right as you to have affairs ... Be logical, darling ... I guess my life is my own even if it's a mess ... I'd rather have my own mess than anybody else's perfection.'[24] She added that she had no fears about his continued loyalty to Racy Fisher. Furthermore she liked the idea of children – two or three – but not before the age of twenty-five. The letter was very long: Jean took trouble with him, fully aware that for all his wit and charm he was an insecure and prickly character.

Reunited in Paris in the autumn they took a circular room on the first floor of the Hôtel Louisiane in the Rue de Seine. He wrote to MacCarthy to report the acquisition of some unorthodox pets, four ferrets named Chica, Bianca, Paco and The English Rose which were fed on raw liver bought from a neighbouring horse butcher. (The English Rose became the favourite. She 'saw three continents from a warm sleeve' and was taken everywhere in Paris.[25] Her favourite spot was the public garden by Saint-Germain-des-Prés. She was later killed by peasant women in the country.) He added that they spent a lot of time in cinemas, museums, concert halls, restaurants and bars musettes, that Jean imagined England to be populated by Le Touquet colonels while he envisaged an America full of travelling salesmen. In theory, the affair was still a closely guarded secret, not least because matrimony – which they had contemplated from an early stage – was the supreme *trahison des clercs* as far as Pearsall Smith was concerned, and although Connolly did not imagine his marriage would result in anything as drastic as disinheritance, there seemed no reason to doubt that Pearsall Smith would discontinue his allowance. To make matters worse, he anticipated a malicious chorus from 'the pirate gang of London buggers ... headed by Maurice [Bowra]'.[26] It would not be the first disagreement they had had and in any case he was now convinced not only of his generic inclinations but also of his particular taste and thought it advisable that he should marry a literary and bohemian creature rather than an English rose.

Connolly may have thought he was writing to MacCarthy in confidence but his affair with Jean was rapidly becoming an open secret. Patrick Balfour wrote saying that Bowra was possessed of the facts. Bobbie Longden added his report, that 'I Tatti was full of flutter about your love story. Apparently Logan had been writing about it to Mary Berenson and she was very much excited.'[27] Pearsall Smith had maintained contact and the tone of his recent letters seemed cheerful, although he had problems of his own. In September 1929 he sent congratulations for what was beginning to look like Connolly's engagement. In October he commended again the idea of living in Paris ('there are no ladders to tempt one, save the ladder up to the Ivory Tower') and reported that the Clarks, recently seen, were full of enthusiasm for Connolly's journalism in the *New Statesman* and *Life and Letters*.[28] In November he wrote with sombre news, although it was delivered flippantly: the Wall Street Crash had made serious inroads into his finances and he hoped that his protégé could anticipate either prosperous employment or a lucrative marriage in order to resolve what had now become an awkward dependency.

The Noël Blakistons, returning through Paris from their honeymoon that autumn, saw the lovers at the Hôtel Louisiane and found them living in 'fairly sordid circumstances'.[29] Giana Blakiston found Jean 'slow and humorous' and said that she 'adored' Connolly. As for the squalor, as Connolly wrote to Balfour at the time, he and Jean had all their faults in common: laziness, hedonism, extravagance, a love of

travel and of low life. It was inevitable that their surroundings were
never going to be immaculate. After the Blakistons had gone, Connolly
sent his old and now married friend what was almost the last of the
intense and vivid letters which had been the vehicle of their romantic
friendship: 'The trouble is that I'm emotionally homosexual still ...
Every Englishman, don't you think, is really contemptuous of women –
the sanctity of the smoking room is always at the back of his mind.'[30]
Whatever his ideas, however, plans were going ahead. In October Mrs
Warner had written to her daughter saying that she felt Jean and
Connolly were 'suited and should marry'.[31] Mrs Connolly, meanwhile,
was delighted, suggested that The Lock House could be made available
for her son and his prospective wife and promised that she would
attend an American wedding, provided accommodation could be
secured. She had one word of caution, a romantic's reminder of the
potency of first love: 'You must remember you can never expect to get
the same as you felt for Racy again. It is like your first glimpse of the
tropics – even much more beautiful places can't stir you in the same
way.'[32] Her idea about The Lock House was not calculated to impress
them: the avoidance of England was an early-established marital
priority. No plans had been made yet about where they should live, but
Jean had already begun to address practical matters, and when he wrote
to Blakiston from Sledmere at Christmas 1929, Connolly revealed that
she had decided she could not marry without a minimum of £2000 a
year from her family.

At the end of February 1930 he and Jean left Paris for London where
he had to secure a visa and there they boarded a German liner, the
Bremen, for the voyage to America which was to culminate in their
wedding in April. Connolly had begun reading more Henry James, his
mind newly turned to America, and the sights and smells of Paris now
receded. Their disappearance was only temporary, however, and they
returned embedded in the vivid and sunlit snapshots of his nostalgic
memory. Long before he arrived at Stone House at Woodbrook, outside Baltimore, he had ideas of what to expect and had already written
to Blakiston declaring that Jean's mother's house had more bathrooms
than bedrooms and that there were six cars, excluding the butler's.
There were other properties at Cape Cod and in the Adirondacks. Two
days before the wedding he pre-emptively accused himself of going to
America for material gain: having travelled third class with £10 to
spend, he would sail back first class with a rich wife, £300, a new coat,

a set of diamond studs and a new box for the ferrets. The day before, a friend from school, 'Tim' O'Connor, arrived from New York to stand as best man. They were married on 5 April and left at midnight for four days in New York before sailing on the *Mauretania* for London.

A postcard from Jean's sister Annie reported that an old friend of Jean's had by chance encountered the honeymoon couple: 'They were holding hands and gazing at the tall buildings and looked like *school children* – in awe of the grandeur of New York.'[33] Already Connolly had decided that 'it is American good taste that is so deadly, not American vulgarity'.[34] But after 9 April, when the *Mauretania* sailed, he would see no more of it for nearly seventeen years. Did Connolly marry for money? It had been decided that for the time being Jean would receive £1000 per annum from her mother and he cheerfully informed friends of the fact: if he was mercenary, he was not furtively so. It would be idle to deny outright that her affluence was an added attraction, but there was an important mitigation: marriage for love is a modern notion and to the Victorians and Edwardians a disregard for dowries was merely folly. Besides, Jean had no doubt of a return on her investment and despite all subsequent disillusion never doubted her husband's aptitude to amuse.

IV
CONDEMNED
PLAYGROUNDS

CHAPTER NINE

THE CONNOLLYS had only one clear idea for the future as they sailed back to Europe: whatever they did – and there were preliminary fantasies which extended even to making films – it would not be done in England. On arrival they stayed in London in St James's and the happy groom took his wife to Bath, to Big Chilling and to Oxford to show her to family and friends. If Jean liked England, however, she resigned herself to this brief encounter: there was never any intention that they would remain longer than ceremony and propriety dictated, and at the end of May they left for the Continent. Whereas a century before, England's men of letters had been largely content to remain at home and pity the exiles of Byron and Shelley, the literary generation which matured between the World Wars was restless and anglophobic. Connolly's models in expatriation were D. H. Lawrence and Aldous Huxley, but when he crossed the sundering Channel he anticipated the larger literary exodus of the Thirties: Auden and Isherwood, Evelyn and Alec Waugh, Orwell, Graham Greene, Robert Graves, Brian Howard, Peter Quennell, William Empson, even Benjamin Britten and Peter Pears, spent prolonged periods away from England, some leaving never to return. They were impelled by a variety of dislikes – of the climate, the cost, the repressive and archaic morality, the philistinism of officialdom – and if Connolly also nurtured a secret longing to rebel against the patriotism of authoritarian figures like his father and the Wilkeses, he was not alone in the means of his rebellion.

They went to Majorca to complete their honeymoon and there met Tony Bower, an American art critic who was to remain their friend until his murder years later in New York. Beyond that encounter, the holiday was dully content and the account Jean sent her mother – with stories of a villa leased by American lesbians who seemed to require their guests 'to swim in the oily pool, stay for buffet luncheon and play vingt-et-un all afternoon' – sounded more complacent than rapturous.[1] With relief they returned to Paris before beginning a leisurely progress down the Atlantic coast to Biarritz and Bayonne. The scheme was now to spend a year abroad trying to write (although Mrs Warner hoped that her son Tom might join them and be tutored by Connolly) and it was in deference to this ambition that they abandoned the Atlantic coast for the Mediterranean. At Toulon they met Aldous Huxley and his first wife, Maria Nys, who had arrived in the area in April, and soon they decided to settle nearby.

They took a lease on Les Lauriers Roses at Six-Fours, a two-bedroomed house battered by the wind and situated on the sea road east of Sanary, the small fishing village where nine years later Anthony Powell would stage the bogus surcease of his travel writer T. T. Waring in *What's Become of Waring?* They had a garden and a pergola and bought ring-tailed lemurs to join the ferrets. Cassis, Bandol and Toulon were nearby; the great metropolis of Marseilles lay up the coast; and Aldous Huxley, the most famous English writer of the Twenties, was a neighbour. For Connolly's generation, he shone with the brilliance of his early comic novels *Crome Yellow* and *Antic Hay* and although his work had begun to appear more portentous and prolix he remained an immense figure and one for whom Connolly had an overwhelming admiration. Later he would recall that what at the time seemed one of the happiest moments of his life occurred when the Huxleys appeared in his drive in their red Bugatti, Aldous in the passenger seat owing to his near-blindness. This first impetuous overture should have been the beginning of the close friendship which Connolly had envisaged when he took Les Lauriers, but it was not. The wandering genius was now under punishing contract to produce two novels a year: he was then working on *Brave New World* and he and his wife, having paid a courtesy call, kept their distance.

When they realized that they were not going to receive any more visits, the Connollys took to going to the Villa 'Huley', as a local workman, defeated by the writer's name, had painted on Huxley's gatepost. But Maria would intercept their arrival and tell them that her husband was working. Similar prohibitions were in force in the evening: Huxley would not go out to dinner because he had to get up early to write. Connolly was sure that Huxley's wife disliked his, and the novelist's future biographer, Sybille Bedford, who was a regular guest at the Huley in the Thirties, confirmed that the fastidious and elegant Maria found the *ménage* at Les Lauriers squalid: 'Eating your dinner with your fingers reading before the fire meant leaving grape skins and the skeletons of sardines between the pages. The ferrets stank; the lemur hopped upon the table and curled his exquisite little black hand around your brandy glass.' Huxley related that he had once watched Jean distribute raw meat to the ferrets and then wipe her blood-stained fingers down the front of her embroidered Chinese coat. Squeamishness apart, he had other motivations of reticence. As Sybille Bedford remarked, 'Cyril may have reminded him of the attributes of his younger self which he was beginning to wish to slough off, aestheticism, pure art, the love of words.'[2] And when there was contact, the effect could be disconcerting: Connolly remembered one rare visit during which he was so overwhelmed by the detail and catholicity of his guest's conversation that he developed a nervous fantasy that he devoured gazettes and books of reference and after his departure he wrote a poem about the visit, one of the verses of which began, 'How pleasant is the encyclopaedia.'[3]

Pearsall Smith, suspecting perhaps that the Connollys' life at Six-Fours was not without its loneliness and *longueurs*, orchestrated a long-promised meeting with his friend Edith Wharton. Connolly recalled that Pearsall Smith regarded her as 'the social pinnacle of two continents'[4] but learned, shortly before the pilgrimage, that he and Jean were not to enjoy an audience alone but to go with the Huxleys, as though in attendance. Mrs Wharton lived eastwards along the coast at Ste-Claire-le-Château at Hyères. Her superb narrative gift, her understanding of the protocol of old New York and her analysis of the American invasion of Europe had brought her royalties which had been the envy of Henry James and which now allowed her to live in sumptuous perfection. Kenneth Clark related stories about how the books in her library were sprung to retract automatically on the shelves and how footmen restored every newly vacated cushion. The journey there was undertaken in the Bugatti and on arrival the Connollys felt like a supporting act. Conversation languished and their hostess, an expert on East Coast genealogy, intimated disappointment with Jean's antecedents and later pronounced her an 'awful lump'. News of her verdict filtered back to her inadequate guests but Jean had already drawn a cartoon to commemorate the fiasco and when Mrs Wharton contacted the Huxleys again, they were invited alone. Pearsall Smith heard reports and wrote teasingly to Connolly: it was obvious that their hostess had been terrified of them all and had protectively assumed her mask of

wealth and worldliness: they had failed to charm her and made her feel
outdated and like a latter-day Mrs Humphrey Ward.

Meanwhile the feelings which the new arrivals felt for their exalted
neighbours across the bay became, in Sybille Bedford's recollection,
'very, very bitter'.[5] She knew that Connolly had arrived 'a legend
already', that he had hoped that proximity to a successful writer, coupled
with the region's beauty and benign climate, would precipitate his own
elusive abilities. Instead he felt inhibited and cast into futility by the
prolific polymath he wanted to be near; lethargy and the inability to
pursue and complete any literary venture crept in, along with an accompanying anger and a distaste for Huxley's new fiction which Connolly
was to feel until the novelist produced *Time Must Have a Stop* in 1945.
To his diary, he confided, 'The Huxleys have added ten years to my life';[6]
suddenly he was too unsure, too inferior, to read the affair equably and
saw instead a crushing rejection deliberately inflicted.

Yet there was much at Six-Fours to delight. The exotic pets which he
and Jean kept, and which were among their most famous accessories,
gave the couple great pleasure and the lemurs in particular became
mascots of the time. Their appearance enchanted him and he was
fascinated by their charm, their responsiveness to the pitch of every
different human voice, their moonlight chatter and cavortings, their
childlike greed with fig and peach. Most beguiling, however, was the
nimble and nonchalant grace with which they carried their romantic
mythology as selenic symbols and as the reincarnated ghosts and
denizens of the tropical paradise of Madagascar, itself a supposed
outcrop of the lost continent of Lemuria. Many of his friends shared
Maria Huxley's distaste for them, but when Connolly himself came to
look back on his time in the south of France, it too seemed like a
Lemurian kingdom, its potent enchantments engulfed by time's implacable tide.

Those enchantments were physical and sybaritic. The summer
climate of Sanary was glorious, the days were long and self-indulgent;
life, after London, was cheap and easy. Jean cooked well and they could
easily afford the best restaurants in the area. Perhaps above all, the need
for a lovable and loving partner, which had haunted Connolly during
his obsessions with Longden and Blakiston, had been answered – at
least for the time being. He sent a contented account of their existence
to Mrs Warner: Jean was running the house smoothly, even though
their one servant worked only in the mornings; they bathed a lot and

played a great deal of ping-pong; and he had shed some of the weight he had acquired in America. This last claim was no doubt true, but Connolly had lost his youthful slenderness in Jamaica: he might claim later that inside every fat man a thin man was wildly signalling to be let out, but in his case the thin man's entreaties were unheard for almost half a century.

Pearsall Smith came to stay in October and hugely enjoyed himself. Far from Jean's advent leading to any immediate frosting of relations between Connolly and his mentor, estimations seemed higher than ever and Pearsall Smith had gone so far as to write to a friend at the beginning of 1930 to announce the arrival of three new literary stars, Connolly, Kenneth Clark and David Cecil, with Connolly seeming the most able. He found them contemplating the acquisition of a yacht and wrote later urging caution, since he doubted their maritime competence. He may have envied them their extravagant fantasies: his own prosperity was now much diminished and in March 1931 he relinquished the lease of Big Chilling, which had cost £500 per annum to maintain. Beyond the Mediterranean coast, anxieties were beginning to circulate in the wake of the Wall Street Crash; the Connollys may have had the money to ignore the problem but others could not. And if prosperity sheltered them from these anxieties, it removed also the urgency to write and thus the purpose of their exile. Elsewhere his contemporaries were starting to make their mark. George Orwell began his literary career in 1930 in the *Adelphi* and Peter Quennell wrote from Tokyo, where he was now teaching English literature at the university, with news that he was working on a novel which he expected to see published in the following year. He naturally hoped for his friend's assessment of the work: 'I wonder how you would like it, or whether you would tell me if you did?'[7] Connolly replied, saying that he missed male companionship and disliked the French people he had met. When he later praised Quennell's novel, the latter seemed determined to doubt his word: 'Your praises are so unexpected and so generous that I wondered ... whether the intention wasn't perhaps a little ironic!'[8]

The difficulty with life in any sort of paradise lies in the suppression of guilt required by the immigrants. To do nothing happily is an art, since with leisure comes introspection and with introspection comes doubt. The Connollys were not industrious but Jean at least could reassure herself that she was taking care of the house and keeping her husband fed. For the latter there was nothing but lonely literary concentration, and when that proved fruitless, the deliberation of excuses. He continued the journal, and filled it with ideas and musings which he might have hoped to expand at a later date. Indolence preyed on his mind: unlike Huxley, he had no need to work, but unlike Maugham, another neighbour along the coast, he lacked the self-discipline to contend with leisure and turn affluence to art. As a result he fretted and took refuge in self-justification: 'Writing is an accident arising out of certain unhappinesses. To write, to walk, to talk, to drink, to have violent exercise, are all alternative forms of self-expression to someone discontented with the present.'[9] He looked back on this time as one of 'living for beauty' but it was also one of restlessness and he and Jean fantasized about other itinerant lives, in converted Dutch barges, in caravans, in yachts. They even began to think of cottages in Hampstead or more substantial properties in the West Country; and English detective fiction, with its details of village life and cold winters and East End fogs, developed a sudden poetry. Years later, however, when Connolly came to write about his life in the south of France, he looked back on it not as an experimental period for which both he and his wife were in some ways too young, but as a Mediterranean idyll:

> October on the Mediterranean; blue sky scoured by the mistral, red and golden vine branches, wind-fretted waves chopping round the empty yachts; plane trees peeling; palms rearing up their dingy underlinen; mud in the streets and from doorways at night the smell of burning oil. Through the dark evening I used to bicycle in to fetch our dinner, past the harbour with its bobbing launches and the cafés with their signs banging. . .[10]

In the summer of 1931 Evelyn Waugh came to stay. To the novelist Henry Green he wrote describing that stretch of the French coast as being 'full of chums' and mentioned the Connollys, the Huxleys, Somerset Maugham and Alec Waugh as presiding spirits.[11] After his stay at Six-Fours he wrote to thank Jean: 'I did so much enjoy it and it was exciting meeting the Huxleys and going to St Beaune and seeing the brothels at Toulon.'[12] With the retreat of the pleasure-seekers at the end of the summer life would revert to the pastoral rhythms which then still governed the Mediterranean French coast; with the autumn would come isolation and more introspection. Suddenly London beckoned and by the last week in August the Connollys were back in the city.

With nowhere to stay at short notice, and fantasies of Hampstead and Somerset forgotten, they moved into the Cavendish Hotel in Jermyn Street. It was an odd choice. The proprietress, the notorious Rosa Lewis, had been cook and, it was widely assumed, mistress, to Edward VII when Prince of Wales and ran her establishment imperiously yet eccentrically, conniving at the visitors imported by her male guests, on occasion even supplying them, and adjusting bills so that the wealthier inmates unwittingly subsidized the poorer. 'A bottle of wine' always meant champagne but Anthony Powell remembered that the Cavendish had a particular atmosphere – tense, menacing and poignant with a prevailing realization 'that dissipation must be paid for'.[13] Miss Lewis had no interest in writers, despite having housed Thornton Wilder and Aldous Huxley, and her indifference edged nearer to contempt when Evelyn Waugh portrayed her as Lottie Crump in *Vile Bodies*, a treachery that barred him from the establishment for the rest of its life. No details survive of the Connollys' stay there, but at one stage they ran up a large bill which they could not pay and for some time afterwards were accosted, embarrassingly and publicly, by their indomitable creditress.

There were no palm trees in London and the weather was less suitable for Whoopee and Polyp, the lemurs. There were compensations, however, not least the presence of a literary culture. Furthermore, writers less insulated by fame and wealth than Maugham and Mrs Wharton were available for companionship and collaboration. When the publisher Cobden-Sanderson had the bright idea of recruiting a panel of writers to contribute to an occasional volume of essays and poetry there was a wealth of accomplishment and promise from which to choose. When *The New Keepsake* appeared, illustrated by Rex Whistler, Connolly with 'The Art of Travel' was in prestigious company: his twenty-three fellow contributors included Maurice Baring, Max Beerbohm, Hilaire Belloc, Aldous Huxley, Rose Macaulay, Harold Nicolson, Siegfried Sassoon and W. B. Yeats.

Meanwhile, becalmed in London, he and Jean could not remain hotel guests and took a six-month lease beginning in November 1931 at 10 Wilton Mews, a small property off Belgrave Square. Just before moving in, Connolly wrote to Henry Green to arrange dinner and indicated that his new home would be more modern and efficient than charming, since everything ran on electricity. Most of the letter decried the formation in August of Ramsay Macdonald's National Government, a mainly Tory coalition which marked the end of the Labour Party's second brief term

of power and which had been appointed to resolve England's mounting
financial problems. Connolly's socialist sympathies were outraged by the
development but the reversals of the Thirties had only just begun. He told
Green that on the night the election results were announced he and Jean
had attended a gala party at Quaglino's and had been appalled by the
enthusiasm with which the formation of the National Government had
been received. He mentioned also that they had failed to secure early
tickets for Noël Coward's hugely successful *Cavalcade*, the patriotic
extravaganza which coincided with the advent of the new regime and
which was widely seen as having swayed the country back to flag-waving.

Green and Connolly admired and liked each other but moved in
different circles and although the experimental novelist and his wife
appeared from time to time at the Connollys' parties, they were not part
of the group of close friends which re-formed around him now. The
Blakistons lived in nearby Chelsea and the two couples resumed contact.
Giana Blakiston thought the Connollys very happy together. She remembered that Connolly was fond of remarking that both his wife and
Blakiston's were 'masculine in mind and feminine in feeling'[14] and she
could hardly overlook the exotic members of their household, the
lemurs, which had been taught to perch on the lavatory and which would
sit up in front of the fire with their paws outstretched. Mary Lutyens, by
now married to her first husband, Arthur Sewell, was less enchanted and
would ask the Connollys to leave their pets behind when they came for
dinner. There was much exchange of hospitality between Wilton Mews
and the Sewells' flat in the Inner Temple: the couples often met for dinner
or for bridge. They played for small stakes and Mary Lutyens remembered that Connolly and his wife were 'competent players, though not
ruthless experts'. Again, the young couple appeared very happy and
although Wilton Mews always seemed dirty, it had about it a sense of
prosperity, furthered perhaps by the alcohol which its inhabitants
poured so freely. Mary greatly liked Jean. She could sometimes embarrass her husband by a deficiency of sophistication and there was a joke
current amongst their circle that at one dinner, finding some shot in her
pheasant, she had complained: 'Cyril, there's a piece of iron in my
chicken.' Connolly could also be extremely amusing and a delightful
companion and although Mary remembered that he was the sort of
person 'one's mother didn't like', she herself found nothing to criticize in
him except laziness.[15]

*

Others besides Connolly had kept a vigil on the night the National Government had been formed, among them John Lehmann, the young King's Scholar who had convinced himself of Connolly's corrupting influence at school, before progressing to Cambridge and then working for Leonard and Virginia Woolf at the Hogarth Press. He had become a socialist and deplored Ramsay Macdonald's apostasy and the apparent stillbirth of the politics of egalitarianism. Later he would speak of 'the consternation and gloom that settled on all our circle' with the arrival of the new administration. He considered rejecting socialism for Marxism; but more significantly, as events turned out, he began preparing an anthology of new poets which it was agreed Leonard Woolf would publish. *New Signatures* appeared in 1932 and although it contained work by Auden, Day-Lewis, Macneice, Empson, Plomer, Spender and others, it was not its contents that became important but its symbolic reputation. Inaccurately but persistently, it came to be seen as the manifesto of the generation of poets who, under W. H. Auden, were to dominate and articulate the apprehensions of many of the younger members of the educated classes between 1932 and 1939. In the 1930s politics invaded literature in the way that religion had invaded politics in the 1630s: there was no escape from a political commitment and for most writers that commitment lay with the Left. The point is worth making because Connolly was sympathetic to socialism some time before serious recruitment was begun by the rival political and literary camps which animated the literature written before the Second World War. This sympathy, and his broader interest in writing, inevitably led to an interest in the work and personality of Auden, who published *The Orators* two months after the appearance of *New Signatures*. It was an obscure but widely noticed work, and if Connolly read it he cannot have ignored the fact that it drew heavily for its symbolism on the gradations of school success. He was not the only member of his generation who remained haunted by the triumphs of the classroom but more than a year was to pass before he wondered in his journal, 'Why don't I know Auden and Spender?'[16]

In June there was further confirmation that for some writers life was still a great examination waiting to be sat and failed when Wyndham Lewis, whom Connolly had noticed in the columns of the *New Statesman*, published *Doom of Youth*. Strange and unreadable though the book seemed, it was symptomatic of a growing sense that something had gone wrong, that there was a failure of nerve or a suspicion of error

in the course the country had taken since 1919. Connolly did not
review the book, but he was aware of it and some of its ideas lingered in
his mind. He had no desire to meet Lewis, as he did Auden, but one
encounter in the autumn of 1932 did prove auspicious. Ethel Sands, the
hostess and literary socialite he had met through Pearsall Smith, gave a
party to introduce him to Elizabeth Bowen. The two Anglo-Irish writers
were distant cousins and had wanted to meet ever since Connolly
reviewed her first novel for MacCarthy. The introduction marked the
beginning of a lifelong friendship; Elizabeth Bowen being very fond of
Jean also, despite describing her as 'a great soft crook'.[17] Connolly was
becoming a significant figure in the literary world, if more by repute and
personality than by achievement. That autumn also saw the publication
of Evelyn Waugh's third novel, *Black Mischief*, and Waugh's friends
and readers had little difficulty in establishing the inspiration of General
Connolly, a stocky Irishman who is the commander-in-chief of the
Emperor Seth's armies and whose wife – in deference to Jean's sultry
colouring – is called Black Bitch. Christopher Sykes, a friend of Evelyn
Waugh, had dinner with the Connollys shortly after the novel's publication and found them unabashed by the caricatures: 'Cyril "raved" as
they say, he was "in ecstasies" about *Black Mischief*. He said it was the
best thing Evelyn had written ... [He and Jean] both thought that
the general was a great stroke. "We don't mind," laughed Cyril.'[18]

   In April 1931 The Lock House had been sold, an unmourned concession to Matthew Connolly's realization that he was anchored to his job
in London and that Maud, now in South Africa with Brooke, had gone
for ever. In 1932 Jean's father died and although the money which
devolved on her was less than expected, she still had some extra capital
as well as her share of his furniture, which was now shipped to London.
With the expiry of the lease at Wilton Mews the Connollys were once
again wanderers and resorted either to temporary accommodation,
friends or brief Continental excursions as solutions to homelessness.
For part of the summer of 1932 they took a house near Enid Bagnold at
Rottingdean and entertained large groups of friends for the weekend.
On one occasion the young writer and critic Alan Pryce-Jones arrived to
find a house-party which included Brian Howard, Peter Quennell, now
back from the Far East, and Nigel Richards, a famous beauty whose
looks were soon to earn him a place in the fiction of his friends.
Pryce-Jones remembered that the lemurs 'frolicked up and down the
curtains, in spite of, or perhaps because of, a chronic looseness of the

bowel'.[19] Quennell was preoccupied with other reflections. Not having seen Connolly for months, he was struck by a transformation: 'Marriage had changed him; he was growing somewhat solid . . . Not that he had quite abandoned his juvenile romanticism; the worldly-wise hedonist remained an imaginative perfectionist, dreaming of the perfect house he would buy in the perfect landscape, even . . . of the perfectly ordered and attended meal.'[20]

By this reckoning, all seemed set for a gentle mellowing into marital complacency: the critic's writing career would establish itself, books would follow and soon there would be children. Events proved less predictable and by the time he was forty Connolly himself had abandoned the smug assumptions of youth: 'We come to see that our life has no more continuity than a pool in the rocks filled by the tide with foam and flotsam and then emptied.'[21] The cruelties of existence were random and unintelligible: he and Jean had money, leisure, friends, but Jean did not have good health and following several bouts of discomfort and distress she sought medical advice. As a result of the abortion four years earlier, she had to have a further operation now and was told that she could never have children. She consulted a specialist, Dr Giekie-Cobb, and reported his findings to her mother: 'He says my glands are very disarranged but that the particular trouble is that I have overstrained my heart. It isn't in the least serious if I take it in hand.'[22] A therapeutic regime was prescribed: the Connollys were to stay quietly in the country and she was to renounce cigarettes, drink and late nights, rest as much as possible and eat bland food. Such restrictions must have seemed drastic and were certainly beyond the patient and her husband. Her health would continue its indifferent course; more immediately, glandular complications made her fat and for the rest of the Thirties she was a regular convalescent at Brides-les-Bains.

The news was distressing for them both but worse for Jean, who inevitably wrestled with self-recrimination. Enid Bagnold wrote sympathetically: 'What an awful blow for you both . . . the illness and the irrevocability . . . It's so claustrophobia-ing to be told that one can never do a thing.'[23] Maud also sent a message of support from South Africa but privately she was appalled by the announcement and feared for the implications for the marriage. Years later she wrote to her son that Jean's infertility was bound to make her unhappy and that she needed adopted children: 'Poor Jean. I don't wonder she feels sad. I often look back to that time in Paris when you used to come in with your ferrets and Jean used to tell me how she adored you in your beret.'[24] The subject was driven underground slightly, although Giana Blakiston remembered Jean's confiding, 'I'd love to have a little girl like Cyril.'[25] Later, when regrets accumulated and blame was apportioned, Connolly likened the news to the cutting of a ring of bark from a healthy tree.

CHAPTER TEN

AS A DISTRACTION and a consolation the Connollys fled to Greece in February 1933. It was a strange destination – the country was cold and also in the grip of political turmoil, its young constitutional republic beset by monarchist and absolutist intrigue. At first the tourists had other things to think about. But the excitement of abroad, normally so potent for them both, failed to banish their gloom and when Connolly came to describe the holiday in the *New Statesman* in an occasional piece called 'Spring Revolution' he admitted to their melancholy, though without revealing its cause. The weather was too bad for them to go anywhere; they stayed in bed late to shorten the days; they became listless and bored, and staring out of the window 'found the Acropolis and the Parthenon blocking the horizon. A thing of beauty, that is a joy once or twice, and afterwards a standing reproach.'[1] It seemed after a few days of lurking in the Hôtel Grande Bretagne that they might as well have stayed in London: 'As boredom gathered momentum one felt all the ingredients of personality gurgling away like the last inch of bathwater. One became a carcase of nonentity and indecision, a reflection to be avoided in mirrors. Why go abroad? Why travel? Why exchange the regard of a clique for the stare of the concierge?'

Disillusion was broken by two unforeseen circumstances. To begin with, they encountered Brian Howard, now roaming Europe with his German lover, Toni. Howard runs through Connolly's life, and the lives of numerous contemporaries, like a scarlet thread: a reproach to the dull and complacent, a sober reminder to the gifted that it is not so much the possession of talent which is remarkable, as the ability to channel it. He may have been an irritating figure but testimony to his wit, his charm, his inimitable personality, abounds in the gossip, even the novels, of his contemporaries. Connolly was amused by him and enlisted his companionship, even though Howard was chronically

insolvent and Toni had to be subsidized. Jean got on well with homosexual men and soon the four were inseparable. Both Connolly and
Howard had an interest in the *louche* and the back-streets of Athens
proved irresistible: 'Here were bars and taverns where hashish was
smoked and sold, where sailors and lonely young men wove about in
the intricate local dances to semi-Turkish music, or sang the laments of
the Greeks of Ionia.'

These casual excursions were interrupted when an attempted coup
followed the March elections. As rumours gathered the day after poll-
ing, an aeroplane flew over Athens dropping pamphlets which
announced the collapse of parliamentary government. Crowds gathered
in boulevards; impromptu marches began; machine-guns were trained
from the presidential palace and eventually fighting erupted. The coup
lasted only one night: with one man dead and thirty-three injured the
republic bought a reprieve until 1935. It seemed unwise to stay and the
tourists went west, travelling to Palermo, Naples, Capri, Seville and
finally southern Portugal, where they divided their time between sunbathing at Praia da Rocha and drinking and sight-seeing in Sintra and
Lisbon. With Howard's discovery of the casinos and the devaluation of
the dollar the idyll ended, but despite a fracas with a waiter in a bar in
the capital it had been a happy holiday – a contrast to the gloom of
Athens and the sadness of London, and a glimpse of Brian Howard
when he still seemed possessed of promise.

The Connollys still had no permanent home in London, but decided
to arrange their summer accommodation before fixing anything more
settled in the capital. At first they considered renting a property in
Brighton for June and July but eventually decided once again to take a
house near to Enid Bagnold at Rottingdean. 'Mind you pay, darlings,'
Lady Jones wrote, 'it would give me such a bad name if you didn't. Do
quote me to the agents about your respectabilities. I am sure you are not
at all respectable, but that's a matter of standards.'[2] Her anxieties about
their conduct at Rottingdean seem to have been unfounded, although
Jean wrote at the end of the summer confessing that they had given a
local butcher a bad cheque. Mrs Warner came to stay and Giana
Blakiston, a guest at the same time, remembered that she could be a
frustrating presence. On one occasion she accidentally locked herself
into the bathroom and Connolly had to climb through a back window
to rescue her. In September they went to the south of France, stopping
first in Paris. Compelled as ever by the *risqué*, they spent an evening in

The Monocle, a lesbian bar in Montparnasse, and Jean inevitably had the better time, as she wrote to Enid Bagnold: 'I danced with a charming young lady well got up in a suit of English tweeds and well creased trousers and we chatted very correctly.'[3] They also met and befriended the poet David Gascoyne, then seventeen, and he became a regular guest in London over the next few years.

Meanwhile, they had begun the serious business of ending a year's homelessness and finally found a property that suited them: 312a King's Road was situated above a shop and opposite Paultons Square in Chelsea's principal thoroughfare. It had two bedrooms and a spacious studio appropriate for a generous and gregarious couple who liked to entertain. There was staff accommodation beyond the kitchen, but the first couple they engaged as butler and cook had a noisy baby; the second couple, perhaps employed because they were without offspring, left in some awkwardness after he had been discovered trying on Jean's clothes.

They began to give parties and dinners and soon established a reputation as good hosts. Connolly loved to entertain much more than he liked to be entertained: it was an aspect of his generosity which combined with the need for a controlled environment. Even at his own parties, however, he could be nervous and difficult as much as charming and reassuring, and he and Jean must have looked idiosyncratic: she was overweight and he was no beauty. Nevertheless he could often assume a commanding social presence. The writer A. E. Ellis noted that 'none but a fool could have proclaimed unattractive a face so alive, so transparently intelligent. Conventionally good-looking men in Cyril's company showed as much to their disadvantage as tall generals in the presence of Napoleon.'[4] David Gascoyne never forgot the pandemonium which the mongoose, the newest addition to his hosts' menagerie, could cause at dinner-parties, when one course or another would be interrupted by telephone calls from neighbouring hostesses with an unvarying entreaty: 'Oh, Mr Connolly, please come and take your horrible mongoose away, he's given the maid hysterics.'[5] The guests on these occasions were diverse and entertaining, and Gascoyne remembered meeting the Henry Greens, the Anthony Powells and Desmond MacCarthy at Connolly's table. It is safe to assume that the conversation, when not interrupted by the antics of the exotic pets, revolved around literature; and all the time Connolly was supplying and regulating ideas as he governed the talk from his host's chair. In his journal at this time he jotted a pregnant aside, the result perhaps of dinner opinion: 'Favourite daydream – edit a monthly magazine entirely subsidized by self. No advertisements. Harmless title, deleterious contents.'[6]

Evelyn Waugh, now between his first and second marriages, was always pleased to accept companionship in the evenings and the Connollys were happy to extend it to him. In April 1934 they took him out to dinner at the Café Grill and found him with a 'face thinner but broader, less flesh more bone . . . He is our most valued friend . . . Made most of the people we want to see seem dowdy.'[7] There was gossip about Brian Howard and malicious talk about Peter Quennell, and the Connollys mentioned their forthcoming journey to Ireland to stay with Elizabeth Bowen at Bowenscourt. Waugh indicated that he wanted to join them on the journey, but never did. A couple of weeks later he was again their guest, this time at 312a. Connolly liked to boast that the guests at his dinners were chosen as carefully as the instruments in an orchestra, and the dinner which Waugh attended he considered one of the best and most typical that he and Jean gave. Waugh's fellow-guests included the novelist Joe Hergesheimer and a young woman called Joan Eyres-Monsell who was to become one of Connolly's closest friends. She was also a beauty and he noted in his journal that the next morning he had her as well as a hangover on his mind. Waugh's opinions of the evening went unrecorded: he was just finishing his fourth novel, *A Handful of Dust*, and had ahead of him a voyage to the Arctic Circle. That novel was serialized prior to its publication and Christopher Sykes remembered encountering Connolly after the appearance of the first instalment: 'I don't know what's happened to Evelyn! His new novel is all about a happy country family, and a dear little boy – it's dreadful! I see what Madresfield and Belton and all this snobbery have done to him. They've destroyed him as a writer.'[8]

In the interim the visit to Ireland had taken Connolly into very different literary terrain. When the writer and his wife arrived, they found that Leonard and Virginia Woolf were also at Bowenscourt. Connolly's attitude towards Ireland was now profoundly ambivalent: he found the countryside melancholy and many of the houses and settlements derelict, and although Bowenscourt itself was very beautiful there was a prevailing torpor which combined with the mild climate to render activity impossible. He was ambivalent also towards Virginia Woolf. Although he later spoke highly of some of her novels, particularly *The Waves*, he was not one of her partisans, and if she read the *New Statesman* she would have been aware of his position. However good a writer the Juno of Bloomsbury was, she was also neurotic and tormented and needed acolytes, and here before her was a reviewer who was clearly not among them. Connolly noted that the Woolfs seemed shocked by Jean's dress but he admired Mrs Woolf's satirical account of the writer G. B. Stern. He was intrigued that she asked Elizabeth Bowen what 'unnatural vice' was and what acts constituted it and sensed that she was a virginal and shy character. In conversation they agreed that they could not like people if they did not like their books. By contrast, Mrs Woolf found the meeting more traumatic. She could not dislike Connolly on account of his books because he was only thirty-one and – like her at the same age – he had not yet produced any. She had nothing to say about his conversation, which was one of the most praised and admired aspects of his personality, and she took against Jean. Later she sent her sister a fuller account: 'We spent a night with the Bowens, where, to our horror we found the Connollys – a less appetizing pair I have never seen out of the Zoo, and apes are considerably preferable to Cyril. She has the face of a golliwog and they brought in the reek of Chelsea with them.'[9]

Mrs Woolf's hostility reflected Bloomsbury's larger dislike of Connolly and his Oxford generation, which was better travelled, more worldly, more flamboyant, more pleasure-loving and more honestly (and successfully) snobbish than the Bloomsbury Group. However, even among Connolly's contemporaries there were enmities and jealousies. At the outset of their careers, Evelyn Waugh and Peter Quennell maintained a friendship which, while never close, was cordial. When the latter wrote a mildly disparaging review of the former's early biography, *Rossetti*, that entente soured and in later life Waugh lost no opportunity to undermine or ridicule Quennell. Connolly retained the friendship of both men yet happily recorded the aspersions which always seemed to emerge when he found himself with one and discussing the other – occasions when Waugh and Quennell would defame each other's origins and denounce each other as hacks. If Connolly tried to bring about a reconciliation his efforts went unrecorded, and he was not above the cultivation and appreciation of a little friction; their mutual hostility and envy subsumed his own jealousy of their more productive careers. They in turn were both aware of Connolly's position. After his death, Quennell described him as being 'deeply emulous' and suggested that when he lived at Sanary he must have been 'a little annoyed by the news of English life and of their recent successes, that he received from former friends'.[10]

This vigil did not end when Connolly returned to England. In the midst of the literary parties, the holidays, the warm and fleeting summers, he noted in his Journal: 'Peter works from 10–6, in the evening writes articles.'[11] Under a financial pressure unknown to Connolly, Quennell indeed maintained a steady stream of books and reviews which was to continue for many years ahead. Since getting married Connolly had written virtually nothing and this negligence was beginning not only to depress him but to feature in the couple's financial reckonings. By the standards of the time he and Jean were prosperous but they were also extravagant. The house, the servants, the travelling, the entertaining all cost far more than the average writer could have afforded. Connolly, indifferent to the financial standards of the average writer, was now living as comfortably as his paradigm Logan Pearsall Smith, resenting the fact that money cushioned him from hard work but still enjoying the comforts it brought.

Now he not only began to imagine that a return to reviewing might help to stimulate a mind grown sluggish, he also saw it as offering salvation from the first serious financial problem to have arisen since his marriage. In 1934, Jean had undergone an operation which required several weeks of costly convalescence; suddenly the Connollys found themselves in debt. To begin with, they tried to sell £100 worth of stock which she held in a family zinc mine but failed to find a buyer. Then they contemplated selling the car. Then Connolly approached his father for assistance and asked him to guarantee an overdraft of £100. At first he seemed compliant but then decided to renege, telling Connolly, who later relayed the matter to Maud, that his mother owed her every wrinkle to his profligacy. In view of his own marital shortcomings, this reproach was more than harsh; to make matters more final and acrimonious, he also wrote to his son's bank manager with accusations of domestic extravagance. Jean was particularly upset by the quarrel: she no doubt blamed herself for having the operation in the first place and could hardly forget that it was the first time they had approached her father-in-law for support, and his response contrasted badly with every generous provision she had made. There was nothing for it: overtures were made, the *New Statesman*, under its second editor, Kingsley Martin, would be happy to take back its boy iconoclast, and he returned to reviewing fiction early in 1935.

For a moment it seemed like a return to school: everything different, everything the same. In February, confronted by ten new novels of which only one, *Bulldog Drummond at Bay*, now sounds even vaguely familiar, he experienced a sense of mild despair: 'The novels are the same, the writers are the same, the same lovers hold hands on the front of the cover, and the men who were boys when I was a boy endorse each other inside the jacket.'[12] He exaggerated: the diet of books he was sent to appraise was less bland and unwholesome than he at first imagined. In March he liked Christopher Isherwood's *Mr Norris Changes Trains* and while finding it a difficult book to praise 'as it deserves', nevertheless made the important point which only one oblique autobiographer could make of another, that in Isherwood perspectives shift and that the centre of attention is not necessarily the most important figure in a book. In April he looked at William Faulkner's *Pylon* and found that in his most ambitious moments the novelist was unsure and that his emotions could be suspect. Nevertheless: 'The morbidity of his imagination is beyond suspicion, he excels above all in combining a passionate hatred of the city, every sputum of which is familiar to him, with an appreciation of everything that is relaxed, corrupt, and phosphorescent in the southern countryside.'[13] In May it was the turn of *The Destructive Element*, Stephen Spender's analysis of James, Joyce, Yeats, Lawrence and Eliot. Connolly professed himself disappointed by the book's construction and its prose but was nevertheless impressed, finding the work 'the attempt of a patient, intelligent, and deeply interested person to get really underneath the ocean surface'.[14] A good review from Connolly was worth having and Spender was not unnaturally pleased. In his letter of thanks he said he had hesitated before writing, being afraid to 'appear ingratiating'. Nevertheless, 'I cannot remember having read a review in which the writer had taken so much trouble to read and understand the truth.'[15]

In May Sylvia Beach assured Connolly that his column was 'the only bright spot in my deflated life' and urged him to produce a novel of his own 'for me to have at least something to recommend to my '*abonnés*'.[16] In July he wrote about George Orwell's *Burmese Days*. Here finally was an indication of what his old friend had been doing since they had last seen each other and Connolly was delighted, recommending the book 'to anyone who enjoys a spate of efficient indignation, graphic description, excellent narrative, excitement, and irony tempered with vitriol'.[17] Another letter of thanks arrived, and with it Orwell's invitation to dinner, but it fell to Connolly to describe the reunion after fourteen years of the ascetic and the hedonist: '[Orwell's] greeting was typical, a long but not unfriendly stare and his characteristic wheezy laugh, "Well, Connolly, I can see that you've worn a good deal better than I have." I could say nothing for I was appalled by the ravaged grooves than ran down from cheek to chin. My fat cigar-smoking persona must have been a surprise to him.'[18] The dinner marked the resumption of a friendship which ended only with Orwell's death. But Connolly later impressed Anthony Powell with his account of Orwell's 'rigid asceticism, political intransigence, utter horror of all social life'.[19] Powell himself came to see Orwell and Connolly as symbolically congruous and his sometime friend Malcolm Muggeridge would repeat his assessment: 'One lean and ugly and the other fat and ugly; one phoneyly abstemious and the other phoneyly self-indulgent.'[20]

Connolly wrote two or three columns a month for the *New Statesman* and it became clear as 1935 progressed that he was adapting the review form for his own ends. He was happy to include references to his own prejudices: 'For me literature cannot be too esoteric, too much a preoccupation with style and imagination.'[21] He gave his readers a recipe for marital happiness: 'Whenever you can, read at meals.'[22] He alluded to the recurrent theme of his precocious schooldays and the myth of his later writing: 'Whom the Gods wish to destroy they first call promising.'[23] The desire to entertain was paramount; and although he was generous where he could be and scathing where necessary, he was no longer merely vindictive, as he had sometimes been in his apprenticeship. Desmond MacCarthy would no doubt have told him that only a bad reviewer shows off at the expense of his subject but Connolly was no saint and when confronted with piles of demonstrably bad fiction, he found giving a comic turn irresistible: twice in 1935 reviews took the form of lessons in which a comic schoolmaster called Mr Mossbross tried to teach his charges the rudiments of mediocre fiction.

In November he joined Harold Nicolson, Rebecca West and other regular contributors on the books page of the *Daily Telegraph*. Once again his province, over the next couple of years, was first fiction, although there were excursions. One of Connolly's most engaging aspects as a critic was his willingness and ability to educate himself in public. Later, in the Fifties, he would come to see D. H. Lawrence as a genius. But now, five years after the writer's death, he decided it was time for a reappraisal and left the *Telegraph*'s readers in no doubt that he thought him very overrated. His descriptions of nature left a feeling 'of having stayed too long in the Pre-Raphaelite room at the Tate', while the exposure and controversy which had surrounded his later years had led to an inevitable and widespread posthumous disenchantment. But here there was a pattern: 'The more boom and publicity writers have in their lifetime the more heavily weighted their reputation sinks down on to the silent ocean bed after their death.'[24]

Very occasionally, he reviewed the same work in the *Telegraph* and the *Statesman* – he duplicated his disappointment with Orwell's *Keep the Aspidistra Flying* – but in general his offerings for the newspaper were much more sober and impersonal, much less idiosyncratic and memorable, than his work for the magazine. He had gone to Fleet Street in purely mercenary mood: at five guineas for every short review, the newspaper generously augmented his income from the magazine; he told his mother that in November 1935 he had made £50 out of the two publications. He did not have the space at the *Telegraph* and may not have had the editorial freedom that he enjoyed at the *Statesman*. Only at the latter, for instance, under the innocuous title of 'New Novels', could he have flippantly called for fresh curbs on the areas which young and talentless novelists could explore, and that at a time when censorship was tightening its hold in large parts of Europe: he proscribed overused names and the stock situations and environments of contemporary mediocre fiction. He hated 'those horrible bus rides, when the stars are so close, and the young man treads on air ... "Fares please," shouted the conductor for the third time. "Fourpenny to heaven," he answered unthinking.'[25]

His pieces attracted widespread attention but one wonders how many of his admirers read between the lines they found so entertaining. Perhaps they took seriously the pronouncement he made so famously in February 1936: 'Reviewing is a whole-time job with a half-time salary, a job in which one's best work is always submerged in the criticism of someone else's, where all triumphs are ephemeral and only the drudgery is permanent, and where nothing is secure or certain except the certainty of turning into a hack.'[26] Nevertheless, the restricted space he was given ideally suited him: whether he was feeling self-pitying or comically inclined, he was by instinct and classical training a concise writer: as an adult no less than as a schoolboy, essays continued to be part of his weekly requirement. Furthermore, his greatest interest, as these reviews suggested, was himself. By the mid-Thirties he was established as the most precocious and fluent critic of his generation. It would have been a simple matter for him to review more significant work, to chart the progress of peers and contemporaries like Greene, Green, Powell or Quennell, or to move to another journal or newspaper if the *New Statesman* could not accommodate him. Connolly was happy confining himself to the trite and irredeemable because he saw that restriction as giving him the licence to be flippant and extravagant. It allowed him to entertain, to air his own prejudices, to note the gloom and the glories of the literary calling. Above all, it permitted him to write weekly or monthly instalments, depending on whim, which gradually built up a tragi-comic picture, that of the failed writer turned sour reviewer. This was a defiant pandering to public prejudice but it was also a cunning protection, since anyone who dissented flattered him and anyone who agreed could not hope to match him in comic eloquence or mock-despair.

This desire to portray, even invent, himself in his column makes Connolly sound cynical and fraudulent but he was not without interest in contemporary literature. In October 1935 he had written to Henry Miller saying that he was determined to review *Tropic of Cancer* for the *New Statesman*. Its author, who had written one of the more provocative novels of the inter-war era, was astonished and wrote to Lawrence Durrell: 'I don't understand it. If they understand what I'm driving at I don't think they would want very much to review my book. I think they're all fog-eyed.'[27] And when in January 1936 he set out in an article called 'The Novel-Addict's Cupboard' to establish which first editions by modern writers he wanted to own, he revealed sureness of judgement: other critics would also have mentioned James, Forster, Edith Wharton, Huxley; but it was Connolly's prescience in addition to cite Hemingway, F. Scott Fitzgerald and Nathaniel West, the last two writers in particular being almost unknown in England at the time. His comments about writers who had become established were incisive. He pronounced Waugh 'the most naturally gifted novelist of his generation' but anticipated a change, since 'his development has taken him steadily from the Left towards the Right, and Right wing satire is always weak . . . it is going to be difficult for him to continue, since Tory satire, directed at people on a moving staircase from a stationary one is doomed to ultimate peevishness.'[28]

CHAPTER ELEVEN

MEANWHILE SYLVIA BEACH would indeed soon have something to recommend to her '*abonnés*'. Unknown to her, Connolly had turned once more to fiction and although the measure was in part intended as a solution to financial difficulties its origins went back to earlier ambitions. As a schoolboy his literary aspirations had been of poetry. As an undergraduate he had dreamt of archaeology, of enthralling the classical world with exhumations of frieze and colossus. As a fledgling critic he was convinced that fine fiction alone justified a literary career and throughout the late Twenties in numerous little sketches and jottings he had sharpened aptitudes for satire, observation, lyricism and comic dialogue, waiting for the intellectual alchemy which would result in the emergence of a work of art. He was self-critical and had always partly understood why these fine hopes came to nothing – but there was more to it than the lack of application he admitted to or the laziness which his friends diagnosed. The lyricism, the excavations, the analysis for which he was really equipped tended in one direction, towards self-portraiture, but something in Connolly prevented him from seeing his own instincts for self-projection as imaginative or creative and thus restricted him to sterile literary idealism. Besides, romantic fantasies are the most stubborn: delusions of fiction died hard in the literary company he kept.

His status as a reviewer compounded the problem. Having publicly insisted that only the best would do, he could hardly begin his own novelist's career with anything less than dazzling triumph. To that inhibition he added the suspicion of another, that criticism distorted his faculties. The worthless novels he had reviewed in the late Twenties, now gathering dust in junk shops or awaiting the conflagrations of war, had not only exalted the few fine books he had been sent but had set a misleading lustre on the merely indifferent. Thus considered, reviewing was one of the few occupations where practice need not make perfect;

but he knew excuses would count for nothing if he failed. There was only one consoling thought. He would be his own strictest critic. These doubts must have had some bearing on the circumspection with which he turned once again to the hope of completing a novel sometime in 1933 or the year after. He confided his undertaking to Peter Quennell, who encouraged him to persevere and was rewarded when Connolly dedicated the finished book to him, but he did not want his endeavours widely discussed: the greater the expectation, the angrier the possible disappointment; and the earliest surviving reference was made in his Journal sometime in 1934 with an indifference he cannot have felt: 'Rejection of *Rock Pool* by Fabers'.[1]

The problem was less with the quality than with the tone and content. The novel begins with two lesbians dancing together in a foreign bar, as they had done when he and Jean had visited The Monocle: Faber, with T. S. Eliot on its board, had a reputation to consider; so too did the other companies he approached. To make matters worse, negotiations coincided with two important and well-publicized prosecutions, against *Boy* and *Bessie Cotter*. The answer seemed to be either to surrender to the radical surgery and alterations one editor suggested, to change lines like 'I want to have somebody tonight' into 'I don't want to be alone tonight' (a change adopted when the book was finally published in England) or else to let the manuscript languish in a drawer. At least in his unpublished state he could cherish a contempt for his censors and see in their straitened tastes the index of a national meanness. At least he could remind himself, when writing his dedication to Quennell, that he was not the first victim of publishing timidity:

> I know there is a theory that a book, if it is any good, will always find a publisher, that talent cannot be stifled, that it even proves itself by thriving on disappointment, but I have never subscribed to it; we do not expect spring flowers to bloom in a black frost, and I think the chill wind that blows from English publishers, with their black suits and thin umbrellas, and their habit of beginning every sentence with 'We are afraid' has nipped off more promising buds than it has strengthened.[2]

His luck changed, however, with a suggestion from Christopher Sykes, who had just returned from Paris and a chance encounter with a flamboyant figure called Jack Kahane who was the antithesis of the demure discretion of the presses of Bloomsbury and Paternoster Row.

He was a prominent figure in expatriate Paris and numbered Stuart Gilbert and James Joyce among his friends. He was the founder and owner of the Obelisk Press, a small imprint dedicated to the publication of books which violated, however finely, the obscenity laws of England and the United States. At first he had experienced difficulty in finding enough material which was *risqué* without being dangerously porno-graphic and had shown a raffish enterprise by writing such literature himself under the staid pseudonyms 'Cecil Barr' and 'Basil Carr'. These ventures were directed, complete with alluring jackets and protective yellow cellophane, at the restless and prurient fugitives from Anglo-Saxon morality who then haunted the Continental capitals and sold well enough to set the Obelisk Press on a stable footing. Kahane was not entirely cynical, however, and if he was eager to publish Frank Harris's *My Life and Loves*, knowing that any confession from Oscar Wilde's circle would find a furtive clientele, he also released Lawrence Durrell's *Black Book* and Henry Miller's *Tropic of Cancer*. Here, surely, was Connolly's liberator and distributor and he need only think of Joyce to reflect that first publication in Paris entailed no disgrace, indeed had a certain boulevard prestige. He wrote to Sylvia Beach, admitting that his novel was 'smut-bound' and indicating that he was contemplating partnership with Kahane while still hoping for a sale to an American publisher; and when Kahane himself came to London in the early summer of 1935 he and Connolly met.[3] The writer found the publisher 'faintly mephistophelean' but the two men must have liked each other since Kahane, having read the manuscript, invited Connolly to join his *bibliothèque des refusés* and offered him 1000 French francs for rights.[4] Publication was scheduled for spring 1936 and although later he used to tease Connolly and say that his novel was so innocuous as to disgrace his list, privately he liked it and mentioned in his *Memoirs of a Bootlegger* that it was 'as sweet a piece of writing as ever I have seen, the work of an exquisite'.[5]

The Rock Pool is succinct. In its most recent edition, published by the Oxford University Press and introduced by Peter Quennell in 1981, it stands at little more than one hundred pages. At first sight it seems to constitute a cautionary tale, since it follows the inglorious decline of a pompous and self-deluding young Englishman who takes a holiday at Juan-les-Pins with a view to observing and patronizing the locals and ends up being corrupted and ruined by the inhabitants of the artists' and writers' colony in the neighbouring town of Trou-sur-Mer, which owes everything but its suggestive Firbankian name to Cagnes. Connolly, however, lacked the simplicity and the complacency of the moralist, and *The Rock Pool*'s most convincing and memorable aspects are those which reflect not its author's certainties but his anguish and regret. It is not really a book about lesbians or about opting out of Baldwin's England, although Connolly's love of the south, the swallow's longing which eventually led him to list 'the Mediterranean' as his hobby in *Who's Who*, informs every page and many of the finest descriptive passages. Instead it is a book about snobbery, about misogyny, about feeling ill at ease in England yet restless abroad, about being lonely and wanting to belong, about futility under the afternoon sun.

He began the work with the conviction that it would eventually form part of a greater triptych (to be completed by 'The English Malady' and 'Humane Killer') which would concern itself with snobbery, that clean and easy disease which is the greatest obsession of the satirical novelist. Unlike Connolly, Naylor has a job in the City and a private income of £1000 a year but he is nervous and uncertain of his social standing. Connolly had a sharp eye and ear for the manifestations and betrayals of class and his novel contains some subtle and telling exchanges which occur when the English are caught abroad trying to assess one another's claims and positions: 'Naylor suddenly realized that she was middle-class and, worse, was assuming that he was.' There are perceptive and haunting epigrams and observations on almost every page: 'We all find faults, but those who look for gratitude find the ugliest.' 'The punishment of continual philandering, of trying to get every woman to have an affair with one, resides in the successes even more than in the failures.' Similarly, almost every page is charged with a sense of the privileges and penances of evanescence, with a feeling that it is easy to be happy in the past but that the apprehension of present happiness is a greater and more poetic thing: 'With the heave of a dolphin out of the water, the force, the beauty of the present moment seemed to flash into something almost visible and then sink back into the natural current of the afternoon.'

Many of Naylor's circumstances are based on the early career of Nigel Richards, whom the Connollys had befriended through Brian Howard. Richards stayed with them at Rottingdean and saw them regularly in the south of France in the early Thirties. Like Naylor he was a disillusioned stockbroker and when he married abandoned the

City to become a tea-planter in Burma. During the journey out his drunken wife fell into the Brahmaputra river and was devoured by crocodiles but the catastrophe was misreported in London where it was claimed that Richards himself had died. As his novel progressed Connolly therefore felt free to fuse aspects of his friend's life with other, less flattering, circumstances, to practise what he had already observed in other writers of fiction – 'For most authors there is only one way to write a novel, and that is to put their friends ... into it.'[6] Richards, a charming and handsome old Wykehamist with a first from Oxford and a modest private income, thus became Naylor, alumnus of the same establishments, but plain, pompous, a bore. For good measure Connolly endowed his creation with several of his own failings: Naylor is prickly, often lazy, tainted with snobbery and misogyny. Like his author he is beauty's unfailing victim and a figure in whom characters detect an ambivalence: '"I don't care if you do like women – you're queer – one part, if you can call it a part of you, is normal but all the rest of you is queer."' Naylor too was attracted to androgynous women, had had a lonely childhood and saw falling in love as a compensation for earlier emotional deprivations:

> She absorbed all the day-dreams he had ever enjoyed: an only child inventing games in suburban gardens, where the rhododendron and fruition-scented privet yearly bloomed; as a schoolboy, where the bare arms of his neighbours lying across uncharted ink-channels had warmed the desks in summer.

Richards returned to London as *The Rock Pool* was about to be published and coincided with the novelist in the Café Royal. A mutual friend recorded the latter's discomfort: '"My God! I thought you were dead," Connolly exclaimed, with as near as he ever got to a blush.'[7]

It was the end of the friendship and Richards had faded completely from Connolly's life by the time he died in the war. Perhaps it added insult to injury to be included in a novel that falters, for all its perception and lyrical idiosyncrasy. For most writers *The Rock Pool* would seem a fine beginning; to Connolly, freighted with a reputation and exorbitant ambitions, it appeared a minor work and continues to seem so today. The dialogue, apart from occasional exchanges, is unreal. The secondary characters – Rascasse, the painter based on Michonze, Toni and the other feverish and melancholy lesbians – are hollow and now even the quality of outrage which gave Connolly so much initial trouble has turned archaic. As he himself said in a postscript written in 1946: 'Nothing "dates" us so much as an ignorance of the horrors in store.'

With publication now definite it was time to head for the Continent once again. The Connollys had arranged to spend part of the summer holidays with Jean's mother but when they went to meet her off the boat-train in Paris she was carried off the vehicle on a stretcher dead drunk. She had become a deeply neurotic and unhappy woman who always had to go to sleep with the lights on and who was constantly irritable and suspicious of everyone around her. During the course of the holiday her daughter regularly had to help her undress and however carefully they watched her she succeeded in buying bottles of whisky and locking herself in the bathroom to drink them. It was decided that once she returned to America she would have to go to a sanatorium; in the meantime, there was the holiday to survive. The Connollys were in high spirits and despite Mrs Warner's presence and condition they determined to enjoy themselves. They drove from Paris to the Spanish coast north of Barcelona before retracing their journey to Juan-les-Pins. They went to Ragusa in Sicily. They went to Venice, where they stayed at the Danieli, and then drove through Trieste and Yugoslavia before arriving in Budapest to find their hotel enlivened by distinguished guests. 'The Prince of Wales was in our hotel,' he later wrote to his mother, 'carrying on in very Ruritanian fashion with Mrs Simpson.'[8] They returned westwards along a different route: Vienna, Lake Constance, Vosges and Paris, where they saw Mrs Warner off to America. They then inspected Brussels, Bruges and Calais. By the time they returned to London, they had driven 5000 miles and as Connolly told his mother they had done so without any misadventures, not even a puncture.

Jean felt much better since her treatment and had decided to take up ballet dancing, perhaps a little belatedly. They had also begun to think about moving, either to the country, or else to what Connolly promised his mother would be a healthier part of London. The Betjemans were trying to persuade the Connollys to move near to them in Berkshire but Jean was enthusiastic about spending more time at Rottingdean. Connolly thought that too expensive an option but was apprehensive about moving to Regent's Park or Hampstead as 'no one will come and see me there'.[9] In the end they stayed where they were and attempts to regulate domestic expenses were also abandoned. For his birthday in September Maud sent her son some money and he bought a gold-edged tortoiseshell cigarette case. Writing to thank her he admitted that he and Jean needed someone to advise them about household bills and 'what servants eat'. The dinners continued, but now he could face his guests not only as a successful and much-quoted reviewer, but as a novelist about to be launched. When Anthony Powell and his wife came to dinner Powell, who by then had three comic novels to his credit, betrayed the competitiveness of his whole generation as well as the value it accorded Connolly's literary judgement, by asking for a comparison between himself and Evelyn Waugh. Connolly was more diplomat than clairvoyant: 'I said I thought Tony had more talent and Evelyn more vocation. Tony is likely to dry up and Evelyn to make mistakes, but you can learn from mistakes, you can't learn from drying up.'[10]

Powell seems to have no memory of that exchange, but he remembered many evenings at the Connollys', in particular that the 'succession of cooks went up and down in quality, sometimes sharply. Whether or not the proprietor of a mobile coffee-stall got wind of this, one of these was certainly parked every night in a strategic position just opposite the house.'[11] It was not only Connolly's school-friends and the well-established who could expect to be entertained. All his life he was a fervent scout of literary talent and was crucial in the instigation of several careers in the world of letters, among them that of Dylan Thomas. The Welshman was then twenty and had not long been in London. He sent Connolly an inscribed copy of *18 Poems* and was promptly invited to dinner. The other guests included the MacCarthys, Evelyn Waugh, the Powells and Robert Byron but the young man was ill prepared for such celestial company. When asked what he wanted to drink, Thomas provoked what his host later remembered as 'a slight hush' by replying, 'Anything that goes down my throat'. There was more awkwardness later when Desmond MacCarthy found himself discussing Swinburne with the young poet, and in particular his novel, *Lesbia Brandon*. Connolly gathered that Thomas had no idea of the novel's preoccupation with flagellation: 'Desmond drew on the exquisite tact which had enchanted the literary world ... and reverted to the schoolboy language which cuts through age and class — "Yes, he liked swishing." There was a long, even more embarrassing silence. "Did you say swishing? Jesus Christ." '[12]

In January 1936 Rupert Doone's Group Theatre staged the first production at the Westminster Theatre of *The Dog Beneath the Skin* by Auden and Isherwood. It was the first of their collaborative dramas and although it is an imperfect work, its earliest critics were enthused. The *Observer*, *The Times* and the now inevitable *Daily Worker* were delighted, and the *Sunday Times* went so far as to claim that 'This play ought to run for five years.' Unfortunately it ran for only six weeks. This outcome did not surprise Connolly, who attended the premiere on behalf of the *New Statesman*. It would be unfair to say that he was always aloof from fashionable politics – during the later Thirties he was particularly their victim – but he could stand aside, and he recommended that 'Dogskin', as its authors called it, should be turned over to Cole Porter, Cecil Beaton and Oliver Messel 'with a cast of singers and a lavish production'. Complaining that 'the bareness of the stage reflected the poverty of the lines', he admonished Auden for being glib and predictable when he could be great: 'It was irritating to note the didactic quality of these choruses, the authentic rallying cries of homo-communism, and also their slightly forced lyricism.' Convinced that Auden was 'the only poet of real stature since Eliot', he nevertheless made a crucial point which underlay the artistic dilemma of the writers of the Thirties, no matter how great their talent: 'He may be a better man and will certainly be a happier man for trying to get in touch with the masses, but his work will suffer.'[13] Auden and Isherwood and their satellites, guilty about their middle-class backgrounds and convinced that communism offered the only solution to the economic and political problems of the time, were eager to court the values of the workers but could not, since in the stratified society of the Thirties, they never encountered them.

Orwell too struggled with this idealism, although he stood apart from literary factions. He stated that no writer should use language which the working classes could not understand and perhaps more than any of his contemporaries was successful in developing an idiom which was apparently utilitarian but which sacrificed nothing to eloquence or persuasiveness. This polemical instrument was being strengthened and refined throughout the Thirties, although when his novel, *Keep the Aspidistra Flying*, appeared in the spring of 1936 it was not judged an unqualified success. Connolly himself had reservations, as he explained in the *New Statesman*: 'There have been so many novels in which young men and their fiancées sit over the gas fire and wonder where the next shilling is coming from ... the obsession with money about which the book is written, is one which must prevent it from achieving the proportions of a work of art.'[14] He sent a palliative letter to his friend, hoping that he had not been upset and pointing out that more colour was needed to relieve the prevailing gloom and that all bitter pills were better swallowed with sweetening jam.

Far from being annoyed, Orwell was concerned with how to help Connolly launch his own novel. He had written to him in February from Wigan, whither he had gone to begin research into what would become *The Road to Wigan Pier*. He wanted the address of the Obelisk Press and announced that he intended to review Connolly's novel in the *New English Weekly*. Connolly himself had long since become disillusioned with the progress of *The Rock Pool*, which Kahane was shortly to issue in Paris. Scribner's had agreed to publish the book in America but he had decided that the venture was without hope and took every opportunity to indulge in insistent declarations of failure in advance of the publication. He had already written to his mother to warn her that she would not care for the book and now he almost invited Orwell to attack it in print: 'You can have your innings. I think [*The Rock Pool*] is lousy myself.'[15]

Orwell began his review with defiant partiality: 'As Mr Connolly is almost the only novel reviewer in England who does not make me sick, I opened this, his first novel, with a lively interest.' And his expectations were not entirely betrayed, since he found that 'the treatment is mature and skilful.' However, the stern prophet had little common ground with Connolly's hedonists and the book's content worried him: 'The awful thraldom of money is upon everyone and there are only three immediately obvious escapes. One is religion, another is unending work, the third is the kind of sluttish antinomianism – lying in bed till four in the afternoon, drinking Pernod – that Mr Connolly seems to admire.' Orwell's underlying contention was that *The Rock Pool* was outdated when it appeared: by the time his review was published in July, Franco had already raised his insurgent standard in Morocco and precipitated Spain into bitter and portentous civil conflict. The Thirties were becoming a nightmare: escapism seemed somehow unethical. Furthermore, if the characters were morally deficient, Orwell could not forget that they were their author's creatures: 'Even to want to write about so-called artists who spend on sodomy what they have gained by sponging betrays a kind of spiritual inadequacy.'[16]

In his loyal and lengthy appraisal in the *Sunday Times* Desmond MacCarthy conceded that – at 50 francs – the book was double the price of other novels but insisted it was worth it and that he would re-read it for its 'witty precision and spirited, off-hand elegance'.[17] Otherwise *The Rock Pool* became a book which for a long time was scarcely known or available in England, except in what used to be called 'rubber goods' shops. Even his mother had to wait two years before Matthew sent a copy to South Africa but she liked it nevertheless: 'There is a sort of fatalistic sadness . . . all you absorbed when you were younger is in your writing.'[18]

It has had other, less partial, enthusiasts. Somerset Maugham listed it as the modern novel he would most like to have written. Philip Larkin thought it a fine and underrated achievement. And shortly after its publication, Henry Miller sent praise. When he had first met Connolly he had disliked him, finding him 'a god-damned snob, a pretentious sort of cad, a cheap, wise-cracking bastard'. Now, however, he was all enthusiasm: he offered to write a review; he admired Connolly's ability to coin 'startlingly beautiful phrases'; he interpreted the book as oblique self-portraiture and praised the sketch he saw: 'To have put yourself down with such utter truthfulness seems to me positively heroic, considering what your background has been.' Indeed, he even went so far as to find the novel a sort of national panacea: 'It's the sort of book England needs more and more . . . If you can do this for Cagnes Sur Mer what could you not do for old England?'[19]

The qualities of irreverence and provocativeness which Miller liked in *The Rock Pool* were brought to a wider English audience in May 1936 with the death of A. E. Housman, whose fame had steadily grown, since the First World War, to a pitch of unassailable repute. As a schoolboy Connolly, like Orwell, had endorsed this standing but by 1936 he had transferred his allegiance to Modernist poetry and found more to interest him in *The Waste Land* than in the Shropshire laureate's simultaneously published *Last Poems*. The poet's unstinting obituaries suggested that a reappraisal was due and shortly after his death Connolly ventured a few sedate reservations in an article in the *New Statesman*. Half-wittingly, he had attacked a national institution and the response was extraordinary in its intensity and anger.

John Sparrow, a barrister whom Connolly had met as an undergraduate a decade before but would seldom encounter in his apotheosis as Warden of All Souls, sent the *New Statesman* one of many scandalized letters: 'Late for the funeral, Mr Connolly at least had the satisfaction of arriving in time to spit upon the grave before the mourners had departed.'[20] Yet the critic was right to advise Housman's partisans to ask themselves how long it was since they had last read him and what age they were at the time, 'for he is a poet who appeals especially to adolescence, and adolescence is a period when one's reaction to a writer is often dictated by what one is looking for, rather than what is there'. Not all the sceptics were silenced but Connolly was ahead of his time; his arguments ring more true today: we have no personal need of war poets, and that in a sense is what Housman was. As Noël Annan later remarked, 'his *Last Poems* brought tears to the eyes of those of his generation who had seen the young men they loved killed in the Great War.'[21]

If the attack on Housman was construed as defamation of the glorious dead, at least Connolly's next target, another institution, more international this time and more modern, was still alive and writing. Ever since the apparent rebuff at Sanary in 1930 Connolly had felt irritated by Aldous Huxley, by his personality and even more by his recent novels. In 1934 he had written to Asquith's daughter and the MacCarthys' great friend, Princess Bibesco, with the news that he was involved in writing prose parodies and that his first subject would be Huxley, despite his fears that the latter was 'too sacrosanct' for anyone to publish them.[22] He had been invited to contribute to *Parody Party*, an occasional venture bringing together pastiches of various writers, and the almost simultaneous publication of Huxley's latest novel, *Eyeless in Gaza*, gave him his subject and inspiration. Evelyn Waugh admired the result as 'a criticism so penetrating and so savage that in a gentler age its victim would have despaired and pined or perhaps disembowelled himself on Mr Connolly's doorstep'.[23] Connolly remained unrepentant: '[Huxley] had become both very commonplace as a writer and laboured and also revoltingly stupid in his conception of people in novels ... You couldn't caricature *Crome Yellow* or *Antic Hay* – they were too good.'[24] The parody appeared after Connolly had seen the last of Huxley for some years. When contact was re-established, Huxley never referred to 'Told in Gath' and it did nothing to damage their later friendship. It is a tribute to Connolly's charm and companionship that most writers whose lapses in taste and standards provoked his stinging pen maintained good relations with him.

Whatever Huxley's opinions, Leonard Russell and the other editors of *Parody Party* were delighted with the contribution and when the following year a successor to be called *Press Gang* was conceived, Connolly was again called upon to participate. The result, 'Where Engels

Fears To Tread', is one of his most famous achievements and endures as
the final comment on the *salon* Marxism of the Thirties. It purports to
be a review of an aesthete's progress, *From Oscar to Stalin* by Christian
de Clavering, but it was immediately recognized as being a triumphant
comic portrayal of Brian Howard. Most of the piece is taken up with
'excerpts' from the book and sketches the intervals of Howard's career:
the obscure background, the suffocating mother, the father who – like
Matthew – was slightly embarrassing, the outrageous Etonian ('While
the battle of Waterloo was being fought around me, I just sat still and
watched my eyelashes grow'), the peer-chaser of Christ Church, the
London socialite of the Twenties, the talented waster of the Thirties. It
is a masterpiece which not only remains very funny but comprehends in
its brief scope the literary and political illusions of an entire generation.

Its brilliance was immediately recognized and it provoked widespread humour and approval, John Betjeman voicing the consensus
with his congratulations: 'I don't think I have ever in my life read such a
good parody of yours as Brian Howard ... There's a poem by Spender
in this week's New Nation and Statesman which reads just like one of
your quotations.'[25] Howard himself was annoyed: he had always liked
Connolly but after the holiday in Greece the episode seemed doubly
treacherous and it only added insult to injury that in his review of the
compilation Evelyn Waugh praised the piece ('It is left for Mr. Connolly
again to lift the book from the level of paper games to art') and
mentioned that it was based on a character who was a figure of fun to a
small circle.[26] The parody was reissued nine years later and the author
wrote to his reluctant subject stressing that his intentions in 'Engels'
were both kind and admiring. Following years of mockery in Waugh's
fiction Howard was only partly convinced: 'I don't, I suppose, *really*
mind, but now that Evelyn has almost stopped after all these years, the
approach of obscurity was so very delicious.'[27] On reflection he decided
to submit with good grace: it was entirely to his credit that he wrote a
generous view of *The Condemned Playground*, the volume in which
'Engels' appeared, in the *New Statesman*.

It was an aspect of Connolly's critic's mind that part of his literary
intellect was reactive rather than creative, that the art and actions of
others stimulated a brilliant responsiveness. His gift for conversation
was no less characteristic, no less difficult to evaluate, than his parodic
skills. He was famous for his talk: less for the repartee, though that
could be sharp and penetrating, less for the *mot juste*, though other

Above, left: Maud Connolly

Above, right: Matthew Connolly

Right: An early love of nature: the
young Cyril Connolly

The Etonian at fifteen

Right: Connolly
sits between Robert
Longden's knees on a visit
to Hadrian's Villa in the
Christmas vacation of
1922–3

Below: King's Scholars,
Eton, 1921. George
Orwell sits in the third
row, far right, with one
hand extended over his
knee. Robert Longden
is seated at the opposite
extreme end of the same
row while Cyril Connolly
is two boys diagonally
behind him with his
chin in his hand

Left: During the course of one of Sligger's reading parties Piers Synott, Cyril Connolly, Kenneth Clark and Robert Longden form a casual group against the dramatic scenery of the French Alps

Below: Photographed in his place of atonement: Cyril Connolly at Balliol with Robert Longden and an unidentified undergraduate between them

Connolly's mentors:
(*right*) Desmond and
Molly MacCarthy,
(*below, left*) Logan
Pearsall Smith,
and (*below, right*)
'Sligger' Urquhart

A pensive and solitary figure prone to romantic friendships: Cyril Connolly photographed by Noël Blakiston

The prodigy beguiles Walter de la Mare at Garsington in 1928

In Yeoman's Row with Patrick Balfour

In Piccadilly Bright Young Things encounter the proletariat after David Tennant's Mozart party: at right, Patrick Balfour towers over a labourer while in the centre Connolly scrutinizes Cecil Beaton's technique with a road drill

Photographed by Noël Blakiston and followed by a ring-tailed lemur, Brian Howard, Jean Connolly, Giana Blakiston and Cyril Connolly prepare for a round of golf at Rottingdean in the early Thirties

At a party in the Thirties. Back row left to right: Patrick Balfour, Constant Lambert, Angela Culme-Seymour, Dick Wyndham, Tom Driberg, Connolly and Stephen Spender. Jean Connolly and Mamaine Paget are seated in the foreground

Janetta in 1939

wordsmiths envied his descriptive abilities, than for the fantasies he could develop out of the air. He could extemporize whole scenes and episodes of comic exaggeration to amuse his listeners but he surely had himself partly in mind when he described the fleeting fame of the conversationalist in *Enemies of Promise*: 'The only happy talkers are dandies who extract pleasure from the very perishability of their material and who would not be able to tolerate the isolation of all other forms of composition.'[28]

Connolly's listeners were never equipped with pen and paper, with the result that although the stories of his impromptu fantasies are numerous, nobody can remember details. His more playful reviews remain the best indication of that comic skill – among them, the episodes involving 'Felicity', the unlikely heroine who first appeared in June 1936 in a review in the *New Statesman* and who lives with her family, the Arquebuses, in an atmosphere of philistine and suburban jollity in Hampstead. Connolly used the Arquebus family to tease blurb writers, the fiction they described and, ultimately, the philistine and suburban readers he assumed bought the rubbish he was sent to review. Felicity and her family regularly resort to chummy names, fetch out the fish knives and commit one social solecism after another. Of course the idea was snobbish but Connolly's ear for social nuance and distinction had a lynx refinement and in 'Felicity' he created a miniature world which rings entirely true. When in July 1937 *Night and Day* was launched (with a cocktail party for 800 at the Dorchester) the owners hoped to produce a sophisticated weekly that would rival the *New Yorker* and eclipse *Punch*. The publishers, Chatto and Windus, had raised over £19,000 capital to sustain their venture and wanted the best comic writers. Connolly wrote once again about Felicity; John Betjeman explored similar terrain in a column decrying the onslaught of suburban culture. But before the critic had had the chance to develop something larger out of the Arquebus family, the magazine collapsed after six months, a victim of the Depression, of litigation provoked by one of Graham Greene's film reviews, of English indifference to magazine culture. By then, however, on 28 September 1936, Connolly had signed a contract with Routledge and been advanced £75 in anticipation of a new novel.

CHAPTER TWELVE

IN THE SPRING of 1936 the Connollys had travelled on a gastro-
nomic holiday through France with a wealthy younger friend they had
met not long before called Harry (Sir Henry) d'Avigdor-Goldsmid.
Mindful of Proust and Dornford Yates, they made pilgrimages to Illiers
and Pau, and Connolly was in fine form as they travelled south in
luxury with evidence of the advancing spring budding all around them.
Jean once again had digestive problems and d'Avigdor-Goldsmid
remembered that at Tours she ordered noodles while her companions
sated themselves on richer meats. As they drove over the Pyrenees their
car was stoned and they decided to return to Paris but despite Jean's
dietary problems it had been a happy holiday. On this occasion or soon
afterwards d'Avigdor-Goldsmid and Connolly found themselves discussing prostitutes and the nature of the advertisements they placed to
secure custom. The former asked his friend what wording, if any,
would tempt him, and received Connolly's reply: '"What humiliations
you will know."'[1] He was newly restless and this time because his
marriage was in difficulties; already in 1936 he had had an affair with a
woman called Betty Mossop who joined him for a houseparty given by
his friend Richard Wyndham in Sussex. Perhaps there were other
infidelities, but if Jean was aware of them she decided to turn a blind
eye rather than risk any damaging confrontation and as a matter of
course they travelled together to the south of France in the summer.
While lying on the beach at Eden Roc one day they overheard a man
say: 'Well, this is better than Mar-Gate isn-tit?' A young woman
sunbathing within earshot was intrigued and remembered turning to try
to identify the contented philosopher: 'At that moment I caught the eye
of a young rather fat man lying nearby and we both had to laugh. It
turned out to be Cyril Connolly.'[2] The woman was called Peggy Bainbridge and she had recently left her husband, Emerson Bainbridge,
when he had become a Mosleyite fascist. She was young and very pretty

and when she joined the Connollys for a drink she found herself drawn to them both. The feeling was clearly mutual; and a few days later, when she moved further down the coast with her friend Nora Shawe-Taylor, a cousin of the music critic, Desmond, Connolly began to write to her. His first letter, from the Hôtel Victoria at Cannes, told how much he missed her and complained of the dullness of life on the Riviera. Even the refugees who had begun to arrive from Majorca, fleeing the Spanish Civil War, offered no distraction; rather, their presence unsettled his conscience, which had begun to plague him with anxieties about duties in Spain: 'I have a horrible feeling I ought to go there and write articles about it as I know it very well.'

More immediately, Jean's mother was due to arrive in Cannes. She would stay with Jean and her son-in-law on the Riviera until the end of August, after which the party proposed to travel to Budapest. Mrs Warner hated cars, so she and her daughter would make the journey by train while Connolly drove there alone. Now he encouraged Peggy to join them in Hungary, arguing persuasively for the charms of Budapest; the Hungarians were anglophiles who particularly liked English hats, shoes and gloves. 'They kept the English golf pro on all through the war, so they're not really barbarians and we ought to give them back Czecho-Slovakia.'[3]

Mother and daughter went to Hungary while Connolly followed Peggy and Nora to Kitzbühel in the Austrian Alps. There he met Ian Fleming and the two men determined to meet again in London. He and Peggy still contemplated driving to Budapest, but on the road to Hungary their car was involved in a direct collision with another vehicle. There was then a part of Austria where motorists were suddenly required to start driving on the left but Peggy remembered that when they approached this zone – indicated by a large sign in German which neither of them understood – it was raining so heavily that visibility was greatly reduced. Connolly walked from the encounter unscathed but Peggy sustained a broken nose. There was such a delay while the car was repaired that they decided there was no point in continuing to Budapest and resolved instead to head for London. At Amiens, they began an affair which was to last for a year. Like so many other women, Peggy found Connolly enchanting and fifty years later still remembered his sense of humour, his wit, his charm, his conversation. Despite, or perhaps because of, 'his somewhat unprepossessing physique', he had to prove that he could attract young and pretty women. 'He was never a bore and had the gift of making his love of the moment feel that she was the only one who mattered and almost his intellectual equal. He was wonderful company.'[4] Connolly – the 'ugly' victim of Etonian initiations – was never interested in plain women; and as his amorous career became infamous onlookers wondered how he could attract some of the most famous beauties of his own and younger generations. They were forgetful – not only of his charm, but of a significant generalization, that women are much less slaves to beauty then men, its comic vassals.

Back in England he was reunited with Jean, who remained tolerant. They went to stay at Sledmere as guests of Christopher Sykes but according to the account Connolly sent to Peggy, the excursion was not entirely happy. The journey depressed him, not least because it was undertaken on a slow train full of soldiers, and he and Jean argued: she had spent over £15 at Harrods on shoes, gloves and a hat, leaving only £5 in their current account. Once at Sledmere, they joined the other guests at bridge but he and Jean lost the only rubber they played together. Aside from disagreements about hats and gloves, nobody was short of things to talk about in the autumn of 1936: the Spanish Civil War, German reoccupation of the Rhineland, a new socialist regime in France, persistent financial instability, the Italians in Abyssinia, the Japanese in China, darkened every overseas prospect. Even so, matters nearer home temporarily eclipsed even these cataclysms: in October Oswald Mosley marched on the Jews of Whitechapel and throughout the autumn the country surrendered to the Abdication Crisis. In a fragment from a notebook, Connolly decided that Edward VIII was the centre, not of a father cult, like George V, Mussolini or Baldwin, but of a spring ritual: 'He is Adonis, he is Hyacinth, he is Jesus, he is Prince Charming, the sacrificed son.'[5]

For most intellectuals, however, the Abdication was nothing more than a tiresome distraction from immenser issues and towering over these in symbolic significance was the war in Spain. When Franco, backed by the Church, industrialists and monarchists, threw down his gage at the foot of the legitimate Republican government, he stole the attention of a continent. Hitler and Mussolini sent him arms, while thousands of intellectuals north of the Pyrenees saw the conflict as embodying the apocalyptic struggle between right and left and took sides accordingly. In England Wyndham Lewis, Roy Campbell and Robert Graves declared their support for Franco. Eliot and Maugham thought one bad side the equal of the other. The vast majority of writers and intellectuals, however, supported the Republic and denied the ambiguities invariably inherent in warfare. As demonstrations marched and pamphlets harangued, nobody wanted to know that more than a century of internecine problems had brought about the present urgency or that it was not only the factions of the right in Spain who rejected the government's authority. This was idealism's last hour before the big guns rolled and to be seen to be sitting on the fence was itself a sort of bravery.

A widely publicized exodus began immediately. Connolly later called this movement the conflict's 'Rupert Brooke period' and was right to suggest that this war, like the First World War before it, was something of a literary event.[6] Anthony Blunt and Louis Macneice had gone to Spain in 1935 and with the advent of hostilities many writers made personal expeditions, some to watch and report, some to fight. The paradigm was the poet John Cornford, who died there on his twenty-first birthday, but Ralph Fox, John Summerfield and Christopher Cauldwell acted no less immediately. Orwell went at the end of 1936, Auden the following January, then Spender, then Julian Bell. As a prominent writer on a prominent liberal magazine Connolly was in a conspicuous position. Unlike many among his peers and friends he had never become an official supporter of communism or disarmament. At the same time, whether out of conviction or a desire to annoy his father or please his friends or be fashionable, he had aligned his sympathies with the left and had done so publicly – to the extent that it was even suggested at one stage that he should stand as a challenger to Sir Samuel Hoare, Conservative MP for Chelsea. However much he might dread the discomfort or fear the danger, he made three trips, two in 1936 and one in the following year.

Describing his adventures later, he said that his first impression was that friends in England shook hands differently as they said goodbye to combatants and reporters: 'One cannot avoid detecting in the farewell a moment of undertaker heartiness, of mortuary appraisal.'[7] He was struck also by the differences between France and Spain when crossing the border: normally the transition was one from energy and prosperity to sluggish despair; now it was Spain that seemed more alive. Such opinion-broking antagonized Evelyn Waugh, who held aloof from Iberian self-destruction and would later mock Connolly's reporting in *Robbery Under Law*, his own very different account of Mexico's reckoning with right and left: as far as he was concerned it was inconceivable that anyone whose intelligence he respected could assert that anarchy and shortages in Spain were preferable to peace and plenty elsewhere.

Connolly found that English journalists were disliked owing to the non-intervention of the British government and the sympathy Franco seemed to enjoy in Fleet Street. Like Auden after him, he saw the churches blackened and locked but was moved instead, he told his readers, by an atmosphere resulting from a backward people's desire for freedom, liberty and education. Returning a few weeks later, he took Peggy with him to Barcelona and Valencia and she remembered that they befriended a Russian anarchist who gave her a red scarf with a hammer and sickle embroidered in its corner. In Barcelona Connolly witnessed the interment of the famous Anarchist Durruti and interviewed Anarchist militia by candlelight in a train bound for Madrid. He recruited opinions among the freedom fighters, idealists and itinerant musketeers he encountered and inevitably found widely divergent opinions about the war and its likely outcome. He met two members of the Spanish Cabinet, Juan Garcia Oliver, the Minister of Justice, and Indalecio Prieto, the Minister of Munitions, Marine and Air. Oliver told him: 'If I had to sum up Anarchism in a phrase I would say it was the ideal of eliminating the beast in man.'[8]

Connolly returned to Spain early in 1937, this time travelling with Jean and their great friend 'Ran' Antrim, at that time describing himself as 'me good pink peer'.[9] Their destination was Valencia. Aware that suspicion was gaining ground as the situation became more desperate and more complicated, Connolly arrived with a letter of reference from Harry Pollitt, the Secretary of the English Communist Party; his caution was vindicated when shortly after arrival he and his companions were subjected to questioning by a Comintern agent. No less reassuring was the other document with which he had arrived – a letter of introduction from Christopher Isherwood, whom he had recently met in London, to W. H. Auden, who had gone to Spain in the hope of serving with a medical unit as a stretcher bearer but ended up working as a propagandist for the government. Arriving with high hopes, Auden had encountered only disillusion: he had failed to find a role for himself; he had discovered that the politics of the war were vastly more complicated than armchair combatants in England allowed and that the Soviet Union was supplying little aid to its natural allies, the Republicans, because it was eager not to upset the balance of European power. At the beginning of 1937 he was stranded and demoralized in the Hotel Victoria in Valencia with no apparent purpose, his companions Arthur Koestler, there to cover the hostilities for the *News Chronicle*, and Basil Murray, the partial model for Evelyn Waugh's Basil Seal.

Auden was understandably thrilled when the Connollys turned up and immediately opened a bottle of Spanish champagne, a gesture which Christopher Isherwood insisted later revealed the real Auden and not an impostor. Connolly was deeply struck by Auden's features and presence and later revealed that he dreamed of him intermittently for the rest of his life. The poet took a great liking to Jean. She named him 'Uncle Wiz', which stuck, and he said she was the only woman who could keep him up all night. Auden and Connolly's party met again in Barcelona and there was a famous difficulty when the poet retired behind a bush in the course of a walk through the gardens of Monjuich. Militiamen seized him, outraged at an abuse of public property, and only Harry Pollitt's letter redeemed the hope of English poetry. Antrim also encountered difficulties. When they arrived in Valencia, the police not unnaturally wondered what had brought an Anglo-Irish noble to Spain and narrowly and suspiciously interrogated him. Connolly later informed Peggy that the treatment had greatly upset him, 'as he had never been treated except as a peer before'.[10] Apart from their personal difficulties, Connolly reported to Peggy that in Barcelona coal, bread and petrol were unobtainable and that relations between the Communists and the Anarchists were disintegrating into open hostility.

By the time he returned to England he had begun to have doubts, not so much about the validity of the cause as about its outcome. He noted a defeatism in professional middle-class Spaniards who, according to left-wing report in England, were loyal to a man to the Republicans. In Connolly's experience, some would defiantly prophesy a triumph of the embattled government, but quite as many would enquire about employment prospects in England or the possibility of escape to America. This implicit pessimism infected his own assessment of the situation; and when he reported more opinions in the *New Statesman* in January 1937 it was in the context of a broader analysis of his generation's doctrinal choices. Looking back to Oxford, he remembered that politics had scarcely impinged and it was only in the wider world that the first allegiances had been declared: 'The most realistic, such as Mr Evelyn

Waugh and Mr Kenneth Clark, were the first to grasp how entirely the kind of life they liked depended on close co-operation with the governing classes.' He wondered what had made all his contemporaries 'who have not taken shelter in the civil service or the Catholic Church' embrace left-wing politics, and besides identifying the motivations of conscientiousness and expediency he invoked 'the typically English band of psychological revolutionaries, people who adopt left-wing political formulas because they hate their fathers or were unhappy at their public schools or insulted at the Customs or lectured about sex'.[11]

This remark seems to anticipate uncannily the explanations of the spy scandals of the Fifties. More immediately, it irritated Stephen Spender (who in Connolly's view 'took himself very seriously as the blue-eyed young Marxist'[12]) and the poet wrote angrily to Christopher Isherwood, complaining that the critic had been stupid, cruel and destructive. And to Virginia Woolf he added: 'I am sure that Cyril Connolly is quite wrong to have allowed the revolution to "go bad" on him as though it were an undergraduate lunch party.'[13] Others took a different view, among them Leonard Russell, the journalist and editor who had been involved in *Parody Party* and who, in the summer of 1937, solicited Connolly for more contributions to *Night and Day*: 'May I say how much I have admired your recent reviews in the New Statesman? I mean for putting the position of those of us who can't go all the way with the Leftists but yet are on the right side of the fence.'[14] Orwell agreed. He had been shot through the throat while soldiering on the Aragonese front yet had hoped to see Connolly in Spain: 'I would have enjoyed giving you tea in a dugout.'[15] He wrote from Barcelona in June 1937, revealing that although the New Statesman arrived belatedly in the hospitals he was still able to follow his friend's column: 'It is a credit to the New Statesman that it is the only paper . . . where any but the Communist viewpoint has ever got through.' When Orwell next wrote, four months later, he was back in England and his hope had soured: 'Nearly a million dead in all, they say, and obviously it is going to be all for nothing.'[16]

In February 1937 the publisher Gerald Duckworth had written to Connolly about his reports from Spain. He had heard that he was considering writing a wider and more extensive treatment of the crisis and asked for first refusal on the project. Nothing came of the plan, not least because Connolly was already under contract to produce a novel for Routledge. In March that publisher proffered another contract and he received £50 as an advance on a volume of essays, some of which were to be culled from recent journalism, and some of which would have to be written. It may have been seen by both Connolly and his publisher as a way of getting something out while the projected novel was under way. Its provisional title was 'The Little Voice' and surviving papers reveal that its original contents were to include 'Revolution in Athens', '90 Years of Novel Reviewing', 'Felicity', 'Housman' and 'Lytton', later renamed 'The Fate of an Elizabethan'. There was also a plan to add a group of parodies: 'Told in Gath' was to be included, along with new works to taunt Maugham, Hemingway, Yeats, Wyndham Lewis, Virginia Woolf, 'Publishers' Lists' and 'Women Novelists'.

The inclusion of 'Lytton' was not insignificant. In 1933 Connolly had been shocked to learn of the death in an air crash of Viscount Kneb-worth, a dashing and glamorous Tory MP who had been his contemporary at school. His brief life – he had been twenty-nine at his death – had been posthumously recorded by his father, Lord Lytton, in *Antony: A Record Of Youth* and Connolly had reviewed the book when it appeared. It was not in itself of literary significance but its contents kindled Connolly's imagination. Although there were wide divergences between their Etonian careers, Knebworth was in Pop, and was the first of that society to be wooed when Connolly planned his unlikely accession. Knebworth too had apparently dreaded leaving Eton, had seen it as a culmination. It was as though he had died a permanent boy; and that impression can only have been strengthened by the inclusion in *Antony* of an introduction by J. M. Barrie. Suddenly Connolly saw that he and Knebworth and countless others were victims of a shared education, an education which was without practical application ('it was assumed in after-life that ravens would feed us') and which permitted exaltations of an unforgettable and eclipsing intensity. Knebworth's Etonian career had been triumphant; his afterlife, including a flirtation with British fascism, an anti-climax. It was as though he had been crippled by early auguries of fame: 'We hear a lot of criticism of public school education from those who were failures at school – but is there anything in reality more dangerous than early success?'[17]

The spring of 1937 brought further opportunities to ponder Eton when Connolly reviewed a new history of the school. His article appeared in the *New Statesman* and fused his recent reflections and recollections of Eton with the mandatory radicalism of the time, denouncing the fagging system and competitive examinations. He had to be careful in what he wrote. Since his recent reports in the *New Statesman* he was aware that his orthodoxy was under suspicion. Early in March he was criticized in the *Daily Worker* for not giving full support to the right side in the Spanish conflict and now joked that every action had to be carefully considered for its ideological implications: he had spent a recent Sunday afternoon in the neutral waters of the Droitwich brine baths and afterwards had read some similarly neutral poetry by Louis MacNeice. 'So physical and mental pleasure is still permissible without a party ticket.'[18]

Meanwhile he pursued the introduction made at Kitzbühel and befriended Ian Fleming, who then inhabited a converted chapel in Belgravia. Connolly was fascinated by his book collection which – housed on conventional shelves but within black boxes – lent the high galleried room a slightly sinister aspect. Connolly was at that time collecting first editions of T. S. Eliot and was amused that he and Fleming bought from the same book-dealer, Elkin Matthews. Their collections could not have been more different, however, since Fleming only bought books which he claimed represented some original advance by the mind of man and as a result boasted ownership of texts about the telephone, the wireless and the latest researches in physics and biology, not to mention the Communist *Manifesto*.[19]

Connolly and Jean also determined to see more of Auden, now returned from Spain. The great poet had not yet acquired the mellowness and tolerance which characterized his American persona and it took little to excite his uncompromising and radical standards. Once he and Connolly found themselves talking about their families and the critic referred to his difficult relations with Matthew. Auden was adamant: 'Those people just batten on one . . . Stand up to him, make him see you don't need him any more.' Later, when Connolly was having lunch with his father, he decided to heed Auden's advice: returning from the restaurant in Soho, Connolly stopped the taxi-driver outside his own flat without inviting Matthew in for the customary talk over brandy. But the father was deeply hurt and the son deeply guilty: 'I don't know which of us felt more unhappy.'[20] However, when in November, having won the King's Gold Medal for Poetry, Auden was presented at Buckingham Palace by the Poet Laureate, John Masefield, it was in Connolly's tails that he made his bow.

In June 1937 Connolly and Jean went to stay at Lord Antrim's house,

Glenarm, in Ulster. While they were in Ireland, Matthew – having survived the rebuff delivered on his son's threshold – advised them to go south and visit Clontarf, now owned by Connolly's uncle Eddie Vernon but inhabited by his cousin Mona Oulton, whose husband, Jack, ran the place as his own and had sold many of its contents. Matthew continued to hope that Eddie's son, Bobby, who was also his godson, would eventually inherit, but Clontarf was passing irresistibly from Vernon control. That summer Connolly took his good intentions for 'The Little Voice' to the Continent, but it seemed unlikely that he would make much headway, since he and Jean began their holidays by staying with Peggy Bainbridge at Antibes. In March, Connolly and Peggy had travelled to Budapest but there she had told him their affair must end. She had fallen in love with another man and in any case felt sorry for Jean, whom she greatly liked. They left Budapest together; Peggy went to ski in Switzerland and said goodbye to Connolly at Zurich station. A connoisseur of the desolate, romantic moment and a hoarder of the past, he was reluctant to admit the affair was over; indeed, now it was, its sweetness doubled in intensity and the least he could do was honour its glories with the rituals of romance. He wrote a long valediction, its tenth and last stanza characteristic of the threnody:

> We shall have much to remember when it is too late
> The meeting in the *bois* the drive in the fog
> The *gams* the Casanova and the Bauer
> The pernod at the violet hour
> and on my birthday in Nancy
> the sad presentiment of my fate
> and the blackbird singing by the Gellert Gate.
> 'I need you more than he. You need him more than me.'[21]

Most couples would have decided that a clean break was the most satisfactory resolution of the affair but Connolly could hardly travel to the Continent without going to the south of France and he could hardly go there without seeing Peggy. He was still in love with her; as for Jean, she would tolerate his infidelities provided he remained her husband. However bizarre the reunion, there were no acrimonies and no regrets beyond Connolly's romantic sighings for irrecoverable time. Presently they left for the Austrian Alps and Peggy received a postcard a few days later: 'We forgot our comb – would you mind sending it on?'[22] Kitzbühel was small and fashionable; chance meetings were inevitable

and soon they ran into another pleasure-seeking couple, Peter Watson
and his lover, Denham Fouts. The four got on very well and Jean
especially became a regular visitor to their apartment at 44 Rue du Bac.
Leaving Watson and friend behind, they continued to Salzburg, where
they encountered Isaiah Berlin, Stuart Hampshire, and Elizabeth
Bowen, who was particularly glad to see them: 'The Connollys turned
up, looking well in mountain get-ups. Our party didn't get into those as
we were all either too fat or too small.'[23] Everybody enjoyed the
festival, a fact which would have surprised Matthew, who had written
warning his son and daughter-in-law against the 'discordant yowls' of
grand opera, indicating that his preference lay with an afternoon at the
Oval supporting Somerset.[24]

CHAPTER THIRTEEN

THE CONNOLLYS RETURNED to London to an angry letter from Mr Ragg of Routledge Kegan Paul who stated that both the books contracted from the critic had been advertised in their lists of forthcoming publications and that 'great interest had been aroused'. Yet he had not seen or heard from his author for six months: 'Publishers, I hope you know, are patient and long-suffering, but we feel that you owe us some word about these two books.'[1] Connolly had also received a letter from Orwell, who had missed his column in the *New Statesman* and was having his own difficulties with publishers: having seen that the situation in Spain was more complex than opinion in England allowed, he could no longer support the Communist cause unequivocally and this hesitation concerned his old publisher, Victor Gollancz, who distanced himself from anything that might 'harm the fight against fascism'.[2] Orwell was now involved with Fredric Warburg and Connolly wrote not only to reassure him that he had greatly enjoyed his last book, *The Road to Wigan Pier*, but also to stress Warburg's probity and professionalism. He understood his friend's difficulties: he too had discovered that any deviation from Communist loyalty jeopardized understandings with editors and contracts with publishers. The two men seem not to have met again until well into 1938; and when Orwell came to a party at 312a King's Road, he arrived 'looking gaunt, shaggy, shabby, aloof and had this extraordinarily magical effect on the women. They all wanted to meet him . . . and their fur coats shook with pleasure.'[3]

Connolly agreed with Mr Ragg that Routledge had shown great patience, confessing to little or no progress with either the awaited novel or with 'The Little Voice'. He proposed instead the completion of a new type of book: half criticism, half autobiography, which would examine 'a lot of problems, ideas, and situations of today'. He envisaged the inclusion not only of a few parodies but also of several of his recently published articles which would help to explain the development of his position. He admitted that he was not only 'very lazy' but also a perfectionist, and tried to explain that he always wanted to tear up anything he had written. To combat this condition he proposed a new scheme: if he did not produce so many thousand words every four weeks, he would be liable to start repaying Routledge's advance at £10 a month. However, he hoped that the plan would not be necessary and was confident that his new idea was auspicious: it would owe something to Robert Graves's *Goodbye to All That*, as well as to the American notion of autobiography mixed with other disciplines, and would certainly prove more profitable than fiction, 'as I think the novel will have less and less future and be harder and harder to write'.[4] Ragg replied by return of post. He was delighted to hear that Connolly was 'still alive' and drily conceded his perfectionism: 'I was not far wrong when I hinted in my previous letter that while there was a possibility that the deletion or addition of a single comma might be necessary to anything you had written, it would be impossible for any publisher to tear your script away from you.'[5] Connolly, meanwhile, had thought of a sub-title: 'How To Live Another Ten Years'.

Peggy's decision to end their affair was more than a blow to his confidence and *amour propre*, since preliminary work on 'Another Ten Years' had given her a significant symbolic role. A long fragment from a notebook used in the book's composition is more than an extemporization or a train of thought committed to paper; it suggests that the crisis implicit in the forthcoming decade was to be examined and resolved around the career of a woman – or women – Connolly knew:

> I should like to tell you about Beulah … because to answer what will happen to the world in ten years time I shall need a symbol for European civilization … For me she stands for the irresistible appeal of a certain kind of life, for the possibilities and limitations which go with a certain set of privileges. Above all, with those privileges in decline.[6]

Beulah, one gathers, is a 'curfew girl': because after midnight her company becomes dangerous; she drinks too much, she bawls in doggerel French, she haggles noisily over the restaurant bill and leaves with a handsome stranger. She consoles herself with fur coats and a portable gramophone on which she plays Ravel and Tchaikovsky, she keeps a dachshund for company and her estranged husband is a blackshirt. It is impossible to say whether Beulah would have been developed only according to symbolic rather than realistic designs but these brief abandoned lineaments suggest that she was to be a symbol not only of emotional loneliness (for she was conceived when it was no longer possible to disguise the difficulties of Connolly's marriage, either from himself or from friends) but of hedonism and of the carefree life now threatened by external forces. But even as Beulah germinated in his mind he saw that she would have to be jettisoned. The affair with Peggy ended; and as *The Rock Pool* had taught him, he failed with characterization, and for one good reason. As another fragment from the same notebook admitted: 'I am only interested in myself. Have I charm enough, I wonder, to interest you?'

On 18 November Ragg and Connolly were due to meet for lunch at Simpson's. Leaving nothing to chance, the publisher warned the writer that he would expect him to pay for the wine if he had not produced at least another 10,000 words but Connolly cancelled, claiming that his writing day would be lost after any lunch inevitably protracted with brandy and cigars. However, he now proposed a title taken from Sir Thomas Browne: 'In vain do individuals hope for immortality, or any patent from oblivion, in preservations below the Moon.' He would call his book 'Patent from Oblivion, or How to live another ten years'. On 15 December Ragg wrote again. He welcomed the title and was sorry they would not be meeting for lunch in the near future, 'but if I can genuinely feel – and why shouldn't I? – that you will be hard at work writing, with possibly an interval for bread and cheese, then I suppose I mustn't grumble.'[7]

The critic's life was not as free from pleasurable distraction as he would have the irascible Ragg believe and he continued to socialize, although he and Jean began to go out separately. That autumn he went to a party given by John Heygate – the man who had captivated Evelyn Waugh's first wife and later found himself immortalized as the vulgar and fatuous John Beaver in *A Handful of Dust* – and there he was introduced to a pretty young woman called Diana who, at twenty-two, was twelve years his junior.[8] She was at the Chelsea School of Art but their conversation soon strayed beyond artistic discussion and she noted his ability to talk about other people and to sum them up in one amusing line. He did not restrict himself to the observation of others, however: self-scrutiny ranked high in his catalogue of diversions and he was quite capable of infecting bystanders with that interest. She was particularly struck by one remark: 'I'm a highbrow and an intellectual and that's all that matters.' He was supremely charming and amusing and also very candid, mentioning not only the affair that had just ended with Peggy, but also the fact that he was married. Again she found herself impressed: he disdained self-exculpation and, rather than claim that he had been driven to adultery by a philistine and uncomprehending wife, chose to appear before her as a frank philanderer.

They saw each other several times in the next few weeks before he suddenly announced that he was in love with her. Diana had not met Jean, was not to do so until two months after she had met Connolly, and so could not judge the nature of their relationship except through his eyes. At the same time, although she was surprised by the suddenness of his declaration, it seemed also to ring true. As she later remarked: 'Strange though it may seem, considering the amount of times it happened, Cyril fell *tremendously* in love when he did. It was never an "idea" but totally genuine.' He began to besiege her with telegrams and telephone calls and she was won over. They continued to see each other and he began to talk of eventual marriage. Diana, however, was prepared to let matters ride for the time being. Whatever happened she did not want to be responsible for the collapse of his marriage: indeed, on more than one occasion, she was to urge him – unsuccessfully – to part with her and commit himself once more to his wife. Furthermore, she had discovered him to be 'very warm-hearted' but also very difficult. He seemed incapable of avoiding 'quarrelsome' behaviour with those he liked yet with his characteristic self-knowledge he also recognized this weakness and once admitted that he always deeply regretted the unpleasantness he had caused. He had 'a passion for deception' which revealed itself most clearly in his amorous subterfuges yet he could also be defiant. Diana learned that Jean knew of their involvement but gathered that he had refused to renounce her, claiming that she helped him with his writing.[9]

At the end of 1937, leaving Diana in London, Connolly travelled to Germany with Peter Watson. The excursion, planned as a distraction, had its sober moments, the most notable being their attendance in Munich at an exhibition of Degenerate Art organized by the Nazis. The exposition comprised a selection of 'decadent' pictures which had been painted, largely by Jewish artists, since 1910 and which came from German state and provincial collections. Although Connolly had imbibed Surrealism in Paris nearly a decade before, this exhibition marked his first exposure to 'German Expression': he and Watson were fascinated by the Kirchners and Noldes, the Kokoschkas, Chagalls, Marcs and Barlachs, and by the scornful captions with which each picture was equipped. Stern guards supervised their contemptible treasures and Connolly and Watson realized that they were meant to look deeply shocked by each depraved canvas. In Spain Connolly had experienced only the chaos and rumours of war; Germany offered something more ambiguous. The country seemed efficient, stable and newly prosperous; English tourists were well treated and could only guess at the cruel secrets of the guards. Whatever they had expected before arriving in Germany, they now experienced the nightmare for which Communism seemed the only antidote. The episode profoundly unsettled Connolly and provoked him into writing a grim fantasy which he published in the *New Statesman* the following January as 'Year Nine'.

He envisaged a totalitarian state of the future described in the last few hours of the life of the narrator, 711037, under sentence of death because he and his female friend, 711038, had inadvertently strayed into a forbidden basement which housed Degenerate Art and saw work which celebrated beauty, private love, the gratification of the senses. John Betjeman was very impressed and wrote at the end of January 1938: 'I never realized what powers worthy of Swift you had. I always thought you were the wittiest of writers we had. But I didn't know it was in you to make a picture of such ghastly horrors as "Year Nine".'[10] Orwell was even more impressed and took some degree of inspiration from it when, a decade later and with Nazism crushed, he came to envisage a future no less totalitarian in *Nineteen Eighty-Four*.

Connolly returned to work on 'Patent from Oblivion', with intervals for reviewing and other journalism. In February 1938 John Lehmann unsuccessfully tried to coax him into writing an appreciation of the fiction of Christopher Isherwood for *New Writing*. Isherwood and Auden, meanwhile, hoping to gather material for a book, had gone to see the Sino-Japanese war for themselves. On 4 February they sent Connolly a postcard. The poet was succinct: 'The Indian Ocean is crashingly dull.' The novelist was more constructive: 'You're to get that book finished before we return – or there'll be big trouble.'[11] For once, however, Connolly needed neither stick nor carrot to work and wrote to Ragg on 21 March that he was disinclined to include the projected series of parodies, 'Flights into Egypt', for fear they would seem too frivolous for the world into which 'Patent from Oblivion' would be born. He proposed instead to concentrate on sections dealing with his autobiography, which he had decided to call *A Georgian Boyhood*, and with the theme of 'Temptation' as it confronted young writers, and he had already completed 6000 words of each. Orwell meanwhile had written in bleak mood. He had been spitting blood again, but the political crises of Europe distressed him more: 'It seems to me we might as well all pack our bags for the concentration camp.' The only thing to do was to carry on writing. He had heard his friend was bringing out another book and suggested some reciprocal reviewing. He would write about Connolly's in the *New English Weekly* and possibly *Time and Tide* and hoped that Connolly would find time to appraise his forthcoming *Homage to Catalonia*, perhaps in the *New Statesman*. His suggestion was succinct and imperturbable: 'You scratch my back, I'll scratch yours.'[12]

In April Connolly went to France alone, first to the Loire Valley and then to Paris. He continued to feel optimistic about the book and wrote to Jean with the news that he had finished its second section and hoped to complete *A Georgian Boyhood* in a further three weeks. He also maintained contact with Diana and emphasized her importance and inspiration in the parturition of his work: he liked emotional complication and his creative talents were most intensively stimulated when he had – in Peter Quennell's words – 'two faces haunting his imagination'. He returned to England but was back on the Continent in the early summer. On 12 June he was able to write to Ragg from the south of France with the news that the manuscript of the book now stood at about 100,000 words and was more or less complete. He saw no necessity to vet the autobiographical section for potentially libellous remarks as he had changed the names of his preparatory school and of the boys most frequently mentioned. The work was now to be called *Enemies of Promise* and he was pleased with the new title, 'as it does express more than any other what the book is about'.[13] He had sent the work to his sovereign mentor, Logan Pearsall Smith, and was delighted by his reaction: although the older man had appealed for cuts in Part One he was impressed by *A Georgian Boyhood*, which he pronounced a masterpiece. Furthermore he had promised to promote the book with such American publishers as he knew and to campaign for serialization in *Atlantic Monthly*.

Fired with confidence, Connolly confided to Ragg that he had already begun work on another book, a short novel almost all in dialogue and farcical in tone which would readily lend itself to theatrical adaptation. Despite his assurances, however, his publishers remained worried about libel actions and he struggled to soothe them with news of emendations: he had thrice edited the word 'homosexuality' and once 'masturbation' and had strengthened assertions that his criticisms were levelled at all public schools and not merely at Eton. With publicity in mind he had already compiled a list of reviewers and influential pundits and freshly printed copies of *Enemies of Promise* were despatched to Cecil Beaton, Desmond MacCarthy, Osbert Sitwell, Somerset Maugham, Maynard Keynes, Maurice Baring, Harold Nicolson, Raymond Mortimer, T. S. Eliot, Gladwyn Jebb, Enid Bagnold, Maurice Bowra, Stephen Spender, Lord Berners, James Agate, Kenneth Clark and E. M. Forster.

Orwell meanwhile was bewildered. He admitted to being apprehensive at the thought that his friend had found letters he had written at Eton but this anxiety was displaced by a larger confusion. He simply could not understand why anyone should want to describe school life: 'I wonder how you can write about St Cyprian's. It's all like an awful nightmare to me, & sometimes I can still taste the porridge (out of those pewter bowls, do you remember?).'[14] Yet he was no less attached to his similar past: the same letter regretted that rain had stopped the Eton–Harrow cricket match which had begun that morning. During the course of these negotiations Mrs Warner had taken the Villa America, a large house on the Cap d'Antibes which had formerly belonged to F. Scott Fitzgerald's friends the Murphys, and Connolly joined his wife and mother-in-law there for most of the summer. Somerset Maugham regularly arrived for lunch or dinner while other guests travelled greater distances: Maurice Bowra, in festive mood following his accession to the Wardenship of Wadham College, Oxford; Peter Quennell and his new wife; Peggy Strachey and her lover; and Diana, who had reluctantly come to stay following Connolly's urgent assurances, relayed by telephone to London, that he could not remain there without her and that unless she joined the party he would leave immediately to be with her in England.

Despite the apparently difficult mix of guests, the holiday was harmonious, not least because of Jean's calm pragmatism and tolerance. Peggy greatly admired her conduct: 'She seemed to take it all in her stride, being used to his affairs, knowing that he always came back to her in the end.'[15] As for Connolly himself, the sunbathing and

swimming had made him fit and well and he informed Ragg that he had
lost half a stone. His publishers were no less complacent and wrote to
their author on 12 August with the assurance that *Enemies of Promise*
was going to be 'a big success ... It will also lead to endless arguments.'[16] Back in London he prepared himself for publication. An
American sale had not been resolved although in September he learned
that Atlantic Monthly Press Books, a division of Little, Brown, had
made an offer of $250 as an advance on publication with a royalty of
10 per cent. In exchange they hoped for a different title and a shorter
text; but Ragg, mindful of the fact that Scribner's had paid a $500
advance for *The Rock Pool*, rejected the offer without even consulting
his author. When Connolly learned of the overture he confirmed Ragg's
decision: he wanted $600 to cover debts and American tax and sug-
gested that negotiations with New York publishers should be deferred
pending the book's reception in England.

   Enemies of Promise, a semi-autobiographical book, appeared almost
simultaneously with Logan Pearsall Smith's memoirs, *Unforgotten
Years*, and Christopher Isherwood's *Lions and Shadows*, an oblique
self-portrait subtitled 'An Education in the Twenties'. Perhaps autobiography would become a greater fashion – as writers sought to record
experience and memory against approaching destruction – but Connolly's hybrid account was not promoted as belonging to a fashionable
autobiographical school but as an enquiry into the state of literature. Its
structure is tripartite: 'Predicament' examines the challenge of the next
decade and wonders how it is to be survived; 'The Charlock's Shade'
reviews the enemies which young and promising writers must resist if
they are to realize themselves by creating an enduring work of art; and
A Georgian Boyhood reviews its author's early years until his departure
from Eton and the end, as he saw it, of formative experience. Yet there
is an element of ambiguity, of generic confusion, which characterizes
the book and flavours even its opening paragraphs, which have about
them a faintly cinematic quality. With the opening sentence, written at
'the time of year when wars break out', an impression forms of a vast
sweep of space threatened by destruction, and the suggestion persists
until the focus, like a camera, closes on Connolly writing beneath a
plane tree after lunch on an oppressive day in the south of France. The
colophon reveals it to be July 1937; and Connolly declares a decep-
tively modest ambition: to write a book that will last for ten years.
Survival and literature are seen to be entwined: if he survives the next

decade he may write an enduring book; equally he may only survive by writing an enduring book before he himself perishes.

Early drafts reveal the difficulty he had writing his prologue and striking a balance between describing his own professional problems and the larger difficulties of the time, which seemed to many writers to be inimical to creation. Later in the book he would declare his conviction that writers indeed wielded the power to change events, a declaration which seemed like wishful thinking in the face of overwhelming evidence to the contrary. In the meantime, the remainder of 'Predicament' was dedicated to an analysis of style, the most abstract of all ideas and one without an obvious relevance either to Connolly's personal career or to the predicament of literature on the eve of war. The literary period he chose to cover began with the year 1900. Looking at the important books which had been written since the century began, he deduced a system: that twentieth-century English and American literature had veered between two stylistic poles, the ornate, artificial and decorated voice of the 'Mandarin' style and the discreet and colloquial qualities of the 'Vernacular', with Henry James and Ernest Hemingway as the most important exemplars of each. Connolly's ostensible position was one of neutrality: he was merely recording recent literary history. However, he dedicated his book not to his wife, his mother or his father, but to another kind of parent, and another great Mandarin – Logan Pearsall Smith. He drew on numerous examples to illustrate his arguments and wrote best about the authors who interested him; and in so doing he indicated two life-long tendencies. Although he had a romantic interest in English and French Augustanism, he regarded the Modern Movement as particularly his own, perhaps because it coincided with his own life. He also saw writers as a race apart and suggested that they contended with agonies unknown not only to bureaucrats but to other solitary creators like painters and sculptors. His prose was epigrammatic and urbane with tendencies towards the purple when referring to himself. One of the metaphors he frequently employed was that of 'literary inflation', by which he meant that cheap and journalistic over-use of certain words had depleted their meaning, but the analogy is a significant one: *Enemies of Promise* was a book of its financially unstable times. This sense of foreboding prevails in 'The Charlock's Shade' where he lists the enemies of literary promise: politics, journalism, worldly success, sex and its complications, domesticity, and the temporary escapes from

duty and disillusion provided by drink and conversation. He demonstrated the damage any of these forces could do, half aware all the time
that he was really talking about himself and that he could have cited
most of those distractions as explanations for failing to fulfil the
promise of his early years at school and Oxford. 'The Charlock's Shade'
continued the oblique autobiography, making Connolly a prose laureate of the good excuse and the bad conscience.

A Georgian Boyhood, prefaced with epigraphs from Leopardi, the
poet who most moved him in his thirties, Gray and Horace Walpole,
was placed at the end of the book because he felt it would have made
the critical sections seem insipid and dull situated at the beginning. He
stressed, however, that it was integral to the book's design: an autobiography which explained the making of a romantic critic. Indeed *A
Georgian Boyhood* is deeply romantic and conferred a definitive shape
on the legendary self-portraiture which he had practised intermittently
through the medium of reviews. Despite the Augustan implications of
its title, it is very much a modern work, based on an assumption that it
is the misunderstood yet vivid experiences of childhood that are the
most formative and important in life. Freud himself might have
approved this implication and Connolly compounded it by stressing the
anti-climaxes of his later career. Here, after all, was a story where the
hero endured bullying, loneliness, ugliness and misery only to emerge
triumphant as the cleverest boy at the grandest school in the largest
empire ever seen, who is still afflicted with disillusion: after Eton, after
Pop, the Rosebery and the Brackenbury, no other triumphs would seem
as bright or as lasting. He gives no sense of family life in *A Georgian
Boyhood* and never mentions the cousins who were at Eton simultaneously. School holidays, innocent friendships, permissible pleasures and
happiness are all ignored and he concentrates instead on misery and
pain and a few joys that bring guilt in their train. He was inviting
readers to dismiss him as a school snob, somebody who was stuck
permanently in the past and still living off his Etonian triumphs when
others had been able to shrug off that past and achieve distinction in a
bigger and more competitive world.

Connolly was careful to release his book with its dates of composition, July 1937–August 1938, and it is difficult to dissociate it from its
turbulent times. It had been written, he reminded his readers, '*Post
fanum putre Vacunae*', 'by the crumbling shrine of Vacuna' (a goddess
of leisure) and it appeared, 'an inquiry into the state of literature', in the

last week of September 1938. Unfortunately, a literary world which might in other times have been agog was miserably distracted. In Munich the British and French capitulated to German demands for the cession of disputed Czechoslovakian territories. In Paris the former Prime Minister Leon Blum spoke famously of his feelings of 'shameful relief' that another year of nervous peace had been so dishonestly bought. Similar sentiments prevailed in London where Anthony Eden had already resigned as Foreign Secretary in protest at Chamberlain's appeasement of Hitler. Connolly was deeply depressed by his departure and wrote to Jean convinced that it 'means the end'.[17] On the night on which Chamberlain flew back from Munich with his famous promise of 'peace for our time', Diana had dinner with Connolly and Spender and remembered that politics, rather than *Enemies of Promise*, dominated the conversation. There were other matters to think about than books devoted to modern literature, and although Connolly saw his work widely reviewed it sold poorly.

In the *Sunday Times* Desmond MacCarthy devoted almost his entire column to a generous though not unperceptive appraisal. He particularly admired *A Georgian Boyhood*, finding that Connolly's skill as an autobiographer 'lies in his having presented himself as "a case" – that is to say, a boy in relation to a particular environment'. Yet he saw that there was a transcendent quality which complemented the book's subjectivity: *Enemies of Promise* identified the sense of futility which plagued writers increasingly as the Thirties progressed and in so doing acquired a generic or representative quality: 'His book as far as it is autobiographical, is the account of one who was nourished on stones made up to look like bread. Today his generation feel that the free play of intelligence is not enough to live for, and yet many of them can't believe in action.'[18]

In the *Daily Telegraph* Harold Nicolson recommended the book, not least for 'the intellect (the very serious intellect) which lies behind Mr Connolly's impish style':

[He] indicates with glee how powerful was the effect upon his own development of the Etonian's worship of popularity. What he describes as 'school politics' read like some embittered social competition in an Indian hill-station. The admirable bad taste of Mr Connolly's description will lead many to wonder whether Eton is in fact the Athens which we had all supposed.[19]

In the *Daily Express* James Agate declared that Connolly's 'standard of
literary criticism is the highest there is',[20] while the *Daily Worker* found
more to praise in *A Georgian Boyhood*: 'Here you have an analysis of
snobbery, of the roads to social success and social humiliation ...
analysed with a perception, a horror that it is not ridiculous to compare
to Proust's.'[21] *Punch* was kind but anodyne: 'No one concerned with
writing or reading should miss it.'[22] Q. D. Leavis, writing in her
husband's crusading quarterly, *Scrutiny*, was neither. She was annoyed
by what she saw as Connolly's inability to measure literature by purely
literary criteria 'because of an unconscious acceptance of social values'
and was astounded to hear him proclaim Virginia Woolf, George
Orwell and Christopher Isherwood as important contemporary English
writers. What most annoyed her, however, was that *Enemies of
Promise* appeared to exalt what she saw as the mutually promoting
circle of old school and university friends who seemed to regulate the
world of letters. 'We who are in the habit of asking how such evidently
unqualified reviewers as fill the literary weeklies ever got into the
profession need ask no longer. They turn out to have been "the most
fashionable boy in the school", or to have had a feline charm or a
sensual mouth and longer eye-lashes.'[23] Her aspersions about varsity
partisanship overlooked a double-edged appraisal delivered in the
Tablet by Evelyn Waugh, whom Connolly had considered a friend, if
not an intimate, for a decade. Throughout 1938 Waugh had been
conducting a lone campaign to stem the abuse of the term 'fascist', and
his contempt for the fashionable politics of the age, combined with a
scrupulous vocabulary, lent spirit to his prosecution. Frustratingly, his
agent had been unable to persuade any newspaper to commission an
article on the subject but the arrival of *Enemies of Promise* for review
suddenly offered an opportunity for which the claims of friendship had
to be sacrificed.

He began his assessment with praise, happy to admit that he had
found 'phrase after phrase of lapidary form, of delicious exercises in
parody, of good narrative, of luminous metaphors'. He argued that
literary criticism as a whole was in decline, 'But above this there is the
rare Art of Criticism, with its own valuable and distinct literature, its
own aspirations and achievements. The only man under forty who
shows any sign of reaching, or indeed, of seeking, this altitude is Mr
Cyril Connolly.'

Yet he shifted, criticizing Connolly, and the book's production, for lapses in grammar and spelling and for the occurrence of clichés, but making no attempt to identify the author's powerful inhibiting demons. He chastised him for his tendency to examine individual passages from books – since 'the style is the whole ... a sentence which he admires may owe its significance to another fifty pages distant' – and complained of a 'lack of masculinity' in the writers Connolly admired, adding that 'the artists in whom he is interested have nearly all come to feel themselves outcasts and to transpose the antagonism, real or imagined, of society from themselves to their art.' He was free to reject his friend's tastes but it was graceless of him to sneer that 'Mr Connolly sees recent literary history, not in terms of various people employing and exploring their talents in their own ways, but as a series of "movements", sappings, bombings and encirclements, of party racketeering and jerrymandering. It is the Irish in him perhaps.' His final complaint was his most heart-felt: Connolly had given too much attention to fashionable politics, had roamed too near 'the cold, dank pits of politics into which all his young friends have gone tobogganing'. Nevertheless Waugh hoped that he would 'one day escape from the café chatter, meet some of the people, whom he now fears as traitors, who are engaged in the practical work of government and think out for himself what Fascism means'.[24]

Compensation came in the applause and curiosity of other writers. Auden was enthusiastic and found *Enemies of Promise* 'the best book of criticism since the war, and more than Eliot or Wilson you really write about writing in the only way which is interesting to anyone except academics, as a real occupation like banking or fucking with all its attendant egotism, boredom, excitement and terror'.[25] Maurice Bowra was charmed and thought the book reeked of Connolly's 'seductive, cigar-like personality'.[26] Enid Starkie, the French scholar, found that 'it had the kind of lucidity and intellectual integrity, that clear objectivity which one hardly meets elsewhere than in Frenchmen'.[27] Somerset Maugham assured him that all writers could read the book with profit, conceding that there was some validity in Connolly's comments on his own writing. Kenneth Clark preferred the critical sections to the autobiographical, 'as I am one of those stony-hearted individuals (freaks) who never fell in love with a member of my own sex'.[28] Even Virginia Woolf implied the book's importance when she reviewed her changing reputation in her diary on 22 November 1938:

Apparently I've been exalted to a very high position ... then was decapitated by Wyndham Lewis and Miss Stein; am ... unlikely to write anything good again; am a secondrate, and likely, I think, to be discarded altogether; I think that's my public reputation at the moment. It is based largely on Cyril Connolly's Cocktail criticism: a sheaf of feathers in the wind.[29]

Enemies of Promise attracted inevitable attention at Eton. Early in 1939 Compton Mackenzie was invited to address the school's Literary Society on the subject 'What gives life to Poems, Plays and Novels?' His autobiography revealed little about the discussion that occurred but instead he quoted anonymously a letter he received the following day from an Eton master:

> Thank you so much for the interesting and stimulating talk you gave the Literary Society last night. It was the first talk we had had on the theoretical and general side of writing ... I myself happened to have read Connolly's book shortly before and many of the Society had been discussing it in English schools with a master ... and it was most interesting to have another view of the same subject. Your talk, I thought, came to many more conclusions than Connolly's book, which I disagreed with from first to last.[30]

It was not only present Etonians who were agitated. Connolly's school-friend Denys King-Farlow threatened libel proceedings. Maurice Baring was 'staggered': 'I thought College was peopled by spontaneous scholars who loved scholarship for scholarship's sake and worked because they liked it. Now comes your book.'[31] Maynard Keynes praised it highly despite contesting some of its conclusions and questioning Connolly's account of College life:

> After all, only a dozen years passed between my departure and your arrival. The culture of the lilies was exactly what I knew ... But the old College customs you suffered from all came in *after* my time and were unheard of in my day ... One very odd error – that Lytton Strachey was in College. He was of no known school. That part of his life lies in great obscurity – he never alluded to it even as an undergraduate to his intimates. He had poor health and was mainly brought up what is called 'privately'.[32]

George Orwell, now living in Marrakech but taking English newspapers, had seen the reviews and was eager to read the book to see to what extent memories of their education coincided: 'You were in every way much more of a success than I . . . I'm always meaning one of these days to write a book about St Cyprian's. I've always held that the public schools aren't so bad, but people are wrecked by those filthy private schools long before they get to public school age.'[33]

Even if Routledge was disappointed by sales, *Enemies of Promise* had generated controversy, as Ragg had prophesied it would. Connolly had made a minor literary sensation and his publishers hoped that he could be transformed into a more valuable property. Not the least of his achievements had been to set a final shape on a literary genre which had gained momentum throughout the Twenties and which later led Noël Annan to call the inter-war years the Age of Almamatricide: the public school novel which attacked the public school.

In *Enemies of Promise* Connolly had advanced this genre by portraying the most famous of all English schools with eloquent ambivalence and without recourse to fiction or substantial disguise. If he had not specifically said that Eton and schools like it were in any sense unjust, he had deduced a theory which nevertheless constituted a serious and lingering charge, the 'Theory of Permanent Adolescence', which asserted that the triumphs and despairs which public-school boys experienced were so intense as to eclipse all later achievement and in many cases even to retard their development. In itself that was neither serious nor surprising; but those triumphs and despairs centred around repressed desire, redundant and elaborate etiquette, jostling for fickle favour and the muddy conflicts of the games fields. It is significant that within two years of the publication of those views, both George Orwell, in *Coming Up for Air*, and Henry Green in *Pack My Bag* had made charges almost identical with Connolly's. Valentine Cunningham, appraising the trend many years later, noted: 'Once it had been formulated so memorably, Connolly's "Theory" had the ring of truth.'[34]

Sensing his new notoriety, Routledge determined to get Connolly to work on another book at once and he and Ragg had lunch at the beginning of December to discuss the matter. They pondered the idea of a novel but the author's demands proved too steep for the publishers and Ragg wrote on 9 December: 'I feel that we ought not to make things too easy for you and therefore encourage your well-known slothfulness.'[35] He proposed an advance of £200 for a new work which he hoped could be completed in three months but Connolly wrote back saying that he needed more time and more money, especially as Chapman and Hall had already offered him £300, albeit to write on a set theme. In the meantime, with American publication now certain, he had to amend the text of *Enemies of Promise* and revisions kept him occupied, however agonizingly, until he told Ragg that by the middle of December he could hardly bear to open the book any more.

Professional prospects seemed hopeful but domestically Connolly was menaced by confusion: Diana assumed that he would continue to write books; he assumed that he would do so at her side, possibly as her husband; while Jean hoped for his return. Connolly, however, continued to insist to them and to other friends that both women were catalysts to creativity and guarantors of happiness. For Diana – on the threshold of her twenties – the situation was easier to accept than it proved for Jean, who was older, infertile, and an American isolated in an increasingly turbulent Europe. Her patience seemed at times to border on supererogation but finally it snapped and when the lease on 312a King's Road expired at the end of 1938 she decided not to renew it. There were last parties there: Patrick Balfour's wife, Angela, remembered creditors mingling with the guests and pursuing the Connollys round the flat. That autumn, through a mutual friend called Lys Dunlap, Connolly met Gavin Ewart, a young poet who was then Lys's boyfriend. Ewart remembered attending a dance a short while afterwards, and having the solitary Jean Connolly pointed out to him: it was widely known that the couple were more or less separated. Nevertheless they were together in Paris for Christmas 1938 and stayed for part of the time at Peter Watson's flat. David Gascoyne was there simultaneously and never forgot the atmosphere at 44 Rue du Bac, its randomness and chaos somehow suggestive of the mess of the Connollys' marriage and the greater mess of Europe:

> [It] had the air of a stage set, an extraordinary collection of people wandering in and out all day long, dubious friends of Denham's, English pansy or café society friends of the Connollys', the actor Jean Marais ... servants, detectives and police inspectors on account of a theft there at a party on Christmas Eve.'[36]

With nowhere to live in London, with his wife estranged and with international tension mounting daily, Connolly was inevitably restless. He was not alone. In January 1939 Auden and Isherwood sailed for new lives and new personas in the United States: the literary left found itself without rudder or figurehead. Connolly himself returned to Paris in February and worked in dilatory fashion on modifications to the

American text of *Enemies of Promise*. He joined Peggy Strachey and a group of friends at Davos but was miserable and could hardly wait to leave. In March *Atlantic Monthly* decided to serialize an excerpt from *A Georgian Boyhood* in advance of publication. The piece was to be called 'The Fag and the Scholar' and Connolly was paid £200 for it. Both Warner Brothers and Twentieth Century-Fox asked for advance copies with a view to filming *A Georgian Boyhood*. He was thrilled and wrote to Ragg, playful but eager, on 17 May, hoping that something would come of the idea, 'with Shirley Temple as Promise and Ginger Rogers and Fred Astaire as Eton boys'.[37] The idea is remarkable, not least because, had time and place cohered and the film been made, posterity would have been left with the double pleasure of Connolly, in his ill-fitting guise of film critic for the *New Statesman* which he donned later in the year, reviewing the film and contemplating his own cinematic avatar.

His melancholy redoubled when the Spanish Civil War ended in March with Madrid's capitulation to Franco; he wrote to Jean telling her that he could not face returning to England, where Chamberlain had just recognized the new regime in Madrid and where Evelyn Waugh had called W. H. Auden 'a public bore'. Hitler appeared unstoppable and Connolly wondered what would happen if the Germans in Ireland appealed to Berlin to annex their country and Eamon De Valera went to Hitler to secure a guarantee of his country's independence. He went south and by the beginning of April was staying at Cassis in the Bouches du Rhône. Diana often came here: it was a cheap resort where painters and writers congregated to work and soon Connolly began to ponder another novel. He intended to call the work 'Lives of the Weak' and in a letter written on 11 April 1939 he explained his ambitions to Routledge. He envisaged a study of a group of friends and acquaintances linked by their time at Oxford; some rich, some poor, some married, some with mistresses. It was to be a study of the 'invisible rubicons people cross ... a picture of weakness'.[38] He promised that it would not be a political novel and hoped to engage the reader's attention through characterization rather than doctrine. Unfortunately, as was to be increasingly the case, he showed himself more adept at conceiving titles and themes than labouring on the small print and making the idea flesh; and 'Lives of the Weak' remained another of Connolly's fine yet fickle inspirations.

He and Jean corresponded and continued to toy with the idea of setting up home again in London. One of his letters contained a projected budget for their domestic expenses: £13 on rent; £6 on servants; £6 on services; £3 on laundry; £2 on cleaners; £20 on food and entertaining; and £10 on wine – but nothing came of the idea. Jean, now living in Flood Street in Chelsea, had been advised by Peter Watson not to take her husband back and Watson's counsel seemed to be vindicated when the prodigal announced that he had fallen in love again. He had first met Janetta Woolley in 1937 through her half-sister, Angela Balfour, and now, at seventeen, she seemed solitary, independent, intriguing, a beautiful itinerant permanently dressed in a corduroy suit with a French army cloak and a walking stick. Connolly was deeply smitten and wrote at once to tell Jean, begging her not to repeat the information to anybody. Janetta suited him: roaming together, he liked to fantasize, they suggested Verlaine and Rimbaud, and she was right for his unsettled and fretful mood, which he diagnosed as a second adolescence. Jean continued to be tolerant, writing to her errant husband on 15 May to inform him that there was only £6 17s 2d in their current account: 'Darling is le cap Naio fun? Who are you staying with, [Diana] or Miss JW? I am glad you have found somebody else who can read maps.'[39]

Janetta had been staying in Brittany with her mother and had resolved to travel alone across France to Cassis where the latter kept a flat. Learning of her intention, Connolly proposed to collect her and drive her to the south himself and duly arrived in Brittany from Paris, a francophile in his English car, a grey Armstrong-Sidley. His passenger thought him a good driver and noted his habit of whistling tunes during stretches of the journey, which for Janetta had begun simply as a passage across the country. Connolly, however, had other ideas: he would take her through the area he considered his 'magic circle' of beauty and poetic association, a territory which began at Tulle in the north and expanded east to Rodez, west to Tonneins, and south beyond Toulouse, a domain which better flattered the five senses than any other he knew, yet was sacred to the sceptical memory of the great Montaigne and traversed by the nutrient rivers of Dordogne, Lot and Tarn. It remained his undying ambition to own a yellow manor farm within this kingdom but for the time being he would content himself by touring its principal villages and towns with his new disciple. The pilgrimage was not without misadventure. The law stipulated that all aliens resident in France for more than thirty days required a permit and Janetta was travelling without one. When they arrived in Tulle he suggested that she should go to the *mairie* to secure her *carte de séjour* while he attended to necessary business (which in these circumstances usually meant trying to send illicit bulletins to one of the other women on his mind: he was no doubt eager to contact Diana or Jean). Meanwhile police suspicions had been aroused: what was a young girl doing dressed as a boy and aimlessly driving around with an older man but without a chaperone or the necessary papers? She was detained and when Connolly finally arrived in search of her he was subjected to hostile interrogation. His French was more or less equal to the occasion but his equanimity was not; the misunderstanding was resolved but afterwards he was reluctant to allow Janetta to emerge from the car except at night.

Despite that restriction she found him an excellent cicerone – enthusiastic, intelligent, entertaining – and the settlements of the magic circle – Beaulieu, Souillac, Villefranche, Albi – became vivid and enchanted in his company. There was only one difficult moment in their relationship: what did she think of Jean? Janetta said she could hardly judge as she had only met her twice and on both those occasions Jean had been drunk. Connolly was infuriated by her reply, partly no doubt because of his own shame and self-reproach, but the disagreement passed quickly and peace returned as they crossed the Massif Central and began the final leg of their journey, the golden moments of which would return to haunt him when skies were darker and all roads were closed: 'Peeling off the kilometres to the tune of "Blue Skies", sizzling down the long black liquid reaches of Nationale Sept, the plane trees going sha-sha-sha through the open window, the windscreen yellowing with crushed midges, she with the Michelin beside me, a handkerchief binding her hair . . .'[40]

Connolly returned to England at the end of June and Jean herself went abroad. He stayed initially at the Langham Hotel in Portland Place but moved shortly afterwards to a flat at 55 Eaton Terrace in Belgravia. In the last unreal weeks of peace he was obsessed not with the impending maelstrom but with his broken marriage and he wrote to his wife almost every day. Once again, he could not bear to say goodbye or accept that a chapter had closed, and prolonged a severance that had in reality begun two years before. On 9 July he revealed that he had discussed his marriage with the Balfours and had pondered Patrick Balfour's suggestion of a temporary separation. He mentioned that he was suffering from insomnia despite sleeping pills and putting on weight despite his diet. The following day he wrote again, declaring the collapse of his marriage to be the turning point of his life, and stressing that if Jean did not return to him he would suffer from permanent ill health and penury with only an endless regime of hack work to sustain him. He enumerated the affairs of 1936, when his infidelities had begun, and claimed that the liaisons constituted a necessary journey of discovery. Nevertheless, 'I see how our marriage is not just a marriage but the whole youth of two people.'⁴¹ He told her that he owed the completion of *Enemies of Promise* to her because she had given him financial independence and freed him from the distractions of auxiliary journalism. At the same time to surrender Diana would be the most terrible separation of his life and would make him prematurely old and bitter. She wrote back on 15 July from Menton in the south of France: 'It seems to me you [and Diana] are both playing at la grande passion . . . Even if you gave up Diana or she gave up you, I wouldn't come back to you until I had regained some sort of equilibrium. That might take a year anyway. You mightn't want me back at the end of a year.'⁴² He replied on 18 July with the determination to transform their love into 'a power station instead of a waterfall' and proposed a unifying project, a travel book about Mexico.⁴³ She would take the photographs, he would supply the text and the result would be the Left's answer to Evelyn Waugh, whose own excursions in that country, *Robbery Under Law*, had ridiculed the *New Statesman*'s coverage of the Spanish Civil War. On 20 July he affirmed his belief in marriage and said that the obstacles to their reunion were his pride and her sloth, while on 24 July he was more in love with her than he had ever been before.

However, public events were crowding in and threatening escapists everywhere. Suddenly there was nowhere to run: hot remote Mexico receded like a dream and it was not Cyril Connolly but his father who saw ambition fulfilled before war broke out, with the publication of *A Monographic Survey of South-African Non-Marine Mollusca*. Matthew had come late to conchology and never hoped for the sound of the sea in the whorls and folds of his shells: he was a scientist and volunteered his observations in a prose which was factual, soldierly, appropriately desiccated. Feigning modesty, he would sometimes describe his catalogue as a pioneer work but he knew it to be monumental and took to teasing his son that when his fugitive journalism was forgotten his own researches would continue to confer a posthumous fame. He was half-correct: his *Monographic Survey* remains definitive.

His son meanwhile temporarily replaced Desmond Shawe-Taylor as film critic for the *New Statesman* despite an indifference to the cinema barely sweetened by the recent overtures of Hollywood. For several weeks, coinciding with Graham Greene, the film reviewer for the *Spectator*, he attended press screenings and he and Greene often liked or hated the same films. Connolly's criticism, however, was remarkable for its lack of enthusiasm and conviction. Thus, of *Undercover Doctor*, he remarked that 'Janice Logan, as the nurse, is a little wooden, but with nice chin, and not too priggish' while Dorothy Lamour by comparison seemed 'hard and unattractive'.[44] *Tarzan Finds a Son* scarcely excited the critical faculties, although he did note gloomily that 'Johnny Weissmuller is beginning to look old round the neck.'[45] Not surprisingly he preferred French films to English ones because 'unreality is the vice of English films, unreal acting, unreal sentiment, unreal men and women, and unreal thinking is the cause of this.'[46] The accusation seems unfair when one remembers Hollywood's blameless fantasies of the time but perhaps it reflected Connolly's depression at the prospect of house-arrest in a country he had always enjoyed leaving. The employment came to an end in mid-August 1939 and he vacated his plush seat without regret: '[Films] seem to me to point no moral except that the human race is not yet old enough to manage firearms, or handle money or attack the simplest questions of human relations.'[47]

Soon afterwards he went to Ulster to stay with Lord Antrim at Glenarm but found himself bored, restless, confined: while the other guests sought distraction in rounds of golf he despatched more recriminations to Jean. One evening he was talking to the travel writer Robert Byron when news was broadcast of the Nazi–Soviet Pact. More than any other it was the covenant which disarmed the idealists of his generation but in his letter to Jean Connolly professed to find the collusion almost comical: he enjoyed the perplexity of the Communists and the dismay of the Capitalists and wondered why a concordance between Fascism and Communism was more bizarre than any such agreement between Chamberlain and Stalin would have been. But if one day he was cynically amused, telling Jean to decide whether she wanted to spend the war in England, France or America, on other days he was prone to regret and reproach. He insisted on seeing her: he was without home, wife or book to write, and mere letters were inadequate to the delicate negotiations of reconciliation. She must not deny him:

and if she persisted in trying to do so, when he had nothing left but the contents of three suitcases, then his life was pointless and he might as well pre-empt orchestrated extinction and plan his own end. Jean was generous, he was persuasive: she surrendered with the times and agreed to see her husband but insisted that the meeting must occur in Paris. Perhaps now he should heed Diana's opinion that they should stop seeing each other and accept her conviction that his future lay with Jean. But such decisions could wait; and as though preparing for a commonplace weekend, as though he could return again at any time, he happily and hastily embarked on the familiar journey careless of the liberating Channel and without suspicion that soon old love's domain would be inaccessible except in the pilgrimages of his memory.

V
THE IVORY
SHELTER

CHAPTER FOURTEEN

JEAN PROVED less tractable than Connolly had expected. She was disinclined not only to return to him but to indicate any ambitions for the future beyond a desire to prolong her stay in France. Perhaps she was stubborn and indecisive but that rumbling August was not a moment appropriate to far-sighted resolution; in any case she had heard all her husband's assurances before. Her determination surprised Connolly and frustration was compounded by the presence in the city of Peter Watson. It was bad enough that he and Jean had become firm friends and were having a wonderful time without him but what made that imagined exclusion harder to bear was the knowledge that Watson had Jean's confidence and had shown no inclination to take Connolly's side in his marital problems. Indeed he was averse by nature to plotting and resentment: suspecting that his involvement could become a festering misunderstanding, he wrote to explain himself prior to Connolly's arrival: 'Please get it out of your head that I want to see you and Jean separated. I do not and I should be very sorry if it happened and I only wish that a solution could be found and that you could be happy together, as I am fond of you both.' Discussions with Jean had given him insights not only into Connolly's private life but also into his professional anxieties and here too he was prepared for sympathy, assuring Connolly, 'I certainly do not think you should do journalism reviewing now that you hate it.'[1]

By the time Connolly arrived in Paris he had resolved to see not only his wife but his wife's adviser. Perhaps Watson thought they would only discuss Jean but he was mistaken: his friend had other partnerships on his mind and knew the time had come to forge them. For many years he had dreamt intermittently of editing a magazine and now, with a novel behind him as well as a survey of modern literature and a jigsaw in journalism of comic self-portraiture, he needed another challenge. He had no doubt that there was talent in England to sustain a literary magazine, particularly since the recent closure of the *Criterion*, the *London Mercury* and *New Verse*, and was equally confident of his ability to cultivate that talent. He was less certain of the profitability of such a venture: investment was essential and if Watson was indeed sympathetic he would rescue him from reviewing by volunteering funds.

Watson listened politely but he was not to be swayed. He disliked England and whether he went to farm oranges in Arizona or remained in Paris to support a journal devoted to the fine arts, he would continue an expatriate. Connolly countered eloquently: Paris had no need of such subsidy when *Verve*, *Cahiers d'Art* and *Minotaure* flourished. England by comparison was neglected: he should return not specifically to serve the war effort but to join the greater crusade against philistinism. But Watson still said no. The next day, 1 September 1939, German tanks rolled across the plains of Poland, and Britain and France declared war two days later. Connolly decided to return to London at once and persuaded Jean to accompany him, arguing that hostilities could spread unpredictably. By the time Watson arrived in England several days later Jean had left her husband once again, this time to stay with friends in Yorkshire. Connolly meanwhile was cheerful. The declaration of hostilities had at least cleared the air and Jean and he were once more living in the same country. Moreover he could continue to rely on Diana's presence while occupying himself with the important business of finding a bearable job. He contemplated joining a newspaper or possibly the Ministry of Information: journalism, a horrifying prospect weeks before, seemed tolerable now, and at least being a bureaucratic propagandist in government service might offer safety. He had always been a survivor: it had been a need inherent in dormitory education and when he wrote to Jean with mention of his plans the analogy he employed was revealing: 'If we're all back at school one must be a prefect.'[2]

By the end of September, however, he was still unemployed. Watson's predicament was worse, since he was without job or ambition now that hopes of expatriate patronage had been extinguished by new travel restrictions. Suddenly Connolly's position seemed the stronger and when he met his friend at a party given by Elizabeth Bowen he once again brought up the idea of a magazine, stressing that such partnership could constitute their own, more interesting, 'war work'. Bereft of excuses, Watson promised co-operation, and by the time Cyril Connolly left his first wartime party he had his magazine.

His Maecenas, christened Victor William but universally known as

Peter, was five years his junior, having been born the youngest child of Sir George Watson on 14 September 1908. His income was inherited but Sir George's fortune, like the baronetcy which adorned it, was new: in the last years of the previous century he had begun the manufacture of margarine, and his business, the Maypole Dairy Company, seized its opportunities during the butter shortages of the First World War and harvested vast profits from the one thousand company shops which distributed the substitute. In fine self-made fashion Sir George sent his younger son to Eton and there Watson befriended Alan Pryce-Jones, who formed a strong impression of his precocious sophistication and aesthetic refinement. He found him 'a slow-speaking, irresistibly beguiling young man whose face was equally poised between the prince and the frog' and remembered vividly one occasion when Watson invited him 'to visit his room behind schools, leading me mysteriously to his bookcase, thrusting a hand behind the Latin dictionaries and extracting a little bottle, which he unscrewed in ecstasy, murmuring, "Smell this: it is called *Quelques Fleurs*".'[3]

After Oxford Peter travelled in Germany and while studying in Munich bought his first Picasso drawing. At his mother's encouragement, he had begun to take an interest in the arts and she had ensured that he was given an income equal to his enthusiasms. When Sir George died in 1930, leaving an estate of £2 million, his younger son found himself a very prosperous twenty-one-year-old and was free to pursue a leisurely education in the galleries and gardens of Europe. He began this apprenticeship with enthusiasm – by ordering a black and orange Rolls-Royce, having an affair with the stage designer Oliver Messel and exciting the life-long adoration of Cecil Beaton. Like Connolly, Watson was a perfectionist, but his strivings were more tangible; his Vuitton luggage and Savile Row suits have passed almost into legend and by the time the Connollys began to visit his Paris apartment in the late Thirties they could inspect works by de Chirico, Gris, Klee, Miró, Picasso. Watson felt a particular sympathy for the Surrealists but his tastes inclined to the international and modernist generally rather than to the insular and nostalgic. In 1939, however, with his acquisition of an important early Graham Sutherland, *The Entrance to a Lane*, he not only revealed new aesthetic sympathies but also indicated his future importance as a patron of British art in the Forties. Yet he was no mere hoarding jackdaw and his treasures reflected what Beaton saw as a kind of spiritual discretion and generosity: 'He practises no art, but I think him a very extraordinary person. If we are meant to live fully, then surely he is one of the few people who know how to do this.'[4]

By the middle of the Thirties Watson had formed friendships with many of the prominent artistic figures of the time, including the composer Igor Markevitch and the portraitist Pavel Tchelitchew who painted him as a knight in blue armour. Another friend was Stephen Spender, who remembered that Watson hated 'priggishness, pomposity and almost everything to do with public life', and suspected that he had educated himself 'through love of beautiful works and through love of people in whom he saw beauty'.[5] They travelled together through Switzerland in 1938 and Spender afterwards recalled a man whose existence seemed in some ways unsoiled by life: 'When I think of him then, I think of his clothes, which were beautiful, his general neatness and cleanness, which seemed almost those of a handsome young Bostonian, his Bentley and his chauffeur who had formerly been the chauffeur of the Prince of Wales.'

He was a figure of striking attractiveness; women in particular seem to have found his manners irresistible, and almost everyone with the exception of Truman Capote appears to have liked him. Watson could have chosen love, sex and friendship in many quarters but his tastes led him into irregular society: the companions he liked tended to be volatile young men and although he described love to his friend Brian Howard as consisting in the wish 'to do someone some good not to destroy them and yourselves' his emotional career was anguished and unstable.[6] When his life recrossed with Connolly's in the late Thirties he was involved with a handsome young American named Denham Fouts, who at fifteen had absconded with a wealthy businessman before making his way to Paris. By the time he and Watson met in the early Thirties Fouts was said to have attended Nazi rallies in Berlin with a Prussian admirer and to have cruised the Aegean with the no less besotted King Paul of Greece. A third lover had introduced him to drugs, thus instigating a life-long appetite which ended after the war in premature death in a lavatory in Rome.

Watson fled Paris at the outbreak of war leaving his art collection in the care of a Rumanian friend who had promised to organize safe storage. Now, having surrendered to Connolly, he had other distractions and was committed to the birth and well-being of the magazine. Meanwhile his partner was excitable and preoccupied and had already learnt of his venture's first victory. For some weeks negotiations had been underway between Evelyn Waugh, Osbert Sitwell, David Cecil and Chapman and Hall, aimed at instigating a monthly magazine to be called 'Duration'. The rivals had been slow off the mark, however, and when Waugh learned that a parallel scheme had been adopted by what his diary termed 'the rump of the left wing under Connolly', he and his colleagues abandoned their editing ambitions.[7]

It seemed a good omen and Connolly was cheerful. Watson also found these early days of war stimulating and strangely happy but he felt a nagging disquiet about his friend's commitment, which he knew could so easily be compromised either by boredom and disillusion or by further amorous crises. It was no use trying to extract promises; instead Watson's solution was to engage an associate editor, and his choice fell on Stephen Spender. However, the reasoning behind the policy would have to be kept from Connolly, whose pride and proprietorial sense could not wisely be overlooked. In the event Watson satisfied his friend, who professed himself pleased by the idea of a critic and poet tempering each other's editorial judgement. The first hurdle negotiated, Watson had to consider the fact that Spender's marriage had recently collapsed: this might not be the moment to propose a new burden of work. In the event the poet welcomed the distraction; but the greatest difficulty of all lay with the fact that he was already committed elsewhere. John Lehmann had provisionally recruited him as an associate editor of *New Writing*, and though the arrangement seems to have been fiduciary rather than formally binding, Spender indicated that any involvement with Watson's venture would have to be kept secret. Inevitably, Lehmann learned of the negotiations and was hurt by what he saw as defection and unsettled by the fear that Spender would poach contributors and ideas from *New Writing*. The misunderstanding led to what Virginia Woolf chose to call 'a deadly feud' and Lehmann himself recalled that 'the reverberation of the explosion spread over most of our literary world.'[8] The matter was eventually resolved when Spender gave an assurance that he would maintain an involvement with both publications.

Generously he allowed the venture the use of his flat as an office – for the next few years art and literature were to be nursed and defended from Lansdowne Terrace in Bloomsbury – and during the last few days of September numerous conferences were called. Spender and Connolly met on 29 September and the poet confided to his journal afterwards that Connolly 'seemed rather vague about what [the magazine] would cost'.[9] There was also the crucial matter of its title. Discussion yielded numerous astrological and astronomical ideas – 'Sirius', 'Orion', 'Scorpio', 'Equinox', 'Centaur' – before 'Horizon' satisfactorily suggested itself.

With the magazine christened, they were free to devote themselves to matters of editorial design. They met again the following day when Spender stressed the need for articles on culture and war. Connolly's instinct, however, was to avoid the political and didactically selective, to be instead catholic and inclusive and respectful only of quality. As he later said, 'A magazine had to be eclectic to survive. It was the right moment to gather all the writers who could be preserved into the Ark.'[10] It was decided that established writers should be petitioned for contributions, although early overtures to T. S. Eliot and Virginia Woolf were fruitless. In the meantime, the *New Statesman* offered its subscription list and Geoffrey Grigson volunteered similar help from *New Verse*.

On 23 October Connolly wrote to the *Statesman*'s subscribers asking for their support and ideas. Advertisements with subscription forms began to appear in the newspapers and further appeals for contributions were despatched to as many writers as Connolly and Spender could name. With curbs imminent, contacts were all-important: the matter of finding a printer was solved when a friend of Connolly's, Tony Witherby, suggested that his family's firm, H. F. & G. Witherby – due to celebrate its bicentenary in 1940 – should oversee publication. He accompanied Connolly and Spender when they met John Roberts, chairman of the *New Statesman*, and sensed a prevailing good humour: Spender was 'a great giggler' while Connolly 'seemed to have a perpetual smile on his face'.[11] Janetta, now living in Devon, formed a similar impression of happiness when Connolly and Diana arrived for a short holiday. John Piper had been approached to plan the cover of the magazine and Connolly had just chosen the design of the title – it would appear in Elephant Bold Italic and surmount the list of contents. He might well feel satisfied: it was a format which was to remain almost unchanged for the magazine's entire life.

Yet for all these hopeful developments, the days were dark and unpropitious to artistic activity. There was an immediate reduction in the volume of paper available to publishers, who now had to survive on 60 per cent of the quantity they had accepted in 1938, and the *Cornhill Magazine*, *The Criterion*, the *London Mercury*, *Fact*, *New Stories*, *New Verse*, *Purpose*, *Seven*, *Twentieth Century Verse*, *Wales*, *Welsh Review* and *The Voice of Scotland* all fell silent in 1939 and 1940. Writers were confronted by the prospect of conscription; and although it had been agreed at an early stage that the senseless mobilization of creative minds which had marked the First World War should be avoided, and although it was hoped that many writers and intellectuals would serve the war in a more appropriately clerical capacity. Philistinism seemed suddenly to have become an article of war and when the *Daily Express* declared that 'There is no such thing as culture in wartime' there were many influential people who were inclined to agree and who might have argued that the onus was on the creative to discredit that conviction.[12] No wonder Orwell ventured a grim prognosis in 'Inside The Whale', an essay completed in 1940: 'The literature of liberalism is coming to an end and the literature of totalitarianism has not yet appeared and is barely imaginable ... from now onwards the all-important fact for the creative writer is going to be that this is not a writer's world.'[13]

There were no two ways about it: the decision to found a literary magazine in 1939 was defiant if not heroic and recent disappointments over 'Duration' notwithstanding, Osbert Sitwell was delighted to 'hear of something opening instead of shutting'.[14] John Betjeman responded with splendid and approving irony to his friend's request for material:

> If the best you can find to do is some highbrow paper with a communist poet fellow, then take my advice and chuck it up and get a job in the Sussex Light. *There's a war on you know* ... we are fighting for LIB-ERTY to make the world fit to live in for Democracy, to keep our splendid system of local government going, to make the world safe for Slough.[15]

The nervous cheer of Betjeman's comments betrayed a fear of being without place or purpose, a fear to which his and Connolly's generation, now in its mid-thirties, was suddenly particularly vulnerable. However, he and many others drew comfort from an article which Connolly published in the *New Statesman* on 7 October. It was called 'The Ivory Shelter' and in it he foretold the aims and preoccupations which were to shape *Horizon*. He conceded that the position seemed inconsolable:

> As human beings artists are less free now than they have ever been; it is difficult for them to make money and impossible for them to leave the country. Lock-up is earlier every day, and they are concentrated indefinitely on an island from which the sun is hourly receding.

Yet he found hope in this dismay. Artists and writers were now freer because the great betrayal of the Nazi–Soviet Pact and the declaration of war had released them from two oppressive obligations, 'the burden of anti-Fascist activities, the subtler burden of pro-Communist opinion'. Whatever the artist had to do now it was not political: 'The fight against Fascism is in the hands of the General Staff, and there is no further use for the minor prophet.' Writers and artists should now serve only themselves, obey only their own creative promptings and turn their backs on the war. 'Nostalgia will return as one of the soundest creative emotions, whether it is for the sun, or the snow, or the freedom which the democracies have had temporarily to discontinue.'[16]

Two of the most enduring books to emerge from England in the Second World War, *The Unquiet Grave* and *Brideshead Revisited*, vindicated this last claim, but Connolly's article was more than clairvoyant, it was almost dangerously frank. He was neither patriot nor pacifist, and it was Stephen Spender who made the point that Connolly, and the magazine he came to embody, were 'no more against the war than Falstaff or Thersites were against wars they were involved in'.[17] That was well said. Equally, Plantagenet England and Heroic Greece were subject to less inexorable propaganda and less stringent censorship than the participants of the Second World War, and when he spoke so freely Connolly risked official rebuke, possibly even difficulties with the Ministry of Information, which would have to clear the projected contents of the first issue of *Horizon*. A deadline for contributions for that number had been set at the end of November, but shortly after the publication of his article in the *New Statesman* the editor himself almost met a deadline of another sort: on 9 October he and Diana were travelling through Sloane Square in a taxi when an army lorry drove into the side of their vehicle. She sustained a broken pelvis, but as though in possession of a charmed life Connolly walked away from his second car crash unscathed.

By the time he wrote to his mother on 14 October Diana had begun a long hospital confinement. He went to visit her every day at six o'clock but then Jean – largely out of pity for his sudden solitude – moved back to the capital to be with him. He had to secure a London home after months in hotels and friends' flats and learned that by strange coincidence 26a Yeoman's Row was available to let. He and Jean moved into the mews in early October and Connolly found himself sleeping in the very same room he had occupied twelve lost years before. The past, normally so vivid and enticing, did not recur to him; indeed, rather than being nostalgic he felt optimistic about his personal life and equable about the future. He mentioned the accident to his mother and, referring to *Horizon*, said he was also trying to secure some sort of employment at the BBC. She was not to worry about his well-being: after witnessing famine, air-raids and murder in Spain, belligerent London held no terrors for him. He was very unlikely to be killed, 'much too old, adaptable, and lucky for that kind of thing', and he thought of the war as 'a necessary but unpleasant police operation'.[18]

Four days later Peter Watson committed himself irrevocably to *Horizon* by signing a contract with Witherby's for the first four monthly issues of the magazine. He was now obliged to finance the production and distribution of 1000 copies each month at a cost of £33 and it was assumed that other expenses would fall to him, not least stationery, staff salaries and contributors' fees: prose fetched two guineas for every 10,000 words while poetry commanded a guinea a page. John Betjeman advised his friend that the magazine should 'look as much as possible like the *Quarterly Review*, the *Gospel Magazine*, or *Blackwood's*, if it is not to look dated in a few years' time'.[19] Nor were all *Horizon*'s editorial policies clearly resolved. Although Connolly knew instinctively that his publication was not to be political, he had no clear idea in these first weeks about how systematic its coverage of contemporary literature would be. Writing to John Hayward on 19 December, he indicated uncertainty about the place and prominence to be given to book reviews: there were unlikely to be a great many at first because *Horizon* would be too little known to attract free review copies. Nevertheless the first number contained impressive offerings: poetry by Auden, Betjeman and MacNeice; essays by Connolly himself, Geoffrey Grigson and Stephen Spender; and a reproduction of Henry Moore's *Reclining Figures*.

The Ministry of Information approved the contents for the first number and release was scheduled for the middle of December. The *New Statesman*, 'with an almost parental mixture of hope and anxiety', wished the new venture success on 16 December and mentioned that its editor 'has been, and still is, one of our most valued contributors. . . . A monthly magazine such as Mr Connolly can be trusted to produce is seriously needed, and we hope the public will hasten to scan this new Horizon.'[20] Tom Driberg, in his incarnation as William Hickey in the

Daily Express, presently sounded another note of approval, adding: 'Diffidence is more elegant and becoming than blowing one's own trumpet ... Horizon ... new literary monthly, indulges in no highbrow mysticism about its slightly high-falutin name, says frankly that it is "a pleasant, meaningless sound which looks well in print".'[21]

His comment, well-disposed but unspecific, reflected a wider uncertainty: no one knew what to expect when this brave vessel, subtitled 'A Review of Literature and Art', finally appeared, priced at one shilling. Virginia Woolf was churlish: '*Horizon* out; small, trivial, dull. So I think from not reading it.'[22] Desmond MacCarthy warmly welcomed it in the *Sunday Times*. Lord Antrim, stationed abroad on naval service, donated a year's subscription to Brooks's. Harold Nicolson read the magazine and was saddened by its assertion that the present fighting was not inspired by pity or hope, as it had been in the Spanish Civil War. Happily, Mrs Woolf's reservations were not London's. The initial printing scheme had stood at 1000 copies but Watson had been persuaded to increase that total to 2500. Even so, *Horizon* was sold out within days and a reprinting of a further 1000 copies quickly disappeared. The printing of the second number would clearly have to be greater: to begin with there was talk of ordering 5000 copies but its eventual sales – 7000 – doubled the success of the first number.

Horizon opened with 'Comment', an editorial which Connolly contributed each month and which became the organ's most familiar feature. Like its author it was inconsistent and undutiful and over the coming years readers would learn not to be surprised by oscillations between melancholy, boredom, eloquence and provocation. Spender, an earnest visionary, found these mercurial utterances unsettling: 'I, who started out with concern for planning post-war Britain, defending democracy, encouraging young writers, and so forth, was disconcerted to find myself with an editor who showed little sense of responsibility about these things.'[23] Far from conceding such distant imperatives, the first 'Comment' stressed only that events would determine the future stance of artists and writers, who would in turn shape *Horizon*. For the time being, the magazine would subordinate politics to aesthetics. For the time being, too, ambitions were necessarily imprecise: 'At the moment, civilization is on the operating table and we sit in the waiting room.'[24]

CHAPTER FIFTEEN

EARLY SUBSCRIBERS unfamiliar with Connolly's writing in other publications could have turned to his lengthier contribution to the first number of *Horizon*, an essay called 'The Ant-Lion', to establish a stronger impression of their editor's aestheticism. This lovely meditation begins with memories of the south of France in the summer before the war: finding himself on the Provençal coast, Connolly ponders the unchanging and beautiful landscape, 'a region hardly inhabited, yet friendly as those dazzling landscapes by Claude and Poussin, in which shepherds and sailors from antique ships meander under incongruous elms'.[1] Nature and art are seen to be ambiguous because in both beauty and ugliness co-exist, but for Connolly himself it was art which held a particular fascination, even when its preoccupations were sinister. 'The Ant-Lion' is a haunting contemplation – indirect, beautiful and also uncompromisingly personal: because although Connolly appears to speak in eloquent generalizations, the power of art was a force which he felt particularly keenly and which his magazine would channel and celebrate. With or without a manifesto, *Horizon* would become a pamphlet of aestheticism, a vehicle of art for art's sake.

His tone changed again in 'Comment' in February 1940. He had learnt, he said, of complaints about the tone, the cover and the contents of the first number: some had found it regressive and too long; some thought it obscure; still others feared it was both too dull and too short. The only criticism which interested him, however, was the accusation that the magazine lacked editorial direction at a time when guidance was most needed, that it sacrificed too much to literary beauty and artistic escapism. In reply he defended his policy by invoking the case of Auden and Isherwood, now resident in America for a year. Their departure, almost universally condemned at the time, assumed a greater significance when war was declared, and now Connolly called it 'the most important literary event since the outbreak of the Spanish War'.

His remark was widely repeated and no less widely misunderstood – perhaps he approved of their emigration? In fact he was indifferent: as far as he was concerned artists should live where they could best realize their talent, and Auden and Isherwood's Atlantic crossing indicated only one fact – they had accepted that art could not change politics or history – and *Horizon* would follow their apolitical example.

The poet and the novelist were themselves bewildered by Connolly's remark. In distant California Isherwood was annoyed and news of his displeasure somehow reached *Horizon*, constraining Connolly to despatch a letter of explanation. The émigré was easily placated, however: 'Now that you have written, I quite understand that you really only meant to defend Wystan and myself from attacks in the Press. I still think that some of the things you said were open to misinterpretation, and I won't pretend they didn't, at first sight, hurt me very much.'[2] Auden was terser: 'I think it meant to be friendly.'[3] At least there was one reader who was neither confused nor annoyed – Peter Watson, whose initial misgivings turned now to confidence not only in his principal editor but in the purpose and direction of his brave investment, and after seeing the March *Horizon* he declared his approval: 'I find the magazine *excellent* ... [Cyril's] remark about the flight of Auden and Isherwood *very true* ... congratulations for the courage in these times to say out loud such things ... Please tell me who is George Orwell: his article is *splendid*.'[4]

Watson's interest in Orwell was significant. On more than one occasion in his later life the novelist told friends that 'without Connolly's help I don't think I would have got started as a writer when I came back from Burma'.[5] He was more generous than precise, since by the time he and Connolly met again in 1935 he already had a publisher and a small but respectable reputation based on two published novels. Nevertheless his name had hardly percolated beyond literary London before 1939 and if he emerged in 1945 a more famous figure, he owed some of that transformation to Connolly's support. Their wartime collaboration began when in December Orwell told his friend that he had just finished a book comprising three long essays for which he had not as yet found a publisher. *Inside the Whale* was finally published in March 1940 but Connolly expressed an interest in releasing one of its component pieces in his magazine; and although Orwell had reservations about whether the shortest piece, 'Boys' Weeklies', would prove acceptable to the inhabitants and visitors of Connolly's Ivory Tower, his editor was sanguine: he knew good writing when he saw it and sensed immediately that Orwell's prose transcended the apparent triviality of his subject. It was accepted for publication in the March issue and occupied a third of the magazine, alongside Auden's 'In Memory of Sigmund Freud' and contributions by Roy Harrod, Philip Toynbee, Stephen Spender, John Betjeman and William Plomer as well as an illustration of Graham Sutherland's *Association of Oaks*.

'Boys' Weeklies' was the first of several important studies which Connolly published on Orwell's behalf. Concerning 'Such, Such, Were the Joys', one of his most persuasive essays, Connolly was both instigator as well as intendant publisher. He suggested that Orwell should write an account of their preparatory school; his friend completed it thinking it would constitute a 'pendant' to *Enemies of Promise*, and only his anxieties about libel prevented its publication in England prior to his death. Two factors were common to all these essays, the first being Orwell's mastery of the form. Of almost equal importance, however, was Connolly's informing philosophy, which was guided by his determination to provide writers with the space to explore subjects which interested them, rather than compelling them to probe the topical. Such a policy might disappoint a public appetite for analysis of the war or expectations of the peace; but if so, the public would have to be educated. Good writing, however remotely focused, mattered more; he would allow room, paper restrictions or no, to fine work which could find an outlet nowhere else.

In April, eager to join before he was called up, Tony Witherby went into the army. Concerned that in his absence he could not answer for the quality of work his company did for *Horizon*, he advised Connolly to transfer his business to the Curwen Press, a prestigious establishment run from Plaistow in the East End and dominated by Oliver Simon, the master printer who superintended production of *Life and Letters* and *La France Libre* as well as designing the *Wine and Food Encyclopaedia*. Simon, like his new client, was a perfectionist and was proud to boast that he always mastered his subject before paying a formal call on his new employer. Even professionals can be irascible, however, and Connolly remembered that his visits could be tempestuous and that scenes occurred despite an office policy which Connolly, half-jokingly, described as 'never a cross word to the face, or a kind one to the back'. Fortunately, the staff of Lansdowne Terrace realized that Simon's rages signified little more than 'the abuse of a rowing coach to his favourite boat', and on this sometimes noisy understanding the Curwen Press and *Horizon* weathered a number of crises to remain partners until the end of the magazine's life.[6]

The first of these emergencies threatened almost immediately with the German invasion in April of Norway and Denmark and the ensuing need for further drastic reductions in the consumption of paper. All publications were assessed according to their pre-war needs, a system which heightened the conspicuity of new magazines and exposed them to particular suspicions of irrelevance. Negotiations began with the Ministry of Information but it is entirely conceivable that without Connolly's friendship with Harold Nicolson, then an unusually literary and sympathetic Parliamentary Secretary at the Ministry, *Horizon* would have perished in its infancy. Moreover the imperatives of propaganda and secrecy were now added to Britain's moral sanctions and magazines seen to be violating any of these discretions exposed not only themselves but also their publishers to official disapprobation. Connolly could joke, later in *Horizon*'s career, that 'Suppression is the deep unconscious goal of every magazine, its secret death-wish' but he knew that insouciant editing could now carry a heavy penalty.[7]

Oliver Simon was no less aware of his responsibilities. In July 1940 he sent Connolly a brusque note informing him that it would not be possible for the Curwen Press to set a 'mischievous' American article for publication in the magazine. Later in the war, Janetta worked for *Horizon* for a while and remembered Connolly's sudden decision to amend a story by Julian Maclaren-Ross which he was about to publish. Set in the army, the work naturally employed language more appropriate to the barracks than the drawing-room but Connolly knew that the frequent expletive 'bugger' would cause more trouble than it was worth. Late one night he, Watson and Janetta took the long tube journey to Plaistow and although an air-raid broke while they were travelling, and much of the route progresses above ground, they arrived at the Curwen Press with their resolve unshaken to delete every 'bugger' in a typescript about to be set. It was not Connolly's first experience of Maclaren-Ross's indifference to literary restrictions. In June 1940 *Horizon* published his short story 'A Bit of a Smash'. The fiction had originally been entitled 'A Bit of a Smash In Madras', but anxieties about libel had determined the abbreviation. Nor had there been any hope of printing the original opening line, 'Absolute fact, I knew fuck-all about it', the less plausible 'damn-all' eventually filling the breach.

Maclaren-Ross was nine years Connolly's junior and knew him only through the reviews he had admired in the *New Statesman* and through *Enemies of Promise* which he had found 'a tremendously invigorating experience'. Like scores of literary apprentices he had seen the advertisements for material which *Horizon* had placed in the national press and submitted some of his writings. Connolly always hoped to publish new authors but had no interest in doing so unless they satisfied his exacting literary standards. However, the twenty-eight-year-old's work excited him and Maclaren-Ross was summoned to Bloomsbury, only to find his potential editor intimidating:

> His face was round, plump and pale, his shoulders sloped from a short thick neck, and dark hair was fluffed thickly out behind the ears . . . He had a short snub Irish nose and under shaggy Irish brows his eyes, set far apart, looked both hooded and alert. A startled expression, instantly veiled, had entered them when he saw me standing at the door . . . The housemaster's outfit affected by many writers of the Thirties – tweed jacket, woollen tie, grey flannels baggy at the knee – gave him an unbuttoned rather than an informal air. His movements like his voice were indolent, one had the impression that he should have been eating grapes, but at the same time his half-closed eyes missed nothing. He was a formidable person.[8]

He also met Bill Makins, the magazine's business manager, and after noting his 'redoubtable figure: tall, gaunt, with a fierce Highland high-boned face and a dark Elizabethan beard jutting from his chin', Maclaren-Ross took a liking to him and the two men became friends. Yet if he struck the younger writer as daunting, Connolly also liked him since he arranged a night's accommodation in London and invited him to lunch at the Café Royal the following day. Maclaren-Ross arrived to find his editor 'sitting on a sofa near the door with a bulging leather satchel beside him and galley proofs unfurled upon his knee. His round plump face looked mild enough and he even smiled as he saw me, nonetheless he was clearly not a man amenable to direct questioning (though fond of it himself).'[9] A favourite haunt in peacetime, the Café Royal was not abandoned now: Connolly spent prolonged periods in the celebrated Regent Street restaurant, like Wilde, Whistler and Firbank before him, musing, reading or entertaining contributors. There were other resorts besides: the Museum Tavern in Bloomsbury, Olivelli's restaurant in Store Street, the Gargoyle Club, the White Tower in Percy Street and the Eiffel Tower nearby, where lunch cost 1s 6d.

Meanwhile in Lansdowne Terrace a routine had quickly developed despite the growing irregularities of London life and the makeshift nature of the office and its furnishings. Spender could pause during his editing activities and look round to see the trappings of his earlier domesticity put to bureaucratic use: 'The long, black-topped inlaid desk which I had built in Hammersmith was used by the secretary and the business manager. Connolly sat reading manuscripts in the editorial chair by the window, occasionally glancing up to see whether any German aeroplanes were coming over.' As the magazine established itself and advertising for subscribers and contributors became less crucial, Spender was also able to take note of his colleague's developing managerial technique and saw something in this disposition which, perhaps only coincidentally, he described in almost feminine terms: '[Connolly] carried on a kind of editorial flirtation with his readers, so that they were all in some peculiar way admitted to his moods, his tastes, his whims, his fantasies, his generous way of giving of himself, combined with his temperamental coyness.'[10] Watson too adopted metaphors of dalliance: 'Cyril's a brilliant editor because he's like a brothel keeper, offering his writers to the public as though they were the girls, and himself carrying on a flirtation with them.'[11]

Beneath this coquetry, however, Connolly had his anxieties, prominent among them the possibility of national service. In February 1940 he received a letter from his father which began with congratulations on sales figures and a declaration of faith in the policies of Neville Chamberlain. It continued, however, with expressions of concern for his son's status: was he sure that being an editor counted as having a 'reserved' occupation where the incumbent was not liable for conscription? During the Phoney War military needs were satisfied by available men of conscript age. When aggression intensified and the German menace grew stronger, men of Connolly's age were more vulnerable to their country's demands and the fear of being drafted into some uncongenial occupation dogged him for much of the war. But khaki regimentation would never have brought out those idiosyncratic qualities with which he contributed to the quality of wartime life and which were saluted by pilots fighting in the Battle of Britain who, Spender recalled, said 'they felt that so long as *Horizon* continued they had a cause to fight for.'[12]

At first it seems strange that a former soldier like Matthew should appear sympathetic to his son's resolutely civilian status but Connolly senior was an old and lonely man now. Although he corresponded with Maud he was otherwise largely isolated and his son inevitably became more important to him, not least perhaps because he thought at last that he could begin to take pride in his activities. Diana met Matthew and was surprised by what she found: he seemed 'rather pathetic and humourless' and certainly not the impossible figure of his son's anecdotes.[13] Nevertheless she was pleased to note that Connolly began to take a new interest in his father, to see much more of him and to worry about the way he lived. About politics they were Hanoverian: the father's meat was the son's poison; but as long as they avoided such contentions all was well. Writing to congratulate his son on the contents of the February *Horizon*, he had expressed delight with 'Comment', which he thought constituted a welcome change to the 'poisonous pro-Bolshevist sympathies' which he had declared in the *New Statesman*. He also told his son to waste no sympathy over the departure from government of Hore Belisha: 'The only pity is that he was ever allowed to do what he has done towards the ruin of the British Army, and it is one more laurel in the crown of Chamberlain if he has had the sense and courage, as he had in the case of that terrible mischief maker Eden, to have sacked him.'[14]

By the early spring of 1940 Diana had recovered sufficiently from her injuries to begin work at Lansdowne Terrace. She accepted a modest payment and in return was put in charge of the assessment of new manuscripts, classifying material into categories ordained for her by Connolly – 'no good at all', 'doubtful', 'good' and 'outstanding'. The next stage involved trying to persuade her editor to read the manuscripts which she had recommended, a task which she remembered was 'by no means easy'. She noted his journalistic habits – that he would regularly write 'Comment' as the magazine was going to press – and his editorial brilliance: 'His genius as an editor was that he could spot the one thing that an aspiring writer or journalist had been born to describe and commission something from him.'[15] Their relationship continued, as did his intermittent mention of marriage, but all such talk remained academic while he still had a wife, and Jean herself was hounded by indecision. She was now living with friends at Malvern Wells in Worcestershire and could not decide whether her marriage had ended, although she still loved the man whose life she had shared for the last decade. If it was over, there was little point in remaining in embattled

England, yet her future in America seemed unsure. To make matters
worse, transatlantic travel was at this stage still quite straightforward:
she could always come back, whereas a journey undertaken with no
possibility of return, however sad, would at least have reduced the
options of uncertainty. Only one consideration was clear: she would
make any such journey freighted with guilt, since her husband would
see her departure as abandonment.

These agonies were reflected in the letters she wrote in the early
months of 1940 in which she addressed him as 'darling Doodie' and
signed herself 'Doodie'. In February she was still painfully accommodating: 'Why don't you and Diana take a cottage in the country and
I'll come and stay and we'll all be high-minded and Bloomsbury and the
best of friends. You can be Lorenzo and I'll be Frieda and she can be
Brett.'[16] A month later she felt differently, no doubt because he had
declined to discard anything to do with the past, and she saw former
unhappinesses repeating themselves: 'I thought we had agreed to separate anyway for a year until I got over my phobia of living with you. If in
that year you got over your desire to live with me that would serve me
right for indulging in phobias.'[17] Sadly, they no longer bargained as
equals: he might be reluctant to let her go, but in the event of departure
she would relinquish more – an adopted country, a stylish writer, a
circle of friends – and new reconnaissances would have to be undertaken in the knowledge that she was older and could never have
children.

In discussions with Diana, Connolly once again seemed to accept her
solution, that they should separate and that he should return to his
wife. Yet in correspondence with Jean he equivocated – either he could
not live without her or else she was unsuitable to his present needs. One
letter admonished her for shirking responsibility and for having no
willpower to organize anything except the satisfaction of her appetites:
he wanted to write books, edit his magazine, have a stable marriage, to
'vivre bourgeoisement', while she wanted nothing but to be a 'maternal
friend'.[18] An impasse had been reached but it took news from America
that Mrs Warner was unwell to galvanize Jean. On 9 May she made a
new will which identified him as her sole legatee and indicated that she
intended him to receive half her annual income for the remainder of his
life. Two days later, she gave him £200 for good measure. They met
again and on 10 June she assured him, 'I love you and will write to you
every week and will come back to you.'[19] But she was edging further

away. On 14 June, writing from Dublin, whence she sailed the following day, she wrote: 'I can hardly bear to write I am missing you so much already. It is beginning to sink in how very far I am going and for how very long.'[20]

Ephemerality regulated human relations during the war: there was the constant possibility of sudden death and the knowledge, inveterate in the armed forces but now acknowledged by newly uniformed civilians, that a sudden and invariably secret posting could soon entail yet more farewells. Jean intended to return; in fact she was going for good. It is impossible to say what would have become of her had she remained but Connolly's career would probably not have been very different. The marriage had spent itself: she had lost some vital element of self-respect, at least in her dealings with him, and he had more or less abandoned the canons of monogamy and would never again try to be faithful to one woman for as long as he had been to Jean. Officially there was still hope: but the circumstances of the severance – coinciding with the expiry of the Thirties and of the peace – proved for Connolly to be the raw materials of forceful symbol and the occasion for flourishes of regret. He wrote his wife a 'private poem':

> My long dark lovely thinking one
> Whose thinking days seem almost done
> Whose talents rot on the night-club floor
> Whom sloth and lust and pride devour
> The little lie, the sawdust heart
> The easy joke, the postponed start,
> and one last drink before we part.[21]

The farcical nature of life is stronger than the romantic impulses of the individual and the valediction he envisaged was marred by a hideous confusion that occurred prior to Jean's departure. A week before she was due to leave Connolly was staying at the Randolph Hotel in Oxford. One evening he tried to place a long-distance telephone call to Jean but was obliged to wait for several hours for a clear line. By 11.15, still waiting, he found himself alone in the hotel's saloon except for a group of officers of the British Expeditionary Force, who were perhaps celebrating the recent evacuation of Dunkirk. His nervously expectant presence attracted attention and one of the party, a military police officer, demanded his identity card. Documentation revealed his damning Irish name, and his passport, issued in Vienna, established that he had been in Austria shortly before the Anschluss. He was confined to his room under suspicion of espionage and when the police arrived an officer greeted him with grotesque certainty: 'Good evening, sir, I understand you are an Austrian.' He had a copy of the June number of *Horizon* in his luggage but when he produced it to prove that he was not a secret agent he reckoned without its illustration, an unfortunate depiction of androgynous Pre-Raphaelite nudes. The officer said he had seen 'a lot of this kind of business' in Belgium and was almost convinced of his captive's guilt when it transpired that Connolly had been educated not only at Oxford but also at Eton. Suspicion faded immediately and he was released. He wrote a letter to the *New Statesman* which the magazine published on 15 June – the day of Jean's departure – entitled 'Spy-Mania', declaring that the episode was typical of a mounting and unhealthy suspiciousness and that the reverence accorded to his Etonian past was sinister.

CHAPTER SIXTEEN

IN THE WAKE of the evacuation of Dunkirk southern England became more vulnerable to aerial attack but in June that anxiety was eclipsed by the German invasion of France. A generation of British francophiles was stunned when that bastion of culture fell and Connolly himself was incredulous when Paris capitulated in the middle of the month. Surrender was only the beginning and for a while it seemed certain that England would follow in prostration. Diana remembered that the possibility compounded Connolly's fears: the thought of having to fight was bad enough but he became convinced that if the Germans did invade, intellectuals would be eliminated. It was a common foreboding, as Orwell recorded:

> I notice that all the 'left' intellectuals I meet believe that Hitler, if he gets here, will take the trouble to shoot people like ourselves ... C[onnolly] says there is a move on foot to get our police records (no doubt we all have them) at Scotland Yard destroyed. Some hope! The police are the very people who would go over to Hitler once they were certain he had won.[1]

It was a relief when Watson, mindful of imminent destruction, decided to evacuate his friends. He took a house at Thurlestone Sands in Devon and suggested that Spender, Connolly and Diana might stay with him for the summer and continue their work in tranquillity. Thatched Cottage was isolated and the friends found themselves imprisoned by petrol rationing, although at first enforced stillness seemed not to matter: Watson had hired a cook and if his guests felt particularly restless there were always bicycles. More importantly, London, with its confusion and emergency regulations, was remote, and Connolly could indulge a life-long fascination and collect shellfish. This occupation required a transformation into informal clothing and when the cook first saw him in shorts and jersey, clutching a net, she took him for her new employer's gardener. Inevitably, expeditions to the sea notwithstanding, he was soon restless: Diana remembered that he could be impossible – sulking on his bed for hours, dissatisfied with the food, bored by the country, brooding about Jean, ominously engrossed in French poetry – and that it was a relief when they all went home in August.

He had been obliged to return to London at regular intervals: its editor could leave the capital but *Horizon* could not and there were always decisions to be made and authorizations to be extended. His 'Comment' for May was important, appearing when German expansion into Scandinavia and the Low Countries seemed irresistible and when Neville Chamberlain's position as Prime Minister was proving untenable. Connolly noted with pride that although his magazine received between two and three hundred hopeful contributions each month, they were characterized by an apparent indifference to the war. Belligerent declarations tended to come from those too old for military service and he found that this division reflected a larger schism in English intellectual life now that thinkers could no longer agree about Russia, Chamberlain and pacifism. On the first of these issues he was clear: the Soviets were discredited as the inheritors of paradise and Chamberlain was not England embodied but a leader who had a finite term of power. Pacifism was a more complex problem and he made the important point that the horror of violence which fuelled pacifism was as much a cause of the war as its opposite, bullying pugnacity. He was more ambiguous about the part intellectuals should play in the conflict. In one paragraph he chastised them mildly for recoiling from the war 'as if it were a best-seller', in another he seemed to endorse that aversion: *Horizon* could do no more in this hour than monitor the kingdom of art and recognize its adversaries. 'This war is the enemy of creative activity, and writers and painters are wise and right to ignore it.'[2]

It is remarkable that officialdom let his views pass. However, a former journalist on the *Spectator*, Goronwy Rees, now in the army, resented Connolly's tone and deductions and wrote a retort which *Horizon* published as 'Letter from a Soldier' in July. It was prominently positioned, occupying the place normally accorded 'Comment', while that component was put at the back: Connolly had nothing to hide and was eager to display his commitment to free polemic. Rees's reprimand was well-mannered and his grievance was persuasively described: 'A million men, and more, will die and the artist will live and create; and apparently he is to accept the fruit of this sacrifice as a free gift and acknowledge no responsibility to the giver.'

In 'Comment' Connolly acknowledged that Rees had a point, that his magazine had not taken the war seriously enough and that the freedom to create and consume art depended in the end on freedom ensured by fighting. Nevertheless he was adamant that 'though this war is being fought for culture, the fighting of it will not create that culture'.[3] A new contributor to *Horizon*, Clement Greenberg, considered Connolly's dilemma when the July number reached New York and wrote to show his sympathy: 'You're in for politics, you simply have to deal with it, and there's no way out. The great problem ... is how, precisely, the socialist opposition is to go about taking over control of the struggle against Hitler.' Connolly was reassured by this show of support. He had suggested to Jean that she contact Greenberg when she arrived in New York and now a friendship had been instigated: 'I find her nice. By this time I feel almost that I know you in person too.'[4]

In August Connolly put *Horizon* unequivocally behind Churchill as 'the one indispensable leader at this time' and by September the war had arrived in London in earnest with heavy bombing which commenced when the Germans began bombarding the docks on 7 September. That day, Orwell went to have tea with his friend and later described how the journey became memorable with vignettes – sometimes inconsequent, sometimes not – as history unfolded before him: women on the bus mistaking shellbursts in the sky for parachutes; the sudden need in Piccadilly to shelter from shrapnel as though from 'a cloudburst'; German planes darkening the sky; 'some very young RAF and naval officers running out of one of the hotels and passing a pair of field glasses from hand to hand'. That evening in Connolly's new flat – an apartment subsidized by Peter Watson, who was also living in the building, Athenaeum Court, in Piccadilly – Orwell, Connolly and a friend called Hugh Slater gazed from the windows as a conflagration swept the East End. Slater found the spectacle 'just like Madrid – quite nostalgic'. Connolly, less casual, led the way to the roof of the building and on the skyline thought he glimpsed destiny's design: 'It's the end of capitalism. It's a judgement on us.' Orwell bided his time: 'I didn't feel this to be so, but was chiefly struck by the size and the beauty of the flames.'[5] Unknown to Connolly and Orwell, another friend shared their vigil. Forty miles away, Bobbie Longden was master of Wellington

College and responsible for the safety of his pupils: a bomb fell on his school on 8 October, killing him instantly. Connolly was not recorded as attending the memorial service.

The German plan had been to immobilize the docks and thus paralyse the movement of food and weapons but the campaign soon moved westwards. Bloomsbury sustained terrible damage and the area around Lansdowne Terrace was severely disrupted, to the extent that *Horizon* was without an office for most of September. The Curwen Press was bombed repeatedly and 2000 copies of the magazine were destroyed in a raid in October. That month Connolly briefly visited Scotland, 'determined to enjoy everything', as he reported in November's 'Comment', and returned to London to stand in as art critic for the *New Statesman*. His article was mainly concerned with the work of Augustus John: he talked of the artist's 'free bold unforced technique and his everlasting pagan sources' and bemoaned again the problem facing artists and writers – how to function creatively at a time when all was geared to destruction: '[Many painters] have to use bomb flares for sunsets, tanks for cows, khaki blobs of men or dingy lorries for patches of shadow.'[6]

The end of November saw a further expansion in Connolly's activities when he began a significant wartime career in broadcasting with a talk on *The Writer in the Witness Box* for which he was paid ten guineas. The occasion marked the public's introduction to his extraordinary voice, which survives on numerous recordings and over the years lost none of its idiosyncrasy: it was soft, slightly drawling, yet distinctively bland; the delivery, while being precise, contrived also to be faintly languid. It was a voice hard to imagine raised in anger, yet Connolly could intimidate friends and acquaintances very easily. He almost raised his voice in 'Comment' in December when he made the point that since the fall of France sales of *Horizon* had declined by 40 per cent. He added a list of 'distinguished non-contributors' to the magazine which included H. G. Wells, Shaw, Forster, Eliot, Beerbohm, Isherwood and Kenneth Clark, and berated members of the forces for promising, but never delivering, articles on the nature of forces life: 'It is ironical that all we have got out of the army has been a slashing attack on us from Goronwy Rees for frivolously condemning the war as "the enemy of creative writing".'

The reproach preceded important essays by Orwell on 'The Ruling Class' and Peter Quennell on 'Byron in Venice' and had to contend with the British apathy which it denounced. Nevertheless, one detailed and spirited rejoinder was written on 17 December by the writer Julian Symons. He had first been angered by Connolly at the time of the controversy surrounding Housman and the intervening years had done nothing to mitigate his disapproval. His comments took the form of an open letter in which he seized on Connolly's assertion in 'Comment' that 'One of us, *Horizon* or its public, has failed the other.' Symons saw the situation differently: 'I accuse *Horizon* of failing, not a non-existent public, but a standard of literary merit and intelligence. I accuse its editor of slackness and flippancy.' He conceded that 'anyone whose interest in literature is more than [as Connolly had termed it] a "luxury emotion" must be interested in *Horizon*'s future' but thought the outlook bleak and was convinced that the problems which besieged the magazine at the end of 1940 would be worse by the end of 1941. Relations with America would be more tenuous; contributors and subscribers would have disappeared into the forces; money would be scarcer.

He was convinced the publication should strive for greater serious-ness and his conclusion was po-faced: 'What is certain, however, is that if [*Horizon*] remains a monthly it will cost somebody a good deal of money in the next twelve months; or else it will die.'[7] The fact was that Connolly could please neither the serious left nor the patriotic right. Yet even if he had adopted Symons's honourable but slightly earnest recom-mendations it is hard to imagine that more readers beyond the narrow factions of the metropolis would have been converted to his, or his magazine's, cause.

Towards the end of 1940, with a new secretary named Miss Warren imported to help with the running of the magazine, Diana decided to take a holiday both from her work and from London. She needed time to deliberate. Her relationship with Connolly, through gradual deterioration rather than sudden decline, had reached a stage where its problems seemed almost equal to its pleasures, and she used her month in the country to measure its promise and opportunities and set them against the conduct of the man she now knew so well. He continued to talk intermittently of finding a new house where they could start a life together, even though there was no possibility of divorce proceedings beginning against Jean, and predictably 'did all he could to try and persuade me not to end seeing him'.[8] Yet although she was very fond of him she realized she could no longer maintain their relationship. She found his apparent need to be quarrelsome 'too much'; besides, she had a life which predated their involvement and which she had neglected. He wanted an absolute devotion; but by the time she had resolved to spend Christmas with her parents she knew there were other claims on her time. Resolution was one thing, execution another, and he prepared once more to resort to the full battery of persuasive techniques to retain her. He sent letters, threats of suicide, warnings that his art would fail; and mutual friends, among them Cecil Beaton, arrived on embassies to plead his cause. In 1941, however, she settled in a flat in Lowndes Square. She would continue to see Connolly socially, but that was all.

Intercessors like Beaton may not have known that in Diana's absence Connolly had met another woman. Peter Quennell had introduced him to Lys Dunlap, the young woman he had met before the war with her then lover, Gavin Ewart; if there had been any initial interest it was superseded now by strong attraction and soon he was obsessed with her. When Cyril Connolly fell in love he did so utterly and with conviction and it was irrelevant that conditions might force him to make the same professions to two women simultaneously. Indeed obscurely he almost preferred having to do so: love was gradually becoming a triangular condition for him, an intenser reality requiring the involvement of three players, himself and two women. It was a situation which not only ensured almost endless intrigue but allowed him his particular emotional devotions. He could compare his two muses and contrast them: one might embody memories of exquisite happiness, the other anticipated ecstasy; one might be fair, the other dark; one naive, the other worldly; one unobtainable, the other enthusiastic. They had to remain distinct but complementary, some-times flesh and blood, sometimes diametric abstractions; but in their alternating ministrations he saw the guarantee of his contentment and creativity. For his women it was a disposition which must often have seemed intolerable but for Connolly it became a fact of adult life and one which somehow made conventional morality redundant, a redundancy implicit in his artless comment to Stephen Spender: 'I shall never believe in women again. I have been perfectly faithful to two women for two years, and now both of them have been unfaithful to me.'[9]

It followed that he saw no need now to terminate matters with Diana and almost a year was to elapse before he finally agreed to accept her as nothing more than a friend. Meanwhile, he had a new initiate. Lys was twenty-two and Connolly thirty-seven when they met and fell in love. By birth she was half-American, by upbringing from London and Kent, by circumstance without money or social connections. Since her liaison with Ewart she had married a handsome young schoolmaster with theatrical aspirations named Ian Lubbock and just before the war she joined the advertising agency where Peter Quennell worked as a copywriter. Presently, when his flat was damaged during the Blitz, he moved into the Lubbocks' apartment in Holland Park. He and Lys got on well but already her marriage, only two years old, was in decline. Besides his job and his labours with *Byron in Venice* Quennell still found time to perform a number of roles in Connolly's life, including those of literary rival and purveyor of gossip. He had another unofficial function, however, which was to act as a catalyst to desire, love and emotion, to introduce Connolly to women who were his *confidantes* or lovers whom his friend could then woo away.

Meanwhile at the beginning of 1941 Connolly was also preparing to move again, to 102a Drayton Gardens, a studio flat on the peripheries of Chelsea which belonged to his friends Celia and Mamaine Paget, twin sisters now eager to decamp to the country. When he installed himself and invited Lys to move in with him she readily agreed, having reached the conclusion that whereas Lubbock was still too young to settle into married life, Connolly's greater years would make him a more dependable, more accommodating partner. For his part the writer may have thought he was simply acquiring a beautiful girlfriend but Lys soon set about righting the unwelcome disorders of his life. She was a renowned cook and quickly assumed responsibility for entertaining friends, but her efficiency, domesticity and practicality needed greater challenges and soon she confronted his complicated finances. She hired a good accountant and supplied him annually with scrupulous calculations, submitting details of necessary professional entertaining and ensuring entirely legally that Connolly paid almost no tax. It was a perfect arrangement – for a time: he looked to her to resolve details he found too dreary to contemplate; she turned to him for domestic focus, rising cheerfully to stem the artistic chaos and gradually convincing herself that affairs would end at the altar.

He had always been indulged by women and Lys continued that tradition triumphantly. It cost her no effort to spare him the boredom of practicalities; in any case she was unequal to his strategies and his single-mindedness:

As soon as Cyril decided he wanted something, he wouldn't rest until he had it. And he was very good at making you feel guilty for not giving him what he wanted. Like a child, he would beg and beg, and then when you gave in, his attention would go to another thing. Sometimes I think he only really loved me when he thought he was losing me. There were endless scenes.[10]

Inevitably Lys's services were soon enlisted at *Horizon*, where she helped in almost any capacity before becoming its business manager with the disappearance into the army of Bill Makins. Liza Mann, a friend of hers prior to the war, worked in the office in 1941 and was impressed by Lys's control and efficiency. She remembered glimpses of Connolly in the summer working in a lemon-yellow aertex shirt set off by an Old Etonian tie; of Stephen Spender, 'always striding around in a fireman's uniform'; of Dylan Thomas, who 'shuffled in occasionally looking rather the worse for wear'.[11] Not everybody shared her high opinion of Lys, however. Peter Quennell soon produced a new girlfriend, a wanton and feline beauty called Barbara Skelton, who was unimpressed by her (and by so many others), finding her at best 'really quite sweet' and on less auspicious occasions 'tiresome ... trying to make the apt reply to everything'.[12] Janetta thought she slavishly endorsed Connolly's every pronouncement, while Diana, referring to her voice, named her 'Squeaks'.

In January 1941, as the Italians surrendered Tobruk to the British and Churchill and Roosevelt continued negotiating the Lend-Lease Act, war news was swept from the front pages of the tabloids by a sensational scandal in distant Kenya. An older Etonian contemporary of Connolly's, the Earl of Erroll, was found dead outside Nairobi, and the ensuing investigation, which culminated in the trial for murder of Sir Jock Delves Broughton, exposed hedonistic irresponsibility at the highest levels of a British colony to the patriotic censure of Fleet Street. Connolly no doubt welcomed the distraction; but he had other reasons for taking an interest. Sir Jock was a cousin of his first friend at Eton, L. R. Delves Broughton.

James Joyce died in January and Connolly wrote a tribute for the *New Statesman* in which he recalled his meeting with the sublime exile in 1929 and reflected that 'he always seemed to be two men, the legendary Joyce, blind but patient, pompous, cold ... with a strange priestly blend of offended dignity, weakness and intellectual power, and underneath, the warm, sympathetic bawdy Irish character.'[13]

In April further revelations came from overseas. When Stephen Spender married his second wife Connolly offered Drayton Gardens as a venue for the party, confident that Lys would successfully plan the celebration. Between them Connolly and the groom could muster an interesting congregation of friends: guests included Cecil Beaton, Louis MacNeice, Cecil Day-Lewis, A. J. Ayer and John Lehmann, who felt that the celebration, 'in reuniting our literary world, painfully marked the absence of Christopher and Wystan'.[14] Even so, the Julian Huxleys came, along with Peter Watson, Rose Macaulay, Guy Burgess, Tambimuttu, William Plomer and Joe Ackerley. Tom Driberg had some interesting gossip. He had recently returned from the United States and had learnt that Jean was now living in New York and having an affair with Clement Greenberg.

Horizon had published an essay by Greenberg entitled 'Avant-Garde and Kitsch' the preceding April and in New York he was beginning to make his name as an art critic and as one of the editors of *Partisan Review*. After the war, when Manhattan became the capital of the world of avant-garde art, he would become one of its most important arbiters. Meanwhile Jean had fallen in with a group which revolved around Peggy Guggenheim, and for a while the two women shared an apartment at 23 East 73rd Street, an address which Jean gave Connolly, telling him he could always apply there if in urgent financial need. Her affair with Greenberg lasted almost two years and at least in its early stages it was unequivocal enough. He found her 'loaded with sex'; Connolly by now had 'no hold' on her sexually and she had 'no remorse at all' for her extra-marital involvement – indeed it may even have been partially intended as retribution for her own suffering. Jean now suggested that Connolly had lacked 'spine and character' and she was certainly disinclined to reminisce about 'living for beauty' with him in the south of France. She had been anglicized by her years in London but remained more interested in 'the here and now' than in the abstract. Nevertheless, 'she had her piety about culture'. Their relationship effectively ended when Greenberg joined the army in 1943; but although it distressed Connolly he did not allow it to prevent him from befriending his sometime rival after the war.[15]

Meanwhile 1941 had begun well for *Horizon* with the publication in January of Alun Lewis's 'All Day It Has Rained'. The publication marked the wider recognition of a potential laureate of the conflict and seemed to provide an answer to the predictable anxieties of the popular press – 'Where are our war poets?' It also led to the collection of an anthology called *Raiders' Dawn* which was brought out by Allen and Unwin in 1942. 'War poets', as Connolly well knew, were as mythical and lovely as the unicorn and in 'Comment' he tried to qualify what he considered to be the unreasonable expectations of the newspapers: 'For war poets are not a new kind of being, they are only peace poets who have assimilated the material of war.' Lewis went to meet 'the strange nervous *Horizon* gang'. 'I felt as if my khaki were too rough and my boots too heavy to be near them ... I don't think they'll ever lead the people to a new world ... they were very thoughtful in speaking with me, not patronising or off-hand, and Connolly said he hopes to go on printing my work for a long time yet.'[16] Sadly, it was not to be: Lewis was only twenty-eight when he died, in 1944, a soldier and an optimist.

In February Connolly was approached by Tom Harrisson, who in 1937 had instituted that phenomenon of the Thirties, Mass-Observation, to participate in 'a general survey of writing during this war. Not only the writing of our friends and acquaintances, but also numerous books that are now coming out about the Home Front, the RAF etc. Striking feature of the whole position is almost unbelievable mediocrity, sterility.'[17] The invitation was a recognition of Connolly's place at the centre of British literary life, a recognition implicit in overtures also made that year by the BBC. In April he broadcast on James Joyce for the programme *We Speak to India* and seven months later he replied to questions delivered by Canadian servicemen in the programme *Answering You*, for which he was paid eight guineas. Another body eager to recruit his services was that of the National Authors' Committee, which represented many of the important English writers of the time – Beerbohm, Walter de la Mare, Eliot, Forster, John Masefield, Maugham, Priestley, Wells, Rebecca West – and aimed 'to help Ministries which have or may have occasion to call on authors for part or whole time services to find someone suitable and available at short notice'.[18]

The year's most prestigious congregation of writers occurred in the autumn, however, when the PEN Club convened a celebrated conference in London. John Lehmann recalled that the occasion constituted 'a demonstration against the Axis not merely because it was held in battered London and attended by so many distinguished writers from the free world, but also because the refugee writers from occupied Europe who were settled in England used it to send out their challenge to the military masters in their homelands'.[19] Elizabeth Bowen and Roger Senhouse helped Sybil Colefax organize lunches while John Dos Passos, Thornton Wilder and Robert Sherwood travelled from the United States. Connolly found himself sitting on the same table as Stevie Smith, Inez Holden, Guy Chapman, a writer from *La France Libre* and a newly prominent émigré writer named Arthur Koestler. Talk, inevitably, was of survival, though seen from a literary point of view, and presently – for a stake of five bottles of burgundy – Koestler predicted that in five years' time Orwell would be the best-selling author. With clairvoyance he would have stipulated a decade in his wager rather than a lustrum, since by 1951 Orwell had joined the glorious dead and was on his way to literary fame and greatness.

CHAPTER SEVENTEEN

HALF-HUNGARIAN, HALF-JEW, educated in Vienna and formerly resident in Germany, Palestine and France, Koestler had crossed more than national frontiers by the time he arrived in England in 1940. He had been a Communist and it was as such that he had worked as a reporter in the Spanish Civil War and subsequently been incarcerated by Franco. He narrowly escaped execution and when he was released from gaol he still considered himself loyal to the cause. However, he had had time for reflection: he had seen the Communists subjugate Spanish interests to Russian; he had learnt how implacably loyal comrades had been sacrificed on fictitious charges to the inconstant yet paramount needs of the Party; and like thousands of other converts to the cause he had been stricken by a chronic disillusion with the announcement of the Nazi–Soviet Pact. Suddenly bereft of faith, he needed a substitute loyalty and, like Orwell, another veteran of the Spanish war, he became an anti-Communist. It is not clear how he met Connolly but by February 1941, when they were on cordial terms, he had already published his claim on posterity, *Darkness at Noon*, and was working on his next novel, *The Scum of the Earth*. On 9 February he wrote to thank his new friend for recent words of encouragement: he always felt while writing a book that it was 'utter rot' and Connolly's show of support had been much appreciated.[1]

For a year, between digging latrines and performing other duties for the Pioneer Corps, he worked on his manuscript before receiving a medical discharge. By September, and presumably through correspondence, there had been a great advance in friendship: Koestler was welcome to stay in Drayton Gardens when he returned to London and negotiations were underway between him and Connolly to recruit the assistance of other wealthy backers for *Horizon*. A new scheme was under consideration – that each future issue of the magazine should be underwritten by a different patron – and Watson was among its supporters: he had begun to notice the publication's inroads into his resources and was convinced that fresh investment could make all the difference to the venture's survival. Koestler now recommended Mrs B. T. Scoville of Taconic, Connecticut, although with reservations: she was generous in her support of refugees but her munificence should not be assumed and overtures were best made in a spirit of delicacy. (Perhaps she responded unenthusiastically, because the scheme was never implemented.) Meanwhile Connolly gave a large party to introduce Koestler to literary London, a gesture the newcomer always remembered: 'You really took me under your wing in those days . . . I got to know everybody, more or less, through that party.'[2] Eventually he moved into Drayton Gardens, where Peter Quennell had also taken shelter, and relations were in the main harmonious, although Quennell found Koestler 'touchy and suspicious' and incurred his annoyance by revealing to outsiders that he wore a hairnet in bed. Connolly also saw Koestler's difficult side and later complained of 'certain rugosities of behaviour' and of 'the painful sensation of being taken up and dropped, discarded without a fair trial, as intellectually worthless'.[3]

With a spacious and amusing studio and Lys's organizational skills at his disposal, Connolly was able to resume the offices of literary entertainer which he had performed with relish in the Thirties. Like *Horizon* itself, these reunions were more than idle luxuries, more than occasions when beleaguered writers and artists might congregate: they were a modest gesture of heroism, an affirmation that despite chaos and destruction there was still the opportunity for pleasure and amusement. As the war progressed London's increasing shabbiness itself became debilitating and stealthily compounded the larger dangers and miseries. Distraction became vital and Connolly himself developed what he later called a 'colour deficiency', as everything, everywhere took on the grey drabness of bombed buildings. Some sought escape at the cinema or at the famous lunch-time piano recitals given by Myra Hess at the National Gallery but the critic and editor found idiosyncratic respite in the sale-rooms of Sotheby's: 'Week after week I would call in after luncheon, lay out my twopences on a couple of catalogues, and set off round the cases to study.'[4] Inspection was more important than purchase and usually he left deliberately unrealistic bids. On one occasion, however, temptation proved much greater. Sir Hugh Walpole, a pillar of literary London and a friend to *Horizon* (he had donated 'Henry James: A Reminiscence' to the second number) died in 1941 and his possessions were put up for sale. Connolly attended the viewing and fell in love with Chagall's *Le Poète Allongé*, which was valued at £200. He had just received his quarterly editorial earnings for exactly that sum – the picture could be his, but he was more intrigued than covetous and in the end his nerve failed him: if he bought the picture he would be penniless for three months and Chagall's vision seduced another buyer before entering the permanent collection of the Tate Gallery.[5]

Distraction of another kind came in March when Connolly received an invitation from John Betjeman, who was working in Ireland as what he termed the 'UK representative to Eire', to deliver a lecture on the modern novel to the Friends of the Irish Academy. Long since cramped by travel restrictions, the critic eagerly accepted and was no doubt as grateful for the excursion as Betjeman was for his gossip and companionship. The two friends had an entertaining time sight-seeing and carousing; Connolly visited the seminary at Maynooth and frequented the Palace Bar in Dublin. He contemplated Joyce, he saw eighteenth-century architecture, he pondered a civilian culture which he himself had once known and taken for granted. While looking at the luxuries of peace he had the idea of assembling an Irish number of *Horizon*, and when that issue finally appeared, in January 1942, he recorded his impressions in a lengthy 'Comment' in which he addressed the Ulster controversy and decried the role of the British in Irish history. Nonetheless he detected an improvement, not least in London's tolerance of Dublin's position: 'While we respect Eire's neutrality we can respect ourselves, its existence is the show-piece of the Empire's freedom.' That said, the city still seemed to provoke questions rather than answers and he returned to London perplexed. Of course principles had to be defended but 'the lovely island of 1938, with its lights and its crowds, its huge trees and cloudscapes, its shops full of food, and newspapers full of nothing' brought home to him the cost of the sacrifice.[6]

He returned to England to be reminded that not even the dead were safe. The bombs which fell on his beloved Chelsea destroyed more than a playground of his youth when Chelsea Old Church, final resting place of Henry James, was hit. Drayton Gardens was only minutes away: death might come at any time. To compound anxieties he was beset with worries about the continued distribution and paper supply of *Horizon* and if the magazine went, so did his reserved status. Equally there were consolations and he was delighted to learn of an unexpected show of support from America. In March *Decision*, a new magazine published in New York, devoted a lengthy editorial to the virtues of *Horizon*; its editor, Thomas Mann's son Klaus, announced that *Horizon* represented the best of contemporary British literature and culture and asked his readers to send messages, via the British Embassy in Washington, asking for the Ministry of Information to increase the number of copies available for export to the United States. Connolly was delighted and without having seen the encomium wrote to Mann, whom he knew through his brother-in-law, W. H. Auden, to extend both gratitude and editorial advice: contributors and staff were unreliable; copy was invariably delayed; politics were always controversial, their absence more controversial still; editors caught employing their friends, however talented, were quickly damned as clique-leaders. However: 'It is very interesting, like sitting all day under a tepid shower, and sometimes one feels that one is really helping something or someone.'[7]

It was timely propaganda. In July Harold Nicolson, *Horizon*'s champion at the Ministry, was moved to other employment and sent regrets that he could protect no more: 'I am clearing out of here today and I fear I can do no more to help *Horizon*. I am very sorry about it.'[8] The magazine's paper supply was now most vulnerable to misguided bureaucratic economy: how could its claims withstand the stationery requirements of more serious publications? Happily, Nicolson was able to continue indirect support and Connolly had another influential friend in Kenneth Clark. Both were able to indicate the prestige accorded to the publication in America and by December Connolly could announce a temporary respite. Meanwhile, with his marriage Spender was decreasingly involved in the magazine's business and in the autumn, having been called up, he joined the National Fire Service. *Horizon* continued to use his flat but was more and more Connolly's private and idiosyncratic vehicle, since Watson allowed him total editorial discretion. Yet the magazine styled itself 'a review of literature and art' and it was Watson's involvement which essentially justified its artistic pretensions. At his instigation, in 1941 alone readers enjoyed a pageant of contemporary art: John Piper, Augustus John, Henry Moore, Barbara Hepworth, Ben Nicholson and Frances Hodgkin were among the prominent British artists whose work the magazine illustrated and Watson himself wrote an article about the work of Joan Miró, complete with illustrations, which appeared in August. Augustus John began his long series, 'Fragments of an Autobiography'. Most importantly, in May 1941, in an issue which also contained tributes following the recent suicide of Virginia Woolf, there was an article on 'The Euston Road Group', the school of painters which included William Coldstream, Victor Pasmore, Claude Rogers and Graham Bell.

The assessment was the work of a pretty young woman called Sonia Brownell who had almost entered the life of the magazine a year previously when she had applied, through Spender's friendship, to edit a projected issue devoted to young British painters originally to have been supervised by Kenneth Clark. Peter Watson rejected her application but Connolly, who met her at the same time, sensed her capacity for devotion and became in some ways the towering figure of her life: on the threshold of maturity, she was romantically hungry for genius, longing to be dazzled, to fly like a moth to the flame of talent, and now she was confronted by the sole remaining steward of the Ivory Tower. Connolly, ever alert for attractive disciples, would happily accommodate her idealism and Spender recognized the bond that united them: 'No one could enter more enthusiastically into the idea that he was the cause of genius personified and frustrated, than Cyril . . . Understanding the many ways in which [he] was misunderstood provided Sonia with a tremendous brief, which took up much time and energy.'[9] For most of the war she was employed at the Ministry of War Transport but her commitment to the world of art and to its denizens made her a regular auxiliary at *Horizon*: indeed she was often mistaken for a formal employee and by the time Liza Mann left the magazine she remembered Sonia as 'sitting at Cyril's feet'.[10]

Sonia's zeal for the artistic and literary world was a loyalty cultivated in early life to sustain her in philistine adversity. She was born in 1918 in India, the second daughter of Charles and Beatrice Brownell. Her father died when she was only months old; the stepfather she acquired when her mother remarried was a deeply unsatisfactory paternal figure whose alcoholism lost him not only his job but his wife's affection and shortly after they returned to England the couple separated. Beatrice borrowed money and established a boarding-house in South Kensington; with hard work she was able to sustain herself and her children and to send Sonia and her sister to the Convent of the Sacred Heart at Roehampton. Sonia hated her time there, finding its regime oppressive and its teaching doctrinaire: for the rest of her life she spat whenever she saw nuns. Somehow the money was found for her to attend finishing school in Switzerland but there was no question of her progressing to university. She was a victim of the prevailing orthodoxy, that women had no use for tertiary education, and would have to escape her straitened background by another route. Marriage offered an alternative solution and she was very pretty, as Lys remembered: 'There was a lovely glow of health in her appearance. She had a pink-and-white complexion and golden blonde hair that she was quite proud of, washing it every night and doing it up herself.'[11] She was attractive to many men but, perhaps as a result of her convent training, their advances seemed to make her nervous. Nevertheless before she was twenty-one she was living near the Euston Road School and it was there that she met William Coldstream and began an affair that lasted until 1941. By the time Coldstream introduced her to Spender she had modelled for, and slept with, a number of the painters, and earned the accolade 'the Euston Road Venus' – although if they thought her promiscuous they were unjust: they had merely enjoyed the generosity of an insecurity which dictated that if artists needed gratification they should have it.

It is not clear whether she had a liaison with Connolly, although he considered her attractive and liked to joke, perhaps in frustration, about her 'lesbian drives'. Sex, however, was secondary in their relationship. When he met her Sonia was a self-made orphan; for partly selfish reasons, it must be admitted, he gave her a mission in life besides endorsing her francophilia and her conviction that writers and artists constituted an elect. Janetta and Diana liked the newcomer and if Lys ever regarded her as a rival she also knew that the magazine would look far before finding another assistant willing to work as hard and type as rapidly – and all for no reward beyond Connolly's intangible and unpredictable benediction. Their relations had to be amicable; later they developed genuine affection for each other and to amused outsiders fascinated by the loyalty Connolly could inspire in his women friends they became known as 'Lend-Lys'. Watson began by finding Sonia insistent and annoying but her hard work and enthusiasm earned his affection; for her part she revered him for his manners and aesthetic discrimination. Many who did not know her well found her slightly ridiculous. The future journalist Woodrow Wyatt was charmed by her appearance but irritated by her habit of 'using French instead of English whenever she thought she could make a literary effect, and to impress Connolly (successfully)'.[12] She may have been intermittently comic and an incorrigible intellectual snob but nobody could deny that she lived her life with a passionate commitment. She was a large and generous personality and it is a testimony to her self-creation, however irregular, that she inspired the characters of Julia in *Nineteen Eighty-four*, Elvira in Angus Wilson's *Anglo-Saxon Attitudes* and Ada Leintwardine in Anthony Powell's *Books Do Furnish a Room*.

From her unofficial position Sonia was able to throw herself into the causes which Connolly and his magazine were espousing when she first encountered them. Among these was '*Horizon*'s Begging Bowl', a scheme which had first been promoted in January in a half-page advertisement which asked not only for more readers but also more money. It reminded subscribers that each issue cost about £150, a sum which had to be met through the sale of 6000 copies and the revenue from advertising. It was a tight ship; Connolly invited readers to send a tip to any writer whose work they had particularly enjoyed: not more than £100 and not less than 2s 6d. British apathy and meanness united against the plan and by the end of the year he had to report disappointing results. The scheme had originated with the need to raise money to help Dylan Thomas and in May 1940 a consortium comprising Watson, Spender, Herbert Read and Henry Moore had collected donations totalling in excess of £100. The Welshman was incurably insolvent, however, and Connolly remembered at least one occasion when he bought poems straight from his wallet, 'as if they were packets of cocaine'.[13] It was money well spent; Thomas was the most important poet to emerge in the British Isles since Auden and enriched *Horizon* with some of his best writing of the Forties – 'Deaths and Entrances', 'Poem in October', 'Fern Hill' and 'A Refusal to Mourn the Death, by Fire, of a Child in London'.

October saw the announcement of 'Why Not War Writers?', a campaign which aimed to redress the injustice by which painters, in exchange for becoming 'war artists' and painting scenes of the war, were paid, exempted from conscription and allowed time and freedom to pursue their own ambitions when writers were either called up or consigned to the Ministry of Information and thus to the sterility of the over-worked clerk. Connolly announced a manifesto which was signed by various figures including Koestler, Orwell, Alun Lewis, Spender and Tom Harrisson of Mass-Observation but bureaucracy remained unimpressed and in February 1943 he had to concede that the idea had been '*Horizon*'s most lost of lost causes'.[14] Shortly after the publication of the manifesto, however, he received a particularly eloquent unsigned letter which he quoted in full at the back of the December number. The document was forceful: 'I am afraid that I do not believe for a moment that these young men want to write; they want to be writers ... They have been whimpering for years for a classless society, and now that their own class is threatened with loss of privilege they are aghast.' Readers may have been perplexed by the identity of the complainant but Connolly can have been under no delusions: it was his eternal scourge and shadow, Evelyn Waugh, now in the army and thus gleefully able to style himself at the bottom of the letter 'Combatant', a status he was sure his manifesto-writers would never earn.

However, Waugh bestowed favours even as he inflicted ridicule. Only a month prior to the publication of this anonymous letter, *Horizon* had scored a triumph with the inclusion of a fragment of his unfinished novel, *Work Suspended*. The appearance of any new prose by such a master was in itself exciting but Waugh further sugared the compliment by indicating that he trusted Connolly to undertake any necessary editing unsupervised. Rare though this accolade was, it seemed justified when 'My Father's House' appeared to great acclaim. Yet when the novelist's growing number of admirers next took to the bookshops with the appearance in 1942 of *Put Out More Flags* they would see the critic's name maliciously applied to a family of rude, unwanted refugees.

If Waugh enjoyed spiteful teasing Connolly himself was not blameless. The 'Comment' which preceded 'My Father's House' revealed that the November issue was the first number of *Horizon* to contain no poetry. Connolly attributed the absence to the poverty of the contributions received and went on to imagine the archetypal poet responsible for much of the derivative verse which arrived at Lansdowne Terrace. He christened him 'John Weaver' and accused him of imitating Auden and MacNeice while genuflecting before all the fashionable preoccupations: Communism, homosexuality, revolution and religion. Furthermore, having been published in all the mandatory anthologies like *New Verse* and *New Writing*, 'Weaver' had produced 'one volume of verse, with an Introduction by Herbert Read, called "The Poet's Thumb"'. Read, a serious critic, a contributor to *Horizon* and a respected figure in literary London, was understandably annoyed by the defamation and sent a letter of complaint to Connolly, who replied assuring him that when the opportunity presented itself he would repair the damage or retract it. Read protested again and this time drew an impatient denial from Connolly, who insisted that the only injured party was the imaginary 'John Weaver' and that Read was a happy inhabitant of never-never land if he imagined that an institution like *Horizon* – besieged by doubting bureaucrats and chronically hungry for paper – could afford to publish the rhapsodies of complacent poetasters. Relations between the two men had never been enthusiastic. Read had been a literary adviser at Routledge since 1937 and although he seems not to have had many direct dealings with Connolly he may have shared his colleagues' frustration with their author's unreliability. Misgivings were compounded when at the end of November Connolly rejected a poem of Read's which, for all its technical skill, contained pedestrian vocabulary. The latter irritably told a friend that such a rejection called to mind Stalin's dislike of a symphony by Shostakovich which contained tunes he was incapable of whistling. Connolly was unmoved and as late as 1953, when Stalin himself died, he was still contemptuous of Read, 'who has been in at the birth of so many modern movements and avant-garde exhibitions, smiling modestly at the christening and always absent at the funeral'.[15]

CHAPTER EIGHTEEN

IN 1941 CONNOLLY befriended David Astor, a member of the wealthy Anglo-American family which in 1911 had acquired the oldest of the English Sunday newspapers, the *Observer*. Privilege for Astor entailed responsibility; his political sympathies, which at home were Liberal, extended to a passionate hostility to European fascism and a practical commitment to the German resistance to Hitler. He was familiar with the colony of expatriate German intellectuals living in London and asked Connolly to introduce him to Arthur Koestler, who became a close friend, exerting an intermittent but important influence at the *Observer* after the war.

In some respects Astor and Connolly were improbable allies, the former concealing beneath sweetness and perfect manners a moral and political seriousness which was to make his newspaper an asylum for the reforming liberals of the Fifties and Sixties. Once again, however, there was the matter of Connolly's transforming charm. At first Astor found him 'so ugly you could hardly believe it', but soon grew to suspect that he used that appearance as part of his self-projection, as a way of making himself difficult to ignore and to forget. He noted that Connolly's need to entertain was paramount and that it often took the form of stories and dramas fabricated around his friends. Koestler, an unlikely comedian, was a favourite butt, his tendency to arrive at cocktail parties uniformed and close-cropped a declaration of anti-fascist zeal which was cruelly undermined by his impotent travails in the Pioneer Corps. Connolly found such urgency irresistibly comic and was fond of jokes about Koestler's Sergeant-Major and his new vulnerability to nervous breakdowns. Astor remembered imitations delivered in a guttural and imprecise mid-European accent when the conflict in the North African theatre was dominating the headlines: 'Who shall command ze dezzert? Wavell, Orvell or Fyvel?'[1]

Astor was amused by the clowning but looked to Connolly for more than entertainment. Mindful of his commitment to Fleet Street, he was a vigilant apprentice and eager to learn the editorial strategy responsible for the success of *Horizon* – a publication he greatly admired: 'Everybody talked about it. Everybody waited for the next number.' He noticed the simplicity of Connolly's method – his indulgence of his writers' interests – and consciously emulated him after the war when he led the *Observer* to pre-eminence. However, he hoped for more than an editorial education from his friendship: pending his formal accession as editor he was in a position to make certain appointments and project future policy and was eager to begin assembling a panel of new writers. As his own interests lay more with politics than with literature he quickly saw the need for a deputy with proven judgement and connections who could run the literary page. It was a matter of importance: both Sunday newspapers relied heavily for their prestige and success on the quality of their critical articles but Astor was confident that Connolly was equal to the promotion. His editorial skills were already proverbial in London, he knew every writer worth knowing and had the charm indispensable to successful commissioning. In the spring of 1942 he offered Connolly the job of literary editor: his duties would begin at once; his salary – a generous recognition not only of his stature but of the extra burden of work he had assumed – would run to £900 per annum taking into account the £100 for expenses the critic had demanded. Astor had an enormous regard for his new colleague and was confident that his admiration had not led him astray. Nevertheless, for reassurance and for official endorsement, he decided it would be wise to introduce his friend to his father, the proprietor of the newspaper, and accordingly invited him to dinner at Cliveden. The invitation was eagerly accepted and when Connolly and Astor arrived on the appointed night they found that Astor's half-brother, Bobbie Shaw, was also of the party. Astor adored Shaw, not least because he knew that his wit and charm complemented courage and honesty and brightened dispositions of the heart which had already led to imprisonment for homosexual activities and would terminate in suicide after the death of his mother. However, such anxieties had no place that evening and the dinner was a success: Connolly was well received by Lord Astor and seemed to get on particularly well with Shaw. A few days later Astor received a telephone call from his half-brother who revealed, after pleasantries, that he had been astonished when the much-heralded saviour of the *Observer*'s literary page had been introduced: Connolly's face, always unmistakable, was familiar to him from many chance encounters in the illicit crypts of homosexual adventure. But Cliveden had not been the place for recognition and both had been blankly convivial, adherents of a crucial protocol.[2]

The appointment to the *Observer* was timely as the tenancy at Drayton Gardens had expired and Connolly was in urgent need of further accommodation. Fortunately Lys, practical as ever, quickly found their next home – a large flat perfect for entertaining in the upper storeys of 49 Bedford Square. The property was expensive but with a second salary to augment his quarterly £200 income from *Horizon* Connolly could afford it. By May he and Lys were installed and were to remain there until the end of the war. Peter Quennell moved with them to inhabit quarters in the attics and his girlfriend, Barbara Skelton, became a regular, though to Connolly not entirely welcome, presence. Out of jealousy or prurience he would complain about the noises made by the couple's bathwater and seemed generally ill-disposed towards her. Quennell, by contrast, was full of admiration for his friend's domestic arrangements: 'Cyril's household . . . was a constant source of wonder. He kept the war at bay more effectively than any other man I knew.' He did, it was true, endure one night of 'fire-watching' before managing to exempt himself and Quennell remembered that he left for his observations with 'a case of cigars, a hot-water bottle and a heavy tartan rug . . . About his own existence he drew a magic circle, within which he pursued his personal affairs and employed his native power of charming.' The household included the 'white, sulphur-crested cockatoo' which Quennell observed as being hostile to almost all human advances except Connolly's: 'At [his] approach it would immediately sink to the ground, pinions extended, crest thrown stiffly back bubbling and gurgling an insensate song of love.'[3] Connolly had helped his friend retrieve certain objects from the pawn shop and in return for this salvation and for supplying him with bedding and towels, he had laid temporary claim to Quennell's sofa and chair, his china, glass and carpets. The chair, which Quennell himself had designed, was a massive affair with broad seat and low, flat arms across which Connolly laid a board to accommodate books, pens and papers; once installed he would happily work in a semi-reclining posture. The arrangement of loans and mutual dependence worked harmoniously and Quennell's note of protest about time and monies due to the cleaning lady was exceptional: 'As to the question of Mrs Pope – of course I'll pay half her wages if you think that is right but I can't say I agree that I absorb half her time and energy . . .'[4]

49 Bedford Square had a generous dining room and drawing room and guests who came to enjoy the famous hospitality, often on business connected with *Horizon*, glimpsed another cultural headland from the windows of the apartment – the dome which spans the Reading Room of the British Museum. Lunches became a common occurrence, though it was something of a privilege to attend them. Not all guests were bohemian: Edward Hulton, owner of *Picture Post*, Mr and Mrs Hamish Hamilton and Christopher and Elizabeth Glenconner were regular visitors who usually found their host in benign and expansive mood. When Woodrow Wyatt sat at Connolly's table he encountered the familiar public front: 'When I urged him to fulfil his promise, he said, "I can't. I'm too frightened. I criticize others so much that any new book that I wrote would have to be superb or I would be sneered at. I couldn't face that. And I couldn't write a superb book."'[5] David Astor went to lunch to find a very different host. His fellow-guest was Gladwyn Jebb, Connolly's travelling companion in Germany in 1927 and now a member of one of Whitehall's most sensitive ministries, the Foreign Office. The food was delicious but what struck Astor was Connolly's direction of the conversation: betraying awe neither of the man nor of the ministry he represented the critic embarked on a description of the current state of hostilities and demanded that Jebb give some sort of interpretation. In time of war political discussion was both more urgent and more delicate: it was also technically illegal and posters were everywhere to remind the garrulous that careless talk cost lives. But somehow Connolly had retained the candour and curiosity of a civilian and felt free to turn the huge questions of war into salon gossip.

Owing to conscription and the other distractions of the time the internal organization of the *Observer* was out of joint. The editor had recently left, but it had been decided, in view of David Astor's eventual status, that a caretaker editor should steer the newspaper through the remaining years of the war. Lord Astor, the proprietor, felt that his drama critic, Ivor Brown, a respected arts journalist and a good Liberal, should oversee the interregnum, but there had been insufficient consultation between father and son and a brief conference would have revealed obvious problems: Brown would discharge editorial duties but would also continue as drama critic while Connolly, according to the promises David Astor had made him, would have jurisdiction over all the arts journalism. Brown, as editor, would therefore be submitting his writing to a man his junior in years and experience. To begin with, however, all was prosperity. The *Observer* fielded an impressive range of reviewers: Maurice Richardson, Basil de Selincourt, Frank Swinnerton and A. L. Rowse were regular contributors to the books page; C. A. Lejeune wrote about the cinema and Joyce Grenfell occasionally reviewed radio. However, Connolly had been employed as an agent of change and soon justified his salary by importing fine reviewers, among them Waugh, Orwell, Alan Pryce-Jones, Logan Pearsall Smith and Peter Quennell. He also recognized that radio played a crucial part in wartime existence and made the inspired suggestion that Tom Harrisson of Mass-Observation should be appointed the newspaper's official and permanent radio critic.

Osbert Sitwell sent congratulations on learning of Connolly's appointment: 'You are left with the responsibility for CULTURE, or whatever its new manifestation may be.'[6] Connolly needed no guidance when it came to producing an enjoyable literary digest. He wrote the leading review every other week and allowed his fancy to wander across countries and ages, veering between moods of modernism and nostalgia. Where he could be he was kind about his contemporaries and wrote affectionate praise for books by Harold Nicolson and Raymond Mortimer. He did not restrict himself to literary journalism and in August 1942, pondering the dismal state of the West End on a Saturday afternoon, he lamented the absence of organized diversion for Allied troops and suggested a World Fair: the government should secure a permanent site within easy reach of the West End where exhibition pavilions might make 'the people of this country, of the Allies and the Dominions more acquainted with each other's war effort'.

The Astors were well pleased: their new recruit had vindicated their faith and justified his ample stipend and perhaps inaugurated a new cultural elysium in their prestigious pages. As a token of esteem David Astor invited Connolly and Lys to spend a holiday on the estate his family owned on the Hebridean island of Jura. With almost no other destinations open they accepted and travelled to Scotland to join Astor and his other guest, David Owen, secretary to Stafford Cripps, who in 1942 was recalled from the ambassadorship to the Soviet Union to join Churchill's coalition cabinet.

Suddenly, however, an association begun so auspiciously began to go wrong. As early as July 1942 Astor had urged caution where Connolly hoped for quick reform: 'I know it's annoying and tiresome and probably seems very silly to you, but the process of putting any new wine at all into an old bottle has to be gone at slowly.'[7] In September Connolly approached Orwell to review O. D. Gallagher's *Retreat in the East*: the commission was accepted and Orwell was pleased to have 'got in some good cracks at the civilian community in Malaya'.[8] Connolly approved the review but Brown, as editor, vetoed it, fearing that some of its remarks could 'play into the hands of a few ill-disposed Americans'.[9] Connolly then asked his friend to review a book about Shaw but received a blunt refusal: 'I don't write for papers which do not allow at least a minimum of honesty ... I had no idea that silly old owl Brown had anything to do with the *Observer*.'[10] Quennell was invited to write a review about Horace Walpole but when he read it Astor was seized with the uneasy suspicion that while Connolly's association had brought many blessings it might end with the *Observer*'s becoming a broadsheet from the ivory tower. He expressed tentative reservations: it was not merely that he thought the subject matter too arcane for a national newspaper but that he disliked Quennell's writing, finding it 'so consciously fastidious that it becomes clownish'.[11] Connolly responded immoderately and now began to stigmatize Ivor Brown as 'middle-aged, middle-class and middle-brow' and as relations deteriorated in an atmosphere of annoyance and distrust he started to voice his resentment towards the Astors to anybody who would listen. By the summer of 1943 even the gentle David Astor found his patience tried beyond endurance and on 20 August he sent his literary editor a polite yet persuasive reproach: 'You have frequently tried to convince me that I am cynical, unscrupulous, power-seeking, uncouth, barbarous; that I am an enemy of intellectuals and a disparager of art ... These views of me are now given at dinner parties by your friends whom I don't even know.'[12] There was a final meeting at White's Club. Connolly said: 'You've let me down.' Astor replied: 'I only gave you a hope and an intention.'[13] Connolly accused him of malpractice and Astor said that he lied in the accusation. Connolly walked out, leaving Astor sitting in a club to which he did not belong. At the beginning of September Lord Astor fired his literary editor, but not before the latter had reviewed *A Bibliography of the Strawberry Hill Press*, a book which he admitted was 'expensive, difficult to obtain and only of interest to a very few people'.[14]

While Connolly had been engaged in securing Orwell's services for the *Observer* the latter had been employed by the BBC in the Indian Section of the Empire Service. The nature of his programme was notional, since the wavelength never reached India, and realizing this deficiency Orwell commissioned writers to discuss anything they liked. India's loss was broadcasting's gain: he assembled a distinguished range of speakers, among them Forster, Eliot, Edmund Blunden and Herbert Read. He asked Connolly to contribute, and *Literature in the Nineteen-Thirties* was broadcast on 31 March 1942. Already Connolly found the decade a distant one: 'To go back to the Thirties now involves an effort of will and imagination; it is like going back to the dentist's waiting room.' He saw the principal figures of the group as constituting a self-conscious school, a school which had failed, given its aim to subvert the catastrophe of war through writing. It was unfortunate that in the course of his summary he dismissed Stephen Spender as 'an indifferent poet with an outstanding clumsiness of mind and a very bad ear'.[15] Spender was hurt and resolved not to see his tactless friend for a few days, knowing that he was too neurotic and sensitive not to notice the absence. 'Soon I received a letter from him in which he explained that he had been puzzled by my silence; but now he had been told the reason for it he could not understand my avoiding him because he had assumed that I would realize that his remarks were "only for India".'[16]

Meanwhile in February, *Horizon* had published another essay by Orwell. 'Rudyard Kipling' began as a review of *A Choice of Kipling's Verse*, recently edited by T. S. Eliot, but developed into a lengthy celebration of the poet both Orwell and Connolly admired as schoolboys. Connolly's later rejection was part of a larger repudiation of paternal values but Orwell remained more loyal: he was fascinated by popular culture; he had seen imperial service, though not in Kipling's India; and he had an instinctive understanding of those qualities of snobbery and nostalgia which led many of the progressive intellectuals of his generation to denounce the balladist of the Raj. His persuasive defence, another example of Connolly's inspired matching of subject and author, maintained that Kipling was an eternal victim of fashionable politics, although not everybody caught the direction of his sympathy and Duff Cooper sent Connolly a testy response: 'When the highbrows start writing about Kipling they usually disclose the fact that they have not read him. There is no mention, for instance, in Orwell's article of the fact that Kipling was the greatest short story writer in the English language.'[17]

Matthew Connolly, a great admirer of the poet, no doubt read the defence but left no recorded opinions. Relations between father and son continued to be more harmonious, to the extent that Connolly had employed meticulous Matthew to do some indexing for *Horizon* the previous year. He was still living in South Kensington and now found his son's writings more to his taste – in September he commended what he had read in the *Observer* and *Horizon* for being constructive and sensible. His life was absorbed by his conchological activities at the Natural History Museum and beyond his son's company he seems to have had only one other distraction, the nude shows, or tableaux, which were the speciality of the Windmill Theatre in Soho.

Presently he acquired a new colleague at the museum, Tom Pain, another amateur who worked in the conchology department and who discovered a truculent perfectionist whose moods had earned him a forbidding reputation amongst the museum staff. He saw that the Major 'was not an easy man' and adopted the understanding prevalent in the department, that his irritability was exacerbated, if not caused, by discomfort in his legs. Pain sensed that the Major disregarded medical advice, eating, and more particularly, drinking, what he liked, subject to wartime availability. He soon saw that he stood apart from the labours of his associates: 'Connolly worked only for Connolly', his autonomy no doubt a reflection of his stature and authority, and to Pain's amusement he addressed his assistants as 'varlets'. He delivered papers fluently and confidently and could be charming, particularly to pretty girls. He particularly treasured a shell in his own collection which he had found after the battle of Ondurman. Pain only met Cyril Connolly once, when he came to collect his father at the museum, and the latter did little to try to impress his colleague: 'My son's coming today. You'll have to meet him. He's a perfect bloody fool.'[18]

The Major retained contact with Maud and gave her occasional details about the son she so rarely saw. She had heard about Lys, one undated letter revealed, and had said nothing, 'because your life is your own'.[19] Meanwhile thoughts of Jean continued to plague Connolly: the intervening Atlantic had only fortified his determination to maintain communication, however great the difficulties and unreliable the couriers. In June 1942 an unseemly incident suggested that he would be better advised in future to commit his letters to the post rather than entrusting them to personnel posted overseas. He had given a letter to Jean to Brian Howard, whose involvement with a merchant seaman seemed to offer a convenient channel of communication. Shortly afterwards he went out for dinner with Howard, the sailor and the Philip Toynbees. During the course of the evening, inflamed with alcohol, Howard began to quote sentences that sounded familiar to Connolly, including one lament, 'I'm so tired of not being respectable', that convinced him the letter had been opened – and not by any official censor. He was humiliated and angry but memories and hopes of Jean, intensified by absence, fermented in his mind and soon he began to compile a journal and commonplace book which set his own reflections on memory, happiness and loss beside those of the great writers he admired. 'He was suffering,' he later said of himself, 'from a private grief, – a separation for which he felt to blame.'[20] This melancholia, sanctioned and distilled in epigram and apt quotation, was the beginning of *The Unquiet Grave*, which was published by *Horizon* in December 1944.

In professional terms, apart from the disappointment at the *Observer*, Connolly had no cause for regret. Indeed he was now more successful, influential and highly regarded than he had ever been before, a status implied in July 1942 when *Vogue* ran an article called 'Brains To Trust' which claimed that a new fashion for artistic excellence had swept the country. The magazine identified the representatives of this resurgence – Cyril Connolly, Raymond Mortimer, C. A. Lejeune, Rebecca West, Eddy Sackville-West, Cecil Day-Lewis and the RAF propagandist H. St George Saunders – and considered *Horizon*, 'low-priced and high-minded', a typical product of the new discrimination which transcended regions, fashions and classes.

In September Connolly received a very different accolade when, proposed by Richard Wyndham and seconded by Lord Antrim, he was elected to membership of White's, the great Tory club in the famous bow window of which Beau Brummel had sat in unchallenged judgement of all St James's. During the Regency White's was said to be the club from which the socially ambitious might die of exclusion, and although wartime membership conferred a less dramatic reprieve it was still a mark of distinction Connolly treasured. Waugh, elected the previous year, sent congratulations: White's was the only club 'that has the coffee house character – one goes to talk to the other members, not to entertain strangers'.[21] Connolly remained an enthusiastic member, using the club to entertain male friends for the rest of his life. He also gave his father lunch there on more than one occasion, an act which Quennell felt 'demonstrated a certain courage'.[22]

Meanwhile the success which *Horizon* had earned had begun to dull its editor's enthusiasm and in the autumn of 1942 he felt the first stirrings of boredom with the enterprise. In October's 'Comment' he remarked that with the magazine 'an established institution it is beginning to suffer from the atrophy of its years'. Part of the problem was the constancy of circulation: the stimulus of ambitious sales was lacking, as was the fear of unsold copies. In December he returned to his theme of disillusion and wondered in 'Comment' whether the magazine had already seen its best days and whether it was desirable to sustain the enterprise beyond its first fifty numbers. Some of this boredom communicated itself to contributors and Osbert Sitwell sent a letter of sympathetic understanding: 'I do feel intensely for you – 35–40 should be a lovely age, bringing a ripening of the senses and a focussing of the powers; how can it be so now? . . . The only thing we can do is to look at history, and at fate, without a loss of nerve, or any weakening that we can help of mental fibre.'[23]

As a distraction from the labours of the magazine Connolly turned his mind to other literary ambitions. He was still in correspondence with Routledge – and still in debt, owing to an uncompleted transaction from the late Thirties when the publishers had advanced him money against a novel which had never been written. There was also the matter of the collection of essays which had been mooted years ago and provisionally entitled 'The Little Voice'. On New Year's Day 1943 Connolly wrote to Herbert Read at Routledge to explain his position. He still felt it might be possible to write the novel and his only anxiety about releasing a collection of essays and reviews was that his journalism seemed too inconsistent to merit the flattery of hard book covers. Nevertheless, he remained hopeful of honouring commitments: 'The only thing the war has taught me however is to enjoy regular work, and I hope that with this new and unexpected asset, the *habit* of work, I will be able to write more books in the future.'[24] In another undated letter he mentioned his ambitions for realizing several literary ventures related to France: one possibility, which clearly could not be resolved during hostilities, was a book about French rivers with photography by Richard Wyndham; another, more practicable at the moment, was to produce a series of interconnected stories illustrative of French life, a

Gallic *Goodbye to Berlin*; another was to address the long-term nature of the Anglo-French destiny: 'England after the war will be a poorer country, either reactionary (like Hungary) or progressive (with labour government) like Scandinavia. France will be the same. Only real federation and union between the two will make them once more equal to great neutrals like America.'[25]

In March he returned to the pages of the *New Statesman* and wrote its 'London Diary'. In the issue of 20 March he allowed his fancy free reign and imagined how Voltaire would respond to the London of 1943, with its cultural apathy, its anti-intellectualism and the sterility of its politics. The following week, after a visit to Oxford, he declared that the churches, libraries and theatres of the university represented the ideas and freedoms for which the war was being fought. In May, in a bid to create the illusion of travel, he went to Scotland to stay with Lord Glenconner. Work detained Lys in London and she had to content herself with assurances that he would take her on holiday in the south of France as soon as the war was over. At the invitation of the British Council Connolly delivered a lecture at the Franco-Scottish House in Edinburgh on 'French and English Cultural Relations' and in June the talk was published in *Horizon*. For many months now it had been a theory of Connolly's that war shrinks the imagination and that the great literary masterpieces of the past were sometimes prone to assume, if not an irrelevance, then an incongruity in the face of world-wide destruction. In Scotland he renewed his warnings against nationalism and urged the collaboration of French and English artists, but most of the lecture was devoted to a celebration of the Gallic genius. Having invited his audience to roam with him across a map of Europe in search of the birthplaces of vision and greatness he assembled a list of important twentieth-century intellectuals. Finally he came to France: 'Here we find such an astounding collection of great painters and writers ... and we feel like elephant hunters who have been stalking a solitary animal and who suddenly discover, browsing by their favourite river, the majestic herd.' Some of the new names he proclaimed were little known at the time, while others – Aragon, Jarry, Malraux – now seem talented rather than immortally brilliant. He had explanations for the cultural richness he found in France: the French took their artists and intellectuals more seriously than the English and offered their visionaries anonymity, a good climate, cheap food and wine, numerous and inspiring treasure-houses of art and architecture. The writer could use 'the Mediterranean for a sun-lamp, and Paris as his oxygen-tent'.[26]

Such partisanship was symptomatic of the francophilia of his generation and was fortified in Connolly's case by a longing to escape England which had been frustrated for four years. Switzerland, Spain, North Africa, Italy, above all France, were out of bounds, their attractions intensified in the dull unyielding English light, the happiness of their memories amplified by time and routine. Connolly's mood was inevitably *Horizon*'s: it had been one of the magazine's glories that it disdained xenophobia in favour of artistic broadmindedness but now French culture was given increasing prominence in its pages and readers were offered essays on Flaubert, Aragon, Proust, Balzac, Mallarmé, Molière, Magritte, interviews with Gide, poems by Eluard. Arthur Koestler, English only by adoption and so perhaps more aware of the self-deprecating nature of English genius, observed the inclination and saw it as being part of a larger pattern. In November he published an article in *Tribune* which announced that 'the managerial class on Parnassus have lately been affected by a new outbreak of that recurrent epidemic, the French 'Flu. Its symptoms are that the patient, ordinarily a balanced, cautious, sceptical man, is lured into unconditional surrender of his critical faculties when a line of French poetry or prose falls under his eyes.' He denounced Gide, then at the zenith of his English popularity, for 'esoteric arrogance', while Aragon struck him as being no more than 'a competent craftsman, one among the larger frogs of the smaller puddles'.[27] His article was not intended as an indirect onslaught on Connolly. Nevertheless, knowing his friend's insecurity and vulnerability, he deemed it wise to write stressing that no malice or personal attack was intended. The episode led to no ill-feeling, not least because Connolly had learnt by then that the émigré was not always the embodiment of tact and that he often appeared more forbidding and inflexible than he really was.

CHAPTER NINETEEN

IN SEPTEMBER CONNOLLY was forty years old and it may have been in recognition of this event that Evelyn Waugh and Nancy Mitford were invited to dinner to find themselves tempted by truffles and lobster, the delicacies of a distant time. Waugh had come to expect fine food at Connolly's table, with or without rationing, and made no comment about the evening, beyond observing that Lys 'loves me still'.[1] He was himself only weeks away from the same portals of middle age and perhaps reluctant to instigate an analysis which would inevitably entail dismal stock-taking and the suspicion that life is a disappointment. Connolly, however, had no illusions about himself and for all his romanticism was never incapable of standing back in sceptical self-appraisal. Just before the anniversary turned he had been consumed with despair: despite the success of *Horizon* he had felt 'a sense of total failure: not a writer but a ham actor whose performance is clotted with egotism ... Never will I make that extra effort to live according to reality which alone makes good writing possible: hence the manic-depressiveness of my style, – which is either bright, cruel and superficial; or pessimistic; moth-eaten with self-pity.' He saw himself torn between the desire to inhabit the past, thus satisfying the promptings of nostalgia, and to fully experience the present. Unfortunately the second imperative too often took the form of an urge towards sensual gratification: 'Both my happiness and unhappiness I owe to the love of pleasure: of sex, travel, reading, conversation (hearing oneself talk), food, drink, cigars and lying in warm water.'[2]

The sense of defeat which oppressed him as his thirties drained away was not merely subjective. Raymond Mortimer and Elizabeth Bowen spoke publicly about a present reality too monstrous and large to promote the functions of literary creativity, while Philip Toynbee concluded that many writers, inhibited by censorship, paper rationing, conscription and chaos, had been driven into a kind of internal exile where communication with their fellows, the fundamental alphabetic instinct, had been rendered impossible. More than ever a beacon was needed: whatever Connolly's inner suspicions of futility, *Horizon* must continue to show an affirming flame: established writers must be comforted and the unknown given succour if writing were not to be demoted, like food and clothes, to mere utility. Two years previously he had inaugurated the literary career of Denton Welch by publishing the latter's unsolicited account of a visit to the ageing Walter Sickert. In April 1944 he reiterated his faith in Welch's talent by printing 'When I Was Thirteen', a story with homosexual themes which the author had been unable to place elsewhere. *Horizon* had a few letters of complaint but many more expressions of enthusiasm. Welch received fourteen guineas for his offering and a subsequent assurance from Connolly that Hamish Hamilton was thinking of offering him a contract on a volume of short stories.

The critic had long extolled the work of Ernest Hemingway and in May the novelist arrived in London as a war correspondent on the eve of the Normandy Landings. The arrival of any writer was always an occasion for a party and as soon as they had renewed their friendship Connolly initiated plans for a celebration in Bedford Square. Hemingway was enthusiastic, to the extent that he insisted on supervising the drink; John Craxton attended the evening and well remembered the delicious and intoxicating punch which the guest of honour mixed. Connolly also decided to introduce his new friend to the American-born society hostess Emerald Cunard, and took him to the suite at The Dorchester which was her wartime shelter. His reasons for the pilgrimage are obscure but he can never have imagined that he was supervising a marriage of true minds. The Soviets were now allies; but Lady Cunard, eager for an assessment of their national character, may have found the novelist's response – 'There is the pro as well as the con about Russia. As with all these fucking countries' – frustratingly opaque, while Hemingway would not have welcomed her opinion that he was 'androgynous', a view which surprised Connolly.[3] The American left London and was never again to be a major presence in Connolly's life. Nevertheless a friendship founded in abiding admiration had been confirmed: for the latter, Hemingway embodied the glamorous life of action laced with danger and transmuted into fiction, while the novelist caught an enticing reflection in Connolly, who could also be militant and strenuous, though in defence of very different values. Later he would write to salute that integrity: 'I always get involved in wars but I admired the way that you did not. It would be wrong for me not to fight but it was many times righter for you to do exactly as you did ... Cyril we were born into almost the worst fucking time there has ever been. And yet we have had almost as much fun as anyone ever had.'[4]

By the summer of 1944, with the success of D-Day, the war had turned in the Allies' favour and Hitler initiated a last attempt to subjugate London with the deployment of his V-1 bombs. During the Blitz Connolly had surprised friends with his displays of composure and courage but he was unable to continue so imperturbably in the face of this new assault: the 'doodle bugs', as they were known, had roaring engines which fell ominously silent immediately before explosion and by June more than fifty were falling on London every day. Connolly and Lys saw a woman killed in the street right before their eyes and found her severed hand beside a railing. Bedford Square was directly hit and it was then, with great reluctance, that he finally agreed to resort to air-raid shelters during an attack. However, comfort must not be compromised and Lys remembered that he went to the shelter with blankets, a flask, cigars and a hot-water bottle. Even with these accessories the noises, smells and crowds oppressed him and he and Lys braved the remainder of the bombs at home. At dinner in July he complained of the terror to Harold Nicolson, James Pope-Hennessy and Philip Toynbee. Nicolson rebuked him gently and urged him to consider those of his dear ones who were in yet graver danger at the front. But the willingness to count blessings is a disposition inherited rather than learnt; Connolly quickly retrieved Nicolson from error: 'That wouldn't work with me at all, Harold. In the first place, I have no dear ones at the front. And in the second place, I have observed that with me perfect fear casteth out love.'[5]

Meanwhile, beneath these public vicissitudes there lay the flux of Connolly's moods – the depression he had noted on the eve of his birthday and the uncertainties of his marital state. Lys secured a divorce from Ian Lubbock, with Connolly cited as co-respondent; and in 1944 he sent word to Jean that unless she either returned to England or gave proof of a desire to do so, he would instigate divorce proceedings. His marriage had been a dead letter for several years but confronting its collapse was not easy: blame had to be apportioned, the past revisited, and all against a backdrop of derelict reality which must have seemed at times as though it would never end, never allow for the resumption and the hope of pleasure. For all his assurances to Routledge he was undistracted by new literary ambitions and like Raymond Mortimer and Elizabeth Bowen he realized that the visible and discordant interventions of history, far from being inspirational, could paralyse imagination and creativity. While hostilities continued it seemed impossible that novels could be wrested from the chaos: the angry present defied the ordering principles of art. Connolly knew many of the writers who in consequence turned in on themselves and their memories in search of literary material but he was not consciously of their number when he began randomly to keep a journal in 1942. Instead, like Eliot before him, he wanted to shore fragments against his ruins, to capture on paper his moments of happiness with Jean and to cherish the wisdom of his favourite French writers. A year later he found himself with three notebooks full of reflections of his own and excerpts from other writers and it suddenly occurred to him that a kind of plot lay within the anthology. A further year of editing and rearrangement saw him invoke the myth of Palinurus as a structure around which to assemble the *pensées*, and in December 1944 *The Unquiet Grave* went on sale in a limited edition of 1000 printed by the Curwen Press and published by *Horizon*.

The book appeared anonymously, its subtitle, 'A Word Cycle by Palinurus', giving no clue of authorship to those outside the circle of friends and writers associated with the magazine. He took his informing symbolism from the *Aeneid*: Palinurus was the pilot appointed by Aeneas to guide his ship on the voyage from Troy to Italy. Asleep at the tiller, he fell into the sea where he survived three days before being swept ashore and murdered for his clothes by savages on an alien beach. His naked body was left unburied, his spirit therefore being denied repose, and when Aeneas visited the underworld he was petitioned for formal burial by his pilot's spirit, hitherto tenant of an unquiet grave. The legend had always fascinated Connolly; he had alluded to it in his first signed review and now found increasing significance in the myth: 'Palinurus clearly stands for a certain will-to-failure or repugnance-to-success, a desire to give up at the last moment, an urge towards loneliness, isolation and obscurity. Palinurus, in spite of his great ability and his conspicuous public position, deserted his post in the moment of victory and opted for the unknown shore.'[6]

Yet although the pilot is a haunting presence in *The Unquiet Grave*, the book remains Connolly's triumph of self-portraiture. He divided it into three sections, 'Ecce Gubernator', 'Te Palinure Petens' and 'La Clé des Chants', and insisted that the whole represented a periplus, or intellectual voyage, encompassing despair, descent and redemption. The first section ('Behold the pilot') presents 'Palinurus', the creator of the word-cycle – a figure distracted by the imminence of his fortieth year ('sombre anniversary to the hedonist') and convinced that literature has only one lesson for its practitioners: 'The more books we read, the clearer it becomes that the true function of a writer is to produce a masterpiece.'[7] Palinurus is a figure preoccupied with thoughts of abandonment and misery: 'So much draws on infidelity and emotional impermanence. As we leave others so shall we be left.' Between vindicating epigrams and excerpts from Pascal and Leopardi he reveals an emotional pessimism: 'Two fears alternate in marriage, of loneliness and of bondage. The dread of loneliness being keener than the fear of bondage, we get married.' He is also a man plagued by memories of lost happiness: 'Summer night, limes in flower . . . sensation of what is lost: lost love, lost youth, lost Paris.'[8] He finds some consolation, however, in a keen and poetic observation of nature: 'For the hundredth time I remark with wonder how the leaves and sprays of the plane-tree forge the pendulous signature of the vine!'

The first section ends with Palinurus overwhelmed with angst, that condition of guilt and morbid despair which Connolly made fashionable in the Forties, and contemplating suicide. The second section ('Looking for you, Palinurus') is superintended by the spirits of Sainte-Beuve and Chamfort and establishes the origins of the angst which plagues Palinurus: 'Tout mon mal vient de Paris.'[9] The obsession with suicide increases but an intimation of salvation appears: 'Ghosts of the lemurs, intercede for me; plane-tree and laurel-rose, shade me; summer rain on quays of Toulon, wash me away.' Palinurus defines the condition, almost need, of having two simultaneous objects of love: 'The two faces. Everything connected with them is excruciating: people, places, sounds, smells, habits.' Invoking Jean, Bobbie and Diana, he admits to the ecstasy of lost love: 'For a dark play-girl in a night-club I have pined away, for a dead school boy, for a bright angel-vixen I have wept in vain.'[10] The last and finest section ('The key to the songs') contains re-creations of remembered happiness: of driving through the south of France with Janetta on the eve of war; of his earliest days in Paris with Jean; of indulgence plucked before the whirlwind – 'Head-lines about the Spanish war soaked in sunbathing oil, torn maps, the wet bathing-dress wrapped in a towel'. He recollects the ferrets and lemurs, now symbols of guiltless carnality and gratification, and experiences a cath-arsis after reaching forty: 'We must select the Illusion which appeals to our temperament and embrace it with passion.'[11]

Connolly was aware that critics might see *The Unquiet Grave* as nothing more than 'a collection of extracts chosen with "outre-mer" snobbery and masquerading as a book', and Herbert Read, who per-haps had good reason for antipathy, was inclined to agree. He praised the book's treatment of the artist and his position in modern society but felt that Connolly's 'moralizings on life in general are rather superficial, and clumsy in comparison with the quotations in which they are embedded. It is a fallacy to imagine that one enhances one's own jewels ... by setting them in other people's gold.'[12] Read was being both unfair and insensitive. He knew that there was an art to quotation and that it was possible – as demonstrated by T. S. Eliot in *The Waste Land* and Thomas Gray in numerous poems – to form an altogether different whole from the sum of diverse borrowed components. It was not as though Connolly attempted to claim other writers' wisdom as his own; and it would be fairer to see *The Unquiet Grave* as the fruit of a lifetime's discriminating reading rather than an attempt to weave gar-lands from other men's flowers. It might be more pertinent to say that if *The Unquiet Grave* has any coherence then it is a coherence based on self-indulgence and nostalgia. In this regard it has often been seen as a companion volume to Evelyn Waugh's *Brideshead Revisited* which appeared the following year: both were books written after years of deprivation by writers starved of the luxuries and glamour of worlds they either remembered or imagined, although Connolly's nostalgia was without the propagandist ambitions of Waugh's sumptuous yet tendentious fiction; and if *The Unquiet Grave* is a monument to hedon-ism and self-pity, it is a monument nevertheless when much of the war's more selfless writing has been forgotten. Indeed one of its admirers, Gavin Ewart, went so far as to see it as 'the Great Missing War Poem of World War II ... out of the misery, blackouts, rationing, boredom, bureaucracy and bombing of a war which was essentially a Civilian War, out of his lost love, lost youth and exile's longing for France and civilized values ... [Connolly] built an elegiac poem of great beauty and power.'[13]

The limited edition sold out but negotiations had already opened

with Hamish Hamilton, who employed Connolly as a literary consultant, to produce a second edition in 1945 in England and America – the
English edition would be priced at about 8 shillings and its author
would probably receive a flat royalty of 15 per cent. Meanwhile letters
of congratulation gradually arrived from enthusiasts any writer would
be pleased to acknowledge: Quentin Bell, Aldous Huxley, Bernard
Berenson, Nancy Mitford, Hamish Hamilton, Noël Coward and
Augustus John. Desmond MacCarthy was greatly impressed and wrote
to assure his former disciple of having made 'a permanent contribution
to the literature of introspection ... So you need never lament over
yourself as a literary failure.'[14] Matthew found the book 'recondite and
brilliantly clever';[15] Maud, when she eventually received a copy, felt
convinced that it would have an enduring success. Nevertheless she
noted its melancholy and wondered whence it came: 'I cannot help
wondering if you were born lonely.'[16] When the book appeared in
America one of its most eager readers was Jean, who sent perceptive
praise: 'I think you are one of the few people whom self-pity or
unhappiness develops rather than shuts in. Only you mustn't stop there,
let the next grave be a pyramid.'[17] It was not only in New York that the
book earned acclaim and in southern California Connolly could now
number Orson Welles, Joseph Cotten and Tallulah Bankhead among
his admirers.

Gratifying and significant praise came from Edmund Wilson, the
most influential American critic of his day and in some respects a
kindred spirit of Connolly's. Appraising *The Unquiet Grave* in the *New
Yorker* he held it to represent one of the most significant cultural
achievements of the war: 'One used to hear it said in London that Cyril
Connolly was out of key with the wartime state of mind, but I think we
ought to be grateful that ... one good writer has persisted in producing,
not what patriotism demanded, but a true natural history of his wartime morale.'[18] Sadly, the admiration of a discriminating few did not
constitute certain wealth and although 1750 American copies were sold
when the book went on sale Connolly was disappointed by his first
transatlantic royalty statement, which he received on 23 October 1945.
It transpired that his advance, despite having been paid in sterling, was
subject to American tax, and he was left with a net credit of £35 and
ideas about how to negotiate future sales to the United States: henceforth, he assured Hamish Hamilton, he would ask for payment in kind
– two armchairs and a sofa or else carpets by the square yard. He was

able to find consolation in reviews he received in England, however. In the *Tatler* Elizabeth Bowen, conceding that the book was 'not for the vague enjoyment of the many ... but for the exquisite enjoyment of a few', isolated what she considered its crucial achievement: 'The prose style, at once taut and supple, disciplined and sensuous, is of a quality we are seldom given.'[19] In the *New Statesman* Raymond Mortimer suggested that Connolly described the faithless void of the times: 'Lacking Grace to be either Catholic or Communist, Palinurus is doubly outflanked ... Trumpeting of the rogue elephant? Braying of the unfertile mule? Such will be the judgement of the innocent, the hearty, the devout and the envious. But some of us must welcome with pondering gratitude this unknown brother who catches the heart with his penetration into anxieties so akin to our own.'[20] In the *Observer* George Orwell also indicated a belief that the author of *The Unquiet Grave* embodied a prevailing sensibility: 'On almost every page this book exhibits that queer product of capitalist democracy, an inferiority complex resulting from a private income.' He commended the book as a 'valuable document' and applauded its creator for his refusal to 'desert the sinking ship of individualism'.[21]

It might be argued that these tributes were scarcely unexpected: the reviewers, after all, knew and liked the author. However, the ambivalence of friends is more potent than the hostility of enemies and no onslaught Connolly expected could have been as unsettling as the ambiguous regard of his friend Evelyn Waugh, who appraised Hamish Hamilton's reissue of *The Unquiet Grave* in *The Tablet*. He had been sent copy ninety-nine of the *Horizon* limited edition by Nancy Mitford while stationed in Dubrovnik. Lonely Balkan nights found him eager for diversion and he read the book at least twice before annotating it heavily. The review which appeared in *The Tablet* was a more seasoned, less revealing version of these marginalia, which indicated that while he had nothing but praise for his friend's evocative descriptive passages, Waugh was profoundly aggravated by Connolly's observations about religion, politics, psychology and popular culture. Yet he could never dismiss him: he admired his prose too highly and in the midst of his contempt he too acknowledged his status as a figure representative of his age: 'Why should I be interested in this book? ... Because Cyril is the most typical man of my generation. There but for the Grace of God literally ... He has the authentic lack of scholarship of my generation ... the authentic love of leisure and liberty and good-living, the authentic romantic snobbery, the authentic waste-land despair, the authentic high gift of expression.' He vented his irritation in abuse which was not only gratuitous but also tellingly vitriolic, seeing him as 'the Irish boy, the immigrant, home-sick, down at heel and ashamed, full of fun in the public house, a ready quotation on his lips, afraid of witches, afraid of the bog priest, proud of his capers'.[22]

CHAPTER TWENTY

AT THE END OF 1944, as though in answer to the recurrent prayer of *The Unquiet Grave*, Connolly secured permission as a journalist to visit Paris, which had been liberated in August. As the city remained almost inaccessible except to military and government personnel there was something approaching trepidation in the curiosity of its veteran pilgrims, a trepidation succinctly put by E. M. Forster: 'I envy your going to Paris, and I shall know later whether I envy your being there.'[1] Leaving Lys at home, Connolly arrived in January 1945 to discover a city which, compared to London, had largely escaped physical injury. Yet Paris cowered under a more sinister legacy which combined inevitable shortages of fuel and food with pandemic distrust and recrimination. His first report home was discouraging and he asked Lys to assure Peter Watson that he was missing nothing: it was no longer the metropolis they knew but 'an unreal city'.[2] He was fortunate in being able to stay with Duff and Diana Cooper, who had just begun their incumbency at the British Embassy, and he adapted quickly to the island of luxury over which they presided, the only place in the city, Lys learned, supplied with hot water. His hostess encouraged him not only to attend embassy receptions but to give a party of his own, to which he invited several writers including André Gide; literary Paris would not deny him: no one outside France had done more to serve the morale and purpose of contemporary French literature and she noted that Connolly was 'fêted as tho' he were Voltaire returned'.[3]

Beyond this sanctuary the familiar squares and avenues now seemed forbidding, and *Horizon*'s readers later learned that 'the heavy snow and the emptiness made the city resemble Vienna or Petrograd'. With influential friends Connolly gained access to some of its newer and less edifying monuments: 'We were taken to see one of the worst of their torture chambers, the shooting gallery at Issy, a closed shed where not one survivor had been found to explain the meaning of the innumerable impressions of hands on the asbestos walls.' What impressed him most was the perpetuation of literature in conditions of such extremity and despair: he had never doubted the resilience of the French genius but it was only now that he could grasp the bravery of its custodians: 'It is to be wondered that once [the Resistance] had learnt to watch their friends die in agony and to carry their own death with them in a capsule as their most precious possession, any of them could even contemplate literature, as an end in itself and not merely a means for bringing people back to the truth.'[4] Yet when he ran into Hemingway the novelist found him buoyant. For all the horror and disappointment, Connolly was delighted to be out of England and after initial confusion his francophilia was irrepressible. He visited the publisher Gallimard and the critic Jean Paulhan and interviewed the ineffable Valéry shortly before his death: 'As always when meeting these great writers whom for years one has loved and admired there is a sense of inadequacy, for how can one communicate to a small mocking figure across a tea-table the glory of the wake which the passage of the great vessel of his work has left for over twenty years across the ocean of European thought?'[5]

Despite the shortages of cakes and ale the cafés were already in operation and Connolly prowled the Left Bank, frequenting particularly the Café Flore near Saint-Germain-des-Prés and savouring the glamorous difference of French literary life for his report in *Horizon*. The regular presence of Jean-Paul Sartre and Simone de Beauvoir made the Café Flore abidingly famous but during Connolly's visit the philosopher was absent in America. He found Madame de Beauvoir eager to discuss Orwell and Koestler, however, and took away from these colloquies a copy of Sartre's manifesto for *Les Temps Modernes*, the magazine with which he soon consolidated his position in intellectual France. In the May number of *Horizon* Connolly scored a triumph with the advance publication of a fragment of this manifesto, which appeared under the title 'Case For Responsible Literature'. Meanwhile, released from its shackles, literary Paris seemed reborn and the visitor enviously surveyed its tumult and the ambitions of Eluard and Aragon, Sartre and Camus, Cocteau and Genet – and thought dismally of *Punch* and Bloomsbury: 'The English literary world is not a world of ideas but of personalities, a world of clubs and honours and ancestor-worship and engagement-books, where a writer one wants to meet has to be hunted down for several weeks until he is finally coralled at bay under some formidable mantelpiece.'[6] Under the dramatic banner 'News Out

Of France', the whole of the May number of *Horizon* was committed to
a survey of contemporary French genius, with Sartre, Valéry and Jean
Paulhan sharing its pages with Philip Toynbee on modern French
literature, John Russell on the existential theatre and Stephen Spender
on French wartime poetry. The remainder of 1945 saw many articles
which covered the same domain: an interview with André Malraux,
pictures by Beaton of Picasso's studio, an article on Braque translated
by Peter Watson and another by A. J. Ayer on Sartre; essays on
Apollinaire and Gide and Acts One and Two of Jarry's *Ubu Cocu*,
translated by Connolly himself.

Returning to England, he determined that French writers and readers
should know something of English writing during the war and
envisaged a special number of *Horizon*, for sale only in France, to be
called *La Littérature anglaise pendant la guerre*. He drafted a three-
clause questionnaire which was despatched to various writers who were
asked to reply 'with perfect freedom' and promised a fee in return. The
response was gratifying in its promptness and seriousness and the
special number was ready for the summer: the Curwen Press invoiced
Horizon for £372 in July and the Ministry of Information distributed
10,000 copies in France. The questions the writers were asked to
deliberate were obvious enough: the best books published in England
during the war; favourite wartime reading; and the outlook for English
literature and culture. Several respondents, including Philip Toynbee,
Elizabeth Bowen and the distinguished historian C. V. Wedgwood,
nominated *The Unquiet Grave* as their favourite wartime reading. In
general the respondents were pessimistic. Osbert Sitwell was almost
bitter: 'Football, cricket, dog-racing, physical jerks, all will prosper,
and the devastated sites of cathedrals and libraries will, when cleared,
make excellent youth-movement centres . . . the outlook for literature is
good – for those who dislike it.' Graham Greene was no more reassuring: 'I should say that the outlook was far too dark for one to observe
anything at all.' Clive Bell told the same tale: 'The ignorance of the
rising generation is matched by its self-complacency. I foresee nothing
likely to cause improvement.' Even John Lehmann, more optimistic
than most, was cautious: 'Much will depend . . . on men of outstanding
talent or genius emerging to crystallize some of the diverse possibilities
that are in solution in the muddy mixture of the present.'[7]

The war was almost won by the time these opinions were recruited
and writers had the opportunity to learn of even graver problems:

Connolly was visited by Dylan Thomas just after he had seen footage of the atrocities at Belsen and the poet described a vivid image, of a starving man trying to pluck a handful of grass. Such information seemed too large for comprehension and if the contemplative sought instruction from the war, it was of a personal nature. Evelyn Waugh had written at its outset that 'its value for us would be to show us finally that we were not men of action' and admitted that he had taken longer than most to learn that lesson.[8] In that sense Connolly had never been a self-deceiver and no other writer of his age could look back on a war so dedicated to literature.

Beyond the fact of victory it was difficult for anybody to find hope or reassurance from the fallen masonry. Elizabeth Bowen, however, wrote to Connolly shortly after VE Day and told him that she had been trying to identify those people to whom 'one owes something better than mere survival'. Churchill's candidacy was obvious but she recognized another contender:

> I thought, and think, of you: I know that many of us owe you a lot, and I do certainly. *Horizon* has been most valuable of all as evidence of continuity; and you've done so much for this continuity in your person. Your parties had something more than even your and Lys's beautiful hospitality can account for, and something without which even intellectual happiness would be desperate: real spirit . . . There has been no one else who, since 1939, has been, done and made just what, indefinably but outstandingly, you have.[9]

The novelist was indeed a regular guest at Connolly's *salons* and attended parties he gave in Bedford Square for Aragon and Edmund Wilson, neither of which was without misadventure. Aragon arrived with Paul Eluard's wife, whom he later married, and found a distinguished company which included the Hamish Hamiltons and a more than usually drunk Philip Toynbee gathered to greet him. Elizabeth Bowen noted tensions:

> I don't think anybody liked [Aragon] particularly, but everybody was, literally, fascinated. Cyril had invited a ring of poets. Nancy [Mitford] distinguished herself by standing in the middle of the room and saying in her clear, high voice, 'Of course, I think Aragon's marvellous – what a pity we haven't got any poets in this country!' Eliot and all the others merely lowered their heads like tortoises and blinked.[10]

Connolly made the mistake of including Waugh in his plans to welcome
Wilson. The American critic's novel, *Memoirs of Hecate County*, had
recently been rejected by his British publishers, who considered it
obscene, and Waugh was asked to make no reference to the matter. It
was the wrong advice and he bullied the guest of honour mercilessly at
dinner, advising him to seek publication of his book in Cairo. The
following day, having agreed to act as the visitor's cicerone around
London, he stood the 'insignificant Yank' up.[11] Wilson, already suffering nervous anglophobia, was further undermined and found
London dilapidated and bankrupt, its inhabitants provincial and
exhausted. For Connolly, however, he had nothing but praise. He had
himself been an editor on both *New Republic* and *Vanity Fair* and
knew all about the freedoms and constrictions of the job. That Connolly had undertaken such a task during the war impressed him greatly
and he reported his admiration in the *New Yorker* in October: 'It
seemed to me proof of his merit ... that, in the literary and Left
political worlds, almost everybody complained about him and [*Horizon*], but that everybody, at the same time, seemed in some degree
dependent on them.'[12]

Meanwhile Waugh's star was unassailable. May had seen the publication of *Brideshead Revisited* and the accession of its author to international fame. Connolly hastened to read the new work but according
to Nancy Mitford, who eagerly relayed the information to Waugh, he
was ambivalent, finding it 'brilliant where the narrative is straightforward. Doesn't care for the "purple passages" ie death of Lord
M[archmain]. Thinks you go too much to White's. But found it impossible to put down (no wonder).'[13] Waugh saw Wilson's tribute, sensed a
rival for his fame and immediately contacted his agent. Since the
appearance of the article, he complained, 'some Yanks have taken
[Cyril] seriously': could the review of *The Unquiet Grave* which he had
written for *The Tablet* be placed in America?'[14]

Connolly was not alone in his ambivalence towards *Brideshead
Revisited*. However, the novel's preoccupation with a great house was
symptomatic, Waugh felt, of an interest common to many members of
his generation. Elsewhere he had written: 'When the poetic mood was
on us we turned to buildings, and gave them a place which our fathers
accorded to Nature – to almost any buildings, but particularly those in
the classical tradition, and, more particularly, in its decay.'[15] If this
disposition was true of Waugh and Betjeman, it was not irrelevant to

Connolly. All his adult life he fantasized about owning country houses of varying degrees of magnificence: in 1945 his career still committed him to London but he was now a successful man moving into middle age and felt a need for something more substantial than the succession of flats he had previously inhabited. When the landlord of Bedford Square decided to cut short his tenant's lease the matter became urgent – new accommodation would have to be found. The choice was bewildering: the unfamiliar noises of peace echoed along streets and terraces across the whole of London where houses stood empty and awaited owners who had taken refuge in the country or were detained by war work or dead and dispersed across the seas. Preliminary decisions would have to resolve where in the city the search should begin; calculations could be made later about size and expense. It was coincidence which determined locality and appeared to sanction grand aspirations. Janetta was living in Park Road near Regent's Park and had fallen in love with a house which stood at the heart of Nash's neo-classical citadel. Applications to the Crown Estate revealed that it contained four large floors and that a lease of eighteen years was available but the cost was prohibitive and it was clear that she could only realize fantasies of occupation by finding someone to share the property. It occurred to her that if anybody would like to live in such a house it was Cyril Connolly; she broached the matter in a state of extreme nervousness but he saw at once that the arrangement would absolve him of the boredom of conducting his own search, guarantee him a congenial neighbour and most importantly answer longings for a house appropriate to a man of substance. It seemed the perfect solution – but not to Matthew, who wrote trying to convince his son that Regent's Park was 'at the other end of nowhere' and that under a shared roof endless difficulties would emerge: noisy babies, noisy parties, disagreeable subletters; in any case the property was surely much too large for someone as restless and inclined to travel as his son?[16] Evelyn Waugh also tried to sabotage proceedings by warning Connolly that he and Janetta would be evicted by the Crown authorities for cohabitation. Connolly was not to be put off, however, and agreed that if Janetta bought the lease he would rent as her tenant. By early June 25 Sussex Place was theirs.

Frances Partridge went to inspect the house and was 'stunned by its grandeur and beauty'.[17] Three months later, however, returning to see how the occupants had decorated their prospective quarters – with

Janetta having the lower floors opening on to the garden and Connolly the upper storeys – she felt more ambivalent. Janetta's apartments she found 'charmingly alive, fresh', her upstairs neighbour's less so. 'Instead of treating [his rooms] in any way visually, as a painter his canvas, he has stuffed them with symbols of success and good living – massive dark furniture, sideboards groaning with decanters and silver coffee-pots, Sèvres porcelain, heavy brocade curtains, safe but dim pictures.'[18] Not all Connolly's decorative schemes were conventional, however. Finding that the connecting double doors in his drawing room had been irrecoverably panelled in cheap wood, he commissioned the young painter John Craxton to embellish them at his discretion. The result was not, in the artist's words, 'in the least *dix-huitième siècle*', but although it hardly matched the surrounding furnishings his patron 'didn't turn a hair'. The doors were now disguised as a diptych: in one panel a young fisherman was depicted holding a crayfish, while in the other a farmboy stood with a sheaf of corn; incorporating many of Connolly's happiest emblems, the surrounding frieze revealed lemurs, flowers and a bird sitting on the fruit-laden bough of a quince tree.[19]

Sussex Place worked harmoniously, and while Lys ensured the delivery of the milk, paid tradesmen and herself pressed his shirts and collars, her lover was left to contemplate the lot of the artist and to congratulate himself on his standing and success. However much he might regret Jean, however wistfully he might await divine afflatus, for the time being he was happy and only shortages of money could distress him. The grandiose furnishings were deceptive, both to others and to himself: sometimes he was so pressed for funds that he would leave his mail unopened until the collection of sinister envelopes proved too large to ignore; then his understanding landlady would have to open the correspondence and disclose the worst of its demands. Inevitably he fell into arrears with the rent; no less inevitably Janetta felt too embarrassed to press her claims in person and took to leaving reminders on the staircase. She and her young daughter were presently joined by Robert Kee, the future writer and broadcaster who became her second husband, and he got to know his neighbour well, finding him always charming, solicitous and happy to dispense advice to his younger men friends: the famous editor and *homme de lettres*, now portly with middle age, seemed a sweet and sympathetic figure as he padded round the house in his dressing-gown. Almost at once, however, this contentment was threatened from within and without. Dry rot was discovered and the repairs would be both inconvenient and expensive. A building company which had often worked for the architectural firm run by Lucian Freud's father agreed to undertake the job but long before the menace was eradicated the builders went bankrupt and abandoned the site, leaving only green tarpaulins to protect the back of the house from the elements. Restoration was eventually completed but by the time £2000 had been raised to meet the final cost an even graver threat had materialized. The Crown authorities and the Office of Works proposed a scheme now unimaginable – the redevelopment of the entire site surrounding Regent's Park. There was speculation in the newspapers and Matthew began sending anxious warnings in January 1946 but he need not have worried. His son was not complacent and on 21 March 1946 *The Times* published a letter of protest subscribed by four residents in the threatened area, Elizabeth Bowen, Connolly, Lord Glenconner and H. G. Wells, which appealed for restraint: 'Let the new flats and offices go up on the former waste lands and slum territories to the north and east of the Park itself, and let the Nash terraces be spared as a *monument historique* for living in, to proclaim to our own posterity the end of the age of vandalism.' Such proclamations were optimistic but for once protest was effective, bureaucracy recoiled and the attrition of the beautiful and palpable past was temporarily halted.

VI
HIGHBROWS AND
LOWBROWS

CHAPTER TWENTY-ONE

WITH THE FINAL capitulations of the war the Labour Party withdrew from Churchill's coalition to precipitate a general election. For the first time in ten years Britons would have the opportunity to paint their country's political complexion but would re-enact the democratic ceremonies as the inhabitants of a world transformed and a victorious nation bankrupt and exhausted. Some electors may have been bewildered by the choice confronting them, between Churchill – imperial, eloquent, an architect of the victory – and the untried idealist Clement Attlee, but Cyril Connolly, canvassing in June's *Horizon*, was not of their number and would vote without equivocation or secrecy. He had supported Churchill's leadership during the war and hailed him as 'the one man to whom I owe it that I am not in a concentration camp'. Furthermore, the patriotic impulse which now animated the Tories was itself no evil: although *Horizon* had opposed war it had opposed fascism more, 'and therefore recognized the value of that patriotism which derives from the healthy human desire to protect our liberties and to fight for our country against an invader'. Yet he would deny the Conservatives his support. He could not forget that it was they who in the Thirties had recognized and traded with the dictators and could not believe that they were better equipped than the Socialists to engineer the new Europe he longed to see, where dictators, kings, tariffs and passports were banished. The Continent aside, domestic reform was also urgent. Freedom was a necessity and capital punishment an evil but there were also grotesque disparities in wealth and he called for 'a levelling up which Socialism alone will provide'. He could not predict which party would more generously nurture the arts but sensed that Labour alone could accommodate the instincts he saw as prevailing across Europe, instincts towards socialism and coalescence, and warned that rejection of those impulses would result in British exclusion from the inevitable, and in his view essential, 'United States of Europe'.[1]

Attlee would have his vote; and if some of *Horizon*'s readers deplored his defection from Churchill they learned, when counting had ended, that if Connolly had changed, like Dryden before him, he had changed with the nation. The Socialists had secured an unassailable mandate for radical reform and the mood at Lansdowne Terrace was jubilant, with Peter Watson writing to Brian Howard: 'I am amazed, delighted, but apprehensive . . . However, it is the most hopeful Event since the end of the war, and perhaps *more* important.'[2]

Connolly continued to give much thought to the kind of society which he felt should obtain in England and eventually announced his conclusions in 'Comment' in June 1946. He reaffirmed his commitment to a reform of the penal system but envisaged difficulties: since 'flogging, or being flogged, for many Tories is the first real experience of their life', he suggested that a reform of the prisons could not be implemented by any parliamentary party educated primarily at public schools and thus accustomed 'to the deterrent of a barbarous severity'. There were many other liberties which characterized what he termed a 'civilized community' and now he drew up a charter, the conditions of which included: no death penalty; model prisons; no slums; 'vocations for all', which suggested a belief in more professional training; freedom of opinion; no racial discrimination; reform of the laws relating to divorce, abortion, homosexuality, licensing and Sunday trading. There was wisdom: 'The acquisition of property to be recognized as an instinct which is, like the wish to excel, beneficial in moderation.' There was nonsense, since as well as calling for free health care, he hoped for 'light and heat supplied free . . . clothing, nourishment . . . almost free. Transport as near as possible within the reach of all.' Evelyn Waugh fulminated against his friend's 'fatuous article'[3] and wrote a hilarious and withering response in *The Tablet*. Connolly sent dignified congratulations: he would certainly have printed it in *Horizon* had its author suggested and only minded the earlier review of *The Unquiet Grave* because 'I thought you fought unfairly i.e. pretending not to know who Palinurus was so as to insult me.'[4] Connolly had the last laugh: apart from fantasies about free heat and light, many of his ideas were enacted into law by most of the western democracies long before his death or Waugh's.

Of all the necessary liberties, the freedom to travel was perhaps closest to Connolly's heart: for all his electioneering he decided, while the campaign was underway and Sussex Place was being decorated,

that he would seek permission to go abroad again and was thus agreeably disenfranchised when the nation summoned Attlee to govern.
Watson was keen to visit Paris, not least to see what had become of his
property, and having persuaded bureaucracy that they were required in
France on *Horizon* business, the two friends arrived in the city in July to
find the apartment in a sorry condition. Flimsy tokens from former
times had eerily survived an apocalypse: Connolly found a sprig of
mistletoe which he had watched Jean hang for Christmas 1938 as well
as a photograph of his wife taken by Man Ray and now fading sound-
lessly in the place where he had pinned it in 1939. The flat was filthy
and its treasures – unsurprisingly – had vanished. Sherban Sidery, the
guardian Rumanian, claimed that the paintings had been stolen but
pawn tickets told another story. Watson made some attempts at
reclamation and was able to persuade Bérard to let him buy back his de
Chirico, but most of the items proved irretrievable. Despite these deprivations they stayed in the Rue du Bac, though Connolly complained to
Lys that the apartment, lacking hot water and clean linen, was 'terribly
depressing'. Before long he had implicated his friend in this decline and
told Lys that whereas before Watson had seemed the epitome of stylish
living he now symbolized 'morbid discomfort'.[5]

While the business of reclamation occupied his friend, Connolly
socialized and explored Paris. Gide was jolly over lunch, Balthus
depressing over dinner; and there were excursions with Christopher
Sykes, A. J. Ayer and Diana Cooper. The weather was hot and dry and
he reported to Lys that the intense green of the trees and the bleached
beauty of the architecture suggested a southern city like Rome or
Marseilles. He enjoyed the revelries of Bastille Day but noted a sinister
change. 'The whole atmosphere,' he later reported in *Horizon*, 'is subtly
Balkanized.' The black market flourished, the shops were empty, the
trains appalling, the disparity between rich and poor immeasurable –
and everywhere lay the corrosive residue of distrust. He pondered
various solutions, including the benefits a large influx of money would
bring, but economics gave way to eloquence and melancholy:

> But by then I was walking along the quays of the Seine, it was after
> midnight, the opaque green river slid by the immense poplars, and I knew
> that my reflections on these political nostrums were a kind of middle-
> aged mumbling over the grave of youth, for even were this young man's
> Paris to be resurrected, who can give back the eyes and heart which first
> explored it?[6]

Before their departure Connolly and Watson had considered following the Irish number of *Horizon* with a further issue dedicated to a
particular country but a combination of diplomatic, financial and
bureaucratic factors limited the areas in which they could roam for
material: France had already received too much attention; the other
European nations were no less exhausted by war; and the editors found
themselves obliged to search for culture in undesecrated Switzerland.
With Paris full of disappointment they left for the frontier after only a
week: the 'Swiss Number' which resulted from their researches appeared
in February 1946 and although its contents were not inspiring, its
'Comment', where Connolly recounted his impressions of Switzerland's
strange prosperity, redeemed the venture entirely. More disciplined, less
lazy, and confined to the civilized staging-posts of the Grand Tour, he
could have been a great travel writer: his eye for beauty, his tendency to
translate sensual gratification into haunting lyrical tribute, his undying
interest in what was foreign but not alien, his wandering heart, which
like a child's rejected routine for diversity and surprise, gave him the
virtues of a great literary itinerant:

> Such intoxication to those deprived of it since 1939, that every sleeper on
> the track, every cable and pylon, every newly born aroma of mountain
> sunlight and fir-forest and the name of every station seemed the last
> unbearable saturation-point in the rebirth of feeling – and then when this
> saturation seemed reached came the spectacle, quivering in the noontide
> haze, blue as the Aegean, green as Cumberland, shot by the copper
> sulphate and azure of the sky, of the blue-green iridescence of the
> vineyards tumbling down, between their limestone walls with the name of
> the grower painted on them in bright black letters, into the lake of
> Neuchâtel. This dazzling lake, first reminder that fresh water can be
> coloured, we follow through the afternoon heat, until we really can feel
> nothing any more. The names become German, the vines vanish and
> suddenly we are on the hotel balcony in Berne.[7]

These rhapsodies came at a price, however, as Watson was later to
reveal when describing the holiday to Cecil Beaton:

> [Cyril] is so vain and touchy, so anxious all at the same time . . . Of course I
> know he is everything I am not, impulsive, enthusiastic, quickly deceived
> and satiated, easily distracted from one thing to another. He can never get
> over the fact that I *won't* behave like a conventional rich man, always go to
> the best restaurant, hotel, travel first class etc. . . . He just makes me feel
> deeply unhappy after a time, all that welter of unsatisfied desires, jealousies.[8]

The rift was neither serious nor lasting and visiting misfortune assumed another guise: Watson developed jaundice and was prevented from leaving Switzerland. Connolly returned to London alone and heard nothing more until a bulletin in early September alerted him to a decline in the patient's condition. By mid-October Watson was very seriously ill and friends in England began to fear for his life. Cecil Beaton and Connolly offered to travel to be with him but their overtures were declined, the latter receiving a wise rejection from the invalid: 'You would die of boredom and I of anxiety neurosis!'[9] In the event Watson was bedridden for six months and his appearance when he returned to London caused dismay. Lys found him irrevocably altered and to Brian Howard Watson disclosed intimations of mortality: 'How terrible it is to grow old. One loses so many tastes one had and seems to get no new ones at all. Wisdom doesn't settle anything – it only removes one from old friends and prevents one from making any new ones . . .'[10]

Connolly meanwhile was buoyant. Labour was in power; Sussex Place was habitable; there was a sense of new openings and possibilities. Paper rations were relaxed and *Horizon* could look forward to a 33 per cent increase in volume. Both editors sensed that the increment should be used to produce more copies rather than a larger magazine but disagreed as to where those extra copies should be sold. From Switzerland Watson proposed an enlargement of the domestic sale, arguing that exports entailed more administrative expense. Connolly, however, saw prestige in a greater presence in France and America and it was his conviction which prevailed. The Hamish Hamilton reissue of *The Unquiet Grave* appeared now and helped to justify feelings of optimism, not least because the cover illustration commissioned from John Piper seemed to the author to capture the essence of the book 'with genius'.[11] Hamish Hamilton was also supervising the American production of the book and – hoping perhaps that Connolly's hour had finally come – made attempts to acquire the rights to *Enemies of Promise*. When these negotiations failed he decided instead to purchase *The Rock Pool*, which he wanted to reissue in an expensive, limited edition produced by the Curwen Press and illustrated by Anthony Gross. Connolly was enthusiastic and suggested that Lucian Freud or John Craxton should be approached to design a cover. In the event the first English edition of the novel, appearing in 1947, settled down to modest notoriety unadorned by such illustrious decoration.

The new edition of *The Unquiet Grave* appeared simultaneously with the collection of essays which Routledge had been struggling to bring to birth since the beginning of the war. The project's working title, 'The Little Voice', had been insufficiently resonant and the collection now appeared as *The Condemned Playground* and brought back into print a selection of Connolly's best work from the *New Statesman* and *Life and Letters*. The author wrote an introduction which sketched his critical disposition. Seeing art as 'man's noblest attempt to preserve Imagination from Time', he stressed that his writings had been informed by a sense of evanescence and decay: 'I feel I am fighting a rearguard action, for although each generation discovers anew the value of masterpieces, generations are never quite the same and ours are in fact coming to prefer the response induced by violent stimuli – film, radio, press – to the slow permeation of the personality by great literature.'[12]

Reviews were generally favourable and friends were happy. Pearsall Smith wrote to say he was enjoying the collection's 'brilliant, witty and glowing pages' and John Betjeman was delighted: 'I think those short articles are just your medium – for you have a gift of parody which never goes on for too long and which less talented men would expand into a book ... No one would think that you in that huge coat and with no hat on your head and going off to Soho to lunch would notice everything as you do.'[13] Once again, however, Julian Symons sounded a dissident voice. He was sent the collection to review by a periodical called *Now* and felt old resentments surging:

> Reading *The Condemned Playground* revived all the indignation I had felt on first looking at *Horizon* at reading pieces that I thought at best frivolous, at worst silly or contemptible ... I remember Orwell reading the review and saying with his grim smile: 'Very good, but you shouldn't have suggested he was rich. He has no money.' In my innocence I had supposed that somebody who lived like Connolly must have a sizeable income.[14]

Jean was among those who sent letters of congratulation but the town from which she wrote was inconducive to enthusiasm. She was in Reno, Nevada, to secure a divorce, and even literary achievement seemed inextricable from the arguments of severance: 'You are a great successful man now. Not for you a middle-aged poorish American expatriate on-the-town girl, romantic, insufferable.'[15] She was melancholy but not abject and warned her husband that even if he refused to sign the papers she despatched she could still obtain a divorce by default. Her determination was unmistakable and soon Connolly discovered its cause: shortly after the end of her liaison with Clement Greenberg she had fallen in love with Laurence Vail, an American Surrealist poet who had enjoyed prominence of a sort in bohemian Paris twenty years previously, and now she intended to marry him. She would be his third wife: by Peggy Guggenheim and the writer Kay Boyle Vail had six children and Jean would finally acquire by proxy the family she had longed to have in England. At first sight her decision seemed a deliverance for Connolly – now he could consider marriage to Lys and do so moreover in the knowledge that he was innocent of the instigation of proceedings. Characteristically, however, he sought complications: it was painful and wrong to put away the sunlit past which his wife embodied. It was also humiliating, since Jean's initiative seemed to reduce him from irreproachable egotist to acquiescent pawn. Above all it invited further risk – his wife had been a bulwark against the commitment which Lys demanded and which something within him shirked.

He was powerless, however, and despite trying to lodge reproachful obstructions he learned that on 7 January 1946 Jean's divorce had become final and she had married Laurence Vail. With her new husband she returned to Europe to reclaim his Paris apartment and the house at Mégève in the French Alps which, after his children, Vail had named 'Les Six Enfants'. Her adoptive family all grew to adore her, the older ones in particular welcoming the thirty-five-year-old more as a stepsister than surrogate mother. Sindbad Vail, Laurence's son by Peggy Guggenheim, married in the same year as his father, and his wife, Jacqueline, at once befriended Jean: 'I took to her on the spot. Fairly tall with a full-blown figure and a bob of dark brown hair, she struck me as immensely attractive. She also had that heavy-lidded dreamy gaze which sometimes comes with severe nearsightedness ... She was intelligent, witty, warm-hearted and so insecure! ... She was so fond of Laurence she'd put up with anything, even tried ski-ing and mountain climbing, not her forte. In his off-hand way, I suppose [he] was attached to her.'[16]

In London preparations for marriage were also under discussion, only to be frustrated by the discovery that although Jean was released, her first husband was not, and could be freed only by divorce in an

English court. The amount of form-filling required to resolve this technicality proved too much for a determination to marry which was strong only in one quarter, and for the time being Lys decided to content herself with becoming 'Lys Connolly' by deed poll. Meanwhile Jean's divorce, at first a rejection and a betrayal, became accepted: nothing could take away memories and she was safe now in the immutable past. Clement Greenberg presently sent consolation: while Jean was 'one of the most fascinating creatures that ever walked the earth', hers was a love which 'consumed' and 'everyone who is ever in love with [her] contracts a mother neurosis'.[17]

At the beginning of 1946 it was announced that the trials of the surviving Nazis would be held in March at Nuremberg. Prominent figures from the Allied nations were invited to attend the hearings but although Evelyn Waugh and Rebecca West both accepted the invitation Connolly decided to remain behind, detained by 'a vein of squeamishness'.[18] Ernest Hemingway pressed him to go to Cuba. Bernard Berenson wanted to see him in Tuscany. Sadly the cash and the permits required were lacking and in February he and Lys opted for more sober adventure when, bolstered by a loan of thirty shillings from Arthur Koestler, they spent a weekend in Wales. It was hardly his ideal escape but Connolly put a brave face on it and promised Koestler that it was all in the way of rehearsal for sunnier explorations. Writing to thank their creditor, Lys told Koestler that part of his loan had paid for a 9s 6d half bottle of claret on the homebound train. She also informed him that some of Matthew's furniture had been installed in Sussex Place. After fifteen years in storage it was filthy but not all was chaos: 'We have a char at last and she brings us breakfast in bed.'[19]

Although for Lys breakfast in bed was a prelude to a day in the office for Connolly it led increasingly to house-bound meditation. There had been a novelty in *Horizon*'s success and an excitement in its salvation of culture which with the peace had begun to turn to stale obligation, and the magazine saw less and less of its editor. Besides, he now had another commitment: as long ago as 1944 negotiations had begun with Hamish Hamilton for the production of a critical biography of Flaubert, with the publisher then offering an advance of £300 and a royalty of 15 per cent and by 1946 expecting to receive a study of 60,000 words. In March the American publisher, Harper's, wrote asking for details of progress and in May Hamish Hamilton was disconcerted to learn that Connolly was talking of abandoning the book because he had heard that Enid Starkie had announced identical ambitions. Hamilton knew of his author's veneration for Flaubert and was prepared to fight for the project. He wrote to Enid Starkie and received an assurance that she had no such intentions, 'though she adds that she once said to you, jokingly, that if you did not hurry with your book she might do one first'.[20] It was only to be expected that with such an obligation Connolly would not see the need to go daily to Lansdowne Terrace. Unfortunately, left alone, he became a dilettante and dissipated the challenging hours which every writer dreads. He could spend mornings pottering among his books and because he thought constantly in terms of words he was always polishing mellifluous sentences and hoarding them against later literary need. He loved to explore London or think in his bath or make endless lists – of books to write or countries to visit or ideal dinner parties or best friends or worst enemies – but such elegant marginalia amounted to little when surrounding a blank page.

Many of the reveries Connolly enjoyed focused on the sudden acquisition of wealth, and there was one figure whose financial intentions he never forgot, Logan Pearsall Smith. In March his old mentor died after a twilight darkened by what he himself termed 'interlunaries' of unreason, and Connolly accepted an invitation from the *New Statesman* to write his obituary. He had remained fond of his first employer, even though he had seen less of him during the war, and it was a matter for regret that although they had spoken only the day before the older man's death their conversation had been marred by Pearsall Smith's strident manner. He had just read Orwell's recently published *Animal Farm* and demanded information about the author. Connolly lacked the time for detailed gossip and promised more information the next day, only to hear the implacable sneer that Orwell 'beat the lot of you' and the crash of the receiver.[21] His obituary made no mention of these tumults of mood and instead praised Pearsall Smith's commitment to seventeenth-century literature, his generosity to young writers, his perfectionism. Connolly had been the earliest beneficiary of these attentions but other protégés had followed: Robert Gathorne-Hardy, the historian Hugh Trevor-Roper, the critic John Russell. Connolly himself never forgot one aspect of his apprenticeship – the Sunday morning walks through Chelsea when the older writer would indicate property he owned and promise that it would eventually devolve on his companion. Gathorne-Hardy, who served a much longer and more arduous term, received other assurances of wealth but their expectations were dashed when the eagerly awaited will named the young John Russell as Pearsall Smith's legatee.

The deceased's sister Alys was among those astonished by the bequest and sent Connolly her sympathy: it was all 'an irresponsible and malicious final joke . . . I *simply can't bear it,* tho' I know he was crazy'.[22] She was not alone in her consternation: Connolly complained to Gathorne-Hardy; Gathorne-Hardy complained to Connolly; and John Russell offered an interpretation more exquisite than explanatory: 'I just happened to be the last *biche* in the Parc-aux-Cerfs.'[23] Meanwhile, disappointment dampened Sussex Place: visions of the perfect eighteenth-century life re-created above Regent's Park collapsed amidst mundane worry. How could one survive as a writer?

Connolly decided to compile a questionnaire which would enable writers to compare their expectations. The responses might also be read by influential people and engineer bureaucratic enlightenment: if the government was to pay for so much else, was it unreasonable to hope that it might also subsidize writers? The questionnaire was despatched to all the writers he could contact and asked them to deliberate the following problems: the income necessary for survival; whether such an income was obtainable through 'serious' writing; if it was not, whether a secondary occupation was legitimate; would such a secondary occupation sap literary energy; should the state offer support; did the respondent have any advice for the young writer about to turn his first professional sentence? When 'The Cost of Letters' appeared in *Horizon* in September Connolly was able to publish a wide-ranging and illuminating response which returned a gratifying consensus – that it was almost impossible to make a living from writing. Orwell knew why: 'The average British citizen spends round about £1 a year on books, whereas he spends getting on for £25 on tobacco and alcohol combined.' State subsidy was viewed uneasily and ideas varied as to the amount a writer needed for survival. Elizabeth Bowen wanted £3500 a year, Orwell £1000, Robert Graves suggested living off friends. Laurie Lee thought time a more valuable commodity than cash. V. S. Pritchett was stern: 'The failures of overwork are fewer than the failures of idleness.' Julian Maclaren-Ross voiced the writer's eternal ambivalence for his publisher: 'Don't listen to [his] sob-stories about how little he can afford. He'll have a country house and polo ponies when you are still borrowing the price of a drink in Fitzrovia.'

Connolly included his own convictions, although some seemed flippant: his second occupation for a writer was 'a rich wife'. He wanted writers to have a year's paid holiday and an entertainment allowance as well as a daily net income of £5 which would purchase 'leisure and privacy' among other essentials. Desmond MacCarthy pointed out that expectations, and thus the sums involved, were hopelessly subjective: he was himself profligate compared to E. M. Forster but thrifty by the side of Connolly. Koestler also thought the questionnaire too simple to answer well and decided not to reply rather than submit 'whimsical or aphoristic things'.[24] Diana Cooper, in more ways than one remote from the debate, read the findings in Paris and applied to Waugh for derision. He did not fail her: 'It is all balls when Cyril Connolly preaches about the economic status of the writer. He is wholly absurd in his serious moments which become more and more frequent. I think he sees himself as a sort of Public Relations Officer for Literature ... He is a droll old sponge at his best and worth six of Quennell.'[25]

CHAPTER TWENTY-TWO

IN THE SUMMER Connolly honoured a long-standing promise by taking Lys to the Continent. The holiday, undertaken as a substitute honeymoon, began in France and continued in Corsica and Switzerland where the couple were joined by John Craxton. The painter met his friends knowing that they both held strong views about an artist's appearance. Once he had incurred Connolly's displeasure by growing a moustache, which was considered 'too airforce and unattractive' for his calling. On another occasion Lys suggested that he should wear white powder on his face 'to make yourself look more pale and interesting'. In plentiful Switzerland Craxton found himself insatiable for confectionery unimaginable in England. Connolly considered the appetite 'very adolescent' and when the painter tried to tempt him to similar indulgence he received a skittish rebuff: 'No, my dear, I get *my* sugar from alcohol.' If these verdicts seemed capricious, however, the younger man was inclined to accept them. Where Switzerland was concerned his fellow-traveller not only seemed omniscient but also ready to mock lapses of knowledge in his friends: to question his pronouncements on pastries might imply doubts about his familiarity with mountains, wines and churches. This balance of belief held until one morning Craxton stumbled into Connolly's room to find him furtively studying the *Guide Bleu* to equip himself for further authoritative performances.[1]

Connolly broached a bold scheme for the autumn: he proposed crossing the Atlantic with Watson to gather material for a special American number of *Horizon*. After their travels in Switzerland Watson may have had his doubts but knew that the magazine could never rest complacently and that it (and Connolly) had been the subject of increasing curiosity in the East Coast literary establishment. Besides appearing in articles in *Time* and the *New Yorker* Connolly had seen his picture on the cover of the *Saturday Review* and had provoked an extraordinary encomium in the *Atlantic Monthly*. 'Meet The Modern Ego' was written by Jacques Barzun, Professor of Cultural History at Columbia, and made flatteringly ambitious claims. It seemed that Connolly had 'a representative modern mind: a mind so full of our own high and low spirits, our own anxiety – and at the same time so competent in self-analysis – that to read him is to explore many neglected corners of oneself'.[2] America was generous but she was also impatient and soon forgot her favourites: now was the time to travel, and on 19 November, with Watson at his side, the chubby forty-three-year-old *zeitgeist* boarded the *Franconia*. He spent much of the voyage reading Baudelaire and Baedeker but as he later admitted in *Horizon*, by the time he saw the first lightship of Nantucket he was ready for distraction, particularly as there was no alcohol on the ship: 'No more dormitory life ... no hurried monotonous meals ... no more scrambling for chairs, or searching for conversation ... Tomorrow our personalities will be handed back to us.'[3]

The travellers were met in New York by Auden and Tony Bower and had lunch on Third Avenue before repairing to their respective hotels – Watson to the St Regis in midtown Manhattan, Connolly to the Grosvenor in lower Fifth Avenue. Later he would tell his readers that Auden's welcome suggested that extended in a Disney film by the town mouse to the country mouse. Privately he found his host charming – less self-conscious and more battered and American than ever – and listened eagerly to his reasons for emigration: he had anonymity in New York and that year alone had earned $10,000. It was obvious that any questionnaire about the cost of American letters would reach different conclusions from those recognized in London. Connolly was in no hurry to make pronouncements, however, and his final American impressions were not released until October 1947, when *Art on the American Horizon* was published. His prolonged introduction constituted one of his most inspired pieces of literary sight-seeing and so impressed Christopher Isherwood that he told Connolly it 'belongs in an anthology of visitors' impressions of the US. (Along with Huxley's drive into Los Angeles, Lawrence's description of the Colorado desert, Dickens.)'[4] Sixteen years before he had sought the summits of the buildings with his eyes; now fame gave him different vantages:

If one need never descend below the fortieth floor New York would seem the most beautiful city in the world, its skies and cloudscapes are

tremendous, its southern latitude is revealed only in its light (for vegetation and architecture are strictly northern); here one can take in the
Hudson, the East River, the mid-town and down-town colonies of skyscrapers, Central Park and the magnificent new bridges and curving
arterial highways and watch the evening miracle, the lights going on all
over these frowning termitaries against a sky of royal-blue velvet only to
be paralleled in Lisbon or Palermo.[5]

Sadly the fortieth floor had to be relinquished and soon he found
himself 'slave of telephone and engagement book. Europe is a dream
and Auden's anonymity equally remote.' He sensed that the city's book
business was more interested in serial rights, cheap editions and book-
of-the-month clubs, prestigious offices and a courtship of Hollywood
than it was in literature. He was also surprised to note that 'in the one
country left where necessities are cheap ... to be poor is still dis-
graceful'. Manhattan was a metropolis 'continuously insolent and alive'
yet his observations were ambivalent – he found the rich joyless and
sensed that behind their energy and prosperity the middle classes concealed tendencies to drinking and despair. These observations were not
conducted in solitude, as Watson suggested to Brian Howard: 'Cyril's
triumphant progress here must be seen to be believed. The Director of
the Metropolitan had us to lunch and gave us a personally conducted
tour of the Museum, and everything else is rather on that level. It's
much too much for me.'[6] His companion had come to be lionized,
however, and accepted all invitations. At Harper's Cass Canfield had
told his staff prior to Connolly's arrival that 'the more attention we can
pay him, the better',[7] and now, relentless in his ambitions to secure
rights to future books, he gave a large cocktail party on 3 December,
aware all the time that Macmillan was also wooing the Englishman. On
12 December Connolly was the guest on the radio programme 'Author
Meets the Critics', where he held an audience for three journalists,
among them Orville Prescott of the *New York Times*. Shortly afterwards, interviewed in the *New Yorker*, he revealed a languor and
self-mockery almost exotic in Madison Avenue: admitting to brooding
and daydreaming in the bath, he claimed that 'sometimes I get one
adjective from an afternoon in the tub' and insisted that his range of
general knowledge came from 'escapist enthusiasms' such as chess,
bridge, rare books, china, and travelling. 'Right now, I am on fish.'[8]

During the war he had read *1 × 1* by E. E. Cummings and was
delighted to discover that the poet and his wife lived near to the

Grosvenor Hotel. A correspondence begun from London was now superseded by a friendship in Greenwich Village – the critic introduced the poet to Auden, another local, and ventured a scheme he had contemplated during his journey which Cummings later mentioned in a letter to his mother: 'Cyril Connolly, the editor of "Horizon" magazine (much the best periodical concerning socalled literature; & published in London) has been wining and dining Marion and me in celebration of a (let's trust) soon-forthcoming English edition of *1 × 1*.'[9] Connolly also saw Clement Greenberg, and although the American was annoyed by the critic's cool claim that 'Jean got tired of you' he nevertheless took to him and was happy to acknowledge that he was 'the most successful English visitor to the United States since Oscar Wilde'.[10] Connolly was equally well disposed and petitioned his wife's lover for a contribution to the American number which was eventually published as 'The Present Prospects of American Painting and Sculpture'.

After three weeks Connolly flew alone to San Francisco and while the architecture of that city disappointed him he enthused over the country-side of the Monterey Peninsula. He visited Henry Miller at Big Sur and told his readers that here was 'one writer who has solved the problem of how to live happily in America'. In Los Angeles he checked into the Beverly Hills Hotel but despite its climate and vegetation the city did not satisfy: 'Those who have loved the Mediterranean will not be reconciled here and those who really care for books can never settle down to the impermanent world of the cinema.'[11] His verdict over-looked the presences of Ivan Moffat and Christopher Isherwood, two immigrants whose friendship he hastily renewed, as well as that of Aldous Huxley, whom he had not seen since their miserable vicinity at Sanary. Contact between the erstwhile neighbours had been recently re-established. In the *New Statesman* in 1945 Connolly had extolled Huxley's *Time Must Have a Stop* and shortly before his departure for America he had received the polymath's impressions of *The Unquiet Grave*: 'There is a distinctive flavour about its weltanschauung – a flavour which might easily become contagious, so that, just as we now note something we can describe as Wertherism, say, or Byronism, future historians of literature may discover lingering strains of palinur-emia.'[12] When they did meet the writers both had changes to observe: Connolly was a touring attraction, the man of the moment, while Huxley had become a secular mystic. Harmony prevailed and the critic later assured his readers that the novelist 'radiates both intelligence and serene goodness'. Yet encounters with these expatriates only served to emphasize Connolly's unlikely kinship with another admirer who sought him out. Orson Welles was already the most famous failure in Hollywood: but he too was a showman, an Irishman and a misfit inside whom a thin man was wildly signalling for release; he too half-enjoyed embodying a cautionary tale, as the favoured and forsaken of promise.

Connolly returned to London in January to find the city almost immobilized by severe weather and a continued scarcity of fuel and there was little to alleviate the ensuing gloom before February's announcement, made by the French ambassador, that he was to be awarded the Légion d'Honneur in recognition of his services to French culture during the war. He had to wait until July for his investiture and received his honour simultaneously with Harold Nicolson, who praised the embassy's hospitality – *foie gras*, braised tongue and cherries stuffed with toffee and stewed in brandy – to Vita Sackville-West. Unfortunately Matthew did not live to see the investiture: he was found dead in bed on the morning of 27 February. His lucidity was true to the end and only the year before he had begun another eccentric career with the completion, for the Wine and Food Society, of a pamphlet entitled *Pottery, or Home Made Potted Foods, Meat and Fish Pastes, Savoury Butters and Others*: 'How delicious to a schoolboy's healthy appetite sixty years ago, was a potted meat at breakfast in my grandmother's old Wiltshire home. Neat little white pots, with a crust of yellow butter suggesting the spicy treat beneath, beef, ham or tongue, handiwork of the second or third kitchenmaid.'[13]

Before 1954 and the end of food rationing such reminiscential cookery remained the easiest form of culinary indulgence and here revealed the inner voluptuary. In other ways, however, the old soldier never denied his Spartan training and when Maud learned of his death she remembered his life-long aversion to pyjamas and bedroom fires and suspected heart failure induced by intense cold. He had expressed a wish to be buried with his mother and grandfather in the cemetery of Bath Abbey but heavy snow and the distance depleted Matthew's mourners and Connolly arrived with Lys to find that besides Mrs Pain only a verger and a curate would mourn his father's passing. Maud had to rely on a letter to learn not only of the burial but of her son's regrets in the cemetery: 'The grave was so deep, cut right through the Bath stone, and the coffin looked quite small at the bottom of it. It was like being left as a little boy at a new school. I thought – such a final helpless parting.'[14] Jean, sending immediate sympathy, rejected the pieties of the moment: 'Don't let the feelings of guilt you speak of increase your misery, after all, he was a sad and pathetic old man but was often not v. nice, either to you or to your mother.'[15] Not the least of the regrets involved money. Maud had been named as sole beneficiary but had asked her son to act on her behalf while she remained in South Africa and to take whatever he wanted from among his father's possessions. She was not an avaricious woman and beyond regretting the dissipation of the £10,000 which Matthew had inherited from his mother she laid claim to nothing apart from his marriage settlement of £4000, which she proposed to invest in South Africa and combine with her soldier's widow's pension of £70 to secure an income for her old age. There was little besides: 500 war saving certificates, £100 in the bank, £100 owed by a stamp dealer, reference books deposited with the conchology department. The mineral collection was to go to Bath Museum while his accumulation of 14,000 shells devolved on the Natural History Museum.

Emergency fuel regulations led to the cancellation of the March number of *Horizon* and even the BBC felt besieged when the Third Programme had to be suspended for two weeks. With the loosening of fuel restrictions and the resumption of comprehensive broadcasting Connolly was approached for his services and delivered two radio talks within the next year – *The Case for Prose*, for which he was paid thirty guineas, and *Latin Elegiac Poets*. Meanwhile *Horizon* was back in business and in April he expressed his disillusion with England, which after a holiday in America seemed particularly depressing. Across the Atlantic 'one is conscious that everyone is tuned up to a positive individual quality'. In England, however, 'most of us are not men or women but members of a vast seedy, over-worked, over-legislated, neuter class, with our drab clothes, our ration books and murder stories, our envious, stricken, old-world apathies and resentments'.[16] Yet if 'Comment' made depressing reading, the magazine as a whole was redeemed by its leading contribution: Connolly had asked Auden for a poem 'that would make me cry' and the result, dedicated by poet to critic, was an exquisite meditation – 'The Fall of Rome'.[17]

In June he and Lys were invited to stay at Piers Court, Evelyn Waugh's house in Gloucestershire, but any expectations of suspicion and recrimination following disagreements over *The Unquiet Grave* proved unfounded. Waugh thought the couple 'pleasant guests' and seemed unperturbed by Connolly's revelation that he had declined an offer recently extended by the *Daily Express*: the post of principal literary critic, with a generous salary of £3500, in succession to the distinguished James Agate. Other confessions made a greater impression, however: 'Cyril recanted his socialist opinions, saying that his father's death had liberated him from guilt in this matter.'[18] The apostasy was music to Waugh's ears and he can only have been delighted when in July's *Horizon* he saw his friend confirm his defection in immutable print: 'The fact remains that a Socialist government, besides doing practically nothing to help artists and writers (unless the closing down of magazines during the fuel crisis can be interpreted as an aid to incubation), has also quite failed to stir up intellect or imagination.' The weekend was a success: once again the ambiguous friendship was whole and shortly afterwards Connolly sent his host thanks and praised his *'train de vie* – fine books, fine wine, fine view'.[19] During the course of the visit he had suggested that his friend contribute an essay to the *Horizon* series 'The Best and the Worst', in which a writer selected a contemporary author whose literary vices and virtues formed the subject of a study deliberately ambivalent and inconclusive. (Rose Macaulay had written about Waugh in December 1946.) The novelist mischievously chose to write about his friend, the priest Ronald Knox; Connolly prevaricated by letter: would he muster the necessary equivocation? Encomium alone was on offer, however, and knowing that no self-respecting editor would reject an offering from Waugh's Augustan pen, Connolly acquiesced and 'Ronald Knox' appeared in May 1948.

This contribution alone was exciting but Connolly was in the mood to press more exorbitant claims. In July Peter Quennell's *Cornhill Magazine* published an abridged version of Waugh's novella, *Scott-King's Modern Europe*. At Piers Court he had learnt that Waugh had completed preliminary work on another brief fiction and sensed that cautious petitioning would secure the work for his own magazine. Meanwhile other supplications had to be made more publicly. Almost every commodity was now scarce and in September further restrictions were imposed on the consumption of meat, butter and petrol. Connolly was not one to accept deprivation philosophically and responded with the introduction in September of *Horizon*'s 'American Begging Bowl'. The prominent advertisement was laconic but frank: 'We English are never so happy as with our backs to the wall, and an understanding Providence has ordained that we need seldom abandon our favourite position.' American readers were asked to send food parcels to any writer they admired, care of Lansdowne Terrace, whether he or she contributed to *Horizon* or not. The idea seemed entirely practical, coming as it did while *Art on the American Horizon* was being prepared for distribution in October. Not all journalists knew as much about honesty or as little about misplaced pride as Connolly, however, and in the *News Chronicle* Ian Mackay was scandalized: 'When the new *lazzarone* go on the scrounge they do the thing de luxe with a chromium-plated begging-bowl, and even when they are whimpering "Baksheesh" on the Transatlantic telephone as sickeningly as any scurvy supplicant on Port Said pier they do it with an Oxford accent.'[20] Nevertheless the response to the appeal was generous and Connolly was soon inundated with parcels. It was widely rumoured that not all the offerings delivered to the office reached their specified destinations but when Edmund Wilson eventually asked Peter Watson whether it was true that Connolly had taken provisions sent for other writers Watson's conscience was more or less clear: 'No, only the *foie gras*.'[21]

Towards the end of September *American Horizon* went on sale but although it contained contributions from Isherwood, Auden, Marianne Moore, Wallace Stevens, John Berryman, E. E. Cummings and other distinguished figures, Isherwood himself wrote that nothing seemed to be 'in the same class' as Connolly's introduction.[22] Clement Greenberg reacted similarly: he had found the issue uneven, 'the fault of the people who failed to write for it, not yours'.[23] There was little time for disappointment, however. The second draft of Waugh's new work was complete and he offered it to *Horizon* for publication on condition that it appear intact and in haste. He waived payment, 'other than your kind continuance of my "subscription"', and even allowed his friend to correct, edit and preface the work at his discretion.[24] Generous though these terms seemed, they were not entirely selfless. *The Loved One* was less demure than its title suggested and its bleak satire of American funeral ceremonial had already led to rejection from several publications in the United States. Waugh liked Connolly and trusted his literary judgement but he also needed him and had turned to his magazine with the conviction that its readers were made of 'tough stuff'.[25] Connolly read the second draft and accepted the work at once. *The Loved One* seemed one of his friend's 'very best' endeavours and he would be 'honoured' to publish it, subject to a few modifications.[26]

The author was all compliance and even when the typescript was mislaid at *Horizon* he remained equable. In December Connolly wrote with offers of an American food parcel and with the hope that Waugh would join him in campaigning for paintings of writers rather than soldiers on the walls of White's. The novelist reassured him: 'We will live to see those hideous paintings moved and ours in their places.'[27] As for food, he had a supply of butter but would welcome any other provisions. Food was despatched to Gloucestershire but even as he made his preparations for Christmas – which he and Lys spent with Dick Wyndham at Tickerage – Connolly began to worry that *The Loved One* might be libellous. On New Year's Day 1948 he wrote to Waugh with a solution: he would write a preface establishing the novella as 'a Swiftian satire on California burial customs. The mention of Swift sets a precedent for a certain savagery.'[28] While it seemed certain that the story would arouse much controversy he was sure that 80 per cent of *Horizon*'s readers would be appreciative. On 2 February he wrote again and told Waugh that he had decided to risk libel proceedings in America: the magazine was insured and in any case held no American assets. A print run of 9500 had been fixed – 1500 copies were destined for America while Blackwell's in Oxford and bookstalls in the London train stations had asked for extra deliveries. There would be no review copies and a paper shortage had compelled Connolly to abbreviate his introduction, which 'is now so telegraphic as to have lost all literary flavour, but I think it says the essential things and takes the reader's hat and coat away before sitting him down in his two-and-sixpenny seat'.[29]

A few days later the special number of *Horizon* appeared, selling out overnight in England and appearing to acclaim in America. Nancy Mitford sent immediate congratulations to Connolly for what had been a publishing coup – *The Loved One* was undeniably 'strong meat': 'But I suppose so much modern literature is about torturing and beatings up of people still alive that what happens to the dead is quite immaterial ... oh dear it makes everything I've written lately look so dusty and redundant.'[30] All talk of libel proceedings faded in the general enthusiasm and it was left to Peter Watson to express a heartfelt disapproval: 'It is neither farce nor tragedy. Well-written, icy-cold but it just lacks all human feeling. How he hates everyone! I should not wish to be him. I just don't understand how he can be religious in any way. I am sorry a whole issue has to be devoted to it. It is just not on anyone's side and certainly not God's!'[31]

It had been a triumphant publication and one of the finest moments in peacetime *Horizon*. Yet even before the success had been scored Waugh sensed incipient disaffection behind the merriment: 'I see Cyril's boom fading, *Horizon* losing subscribers, income-tax officials pressing him, inertia, luxury and an insane longing to collect rare things.'[32] Not all Connolly's complaints were so abstruse. For some time he had been over-weight and at the beginning of February he was plagued by listlessness and fatigue, recurrent dental problems and blurred vision. During the war, when he had experienced a similar malaise, Lys had arranged for a period of abstinence at a health farm at Tring in Hertfordshire and now she coaxed him once again into submitting to its regime. His friends seized upon the news and turned at once to malicious fiction. Writing to thank Waugh for a copy of *The Loved One*, John Betjeman attributed Connolly's withdrawal to a heart attack and Waugh gleefully fell in with the diagnosis, despite his recent association with *Horizon*, and was po-faced in reply: 'If he has had another seizure it is really all up with him. I wish I could get Lys as a cook.'[33] Reports of doom proved premature: Connolly made good use of his confinement to revise *Enemies of Promise*, scheduled to be reissued later in 1948, and could now wear suits which had been tight for two years.

Waugh could mock but the critic told him that although the treatment had been 'horrible' he now felt rejuvenated, having lost one and a half stones and been denied alcohol and cigars. His new policy was to eat judiciously for breakfast and lunch and drink as much as he wanted in the evenings. 'My platonic idea of myself has been of a personage much thinner than the armchair figure with which you are familiar. I am only trying to live up to my ideal.'[34] Waugh was preoccupied with other idealisms and stories began to circulate that he was a party to a doctrinal conspiracy in which numerous Roman Catholics were entrusted with the conversion of distinguished Anglican malcontents prior to the *Annus Sanctus* of 1949–50, a campaign in which he had been given the greatest challenge – the conversion of the editor of *Horizon*. Waugh's friends assumed that his latest reconciliation with Connolly had no other object and when Randolph Churchill encountered the critic he taunted him with the general suspicion, only to report to Waugh later: 'He vehemently denied that he was in any danger and stated that he had been disgusted by the fact that nobody any longer talks of anything except religion ... He makes an exception in your case and says that since you are a genius you are entitled to have your own opinions.'[35] Later in the year, when they coincided at White's, Waugh told Connolly that he was going to Rome for the Holy Year and intimated that if his friend wanted to accompany him, he would be happy to underwrite expenses. For once Connolly decided to remain in England.

CHAPTER TWENTY-THREE

MEANWHILE the therapy at Tring could not have come at a more inconvenient time since in March the London County Council decreed that Stephen Spender's flat, which had doubled as the *Horizon* office since 1939, was needed for housing. Lys rose to the challenge, however, and soon the publication was preparing to move to two large rooms on the first floor of 53 Bedford Square which Peter Watson set about transforming into an environment befitting a magazine of cultural prominence. He removed paintings from storage and arranged them on the walls and bought a large eighteenth-century break-front bookcase in Edinburgh. Most generously, he commissioned Diego Giacometti to design his first chandelier, although when the finished artefact arrived it proved to be almost too large and heavy to hang and was finally installed only six months before the offices were closed. It was an eclectic arrangement but even though the office desks were new the original fireplace combined with the furniture and pictures to lend the headquarters something of the atmosphere of a private drawing room.[1] Even as the move was completed *Horizon* braced itself for its hundredth number but April's centenary 'Comment' found Connolly reluctant to celebrate. He saw cultural decline on every front and was at least partly inclined to blame public indifference. Since his magazine had begun Joyce, Yeats, Virginia Woolf, Wells, Valéry and Freud had all died, yet such artists as rose to replace them were disinclined not only to contribute but even to create: although 'six eminent poets' had been invited to submit material for the centennial edition only Edith Sitwell had work to hand. 'All the others are hard-working officials, publishers, teachers, etc., in fact culture diffusionists, selling culture for a living like the Aga Khan his bath-water.' The underlying accusation was clear: those who had abandoned the hard solitude of creativity for salaried companionship at the BBC or in the new universities had done more than neglect their artistic obligations – they had compromised.

Moreover, while subscriptions continued to climb in America, in England they were dwindling. Besides, there was little point in an arts magazine when, with the first frosts of the Cold War, it began to seem as though enduring peace could never be more than the dream of a warring generation. Until now the publication had survived on the generosity of its proprietor and the determination of its editor but those sustaining forces should not be taken for granted: 'We would be rash to prophesy for *Horizon* a further existence of more than two years. This will enable us to have covered the whole of the forties and to have enslumbered the arts, like a skilled anaesthetist, into final oblivion.'[2] In June, as the guest of honour at a dinner given by the Oxford University Writers' Club, he shared his doubts with a group of undergraduates which included the future broadcaster Ludovic Kennedy, who as secretary recorded the evening:

> Mr Connolly having the reputation of a gourmet, we gave him in Pembroke the best dinner we have yet had. Mr Connolly honoured and shamed us by appearing in a dinner-jacket. We had half-expected [him] to adopt an aggressive attitude and quote freely from obscure Latin and French poets. On the contrary, he was mellow, informative and extremely practical. He was both impressive and depressing, saying that the prospects for the creative writer were harder today than they have ever been.[3]

Whatever the quality of the food, there was no shortage of wine and Connolly drunkenly told Maurice Cranston that for all his francophile writings he could hardly speak any French. He could have committed greater indiscretions, not least repeating what he had already told Cass Canfield while in New York, the essence of which the American relayed to Hamish Hamilton: 'He feels that the job of editing a monthly takes up too much of his time and energy. Accordingly, his tentative idea is to switch from magazine to book editing. I gather in 1950 or thereabouts he will embark on a program of publishing eight or ten books a year.'[4]

Amongst the contents of the centennial number, along with essays by Bertrand Russell and Lionel Trilling, Robin Ironside on 'Balthus' and Rex Warner on 'Greece', was a short story entitled 'Crazy Crowd'. It was the work of Angus Wilson, and his discovery by the magazine – one of the major achievements of its twilight – mitigated Connolly's bleak claims of cultural stagnation. Wilson worked at the British

Museum and saw writing as nothing more than a diversion from his curatorial duties, an attitude he continued to hold even when a mutual friend asked if he could show some of the unpublished stories to the celebrated editor of *Horizon*. Connolly's assessment was less diffident than the unknown author's and he at once agreed to publish 'Mother's Sense of Fun' in November 1947 and the second story five months later. This exposure led to enquiries from Secker and Warburg, the publication of Wilson's first set of stories, *The Wrong Set*, in 1949, and a literary career which placed him at the heart of British letters during the Fifties and Sixties. As he himself admitted to his first editor, his life could have been otherwise: 'If I had not been chosen by you for publication in Horizon it is almost certain that my writing would have petered out as the unfertilized hobby of a man who was looking for some means of self-expression but never found it ... I think I have contributed much that is worth having done. *None* of it could I have done without your encouragement.'[5]

At Sussex Place meanwhile one literary party succeeded another. When Dick Wyndham took along his daughter Joan she found a group of 'terrifyingly smart and intelligent people' eating ortolans. Koestler was kind and avuncular during dinner; Spender and Quennell appeared later. 'Everybody was being terribly bitchy about everybody else. It was like being in a nest of intellectual vipers ... As for Connolly, he was known as "Squirrel". When he went out of the room a young man leapt onto a stool and did a wicked impersonation of him and everybody screamed "Oh, darling, you've got Squirrel to a T!"'[6] Elizabeth Bowen, Louis MacNeice and Lucian Freud joined the throng which gathered to welcome Auden and Chester Kallman and perhaps showed more tact than Connolly, who asked Kallman, 'How does it feel to be the male Alice B. Toklas?'[7] In the autumn Aldous and Maria Huxley were the pretext for another large gathering. On a further occasion Alan Pryce-Jones brought along Alan Ross, a young protégé from the *Times Literary Supplement*. The newcomer had just made his first appearance in *Horizon* with an essay on Nathaniel West and now found himself with Anthony and Violet Powell, Patrick Kinross and Henry Green. He was struck by his host's idiosyncratic hospitality: 'On that same evening Cyril, one of whose most engaging qualities was the trouble he would take when his interest was aroused, spent a long time away from the party showing me round his library.'[8] Yet another celebration took place in December to mark T. S. Eliot's acceptance of the Nobel Prize.

The occasion merited black tie and at the end of the evening the guests were privileged to witness the poet singing 'Under the Bamboo Tree' from *Sweeney Agonistes*.

Connolly's entertainments depended on unstinting practical assistance which for the last few years had come from Lys, who had performed countless other thankless tasks on the assumption of eventual marriage. Although Connolly's divorce became final in June 1948 it was clear to onlookers that initial passions were long dead between him and the woman he saw increasingly as embodying the ebbing Forties. Her time had run out. At first Lys was able to take comfort from the fact that Jean could no longer be invoked as an excuse for marital delays but she began to sense her lover's change of mood and to doubt the promises he had made. He prevaricated and old friends drew knowing conclusions: Peter Watson found her crying twice in the *Horizon* office and Sonia efficiently reported events in her correspondence: 'Lys is more like a sad and bedraggled sparrow than ever, keeping up an unceasing chirping about "true love" while contemplating the ringless finger – and there's NOTHING one can do about it.'[9] Eventually she did acquire a small ring but there was little triumph when she showed it to Janetta: 'This is all I've got and I've had to buy it myself.'[10]

In May Dick Wyndham was killed while covering fighting in newly proclaimed Israel for the *Sunday Times*. When his will was read Connolly discovered that he had inherited his cellar of 400 bottles; meanwhile, at the funeral, his eyes met those of the painter Anne Dunn, the eighteen-year-old daughter of the financier Sir James Dunn. They were introduced afterwards and a few weeks later, during the course of a party, she was approached by Sonia Brownell who told her to abandon the man she was with and accompany her and Connolly to a nightclub. As she got to know the famous editor she found Lys 'exquisite'; but if he was fond of her he also clearly found her exasperating and both parties gave the impression of sensing that the end was near. Nevertheless for a while they continued to socialize together and took to frequenting 'Antilles', a nightclub in Soho, with Anne and her lover Lucian Freud. The men got on well: the critic later bought Freud's portrait of Anne while the painter 'adored' Connolly.[11]

Emotional turbulence echoed and complicated literary indecision. As though a serious study of Flaubert were not sufficiently ambitious, Connolly had already decided that the scheme would be enriched by the involvement of Baudelaire before being seized with more glamorous yearnings which might take him to France for most of the year. He was already committed to a July holiday at Somerset Maugham's and soon *Le Tombeau de Palinure* was due for publication in Paris. The right scheme, sandwiched between these prestigious dates, would not only finance his travels but also free him from Lys's reproaches. He broached his plan to Hamish Hamilton: only a travel book would clear his mind in preparation for 'Flaubert' and only a travel book about France seemed desirable. Specifically he proposed 'a hymn of gratitude with good maps':[12] a study of the magic territory which he knew extended for 100 miles around Bordeaux and at the very centre of which stood the Chapon Fin, the great hotel and restaurant which at varying times had beguiled Edward VII, Sarah Bernhardt and the whole French Cabinet, to say nothing of Cyril Connolly when an itinerant under-graduate. He would need two months for research and £300 for pay-ment and expenses but in return Hamish Hamilton could expect a manuscript of 70,000 words in the spring of 1949 which would have a passionate and idiosyncratic excellence. Connolly had luck as well as charm: Harper's would also be involved in the scheme and from New York Cass Canfield – advancing $1000 for 'Flaubert' and the travel book – seemed to suggest that he had only to ask and funds would be made available: 'I can't tell you how pleased we are about this new project. To publish a book by you is an exciting event.'[13]

Leaving Lys and Sonia in charge of home and office, he travelled in June, staying in Paris before continuing to Bordeaux and the Dordogne. Returning to the capital to collect Lys, he made contact with Edward and Nika Hulton and together the four friends headed for the Villa Mauresque, where the Connollys were expected for a fortnight. On one occasion during their stay the Windsors came to dinner and Maud learned that 'I like her very much.'[14] Afterwards they went to stay with Lady Kenmare at Cap Ferrat before Lys returned to London in August and Connolly headed for Bordeaux to begin the book. Photographs were required with the text and it had originally been agreed that Wyndham would take them. Casting around for a replacement, Con-nolly thought of his old friend Joan Eyres-Monsell, whose photography had appeared in *Horizon*, and she agreed to join him in France. They spent most of August travelling through Gironde up the Atlantic coast to La Rochelle and going inland as far as Toulouse, and although very little work was done Connolly soon saw his expenses climbing. He applied to Hamish Hamilton for a further £50 – unsuccessfully – and also despatched assurances to Lys that his relations with Joan were strictly artistic and professional. His claims were not entirely true: Joan was already involved with her future husband, Patrick Leigh Fermor, but the fact that she was unobtainable made her doubly attractive to Connolly, who sent confessions to South Africa: 'I chose an old flame of mine and fell very much in love with her.' Nothing had come of it: they were merely closer friends but he now knew that he could not marry Lys: 'I should only be unkind to her – she is so devoted to me and belongs to all the everyday part of my life – but Joan is like Jean a very intelligent and remarkable person.'[15]

The book was abandoned in lethargy and despair but hope sprang eternal and even his mother expected a daily breakthrough: 'I *know* you have not yet written what will bring you world fame . . . if you have genius of any kind you also have a complex character that even yourself may not be able to understand.'[16] In a sense she was right: for all the acuity of his self-analysis in private letters and public writings he continued to deceive himself as to the nature of his talent, continued to accept the sovereignty of fiction and to hope that one day he would be its practitioner. 'Happy Deathbeds' was his attempt in 1948 to transfer the characters and friendships of *Horizon* into a fictional narrative: Elsa bears a strong resemblance to Sonia while Paul is the rich homosexual whom she loves and who owns the magazine. The main character, however, is Brinkley, the editor: he alone seems real simply because he has the implausibility of reality, and he alone acts with the inconsistency which characterizes the living. It is he who dances round success: 'Hating blame, he yet found praise all dust and ashes.' It is he who suspects that the discovery of talent is no more than a sentence to futility and frustration. It is he who knows that he behaves selfishly and inexcusably towards those who love him, who analyses himself so well without being able to recant his imperfections.

That manuscript too was abandoned and before long so was Lys: Connolly returned to Paris without her but did nothing to conceal the pleasures of new bachelorhood and sent bulletins full of chance encounters, surprising telephone calls and nostalgic laughter with old friends. Joan was there and he saw a lot of Jean besides. Even a difficult encounter with Nancy Mitford did little to dampen proceedings and Lys finally decided in November that she must go to Paris to reclaim him. They were reunited and returned together to London where he interviewed the visiting Aldous Huxley for *Picture Post*. That same month an article in *Time* suggested that Connolly was a representative European thinker: along with J. B. Priestley, the British anthropologist Geoffrey Gorer and Jean-Paul Sartre, he was identified as a *savant* who took a dim view of American civilization and saw the United States as 'the playgirl of the Western World – and not even a pretty one – with plumbing instead of arteries, ice water instead of blood, neuroses instead of a heart and a radio instead of a brain.'[17] International salutations, however fatuous, were always welcome, but less agreeable news came from overseas at the end of 1948: on 27 December Christopher Brooke died at home in South Africa having been nursed through a long illness by Maud, his lover and companion of over twenty years. In *The Bugle* his obituary paid tribute to his service in the army, his bravery, his horsemanship and the trouble he took 'to help any member of the Regiment who felt he was being unfairly treated or who was in any difficulties'.[18] Apart from all considerations of loneliness, his death enforced a greater degree of financial prudence on Connolly's mother, who now decided to adopt South African citizenship in order to avoid English death duties and who, worrying increasingly about her son's solvency, wrote in April 1949: 'I should *hate* to live to be so very old so I hope I won't – and I am so afraid if by any chance you were unable to write, you would have nothing.'[19]

Meanwhile the interests which had converged behind *Horizon* were beginning to disperse. On 1 January 1949 Peter Watson departed aboard the *Queen Mary* for almost four months in America. He had watched his friend's dealings with Jean, Diana and Lys and known of his occasional and pragmatic encounters with Sonia while at the same time pursuing an emotional career no less anguished. With Denham Fouts in America he had been isolated throughout the war but when he remained in New York after Connolly's departure in January 1947 he fell in love with an aspiring poet named Waldemar Hansen, a cultivated and sensitive twenty-four-year-old who was far removed from Fouts's philistine self-destruction. Hansen joined Watson in London in 1947 and the two men lived happily until the American's return home the following year. Fouts died in Rome and even before being reunited with Watson in America in 1949 Hansen knew that his lover had been deeply upset by the news. He was completely unprepared, however, for Watson's revelation that he wanted their affair to end: he was involved with another man named Norman Fowler, with whom he had had a

brief fling several years before and who was himself a former lover of
Hansen's. As if these preoccupations were not enough, Watson was
increasingly involved with the Institute of Contemporary Arts, of which
he had been a founder member in 1947. Now more funds were required
and a permanent home needed if the organization was to expand
satisfactorily. He wanted to help and had to acknowledge the fact that
he had other claims on his time and money than the future of a
magazine to which his colleague was decreasingly committed. Connolly
turned up at the office less and less; his 'Comments' were now blatantly
intermittent. The bills still had to be paid, however, and Watson began
to find the imbalance in obligations annoying, writing to Hansen in
July: 'A rather terrible showdown with Cyril is about to happen. Either
the magazine will end in November or continue under very different
auspices. He has behaved with shattering cynicism and it has upset me
very much.'[20]

Yet whatever the degree of his frustration he found it impossible to
make his friend commit himself about the magazine's future: Connolly's
usual aversion to decisive farewells surfaced and besides he had his own
set of emotional distractions. Tried beyond endurance, not least by his
growing infatuation with Anne Dunn, Lys had left him to spend more
than a month in Italy, only to be pursued by letters of manipulation and
reproach. She should have known the audacity of his overtures even
before she read them, should have known that his technique – of
appealing to maternal protectiveness while at the same time detailing his
trespasses with insight, defiance and knowing self-pity – would win her
over, but perhaps she still wanted to believe and to forgive. She returned
but he continued to be restive, happy to delegate all *Horizon* work to
Sonia while he dissipated the day and thought of Anne.

While this carousel revolved, Sonia maintained her loyal watch at the
office and *Horizon* continued to appear, even though its most impor-
tant contributions – fiction by Truman Capote, 'The Lesson and the
Secret' by Lionel Trilling, Lawrence Durrell on Henry Miller, 'The
Oasis' by Mary McCarthy – were increasingly transatlantic. In October
Waugh paid a surprising visit to the office – as though inspecting an
exhibition shortly to close – and relayed his findings to Nancy Mitford:
'I saw the inside of *Horizon* office full of horrible pictures collected by
Watson and Lys and Miss Brownell working away with a dictionary
translating some rot from the French. That paper is to end soon.'[21] At
first the talk among the partners avoided mention of outright closure:

Watson toyed with perpetuating the venture under Stephen Spender's direction, an idea that prompted Connolly's irritable and unfair aside to Waugh that the poet had 'generously offered (behind my back) to take my place as Editor pour l'amour de l'art';[22] and Connolly himself thought a new management might be inclined to retain him to edit a quarterly publication. Then he met John Lehmann and 'offered me *Horizon*, over a bottle of champagne at the Athenaeum, at a reduced price . . . I suggested to my backer in Purnell that it would be well worth buying for the small sum involved; but nothing came of it.'[23] The Rothermeres were known to be watching developments with acquisitive interest. The *Observer* even went so far as to ask Alan Ross if, in the event of purchase, he would be interested in assuming the editorship. All negotiations had effectively foundered, however, when the magazine's most stalwart foot-soldier, Sonia, finally accepted George Orwell's proposal and married him in October. *Nineteen Eighty-Four* had been published in June to great acclaim but it was increasingly clear that its author had little time left to live. Word inevitably spread that she had married a dying millionaire and for years she was dogged by accusations of mercenary opportunism. Connolly told Waugh that he found the marriage a 'grotesque farce'. 'I can't really regard it as an act of self-sacrifice so much as a panicky acceptance of a new job because she is losing the old one.'[24] Annoyance and jealousy spurred his cynicism: it was unsettling for someone as possessive as Connolly to reflect that she who had been so devoted for so long could so suddenly acquire new purpose. Equally, if there was any truth in his sneer he could at least have admitted that her new career would be no better paid than her last: marriage to Orwell did nothing to make Sonia rich, since the Orwell Estate was impoverished until the paperback publication of his novels many years later. Whatever her motives, however, the implications were clear: henceforth, whatever the magazine's future, she would have other vigils to keep.

November's 'Comment' confirmed what literary London already expected, that *Horizon* would close at the end of 1949, when an era would end with the decade. The news brought letters of regret. Augustus John thought the publication irreplaceable: 'Our civilization grows more and more to resemble a mixture of a concentration and a Butlin camp and without your unique magazine there won't be much of a view left or means of escape to open country.'[25] John Betjeman was no less inconsolable: 'I know that to appear in Horizon was a real honour . . . I think I was taken seriously first (and therefore took myself more seriously) after you had had the courage to print my poems.'[26] A double number, serving December 1949 and January 1950, was as international in range as its predecessor 120 issues previously, and besides essays on Francis Bacon and the Marquis de Sade and poetry by Cecil Day-Lewis and Octavio Paz, it contained a last 'Comment': '"Nothing dreadful is ever done with, no bad thing gets any better; you can't be too serious." This is the message of the Forties from which, alas, there seems no escape, for it is closing time in the gardens of the West and from now on an artist will be judged only by the resonance of his solitude or the quality of his despair.'

They were to prove the most famous and enduring sentences Connolly wrote in the magazine's service, gloomily portentous to those who found them lacking in precise meaning, evocative and prescient to those who doubted whether the new decade would inaugurate a reversal in the decline of European culture and vitality or arrest the transatlantic exodus of power, initiative and prestige. Whatever their meaning, however, it escaped the consortium of enthusiasts which had made the magazine possible: in January Watson was in Brazil with Norman Fowler, Sonia was fraught in anticipation of imminent widowhood and Lys perplexed about her future since the man she had hoped to marry had fallen in love with another woman. Nevertheless she loyally stayed to help with terminal administration, her assistance unspecified in Connolly's inimitable recollection: 'We closed the long windows over Bedford Square, the telephone was taken, the furniture stored, the back numbers went to their cellar, the files rotted in the dust. Only contributions continued inexorably to be delivered, like a suicide's milk.'[27] Time would tell if he was wrong in his decision to jettison success for the uncertainties of another professional life but perhaps after all volition had yielded to inevitability, perhaps he was bound to go, for the Forties had taught another lesson besides: that all redoubts not captured are in the end abandoned.

VII
'DEAR, DAMN'D, DISTRACTING TOWN, FAREWELL!'

CHAPTER TWENTY-FOUR

IT WAS PETER QUENNELL who christened Barbara Skelton 'Baby', although it was hard to imagine that she was ever pink, predictable, shapeless and defenceless. Her mother had been a Gaiety Girl and a beauty who liked to claim that her eyes were the blue of blue hydrangeas: while performing in *The Merry Widow* she had accepted a backstage bouquet from Eric Skelton, a young officer of some means with an interest in cricket and actresses and a direct descent from the dramatist Richard Brinsley Sheridan, and they were subsequently married. While stationed in Barbados he developed malaria and following a heart attack was retired from the army to spend the remainder of his life officially frail and unfit for strenuous activities. He was a victim of the Wall Street Crash and the Skeltons moved around Kent and Berkshire – where Barbara Olive was born on 26 June 1916 – before settling, with the birth of another daughter, Brenda, in London. By then, however, Barbara was already precocious in moodiness: 'Bun-faced, with slanting sludge-coloured eyes, I was probably a great disappointment to my parents.'[1] The feeling was mutual and she seems to have spent her earliest years either bored and frustrated or else in paroxysms of fury brought on by parental neglect, criticism or contradiction. She was four when she ran at her mother with a carving knife and no older when a scene she created attracted a crowd and a curious policeman who was enlisted to help control her. After a succession of educational establishments, with expulsion from one and anorexia along the way, she left school altogether at fifteen.

The boredom and restlessness she had suffered in the provinces she took with her to the metropolis. Her liaison with a wealthy friend of her father's resulted in an abortion but when furs and continental holidays could no longer keep tedium at bay she terminated the affair without securing any financial settlement. She was subsequently in India where her relations with an officer led to his court-martial. With the war she was back in London: whatever the fortunes of the Allies she insouci-antly followed her own interests even as those interests pursued her: Osbert Lancaster chased her round a sofa; the artist Feliks Topolski and other lonely wartime itinerants proved more determined. So too did Peter Quennell, who also christened the twenty-four-year-old 'Skel-tie', thus suggesting the speed and careering randomness of her progress from job to job – model, truck-driver, secretary – and from man to man. The young diplomat Donald Maclean sponsored her application to the cipher department of the Foreign Office and she was posted to the British embassy in Cairo, where her cryptographic accomplishments were overshadowed by her liaison with King Farouk. Officialdom frowned when the king himself flogged her on the steps of the palace with the cord of a dressing-gown – she was subsequently asked to leave Egypt – but Farouk always remained in affectionate if distant contact, and besides one small complaint – 'I would have preferred a splayed cane'[2] – Barbara was without regrets: the fact was that despite being mean, spoilt and infantile of humour, Farouk *amused* her.

Her memoirs – and the memoirs of those who encountered her – reveal numerous occasions when, owing to boredom, frustration and irritation, she resorted to sulking, tantrums, defiant rudeness, even physical violence, and gave no care to the impressions onlookers formed. She was arrestingly good-looking: her eyes were green, her features angular and her figure, formerly the inspiration of Schiaparelli, remained the envy of London. As a vagrant she was difficult to describe, and in their attempts to define her some of her contemporaries turned to the animal kingdom for illumination. The painter Michael Wishart, having been her lover, later spoke of her 'chameleon adaptability and ruthlessness'[3] but her wanton behaviour and lissom shape were scarcely reptilian and Cyril Connolly himself was nearer the mark when, long after initial infatuations, he discussed her with Edmund Wilson: 'Lys had been a Shetland pony; B[arbara] was a lioness – her silvery hair and her greenish and feline eyes – her friends complained that she bit them, but then she would come back and rub against you.'[4] It was no doubt partly her own fault that such metaphors of wildness obscured a crucial fact: she longed to be tamed, to cook, to run a home and to have children, to create the stable domesticity she felt she had been denied as a child but which only men she would have found boring were likely to provide, and even Connolly, her first husband, the man she revered above all others and the one who came closest to providing that arrangement, proved unequal to accommodating her humours or pre-dicting the directions of her frenzy.

They first met in 1941 when Peter Quennell brought his friend along to a flat in Mayfair where Barbara was also having a drink. Her erotic tastes were still conventional and she gave little thought to the editor of *Horizon*, preferring instead to contemplate Quennell. On Christmas Eve 1941 she went to dinner at Drayton Gardens and recorded in her diary that Connolly had managed to procure some good ham which had been served with large amounts of wine and rum. The company – Lys, Mamaine Paget, Arthur Waley, Quennell, Joan Eyres-Monsell and her husband John Rayner – sounded convivial, but Barbara reflected that 'Cyril always manages to create a strained atmosphere' and per-haps as a result found herself so intimidated that for most of the evening she spoke infrequently and then only in whispers.[5] A few days later she coincided with him again when she and Quennell, Lys and Connolly all had dinner with Augustus John. This time Connolly seemed 'more human' but he remained a distant figure and she could form no further impressions until they met again in the late Forties. Their second introduction was the work of another mutual friend, Natalie Newhouse, who later married the actor Robert Newton, and occurred when it was widely known that Connolly and Lys were on the verge of final parting. When Natalie told the ivory tower's custodian that Baby had a passion for learning facts, Connolly's interest was aroused, and at the beginning of 1950 Waugh wrote to Nancy Mitford: 'G. Orwell is dead and Mrs Orwell presumably a rich widow. Will Cyril marry her? He is said to be consorting with Miss Skelton.'[6]

Connolly had looked to Mrs Orwell for unswerving commitment and veneration but Baby would meet other needs: he had seen enough of her dealings with Quennell, knew enough instinctively about the capacities and potential of women friends to realize that she would provide him with the complications necessary to his emotional life. In March 1950 Barbara received a telephone call in which he revealed that he was alone in Sussex Place – Lys having gone out to dinner – and that while she played merry chess with a friend he sat in cold and miserable penury. In short, she was 'a selfish bitch',[7] yet when Barbara arrived prepared to flatter she found him exultant and ready for bed, not recrimination. A few weeks later, he rang to reveal that he had devoted the previous night to giving all his women friends marks for attractiveness, loyalty and spirituality: she eclipsed Sonia as the most attractive while Joan and Lys were judged the most loyal. Quennell had seen his friend pit women against one another before while employing complaints of deprivation to move them, but he nevertheless watched developments with interest and archly asked his former girlfriend for news of her progress: 'Has Baby read her *Palinurus* yet?' More than mere flippancy informed her reply: 'Why should I read it, when I live it every day?'[8]

With no work to occupy him and all ambitions temporarily in abeyance, Connolly had time for emotional games. Furthermore, Sussex Place was increasingly unwelcoming: Lys had already begun the search for a new job and a new life and had no inclination now to pamper the house she had once imagined she would occupy more permanently; its echoing chambers made him feel solitary and restless, and as always in such a mood his thoughts turned to travel. In March he went to Paris, and besides having dinner with Waugh, bound for Rome and Holy Week, he visited Jane Bowles, whose husband Paul, an accomplished composer, had also earned great acclaim the previous year with the publication of his first novel, *The Sheltering Sky*. The author had arrived in London to help advertise his work and in so doing had hastened to declare his respects both to Connolly and to the memory of *Horizon*. The critic had liked the novel but perplexed the young American prodigy by saying that he considered it too good to review. The meeting in Paris was not a success. Connolly announced himself to the concierge as 'a friend of Bowles', but as the latter told Lehmann in a subsequent letter, his wife had no interest in his friends. 'She is also very near-sighted and has a foul memory besides . . . she was sure he was a musician of some sort, come to pay his respects.'[9]

The main attraction in Paris, however, was Jean, and even as he travelled Connolly reminded himself of the certainty of her compassion: she had always understood him and would be sympathetic to his needs for a new mate and career and would counsel how best to manage Baby's waywardness or Lys's impatience. However, his former wife was in a sorry condition – she drank relentlessly, her make-up ran, and despite a diet dominated by artichokes, which were said to fortify the liver, she was badly overweight. Connolly found this deterioration doubly unsettling: she was too young for her present condition and her outer decline or inner malaise reproached his fame and prosperity and rekindled memories of guilt and regret.

Yet if he was distressed it was partly his own fault: confrontations with the past are especially disappointing to the nostalgic and he had sought Jean out as much in the hope of reclaiming lost time as for the charms of her company or the generosity of her marital advice. Perhaps at least there was an appropriateness to the fact that reunion occurred in Paris, home to more and more ghosts – Logan's, Joyce's – and setting to numerous memories grown sepia and faded with time. Spectres scattered with the sudden arrival of Barbara, who had been touring France with Peter Quennell in her red convertible Sunbeam Talbot. Not wanting to be worsted by his old friend or left out of the fun with Baby, Connolly decided to follow her when she progressed to Geneva, where she was due to meet John Sutro, the prosperous cinephile and writer who had founded the Oxford University Railway Club. When he arrived he booked into a hotel opposite theirs so that he and Barbara could signal to each other from their rooms. Meetings had to be conducted in secrecy and she would escape Sutro by claiming a booking with her hairdresser. When they met she and Connolly would have tea and caviare and he would consult his guidebook for advice about where she and Sutro should eat that night. When Sutro returned to London the conspirators took to the Sunbeam Talbot and toured Switzerland, visiting Madame de Staël's château, Rousseau's house and the Monastery of Chartreuse.

They returned to England separately – he joined Lys outside Marseilles while in Paris Baby flirted with lesbianism, though 'I just saw her as another man with breasts.'[10] Back in London, although not officially cohabiting, they saw increasing amounts of each other and when not at Sussex Place could often be found at Barbara's flat at Queen Street in Mayfair whence Janetta and Robert occasionally received telephone calls in which their neighbour would say no more than that he was ringing from 'a pink boudoir'.[11] Barbara also had a small cottage outside Hastingleigh near Ashford in Kent which she had bought for £400 before the war and this too became a regular resort, although its rechristening, from honest Oak Cottage to the distinctly more ambivalent Oak Coffin, indicated that Connolly was not always in the mood for country pleasures. One entry in Barbara's diary revealed eager participation: bare-foot and with rolled-up sleeves he clipped the hedge and said he found the air beneficial; but on another occasion enthusiasm forsook him: 'An hysterical quarrel as I wanted to go to the country and Cyril didn't. He kept sneaking out to telephone Lys.'[12] He could not readily forget the pleasures of metropolitan life: good air was all very well but remained less entertaining than hosting a lunch at the Ritz, with Evelyn Waugh among the guests, as he did in the summer, or attending a lunch given by Raymond Mortimer for the visiting Aldous Huxley the same season – Huxley himself led the applause when Connolly declared: 'Longevity is the revenge of talent upon genius.'[13]

On 16 July, after a week of illness but little pain Jean died from heart failure. She was thirty-nine years old. At last she would take her final place in Connolly's pantheon, not as the woman who had refused to go back to him in 1945 nor yet as the declining figure he had seen four months previously, but as the embodiment of youth and its promise. Lys also was soon to disappear from his life, though with less finality: she had secured a job in the London office of the *New Yorker* and at the end of 1950 announced that she was moving to New York to work for the publisher Doubleday. Once again Connolly's 'desertion complex' was aroused but for once it seemed that he had lost the initiative: Jean was now beyond any appeal or manipulation and even Lys was acting with an independence and determination she had never shown before; the man who had been surrounded by muses a decade before found himself temporarily forsaken. Of course there were women like Sonia who adored him and would do anything he asked; equally there were the distant or impracticable goddesses like Anne about whom he could continue to fantasize; but he had to recognize that there was only one woman in his life in the summer of 1950 and she promised nothing if not turbulence. Overtures of marriage were made with a caution and contradiction which Barbara recorded in her diary: the first came in July when he announced that wedlock was impossible, 'as we don't get on all that well when things go wrong and you couldn't bear being poor. After all, it's not as though anyone is likely to leave you any money we can count on.'[14] A month later he returned to his theme: about to go and stay in Scotland, he suggested that they live together preparatory to marriage. 'He can't live alone at Sussex Place and [says] that if he doesn't marry me he will marry someone else.'[15]

In Scotland he stayed with Lord Glenconner at Glen and told Barbara pointedly that the beautiful Clarissa Churchill, niece of the statesman, was to be of the party. In the event she never arrived but the disappointment was forgotten almost as soon as he returned to London when King Farouk summoned Barbara to join him on his progress through the casinos of Le Touquet and Deauville. Connolly at once saw advantages: whatever her mischances with roulette or baccarat, royal favour – itself a game of fortune – might secure them other winnings: a winter holiday in Egypt, the odd fur coat, French currency for future excursions. Furthermore, he reminded her, 'a King's a King'.[16] Such was his enthusiasm that he accompanied her to the airport and then secured a commission from the *Daily Mail* to report on the royal itinerary. Baby joined Farouk's retinue at La Baule. He told attendants that she was 'a real minx' and gave her 1000 francs every evening to chance at the tables, but Connolly arrived only to learn that the king had a horror of writers and journalists and would not grant an interview. The next day his entourage, with Baby in attendance, departed for Biarritz and Connolly had to look for consolation in the cufflinks which Barbara bought for him out of money hoarded in the casino. Farouk eventually took his court to Cannes, leaving his minx to reunite with her other admirer and travel back with him through the Dordogne to London. When she collected her luggage – sent ahead to the Egyptian embassy – she found with it a crate of mangoes for Connolly, the tribute of one hedonist to another.

In September they became secretly engaged and he went to Paris once again to present his fiancée with a ring. He travelled with Janetta, who had left Robert Kee and was going to meet her next husband, Derek Jackson, and on the ferry kept them both amused with role-playing and impersonations. A few days later a group of friends went to a nightclub and everybody became very drunk: Barbara was a conspicuous figure on the dance-floor and conferred lavish attention on all the men present apart from her future husband. Decisions had already been made, however, and on 5 October, to the surprise of many of his friends, Connolly married Barbara at Folkestone registry office. He gave his profession as 'publisher' to the attendant clerk; she could only remember her father's army rank and not his regiment, a lapse which outraged her new husband. The ceremony was witnessed by the bride's village policeman, W. W. Boot, and a casual pedestrian importuned on the moment by the groom. The couple argued before and after solemnities. The *Daily Express* indicated a desire to write an article about the alliance but then thought better of it, and although Barbara was amused to see her husband scan the other newspapers in hopeful fear of publicity, Fleet Street remained aloof. The marriage proved of consuming interest to Evelyn Waugh, who wrote to Diana Cooper with the news that 'Connolly is married to a concubine of the Emir of Egypt's' and that he had suffered another seizure requiring further incarceration at Tring immediately after the service.[17]

Only five days after his wedding Connolly told his new wife that marriage made him feel 'trapped'. She too had misgivings and felt 'very restive and dissatisfied, saddled with a slothful whale of a husband who spends his time soaking in the bath and then plods despondently to White's where he studies the racing form'.[18] Not the least of his anxieties was the future of Sussex Place. Now that the Kees had separated it became clear that radical revision of the tenancy would be necessary, but beyond negligible royalties he was earning nothing and nor was Barbara. Her solution was that they inhabit the top floor and let the remainder of the house but her husband hoped that they would be able to retain the principal reception rooms if the house was divided into three. The problem was the occasion for strident confrontations but by the end of November the lease was up for sale and he and Barbara would continue temporarily with the use of the flat in Queen Street. It was the end of expansive ideas and the final farewell to the age of *Horizon*, but when he wrote to Hamish Hamilton on 24 November to discuss revising *The Unquiet Grave* he revealed his new enthusiasm – gardening, and in particular shrubs and creepers, and wondered if his publisher had any idea where he could buy a weeping silver lime. He was still nominally preparing 'Flaubert' and pleaded domestic turbulence: 'I feel very badly about Lys and therefore very badly about marrying Barbara though I think it will turn out all right hence my general furtiveness and persecution mania.'[19] John Lehmann was also a party to Connolly's horticultural designs and having recently planted a garden at his cottage was the object of friendly rivalry: 'One day he challenged me to a contest of Latin names of the most desirable rhododendrons, magnolias and camellias. I had delved as deeply into the catalogues as he had, and I think I held my own fairly well, perhaps to his surprise.' Lehmann cared more for his friend's literary aptitudes and listened eagerly to news of his next venture: 'He already had plans to write a novel, a successor to *The Rock Pool*, and he told me that he had invented a new "internal daydream" technique. He confessed, however, to a snag: his imagination conjured up the scenes he intended to create so vividly ... that he just lay on his sofa and chuckled at the brilliant show his fancy was putting on for him.'[20]

The Connollys' first married Christmas was spent sociably: there were dinners with Sir Oswald and Lady Mosley and John and Penelope

Betjeman and in January 1951 they went to stay with Robin and Mary Campbell in Wiltshire. Campbell had been a war hero and an intermittent contributor to *Horizon* and now impressed Barbara as a good host, 'easy, informal and no heckling in the mornings to get us out of bed'.[21] The Campbells took their guests for dinner with Ralph and Frances Partridge, and although the latter felt 'faint resentment at the way everyone lays out the red carpet for Cyril just because he seems to expect it' she nevertheless fell in with the tendency and cooked a good dinner. '[Cyril] has become quite humpty-dumpty shaped, his egg head backed by a wild tangle of hair and merging necklessly into the larger egg of his body. Barbara ... is pretty but aggressively silent; she absolutely refused to be drawn into the conversation.'[22]

The good food was welcome. Life in Queen Street, Oak Cottage and Sussex Place, which they continued to use while it was on the market, was increasingly trammelled owing to financial difficulties, and although Barbara enjoyed spending prolonged periods in the kitchen trying to tempt her husband's exacting palate, she referred frequently in her diary to trips to the pawnbroker and shortages of lavatory paper. Despite insolvency they retained a cleaning woman for the Mayfair flat and until that property was surrendered in retrenchment in March Mrs Munro was Barbara's confidante, revealing that although she thought Mr Connolly had a kind face she also found him selfish and lazy. Maud arrived from South Africa at the beginning of 1951 for several weeks in England, determined to inspect Matthew's gravestone and her new daughter-in-law and eager to spend time with her 'darling Sprat'. Concerning Barbara she was non-committal or silent in the letters she sent subsequent to her visit but time would overthrow her reticence. In May she sailed back to solitude and remote adoration; but Barbara continued to remember the lunches and dinners they all three had together, when Maud's adored son 'barely looked up from his plate'.[23]

Even as Mrs Connolly experienced the novelty of post-war England and noted the changes in her son, Nancy Mitford was revising her forthcoming novel *The Blessing*, and giving particular attention to detailing the character who appears in its closing chapters: Ed Spain, otherwise known as 'The Captain', an Old Etonian and Oxford graduate who runs a London theatre which specializes in the production of 'highbrow' plays. Spain 'was a charming, lazy character who had had from his schooldays but one idea, to make a great deal of money with little or no effort, so that he could lead the life for which nature had

suited him, that of a rich dilettante'. He disdained intellectual compromise: 'The Captain had too much intellectual honesty to pander to an
audience by putting on plays which might have amused them but which
did not come up to his own idea of perfection.' He too had a band of
faithful female acolytes and 'his keen blue eyes looked as if they had been
concentrating for many years on a vanishing horizon'.[24] If her final
caricature of Connolly was merely playful, its lack of cruel detail had
nothing to do with Waugh, who wrote advising Mitford on more than
one occasion to 'soften and fatten' the Captain.[25] The book appeared in
April but Connolly betrayed no suspicion of collusion when he gave
Waugh his opinion of the novel: 'She keeps at it. I suppose she is
constantly terrified by the thought of poverty in old age.'[26]

Connolly's presence in *The Blessing* may have been disguised but that
month he appeared with no distracting embellishments in another book,
Stephen Spender's autobiography *World Within World*. At forty-two the
poet was perhaps a little young for such solemn retrospection but the
turbulent events which he and his contemporaries had survived seemed
already to be vested with the distant glamour of history, and to acknowledge that temporal remoteness was also to declare membership of a
middle-aged literary generation. Certain of his involvement and no
doubt curious to see himself through time's telescope, Connolly read the
book with interest and was pleased to see that the *Horizon* years were
recorded with seemly reverence. He applauded *World Within World*
while feeling in some ways ambivalent about its author, who seemed
alternately 'an inspired simpleton, a great big silly goose, a holy Russian
idiot, large, generous, gullible, ignorant, affectionate, idealistic' yet at the
same time 'shrewd, ambitious, aggressive and ruthless, a publicity-
seeking intellectual full of administrative energy and rentier asperity'.[27]

Meanwhile, although such publications endorsed his importance
among the members of his literary generation, his domestic realities
were less auspicious. Inclined to sloth yet possessed of a nimble, nervous conscience which punished him even more than his shortages of
cash, he continued to indulge in self-reproach and self-pity and Barbara
confided in her diary that 'on bad guilt days, he remains in the bath and
groans'.[28] She now referred to him as 'Pop' or 'Pungle' and her solution
to the encircling gloom had been to prevail upon John Sutro to bring
her a coati – a small raccoon-like creature – from Uruguay. While her
husband, assisted by Mr Coombes the gardener, absorbed himself in
the adornment of lawns and borders, she looked to her exotic pet for

solace: 'I don't know what we would have done without the coati and its enchanting ways. Such a relief to the monotony and poverty of our existence at the moment, always running out of money, and Cyril just sitting brooding like a furious fallen emperor.'[29] Suspicions of exile and decline were confirmed in November with the sale 'at a considerable loss' of the lease of Sussex Place.[30] Following payment of various bills the sum was depleted still further. Nevertheless, determined to keep his china, furniture and books with him, Connolly insisted on the enlargement of Oak Cottage: all the walls were built out by six inches, the roof was repaired, a new boiler installed and calor gas fitted in the kitchen and sitting room. Evacuees from metropolitan life, they were now dependent when called to London on the hospitality of friends. None was more insistently loyal than Sonia and they often stayed with her, despite the discomfort of the bed. For her it was an honour and an obligation, the least she could do: she was greatly distressed by her friend's plight and eager that others share her concern, as Spender learned in December 1951: 'Sonia got rather drunk ... As self-revelation of her feelings, she provided a description of Cyril's poverty ever since his marriage ... She is obsessively interested in her friends' marriages – especially in those that don't succeed.'[31]

However, Connolly had begun a new career, and although it would never make him rich, never even pay as much as the lucrative American lecture circuit which many of his contemporaries were to join, it nevertheless gave him a degree of exposure and influence the late twentieth century rarely conceded to its men of letters. In September 1950 he had started to review occasional books for the *Sunday Times*, then the family business of Lord Kemsley and the only weekend rival to the Astors' *Observer*, and in the spring of 1951 the newspaper suggested that he join its regular staff of critics, an august and fastidious panel which, under the captaincy of Desmond MacCarthy, included L. P. Hartley, Raymond Mortimer, A. L. Rowse, John Russell and C. P. Snow. His debut was devoted to an assessment of Hemingway's *Across the River and into the Trees* and although he disliked the book he exalted the novelist as a man of action who had inspired other writers whose yearnings for adventure had conflicted with their sedentary calling. A month later he reviewed a new omnibus edition of Galsworthy's *The Forsyte Saga* and while he reviled the writer once more he suggested that his Forsyte novels would make admirable cinema, an idea the BBC was to adopt to great acclaim fifteen years later. In 1951 he assessed Stephen Spender, the Wallace Collection, Marianne Moore and F. Scott Fitzgerald, indicating enthusiasms for twentieth-century literature and French eighteenth-century art which were to characterize his column for its duration. He also revealed an ability which veteran admirers of his prose had long cherished and which any reviewer would envy: the gift of turning a perfectly balanced and poetic sentence which was both memorable and idiosyncratic.

Baby took comfort in the new standards of living which the appointment promised and remarked in April that at least now they would be able to buy lavatory paper rather than resorting to magazine covers. That summer, in recognition of the success which *Brideshead Revisited* and *The Loved One* had enjoyed in America, *Time* decided to publish an article on Evelyn Waugh and immediately commissioned Connolly – the novelist's only friend besides Graham Greene who could boast any prestige in Greenwich Village or the campuses of the Ivy League. The contract was agreed and the fee set at $1000, but it would not be easy money. Connolly broached the matter with Waugh who promised co-operation but harboured suspicions and threatened recriminations when writing of the matter to Graham Greene on 21 August: 'Connolly has many injuries to revenge. I can't blame him if he takes the opportunity, tho I may have to horse whip him on the steps of his club.'³² Barricaded by anger and suspicion, a greater source of misery and pain to himself than he was even to his vigilant friends, Waugh was unlikely to bare his breast for a publication or a nation he held in contempt. The money involved lent force to Connolly's charm and persuasiveness, however, and Waugh agreed to look at a first draft which had already been submitted to *Time*. Connolly heard from T. S. Matthews, commissioning editor at the magazine, that his first draft included too much about ancestors and family trees. The essence of the appraisal should be devoted to an evocation of the novelist's character and working habits, as well as supplying a digest of his achievements: 'I must remind you that most of our nearly 2 million readers have probably never heard of Waugh, let alone read him.' That said, he greatly admired the introduction, which 'is just about perfect ... The main lack in the piece as it stands is, perhaps, its failure to live up to the promise of this first paragraph.'³³ Dutifully, and with the prospect of trespassing on dangerous ground, Connolly returned to his famous victim and applied for information concerning the collapse of his first marriage. Reluctantly and confidentially Waugh told him that the partnership had been nullified because he and his first wife had made an agreement never to have children and never to have sex without contraceptives, thus leaving their union unconsummated. He added a gleeful coda: 'I am afraid you have little cheer of your thousand bucks. The Americans have lost interest in me.'[34] It was true: although Connolly was pleased with the result and received his $1000, the assessment was never published. *Time*'s readers no doubt never knew or cared but they missed an interestingly equivocal documentation: Connolly's sketch was unattractive but not insulting and never forgot the sympathy due to each self-lacerating bully: '. . . a short, stout, militant, brick-faced figure with a neat moustache, smiling at the thrust he is about to deliver . . .'[35]

CHAPTER TWENTY-FIVE

CHRISTMAS 1951 had proved miserable; Connolly read Baude-laire and Barbara drank gin to help forget the heavy snow and pressing bills which arrived at Oak Coffin. However, at least now he was committed to producing a weekly review for the *Sunday Times* until Raymond Mortimer returned from holiday, and a fortnightly one thereafter, and on the strength of that security was able to negotiate a larger overdraft with his bank manager early in 1952. Besides the portrait of Waugh he had also undertaken to do some broadcasting for the Third Programme and the first of these transmissions went out on 16 March and addressed *The Infiltration of American Culture*, which Connolly saw as both benign and inevitable: Europe had destroyed numerous civilizations and could scarcely complain now of American hegemony and its attractive blandishments – its gadgets, its demotic language, its jazz and thrillers. The broadcast was a success and was followed by appearances in further talks in May and October, *European Letter Box* and *New Soundings*, which carried a standard fee of ten guineas and the fare from Kent. He also began a diary to record the progress of his marriage, convinced that otherwise posterity would be left with nothing but Barbara's account. Only hers has so far come to light. On 23 November 1951 his first words to her had been: 'Why don't you drop down dead?'[1] By March nothing had improved: 'Cyril hardly speaks now when we are alone except to correct something I have said ... He is my father-figure in the form of a pedantic schoolmaster.'[2] She continued to find distraction in her menagerie – besides the coati she now kept Chinese fowl – while he fantasized about moving to Georgian rectories or Regency manors and occasionally scraped money together to buy eighteenth-century silver as a substitute for its architecture.

Early in April he and Barbara had dinner with Ann and Ian Fleming, newly married after her divorce from Esmond Rothermere, at White

Cliffs, their house near Dover. The two men had always got on well and as foreign manager to the Kemsley newspapers and a favoured protégé of Lord Kemsley himself, Fleming was in a position to champion the critic whenever struggles within the *Sunday Times* threatened his prestige. During the course of dinner conversation turned to Fleming's involvement with a small publishing imprint called the Queen Anne Press and his plan to recruit work from writers of quality which could then be published in elegant and expensive collectable editions. He had decided to approach Betjeman, Quennell, Waugh and Patrick Leigh Fermor; perhaps Connolly might also be interested? Yes, of course he would be; and on 10 April Fleming sent him a letter of confirmation, adding: 'Please do bend your mind to this very attractive project which will give please [sic] to all of us and be a nice surprise for all those who live at the foot of the volcano.'[3] A week later he wrote again. He had discussed the matter with Hamish Hamilton, who would be happy to publish a popular edition of the story, and recommended that Connolly campaign for 20 per cent royalties on that edition 'instead of [Hamilton's] usual miserly fifteen per cent'.[4] Now all that remained was to write the story. The latter publisher was pleased to find any ally keen to extract work from his mercurial author. He was simultaneously trying to persuade Connolly to bring out a volume of recent articles from the *Sunday Times* but the critic – already toying with the title 'Ideas and Places' – thought such a venture would seem hasty and ill-judged and argued that a selection of his 'Comments' from *Horizon* would be a better idea. George Weidenfeld, a young publisher he had met through Clarissa Churchill, agreed, and it was he rather than Hamilton who published *Ideas and Places* the following year.

At the end of May the Connollys went to Paris to attend a cultural summit sponsored by a wealthy American called Fleichman and although Connolly was not invited to speak he enjoyed the holiday and was happy to revisit the bookstalls and restaurants and to see Sonia and Tony Bower at the Deux Magots. They arrived home to discover that Desmond MacCarthy had died of pneumonia on 7 June: he was the last of the mentors to go and with him went another member of Bloomsbury, another of Chelsea's men of letters. For twenty-four years he had dominated his page at the *Sunday Times* and it was as an exhaustively read gentleman that he had surveyed contemporary literary endeavour, avoiding dogma and asperity and an unseemly courtship of modishness. With his death Lord Kemsley offered his widow a pension of £260 per annum and his empire was divided between his former pupils; henceforth Raymond Mortimer and Cyril Connolly would be the newspaper's principal literary journalists and would guard the tradition which Gosse had begun and MacCarthy continued of communing, as sensitive men of the world who disguised seriousness and rejected high-mindedness, with an invisible audience grateful for urbane Sunday society. They would not hope to replace him, however, as Connolly suggested in a generous yet heart-felt epitaph: 'He belonged to a larger age ... he had read everything and he was wise, just and kind, with a talent for epigram.'[5]

He settled, with Mortimer, into the new routine of greater eminence at Gray's Inn Road but he was dogged, like his countrymen, by a mystery, and one moreover involving two men he knew. On 7 June 1951, a year to the day before MacCarthy's death, the *Daily Express* carried headlines that two British diplomats had unaccountably disappeared on French soil. Having caught the cross-Channel ferry on 25 May, Guy Burgess and Donald Maclean travelled by taxi from St-Malo to Rennes before vanishing on the express train to Paris. Their mysterious departure made headlines around Europe and for several months afterwards anxious report sighted them in Paris, Brussels, Cannes and Prague, when in fact the fugitives had embarked on the journey to Moscow and to enduring notoriety well before their story broke in the press. Not all was innocent conjecture, however, and at the first fever of speculation, on 8 June 1951, Harold Nicolson confided in his diary: 'Everyone is discussing the Burgess/Maclean affair ... I fear poor Guy will be rendered very unhappy in the end. If he has done a bunk to Russia, they will only use him for a month or so, and then shove him quietly into some salt mine.'[6]

Fleet Street inevitably lost interest but in literary London, which forever flirts with politics and diplomacy, the truants remained the subjects of intense speculation, especially as it transpired that Burgess had once admitted espionage activities on behalf of the Comintern to an incredulous Goronwy Rees and tried to recruit him to the cause. Listening to the gossip, Connolly was fascinated and may have reflected that all his generation, even its most innocent members, were somehow implicated in the scandal: after all, Auden was questioned as the friend Burgess had tried to contact prior to his flight and both Harold Acton and Brian Howard were mistakenly identified as the missing diplomat. If the rumours of espionage were true, the episode could have far-reaching consequences; but it was not merely for that reason or for the fact that he had befriended Donald Maclean in particular that he decided to turn his curiosity to literary account. As usual there was a personal element: he too had once been intended for diplomacy; he too had been sympathetic to the ambitions of the left. Perhaps in other circumstances his own identity could mysteriously have vanished on a fast train to Paris.

The very idea of Cyril Connolly as a spy sounds fantastic but Burgess himself seemed an improbable agent – dirty, bibulous, indescribably *louche* and blatantly disreputable – and as such antipathetic to the critic. He was eight years younger and scorned *Horizon*, which he found stale and timid, but seems to have liked and respected Connolly himself. On their rare encounters, however, his manner generally disconcerted the older man: during the Spanish Civil War, when he was working at the BBC (and sporting the camouflage of fascist sympathies), he appalled Connolly by his praise of Hitler and his talk of attendance at a Nuremburg Rally, and when they encountered each other on 9 May 1951, when the diplomat was briefly in London between his disgraced return from the British embassy in Washington and his dramatic disappearance, Connolly once again noted with some distaste Burgess's 'usual shaggy, snarling-playful manner'.[7]

Maclean, however, he knew much better. They had often encountered each other in Chelsea in the late Thirties and although Connolly could not always accept the younger man's politics, he found him gauchely sympathetic: 'He did not seem a political animal but resembled the clever helpless youth in a Huxley novel, an outsize Cherubino intent on amorous experience but too shy and clumsy to succeed.'[8] In 1948, when Maclean returned from a spell at the embassy in Washington, he held a dinner to which Connolly was invited and the critic was pleased by his host's enthusiasm for *Horizon*. In November 1950 they met again over lunch at Maclean's club, arguing politely about colonialism and the Korean war, and in early May 1951, when the diplomat turned up at Sussex Place drunk and in search of a bed, there was no reproach in the welcome Connolly extended: Barbara noted how 'Cyril put him to bed and took him up some Alka Seltzer, which is more than he would do for me!'[9] Their last encounter, a fortnight later, was again unplanned: they met in a Soho street as Maclean made his way to his birthday lunch. It was Friday, 25 May, his last day in the West, but to Connolly he appeared no more than genial and a little tired.

In the summer of 1952, preparing to write about the mystery,

Connolly pondered the events of the previous spring and advertised for information among his friends. Many had theories, some were wise after the event, and it was clear that such hard facts as there were could only come from government servants. It was not a good moment. Suspicions and recriminations continued to multiply across Whitehall as the possibility remained that the two men had indeed finally gone home to their Kremlin controllers. Meanwhile, in the inner chambers of Intelligence, nobody could forget that Maclean, long under observation, had vanished only a weekend away from official investigation, as though warned by an accomplice. And why else had Burgess fled, unless he too had indiscretions to escape? If the worst did come to the worst and these possibilities were realized, the implications for Anglo-American relations would be serious. In the meantime the departments involved decided on a public position which was partially true – that they too were ignorant of the diplomats' whereabouts and that there was nothing more to be said – and kept faith with the only certainty, that prying journalists, whoever their friends and whatever their stature and aesthetic credentials, should be discouraged.

Armed with a commission from the *Sunday Times* which also catered for generous expenses, Connolly refused to be deterred and Barbara noted his obsession: 'Nothing *but* Burgess and Maclean talk now all the time . . . It has given [Cyril] an excuse to see a lot of people who could provide information. Expensive restaurants, caviar, champagne dinners and endless long distance telephone calls.'[10] As various interviewees proved evasive and discouraging, however, he began to sense that the double doors of Whitehall were not going to yield: one ambassador asked him on no account to mention Kim Philby, since it would be unfair to involve him merely on the grounds that he had once had Burgess to stay in Washington; a second insisted that he should not involve Maclean's wife and a third declared that Maclean himself was incapable of dishonourable behaviour. Connolly's deliberations were published in two parts in the *Sunday Times* in September 1952 and despite being more speculative than precise they included a defence of the writer's inconvenient curiosity which could still stand as a professional testament for many journalists and biographers in the long argument about the shifting demarcation between private business and public interest: 'Something of what I have put down may cause pain; but that I must risk, because where people are concerned the truth can never be ascertained without painful things being said.'[11]

Cyril Connolly in Spain to cover the Civil War for the *New Statesman*

In Davos in 1939. Left to right: Eddy Sackville-West, Peggy Strachey, Connolly, E. Curwen, Diana Romilly, Basil Leng, Muriel Wright and Tony Bower

Barbara Skelton sunbathing in Feliks Topolski's garden

Lys Lubbock in 1941

Peter Watson was infallibly stylish

Connolly and his long shadow on a Spanish beach in the Fifties

A Soho rendezvous with Caroline Blackwood

Men of letters: Connolly with Peter Quennell

Bushey Lodge in the Sixties

The Oxford University Railway Club reunion in 1963. Standing left to right: Roy Harrod, Desmond Guinness, Evelyn Waugh, Lord Boothby, John Sutro, Harold Acton, Connolly, Henry Harrod, Giles FitzHerbert, John Sparrow, Lord Antrim, Auberon Waugh, Dominic Harrod. Seated: Christopher Sykes, the chef, Lord Bath

Inspecting the stables at Lismore Castle with the Duchess of Devonshire. Royal Tan, a gift to the Duchess from Prince Aly Khan, won the Grand National in 1954

Cyril and Deirdre Connolly at Bushey Lodge

With the Augustus John drawing behind him and Matthew at his knee
Cyril Connolly sits for the *Sunday Times* at Eastbourne shortly before his death

His account fused anecdote, reminiscence, biography, autobiography and lyrical parenthesis and quoted approvingly the opinion of a psychologist involved in the case, that both men harboured a strong resentment of feminine domination. Connolly himself felt encouraged to import semi-Freudian technique and decided that if they were indeed traitors their actions owed a lot to family feeling: 'Before we can hurt the fatherland, we must hate the father.'[12] In the end he was inclined to absolve them, if only because they both seemed too humanly distracted to cultivate the spy's exquisite detachment, and concluded instead that a fear of America's belligerent overseas policy and its influence with the Foreign Office had led them to a panic-stricken decision to abandon their diplomacy. He ventured no speculations about their present whereabouts and although he was sure they would reappear – 'haunting the Old World's pleasure traps about the season of their disappearance, bringing with them strawberries and hot weather and escapist leanings: a portent of the middle summer's spring' – his forecast of the circumstances was more poetic than accurate. Nevertheless his report, as Barbara noted in her diary, was 'a great success'[13] and his fine character sketches of Burgess and Maclean held good even after their dramatic reappearance in Moscow in 1956 had added another chapter to the worst spy scandal in British history. Tom Driberg, who knew Burgess and later visited him in exile, was alone dissatisfied with Connolly's account and felt that his friend's report was disabled by his 'fear of the real world'.[14] Ian Fleming disagreed and at the end of 1952 agreed to publish the two articles in expanded form at the Queen Anne Press: *The Missing Diplomats* would appear with an introduction by Peter Quennell.

Many of the details of the treason remain obscure but as the truth gradually emerged the flight of the diplomats developed beyond an establishment scandal into a paradigm of national self-doubt: if the sons of the most ancient schools and universities could no longer believe in the system from which they had sprung, where might doubt and disaffection not end? The blow of treachery fell hard and would continue to trouble the diplomats' thinking contemporaries, unsettling their failing patriotism and intermittently infecting their writing: themes of betrayal would inform the fiction of the Fifties and would even propel the action of the later volumes of *Sword of Honour*, the tripartite study of army life which Evelyn Waugh began in September 1952 with the publication of *Men At Arms*. Connolly was not alone in finding his friend's latest novel uneven; and while both the *Spectator* and the *New Statesman* voiced reservations, Connolly was the critic who expressed his misgivings most forcefully. He felt that Waugh had failed to establish relations between his military characters and had proved unequal to the reconciliation of love and aggression achieved by Hemingway in the novel he reviewed simultaneously, *The Old Man and the Sea*. The first hundred pages were excellent but he admitted that what followed had bored him: 'One raises the silver loving cup expecting champagne and receives a wallop of ale.'[15] Waugh could dismiss the opinions of other arbiters but he had known this commentator too long and admired his writing too much to ignore his criticism. His acknowledgement was lofty but not indifferent: 'I thought your review of *Men At Arms* excellent. It is a pity you called "Apthorpe" "Atwater" throughout . . . because it will make your readers think you did not give full attention to the book. You plainly did, and have clearly defined all that I dislike [in it].'[16]

He nevertheless hastened to despatch a signed, complimentary copy of the novel to Oak Cottage, although the inscription – 'To Cyril, who kept the home fires burning' – was flagrantly double-edged, referring half-playfully to a claim once made in 'Comment' that the civilians had the worst of the war, and to Connolly's short-lived career as a fire-watcher. The barb went home and Ann Fleming was happy to report to Waugh that she had found Connolly 'hopping mad with rage'.[17] The novelist sent disingenuous mollifications: there had been a misunderstanding and he was sorry for any unintended slight; he had merely wanted to acknowledge his friend's wartime contribution in providing 'a delightful salon for men on leave, giving them a further choice than Emerald's oven and Sybil's frigidaire'.[18] The torment would continue with *Officers and Gentlemen*, the second volume in the trilogy, which opened with a party of progressive novelists trying to be firemen and failing to extinguish the flames which were consuming the morning room of Turtle's Club. Shortly afterwards Waugh spent a weekend at Mrs Fleming's and along with his hostess and her other guests – the Duff Coopers, Joan Rayner and Patrick Leigh Fermor – went to tea at Oak Cottage. *Men At Arms* was forgotten or at least ignored but Barbara noted that despite her husband's endeavours – he retrieved the silver teapot from the pawn broker, lit fires and spent most of the afternoon arranging the tea table – their guests were slightly disappointed: '(a) they had expected our surroundings to have been far more squalid, (b) because Kupy [the coati] had not come out of her hut and bitten someone's penis and (c) because I had not been thoroughly rude to everyone.'[19] Ann Fleming overcame her disappointment the following month, however, when she invited her neighbours – without coati – to spend Christmas at White Cliffs, and she and her guests, Peter Quennell and the Duchess of Westminster, were reunited for dinner at Noël Coward's on 27 December.

The first invitation of 1953 came from Malcolm Muggeridge who wrote as editor-designate of *Punch* wondering whether Connolly would care to assist him in the revival of the magazine. In the event his only appearance in its pages was unwitting – as the object of a somewhat toothless pastiche written by Muggeridge's new literary editor Anthony Powell to coincide with the publication later in the spring of *Ideas and Places*. There were dinners and lunches to ease the passage of January – with the inevitable Flemings, with neighbour Eric Wood, and with the writer Jocelyn Brooke whose *Orchid Trilogy*, completed two years previously, established his position as a celebrant of rural Kent and indicated that like Connolly he was a confirmed autobiographer. At last February arrived and six days later they were away: a boat across the Channel, a train to Paris, a connection to Madrid, where they were met off the train by Bill Davis, husband of Jean's sister, and escorted to the apartment he and his wife kept in the Spanish capital. When the travellers went to bed Connolly startled his own wife by producing a pair of orange silk pyjamas, black-trimmed and initialled, which she forbade him to wear while they were sharing a room as they made her dizzy. Equanimity was restored the following day when they lunched outside Madrid and then continued to the Prado, where Connolly was engrossed by the impenetrable Gothic dreams of Hieronymus Bosch.

Annie Davis was younger than her sister, and had hardly known her brother-in-law until they met again in Paris after the war. By that time she had married Bill Davis, a New Yorker of no apparent profession whose father had been a successful Chicago lawyer, and developed into a relaxed, gentle and generous spirit with a striking American-Indian face and a slowness of speech and manner which belied her quick eye and sharpness of observation. 'Whereas one's heart slightly sank when Bill sat down next to one,' Frances Partridge remembered, 'it rose when Annie did.'[20] Although Bill was kind and generous and loyal to his friends, interested in literature and devoted to Spain, he could also be boorish, snobbish and aggressive. Nevertheless Connolly grew to be very fond of him and to adore Annie; love was reciprocated and for many years they lavished loyalty and hospitality upon him. After a few days in Madrid the four friends headed south; for Connolly himself the mere direction was propitious – a spiritual repatriation – and Barbara recorded his delight as they reached Andalusia: 'Pop ... tells us to cry out when we first see some sign of a southern climate. The person who pipes up first is rewarded with ten pesetas, the unobservant ones paying the forfeit. The first sign being a palm followed by an aloe, Pop is the first to spot both and cries out, unable to stifle his pleasure at his own cleverness.'[21] Between playing games of observation and squabbling in the car they visited Ubeda and Torremolinos but were depressed in the latter town by pioneer English tourists and headed for Malaga to have the car repaired and to inspect the cathedral and the Riberas and Zuburan in the museum.

Connolly had resolved to introduce the Davises to Gerald Brenan, the Bloomsbury maverick and hispanist who had moved to Spain many years previously and now lived near Malaga. The two couples paid a visit for tea and the visit was a great success: their host was talkative and intelligent, his guests the first company he and his wife had seen for five weeks, and Barbara noted that he 'was terribly pleased to see people, just as Cyril is after being deprived of company for five days'.[22] Connolly had reviewed Brenan's *The Literature of the Spanish People* in the *Sunday Times* two years previously and in 1957 he would praise him as 'a poet and a romantic preserved by his irony and scholarship from inflationary looseness'.[23] Bill and Annie were thinking of acquiring a house in Spain and the meeting with Brenan led directly to their buying La Consula, a large nineteenth-century villa with balconies and pillars complete with vast garden, tennis courts, swimming pool and a huge avocado tree. Meanwhile the tourists progressed to Gibraltar and Cadiz but Barbara's thoughts had begun to turn to nightclubs and to impatience with her older companions. Between Cadiz and Seville disenchantment spread and both she and her husband began to feel that Spain was 'blighted': its architecture and scenery were superb but its people merely 'gibbering monkeys'. Their disillusion was short-lived, however: they would both return many times, Connolly himself becoming a regular guest at La Consula. Indeed such was his enthusiasm that he delegated Brenan to look for a property on his behalf. The latter told him that for £2000 he could have the house of his dreams in the south and would certainly have welcomed his proximity, not least because the two writers had a communion of interests. Besides: 'You are the only person whose opinion I would take because you are a Romantic at bottom like myself and do not think an interest in oneself is a thing to be ashamed of.'[24]

CHAPTER TWENTY-SIX

THE COATI had matured in its owners' absence and its newest activities were the stuff of correspondence from Mrs Fleming to Evelyn Waugh at the beginning of April: 'Cyril knew she must have a mate or satisfaction, he was unable to provide either and now the animal hates him, has bitten him to the bone twice and chases him snarling round the house; Barbara's comment is that the house is full of unsatisfied women.'[1] Spring gave way to summer and while Britain prepared itself for the coronation of Elizabeth II Connolly braced himself for the reception in May of *Ideas and Places*. In the *Sunday Times* Maurice Bowra did not disappoint: 'Few living writers can make a landscape live so vividly before our eyes ... [the author] is a most unusual creature, a true original, a man of letters who follows no path but his own.'[2] In the *Observer*, however, Philip Toynbee sounded a jaundiced note:

[Connolly] can be treated as the panjandrum of the decade, or as a sparse and rather lonely writer, crying in his self-created wilderness ... Palinurus is perhaps a more satisfactory figure than Cyril Connolly and Palinurus is defiantly unsuited to being a leader of opinion. The ideas, in fact, wear worse than the places ... Hatred of England, an adulatory and snobbish love of France, embittered and boring connoisseurship of food and wine, an inaccurate and unsupported *laus temporis acti*, these are some of the errors of taste and judgement which can no longer give pleasure ...[3]

Toynbee learned well the price of such disaffection and still remembered its consequences even when he wrote Connolly's obituary – 'instant ostracism, though never for long, and a barrage of quickly reported, malicious comments'.[4] Having inflicted his wounds he would not escape such treatment now, and Barbara recorded the eclipse of happiness: 'All through the day, Pop's hurt feelings exposed in different shades of pink all over his face. He lies on his bed in his kennel, groaning.'[5] It was not merely the substance of the argument which hurt, however, it was the tone: there was an element of irritable recrimination in Toynbee's review which seemed to sound a note of betrayal. After all, he had been a close friend, almost disciple, during the war and had shared the composition of the brief lament which they had chanted together on a holiday in Devonshire:

> We don't like the sex war;
> We don't like the class war.
> We don't like the next war;
> We don't like the last war.
> WE DON'T LIKE THE WAR.

Now this querulous compact seemed forgotten and Toynbee compounded his disgrace by dismissing *The Golden Horizon*, an anthology of the magazine's best articles dedicated to Sonia which Weidenfeld released almost simultaneously, and the Connollys had the satisfaction of hearing him dismissed at Mrs Fleming's as 'a nasty piece of work'.[6]

June began with the coronation but Connolly was a doubtful royalist and complained to his wife: 'Science fiction – it gets me, Baby.'[7] His mood had scarcely improved a few weeks later when Jack and Catherine Lambert came to Oak Cottage for lunch. Lambert had worked as an assistant editor on the *Sunday Times* since 1948, and from 1960, as arts editor of the newspaper, he was Connolly's indulgent chief and counsellor. It was a beautiful day when the taxi from the station arrived and Connolly himself, shoeless, with socks full of holes and baggy green corduroys, met them at his gate. The Lamberts followed their host into the garden, one corner of which was occupied by Barbara, whom Catherine thought seemed 'like a witch', and another by a run full of the guinea fowl which provided the delicious eggs with which lunch began. As they were finishing their strawberries Connolly said, 'Baby, Baby, can it come out now?' The coati was released and with it pandemonium: the animal leaped across the table, scattering the cutlery, crockery and condiments that obstructed it and their host had second thoughts: 'Baby, Baby, it's cross. Do something!' Barbara pulled on a pair of kitchen gloves, seized the coati by the tail and flung it into the guinea coop, an ejection which provoked a fearful noise but no apparent carnage. During lunch the subject of marriage had come up and the Connollys were amazed to learn that their guests had been married for thirteen years: 'Thirteen years! How can anyone stay

married for thirteen years?' Disillusionment seemed confirmed when
the sexes segregated after coffee. The women remained outside and
Catherine, resorting to pleasantries, admired the garden and wondered
if they employed any help to maintain it. Her hostess was unequivocal:
'No. I work at it three hours every day and I *loathe* every minute of it.'
Meanwhile, the men had somehow strayed to Connolly's bedroom
where a large black flare disfigured a wall and alerted Lambert to the
fact that the room was illuminated with oil lamps, one of which clearly
had an untrimmed wick. Standing at the window he admired the view
but his compliment was also dismally rebuffed when his friend replied:
'Yes, it is beautiful, isn't it, and I *loathe* every yard of it between here
and Folkestone.'[8]

Returning to London the Lamberts dwelt on what they had seen –
separate rooms, parallel disillusion – and abandoned long-term hopes
for the Connollys' marriage. They could not know that both parties
relished complaining and that displays of antagonism were often only
displays and as such an aspect of the fun. Nevertheless discontent was
growing on both sides. He missed London and found the cottage – two
up, two down, with a tiny kitchen and a bathroom built on – claustro-
phobic. She in turn had been aggravated by his nocturnal whisperings
of self-pity – 'Poor Cyril' and so on, with an eye on her to see if she was
awake to hear – and had told him to sleep in the other room. One day
he angrily demanded: 'Why did you entice me away from Lys when all
you wanted to do was to push me out of your bed?'[9] Where sex was
concerned, however, it was not Barbara who had proved coy or unwill-
ing; on the contrary, by her own admission she was obsessed with it
'the whole time'. Her husband, alternatively, 'always had this idea that
it was sapping his mental energy, that it was bad for him'.[10] As a result
he would often only make love once a month in the hope of increasing
his literary output and Barbara would soon seek consolation elsewhere.
Connolly himself did not help matters by brooding on the past and
indulging in fantasies about Lys. He had dedicated *Ideas and Places* to
her and had continued to send her impassioned and manipulative letters
even after her departure for America. In 1953 he wrote that he doubted
if he would ever finish a novel or any other writing; he felt his life was
more or less over and rather than being visited by inspiration he only
had vivid dreams of Jean and of her, in the most recent of which she had
been walking towards him in the brown coat with the velvet collar he
had given her, a yellow scarf on her head. 'It was not a dream but like a

shot in a film-sequence. Ever since I have tried to start this film going again but with no success.'[11] So much for muses of the past; but he had also given thought to their sisters of the future and had begun to turn his interest to Caroline Blackwood, a good-looking and aristocratic young woman whose marriage to Lucian Freud – which he attended in the summer – placed her satisfactorily out of reach and whose zenith in his wistful affections was still to come.

The holiday in Spain had proved more expensive than anticipated and the summer was another period of desperate financial crisis: at one stage they were unable to cash any cheques owing to the steady and unnegotiated increase in Connolly's bank overdraft, and the severance of the telephone line compelled him to borrow more money from George Weidenfeld against the earnings of *The Golden Horizon*. In June, equipped with a loan of £20 from Joan, he went with her, Barbara and Eric Wood on a short holiday in Normandy. In July, at least, overtures came from the BBC which could augment earnings from the newspaper: would he care to participate in a programme to be broadcast to the Far East on the subject of 'peace of mind'? Would he like to follow Gilbert Murray, Cecil Day-Lewis and Kingsley Martin, among others, in talking on a series called 'This I Believe' which was broadcast by the BBC's North American service and reached an estimated audience of twenty-nine million? A more exciting invitation led to his accompanying George Weidenfeld on a cultural programme organized by Unesco and revolving around the musical festivals at Salzburg and Bayreuth, and while the two men went from opera to opera Barbara stayed with Farouk, now living in Rome since his abdication the previous year.

Weidenfeld was hopeful of securing future literary projects from his companion; he carefully watched his moods and reactions and in Bayreuth was impressed by his responsiveness to a world and culture with which he had no prior acquaintance: 'Although Connolly did not speak German and knew nothing of Wagner he had an intuitive sense of quality, an intuitive understanding of genius, of artistic romanticism.'[12] The itinerant meanwhile wrote to his wife in Rome: he missed her very much but found some solace in Weidenfeld's company – besides being a useful interpreter he was tactful and charming and might make his fortune. He was glad to have seen *The Ring* but was tired of 'gazing at fat women berating each another'.[13] Alan Pryce-Jones was also at the festival with his son, David, and the latter noted Connolly's humour and his tendency to extended jokes and word play:

He rarely laughed out loud but had a way of gleaming with the pleasure of anything funny, and meanwhile his shoulders heaved. . . . He seemed like someone from a more expansive age, a survivor stepping through postwar debris. The presence was powerful . . . Trouble was taken with his appearance – a long soak in the bath, expensive clothes. Yet he always looked ruffled, more bohemian than he was . . . A double-chin, jowls, discoloured teeth, straggly hair, a figure tethered by its weight and shape.[14]

Connolly knew much of the classical world but little of the Germanic, and he revelled in the exquisite irresponsibilities of Austrian and Bavarian rococo architecture. The bibliophile Anthony Hobson came to lunch at Oak Cottage shortly after his return and found his host still enraptured by the stucco visions he had seen. He was determined to buy a rococo work of art and if necessary would sell his book collection: 'If I could only prop up one rococo ceiling, I should think my life well spent.'[15] Later, writing in the French magazine, *L'Œil*, he returned to his theme: trying to define the precise appeal which the rococo spirit made to his own and which had begun its seductions when he first explored the Amalienberg Pavilion in 1938 he decided that its essence, crystallized in plaster arabesques, was of sadness disguised as gaiety, the sadness which came with intimations of impermanence but which still aspired to brave and beautiful perfection.

He had further opportunities to urge the heroism of perfection with the visit in September of Kenneth Tynan, the twenty-six-year-old prodigy of theatre criticism who had been fired from his post as drama critic at the *Evening Standard* earlier in the summer and who, through the offices of David Astor, would succeed the lingering Ivor Brown at the *Observer* in 1954. Tynan augmented his income and advertised his brilliance by writing pen-portraits for American *Harper's Bazaar* of personalities which fascinated him and produced about a dozen such essays for his transatlantic readers, amongst them studies of Alec Guinness, John Gielgud, Graham Greene and Peter Brook. His journey on the 7.15 to Ashford was therefore a tribute to more than Cyril Connolly's standing in America: it was a recognition of his status as a showman and entertainer. He arrived to find that his host had brought out champagne, and the two critics, the most famous of their different generations, sat and discussed Spain, bullfighting, Virginia Woolf, Eton, the coati, the guinea fowl and the Chinese ducks. The showman declared a new ambition – the creation of a small garden reserved for poisonous plants – but not all his plans were horticultural. Using the mornings to 'rev up the engine' and reserving the afternoons for writing, he was already working on a new novel about the murder of a man of letters, and proposed to edit an anthology of great short stories. Tynan suggested the inclusion of *Rasselas* but Connolly dismissed that work as 'perfect but dead'. Barbara noted that the younger man seemed shy. His essay, which appeared in March 1954, was written with characteristic verve and authority but suggested that for all his brilliance Tynan, like Toynbee before him, found Connolly difficult to define and place. He was 'either a bon viveur with a passion for literature, or a *littérateur* with a passion for high living. He has never quite made up his mind, and his biography will be the story of his indecision.' It was 'hard to explain his influence to anyone who has not felt the impact of his personality' and confrontation itself merely compounded the problem, since there was a comic aspect to the writer which belied the significance of his aspiration and idealism: he was 'a baggy, besandalled Budda, with a pink child's face, slack jowls, a receding fuzz of hair skirmishing across his scalp, and somewhat sour, blank eyes which express the resignation of one who envisaged himself in a sedan chair sucking on a hubble-bubble and was fobbed off with secondhand Sheraton and cigars'.[16]

The appraisal coincided with Connolly's fiftieth birthday but gaudy ambitions involving a party for forty at the Ritz were abandoned and instead a small group – Sonia, Janetta, Robin Ironside and the Connollys – met at the Etoile to eat ham and melon, *bouillabaisse* and partridge. The anniversary seemed to merit greater observance, however, and at the end of the month Ann Fleming wrote to suggest that she might give a larger dinner. The invitation was accepted and she despatched a choice of menus for Connolly's deliberation: soup, cold lobster, roast partridge and figs flambés; or cheese soufflé, curried sole poppadum, roast grouse, compôte of apricots and crème brûlée. She also proposed a cake 'wreathed in angelica laurels'. The Connollys stayed at the Ritz for the night but Barbara was detained at the last moment with gastric problems. Waugh also was unable to attend but their absences notwithstanding the gathering at the Flemings' house in Victoria Square was convivial and representative and Peter Quennell, Elizabeth Glenconner, Robin and Mary Campbell, Joan Rayner, Maurice Bowra and Clarissa Eden were joined after dinner by Alan Pryce-Jones, Cecil Beaton, Lucian Freud, Caroline Blackwood, Francis

Bacon and Stephen Spender. Since the guest of honour was famously imaginative and generous in his choice of presents for his friends it followed that they would not neglect to indulge him and there were tributes of books, brandy and caviare. Beaton recorded triumphs for Mrs Fleming and her principal guest: 'The talk was on target . . . no one wasting time in banalities . . . Cyril was radiant and feeling very warm-hearted at such a genuine display of affection. His heart and greed were equally overflowing at the tributes given to him.'[17]

The greatest tribute arrived belatedly. On 1 January 1954 the *Times Literary Supplement* devoted an entire page to an anonymous review of *Ideas and Places* and *The Golden Horizon* which transcended appraisal of the books to define Connolly's qualities and achievements. It was possible that his most telling significance would lie 'in contemplation of the writer's situation, his reasons for not writing, the purity of the piece of white paper in front of him'. Yet when he explored beyond such abstrusenesses he disclosed a major virtue which entitled him to the accolade 'great writer': he treated 'all writing as the personal expression of a particular human being in particular circumstances at a particular moment, with all the hundred and one reasons that produce one kind of writing and not another'.

George Weidenfeld would have read the encomium with satisfaction: contracts were signed on 18 January for 'Great Short Novels' and for the murder story, now entitled *Shade Those Laurels*, and praise from so significant a quarter could only be auspicious. The author himself was of course delighted and introduced the matter in conversation with Edmund Wilson when the American returned to England at the beginning of the year. Indeed the transatlantic critic had begun to suspect that conversation with his English counterpart was an unequal business: 'Cyril, like many wits and raconteurs, never listens to anyone else's sallies or stories: his mind begins at once to wander, and when the other person has finished gives a little nod and smile that indicates he has paid no attention.' Wilson was disposed to forgive, however: he admired the egotist's mind, at least as he glimpsed it in his writing and talk, and was happy to make the pilgrimage to Kent to have lunch with the Connollys and with Jason Epstein and his wife. Epstein worked for Doubleday in New York and nurtured plans to send the romantic escapist to the South Seas to write a travel book. Wilson was surprised to hear of the scheme but heard an almost comic integrity in Connolly's own misgivings: 'Cyril said that he didn't like to go anywhere where there wouldn't be a chance of his being able to turn the corner and come upon an old bookshop in which he might find a first edition of Proust.' Barbara he found more challenging: she seemed impossible to talk to yet clearly ruled her husband 'with an iron hand'. He thought she also tried 'to vamp me by lingering glances from her brown long-lashed eyes'. Small wonder at least that he told his fellow man of letters that his wife 'did much to redeem the London literary world from the taint of homosexuality'.[18]

In March the American had the opportunity to digest another opinion of his friend when the *New Statesman* published an anonymous article entitled 'Joker in the Pack'. The writer was John Raymond, a regular critic for the magazine who was also known to be obsessed with Connolly – an obsession which it was thought helped prompt his later involvement with Barbara. He had been a predictable presence at literary parties for many years: when sober he could be personable but his more frequent drunkenness made him vicious and tiresome and his assessment of Connolly, despite its reference to its subject's 'first half-century', seemed pointless and unfocused. He conceded that the critic remained 'the sea-green incorruptible artist, one whose unremitting search for perfection as a writer is among the half-dozen literary inspirations of our time' and was prepared to acknowledge that by the side of his achievements, his sins and self-deceptions were venial: 'To one who has written some of the finest English prose of his generation, a fantasy or two may be pardoned.' Yet the sins interested him more than the achievement. He began by claiming that his subject had lied about his distant undergraduate ambitions to become a diplomat and remarked that such dishonesty was characteristic of Connolly who, with the revised edition of *Enemies of Promise*, had amended *A Georgian Boyhood*'s revelations of his background, painting a grander picture simply to comply with the changing aspect of snobbishness. He had once pretended to be left-wing when in fact, 'like Yeats or Evelyn Waugh, he is a snob in the grand and vulgar way in which only writers can be'. If he had once kept abreast of intellectual tides he still retained a clever and convenient pragmatism which enabled him to retain a rather specious eminence in the world of letters:

> One of Connolly's greatest qualities as a literary journalist is his ability to be plumb on the target where cultural trends and fashions are

concerned. No one has a better knowledge of the poses, the rackets, the gimmicks of Eng. Lit over the last quarter of a century.[19]

Every critic knows that it is easier to damn than to praise but what Connolly's detractors often forgot was that their complaints were stale: it had all been said by Connolly himself and with a persuasiveness and perspicacity that contradicted his own declarations of literary failure. Yet Raymond's article did at least provoke unexpected sympathy from Evelyn Waugh: 'I am moved by disgust to write to you about this week's *New Statesman*. A futile caricature and the text (the first half at least) as caddish as anything I have read in an English weekly.'[20] The affair did nothing to lessen the regard in which Connolly was held in Gray's Inn Road and at the end of March Leonard Russell, who superintended arts coverage at the *Sunday Times* until his departure in 1960 and who had been directly responsible for importing both Connolly and Mortimer, wrote to the former with reassurances of his employment: the initial agreement had been that Connolly should serve the newspaper for three years and that his contract could be terminated with one year's notice on either side, 'which would mean, I hope, that we went on forever'.[21]

Lord Kemsley and his subalterns had good reason to be pleased. Although nominally junior to Raymond Mortimer, Connolly had proved himself the more entertaining and elegant bookman and by 1954 had evolved his characteristic reviewing style. He liked to claim that it was his policy, confronted by a choice of books, to select the more difficult, unless the more difficult addressed a subject about which he knew absolutely nothing: for one thing, when conscientiously practised, reviewing was an educative career; for another, rejecting the more accessible book would enable him also to escape the depression which could result if he found that he had advanced the same arguments, and with the same illustrating quotations, as numerous other critics discussing the same writer. It would have been truer, however, to insist that whenever possible he reviewed books which could tell him more about matters with which he was already well versed. He tended to analyse the same subjects repeatedly, not trusting himself to avoid boredom and bad writing in areas which held no appeal, and votaries of his column soon learnt that he would rather evaluate several books in sequence about English or French eighteenth- or nineteenth-century literature, English or American twentieth-century writers, horticulture, nature, travel, antiques or the rivalries of dandies than one about music, philosophy, politics, oriental culture, most history, most science and most fiction – however elevated the novelist. If he was restricted in range he was also cavalier about the traditional disciplines of his calling: textual scrutiny, the ability to draw analogies with kindred studies, sometimes even the habit of summarizing the book's contents – these were the work of lesser talents. Nor did he wish to seem punitive or didactic. Instead he assumed an equality of education and interests with his readers which lent his paragraphs a tone at once discursive, inclusive, intimate and urbane. When writing about individuals he found particularly appealing, he adopted the role of intermediary between the greatness of his subject and the curiosity of his readers; and it was this unobtrusive familiarity which exempted him from the twin temptations of awe and patronage which beleaguered so many of his colleagues and lent his appraisals a supple and graceful vitality. He had at his disposal a prose which was lyrical but never effete or saccharine and a disposition which knew the transience of all sublunary things. His love of beauty was tireless and his faith in the value of personal judgements (inevitable in an autobiographer) so unshakeable that it regularly committed him to defiant subjectivity, even occasionally to fictitious involvement with his book's contents. *Enemies of Promise* had insisted that 'literature is the art of writing something that will be read twice; journalism what will be grasped at once', yet by some mysterious creative alchemy his particular critical faculties permitted him, when writing on best form, to attain the higher art.

No wonder Leonard Russell wanted him to stay or that Ian Fleming assured him that Lord Kemsley himself saved his reviews to read after every other item in the newspaper. Indeed the magnate occasionally sent Connolly letters of congratulation and they remained on happy, if distant, terms. Once only the critic fell from favour when one of Kemsley's relations overheard him mimicking Brian Howard at a party and, assuming him to be homosexual, reported the matter to the homophobic proprietor. Kemsley had been shocked to learn of the proclivities of another of his leading critics, James Agate, and was now no less disconcerted, and until the pleadings of Fleming and Russell prevailed, Connolly was under a shadow and deemed inferior to the homosexual, but impeccably discreet, Raymond Mortimer. If he never became a close friend of his employer, however, Connolly got on very well with Kemsley's personal assistant, the future columnist Godfrey

Smith, who had joined the *Sunday Times* in 1951. Smith had other aspirations besides journalism and by 1954, with his first novel, *The Flaw in the Crystal*, almost complete, he felt he knew the august critic well enough to apply for advice. Connolly sat him down and delivered a gentle but serious tutorial, explaining that the novel's hero was 'over-talented' and that 'the food wasn't good enough'. Smith's admiration for Connolly's writing was such that he accepted the observations unquestioningly. As their friendship developed he came to appreciate the critic as a wit and raconteur and to understand that his dead-pan and po-faced delivery of jokes confirmed the ancient wisdom that the funniest men never laugh. Finally he summoned the courage to invite Connolly for lunch and having agonized about where to take the renowned gourmet he booked a table at L'Escargot. While nervously waiting, Smith had explored the menu, wondering what his fastidious companion would choose. One quick glance satisfied Connolly, how-ever, and his order – simply sausages – seemed almost impertinently modest. Conversation presently turned to family matters. Smith had three daughters and asked his guest what parental instruction he would dispense, what skills, were he similarly encumbered, would he recom-mend them to acquire. He was surprised by the reply: 'Magic.'[22]

CHAPTER TWENTY-SEVEN

IT MIGHT HAVE struck Connolly as odd, given the disparity in ages between Godfrey Smith and himself, that the younger man already had three children when he had none. Looking at his male contemporaries, the automatic objects of his competitiveness, he might take some reassurance from the fact that when those variously incapacitated by death or disinclination – Orwell, Kinross, Longden and the slightly older Bowra – had been taken into account, only Waugh and Quennell had produced offspring. The latter had a daughter, the former, after a late start, a large family, but neither could be ranked as enthusiastic family men. Connolly himself was not especially dynastic and not especially interested in children but he could not disregard the fact that most people and almost all married couples did tend to have them. With Jean, of course, there had been no appeal against misfortune; and there was no point in speculating what might have happened with Peggy, Diana, Lys, or any of the lesser affairs. Oak Cottage was too small for two occupants, let alone more, and he was too straitened to buy anything larger. Yet, whatever the practicalities and qualifications, the fact remained that he was without a child and thought increasingly that he would like to have one. With two books under contract he also needed muses, and Barbara, being his wife, was unqualified for the part. However, when Lys, an embodiment of yesterday's happiness and therefore supremely eligible, passed through London in April and suggested lunch, he was compliant. After all, the reunion might rekindle the fires of thought and literary belief – but then he learned that she had conditions to apply: 'Let's make a pact not to talk about the past. The present is much more interesting.'[1] The encounter seems only to have fortified his self-pity and nostalgia because when he met Waugh in May the latter found his friend 'in the uttermost abyss of melancholy'. Urban pleasures had failed to restore him: 'We went from shop to shop where Boots examined silk shirts and antique silver & complained bitterly that he could not afford to buy all he saw.'[2] He had permitted himself one telling extravagance, however: the purchase of a silver knife, fork and spoon in a leather case to send to Lys in New York.

There was a limit to the amount of time and attention he could give his former flame once she had returned to America. Caroline Blackwood, however, was very much accessible and the mere fact of her being married, and to Lucian Freud, rather than dampening his interest, was a complicated incentive to desire. Nor was it disagreeable to reflect that she was the daughter of his Eton contemporary, the Marquess of Dufferin and Ava, and a member of the wealthy Guinness family. She had literary aspirations, she was young, good-looking, above all unobtainable: the perfect hopeless love. For her part Caroline soon learned that Connolly was a fine mimic, 'a *raging* snob' and 'a brilliant manipulator of other people's emotions'.[3] But she could not take his romantic ardour seriously for a moment. That was all as it should be: for him the chase mattered more than the clinching victory, and his romantic imagination savoured initial strategies and later London assignations. They met at parties or dinners: soon the next stages of intrigue – letters and presents – would follow. It is a moot point how explicitly Connolly declared his position but gossip began and Lucian Freud, taking the matter rather more seriously than his wife, decided on action rather than complaisance. He hid in a doorway in Soho and emerged to ambush the approaching Connolly with a fierce kick to the shins. If the warning was unseemly it was at least public and unequivocal and marked the end of his friendship with the would-be Casanova. Barbara, a pragmatist in adultery, received the inevitable confession calmly but not passively:

> 'In that case,' I said, 'I shall have to find somebody.' Using the very words of my mother, Cyril replied, 'So long as he is a gentleman, I won't mind.'
> 'Whom do you consider a gentleman? Weidenfeld?'
> 'Too continental. But, so far as a continental Jew can be a gentleman, he fits. And,' Cyril added, 'I would prefer him to most people.'[4]

In July Connolly went on a travel assignment for the newspaper and brought his classicist's familiarity, his poetic eye for the details of Mediterranean life and his romantic conviction that arrival will always disappoint expectation, to a sunny itinerary: Paris, Versailles, Venice, Brindisi, Corfu, Athens, Rhodes, Mikanos, Delphi, Delos and Athens once again. His account appeared in the *Sunday Times* on two consecutive Sundays at the end of the month and shared with his readers his reflections on the slave trade, the cult of Apollo and the evanescence of ancient Greek painting and music. In Athens, where the sculpture shines in permanent assembly, he had a kind of epiphany: 'Here the chain of masterpieces signal to each other down the ages. This is how Greece was; this is what man can do. Apollo is manifest at last with his smile which seems instantly to annihilate all time and all suffering.'[5]

Back in London, over lunch with Aldous Huxley and Raymond Mortimer, he and Barbara gossiped about Bertrand Russell, D. H. Lawrence, Norman Douglas and Somerset Maugham. Connolly's unflagging enthusiasm for exile under a hot sun led the conversation to expatriation and he mentioned the idea of living in California. In October, along with Maurice Bowra, the Connollys stayed with Kenneth and Jane Clark at Saltwood Castle and as usual there were erotic tensions which Ann Fleming heard of and eagerly reported in her correspondence: 'Baby declared that Maurice is frivolous and trivial and cannot be compared to Berenson and Edmund Wilson and to add to the disaster she had never met K. Clark before and finds him a mixture of Berenson, Wilson and Rudolph Valentino, so Cyril is full of woe and says she already sees herself as Lady Clark.'[6] At the end of December the Connollys went to Italy but Rome was bitterly cold and the Sistine Chapel a disappointment: he sulked; she contemplated ringing Farouk; instead they left for the south, visiting Naples, Paestum and Pompeii to research an article for the newspaper. Afterwards they caught the train to Tuscany and arrived for three days with Berenson at I Tatti. They gossiped about mutual friends and their infidelities and the nonagenarian remarked: 'Can anyone be faithful to anyone, anyway? Fidelity belongs to an era of slavery.' News had reached the villa that Connolly was now obese and drinking very heavily – whisky had accordingly been provided – but Berenson found his guest in fine form and asked Barbara: 'Aren't you proud of having a husband who is as well-informed as he is frivolous?' Connolly in his turn had compliments to bestow: he told Baby that in his youth Berenson's house had seemed like the dead hand of the past which might inhibit the creativity of youth. Now, however, he was convinced that 'I Tatti was infinitely more precious than anything *avant garde* which had such a short life.'[7]

Before leaving for Italy Connolly had answered Stephen Spender's pleas by consigning a nostalgic excursion among his metropolitan ghosts, 'One of my Londons', for publication in *Encounter*, the pan-Atlantic cultural magazine founded in 1953 and edited by Spender and the American writer Irving Kristol. The article appeared in January 1955 and Spender was to continue trying to coax more journalism from his friend until the discovery that the magazine was ultimately funded by the CIA led to his angry resignation in 1965. Meanwhile in February the Connollys received a mobile recording unit at Oak Cottage which had been sent by the BBC to prepare *Personal Call*, an interview between Stephen Black and the critic which was to be broadcast on 14 February by the Far Eastern Service. The series of programmes was designed to give Asians an idea of post-war British life and for their benefit the two men reminisced for half an hour about the writer's schooldays, loneliness at Oxford, his arguments with his father about Franco and Churchill, his views about marriage. Black asked him: 'Do you find marriage generally an essential part of your life?' Connolly answered: 'Indispensable, yes. Only children have to have this company all the time.' 'And you think of yourself as a child?' 'No, as an only child.'[8] Shortly afterwards the newspaper sent him to Egypt and his impressions appeared in the *Sunday Times* over three weeks in February and March. A lot had changed there since Barbara's departure more than a decade before and as he roamed Farouk's former kingdom he could contemplate the sad abeyance of royal playboys, the ending in June after seventy-odd years of British occupation of the Suez Canal Zone, or the ambitions nurtured by the new military government headed by Farouk's nemesis, President Nasser. One of the more controversial of these ambitions entailed the submerging of Korosko, Derr and Wadi Halfa, along with various Nubian temples including Abu Simbel, beneath a vast Aswan dam. He made a melancholy inspection of the threatened colossi and although he had praise for many of Nasser's other reforms nothing could reconcile him to destruction in the name of progress of one of the wonders of the world. Readers should quickly see for themselves; and he tempted them to undertake the pilgrimage with accounts of his own Nilotic exaltations. 'Now falls the brief unpaintable twilight'; and he resumed his narrative with descriptions of Cairo, Memphis or Luxor: 'Light meters dangling, guide-book in one hand, fly whisk in other, our noses smarting from mummy-dust, we troop into meals obedient to the gong, while like patient elephants the temples wait for us among the sugar cane.'[9]

   At the end of March he and Baby had lunch in Folkestone with Ian and Ann Fleming, unaware that the latter had hoped to unleash new torments on her neighbour by trying to persuade her husband to name the villain of his recent thriller, *Moonraker*, Connolly Drax. Fleming himself, eager for a quieter life, had settled on Hugo Drax and was no doubt relieved, over a peaceful lunch, to find the Connollys in 'honeymoon mood'.[10] In May the critic made his début on television: the BBC paid him £29 4s 4d to cover train fare, accommodation and appearance in the programme *Press Conference*. The writer Beverley Nichols was among those watching the pioneer performance and sent his congratulations. It had been a privilege 'listening to enchanting conversation without the tiresome obligation to take part in it' and Connolly had acquitted himself well: 'It was a quiet and highly civilized interlude in which, I thought, you had perfectly adapted yourself to the medium – presumably by forgetting about it.'[11] He had continued his regular reviewing in conjunction with these other activities and as usual tended to avoid fiction. There were writers, however, whose creative imaginations could prevail over critical habit, and Evelyn Waugh, who published *Officers and Gentlemen*, the second volume of his *Sword of Honour* trilogy, in July, was pre-eminent among them. Connolly had looked to the sequel to correct the decline he had noted in *Men At Arms* but was disappointed now to register 'a benign lethargy' which he felt made certain passages almost sluggish.[12] Connolly was not alone in his disenchantment; but some mutual friends assumed that his reservations stemmed in truth from irritation with the book's opening jokes at his expense.

The long and public disintegration of the Connollys' marriage dragged itself for months through the cocktail exchanges, the dinner discussions, the letters and the telephone calls of the numerous friends and acquaintances who looked on with amusement, bemusement and eventual boredom. All marriages are in some way mysterious but even in their circle of friends, which was liberal in its interpretation of the sacrament and tolerant of domestic unorthodoxy, their marital arrangements had always seemed both comic and inexplicable. The disparity in their ages, the straitened and country disorder of their existence, the public turbulence of their relations, the absence of children would all have confounded more conformist onlookers, yet none of their friends doubted that there was a bond of feeling between them and none could confidently deny that their quarrellings and inconstancy had been permutations or even declarations of strong mutual affection and understanding. Nothing seemed any clearer, however, when disintegration

began and the protagonists themselves seemed almost passive in the face
of boredom and indecision. With Barbara's revelations of involvement
with George Weidenfeld Connolly desisted in his monotonous praise of
Caroline and changed his mood overnight. The transformation did not
go unnoticed by his wife, who recorded: 'Cyril has become angelic, never
a grumpy word. Now professes to love it here, never wants to leave Oak
Coffin, is disgusted and bored with London ... he would like to kill
W[eidenfeld] and it would break his heart if we separated. It would break
mine too.' Almost in the same breath, however, she had her doubts: 'I
find it increasingly difficult to think of leaving Cyril and yet I seem to
have inwardly made up my mind to do so.'[13]

They continued to live together in the cottage, Barbara nearing
completion of her first novel and her husband working on his: they read
each other's writing, offering corrections and volunteering suggestions,
and even planned a holiday together in Sardinia. Such harmony was
superficial, however, and easily unsettled when their shared publisher
rang to talk only to her: 'Telephone rings at midnight and Cyril gets to
it before I am fully awake. It was clearly W., who hung up on Cyril.'[14]
Sardinia was abandoned and Connolly flew alone to Vienna, where
Nicholas Henderson, then First Secretary at the British embassy, acted
as his host. Despite distractions, his visitor was thirsty for news of
cultural developments within the city and Henderson took him to a
friend's flat to hear some Schoenberg. He also gave a lunch in his
honour but was aware that he was not sufficiently senior to provide a
banquet of the ambassadorial grandeur his guest would have liked. No
sooner had Connolly left than Weidenfeld arrived and revealed, when
he in turn contacted the diplomat, 'I think you should know that I'm
here with Barbara Connolly.'[15] When the lovers returned to England
Barbara sought temporary refuge at Janetta's house in Alexander
Square but thought nothing of involving her hostess in her endless
deceptions. Janetta finally refused to be a go-between and other mutual
friends realized that they would be asked to take sides – although some,
like Robin and Mary Campbell and Bill and Annie Davis, were
staunchly for Cyril.

Meanwhile Connolly himself, never one to contain his grievances,
did not hesitate to turn to friends both for expressions of sympathy and
loyalty and also for denunciations, the more malicious the better, of
Barbara and Weidenfeld. Some partisans would never fail him. Sonia
wrote in July: 'I can't bear to think of your being made to suffer like

this, particularly as you are the only one of us who really understands what love is about.'[16] Waugh wrote to Mrs Fleming: 'You must explain to me why Cyril wants Barbara. It is not as though she were rich or a good housekeeper or the mother of his children.'[17] John Craxton tried at once to divert and reassure his friend: why did he not write more? But Connolly spurned distraction with an unanswerable reply: 'When I've met my Katharine Parr.'[18] Alone and anxious in South Africa, his mother did not escape involvement but had no doubt where to point the accusing finger. On 10 October she wrote: 'I wish you could see Caroline – she sounded so fond of you and you must be so desperately lonely. I *know* there are some losses you can never replace – but there is something about youth that revives one and you sounded to enjoy things so much together.'[19] On 31 October she wrote again, this time with definite advice. Divorce was his only hope of happiness: it seemed obvious to her that Barbara was totally untrustworthy, as he had known all along, and in any case she clouded his judgement and sapped his strength. She would always compare him with Weidenfeld and find him the lesser man; besides, he could never really have loved her or he would have no need of friendship with Caroline. Furthermore in her view: 'She is so smally made I should doubt very much if she would ever have a child – it would be another thing for her to be cruel to – and to bring another edition of her into the world seems a doubtful blessing.'[20]

Even as Maud sent advice her daughter-in-law had finally decided to follow gynaecological recommendation and undergo an operation for the removal of fibroids in Canterbury hospital. Connolly, 'who had always wanted me to have a child', was gentle and attentive and accompanied her in the taxi. 'I found his back view very touching,' she remembered, 'the uncombed hair round a bald patch on the pudding basin head, his coat collar crumpled inward and, when he turned towards me, his pale blue eyes had the pained expression of an injured child, not knowing what he had done to deserve such punishment.'[21] Even in hospital Weidenfeld continued to be the staple of their conversations: Connolly told her that if she married him he would never be faithful and in the meantime, prior to anaesthetic, he told her to make a will naming him as her sole beneficiary: 'It's the least you can do.' In the event the fibroids were removed but Barbara, like Jean before her, had been rendered incapable of having children by a clumsy abortion. It would not be a need for more space that would drive the inhabitants from Oak Cottage. During her isolation and convalescence Weidenfeld had been supervising the publication of her novel, *A Young Girl's Touch*, which appeared shortly afterwards, and Connolly himself had befriended Kenneth Tynan's wife Elaine, herself a future novelist, whom he described as having the face of a girl in a painting by Boucher.

Barbara emerged from hospital to stay in a hotel where Weidenfeld also had a room. Connolly went to Brussels but on his return he too checked into the Westbury. Meanwhile he arranged for Barbara to convalesce with the Davises: southern Spain's autumn sunshine would do her good and in any discussion of her marital affairs the Davises themselves were bound to advise her to return to her husband. He wrote to Bill and Annie ahead of her departure to thank them for their generous accommodation and to ask them not to let her get bored in the evenings. The last few weeks had been hell but at least now matters might be simplified: Barbara would either summon him to join her or leave La Consula to be with Weidenfeld, but either way her preference might clarify an increasingly tedious and intractable puzzle.

By now boredom was affecting friends and onlookers. On 16 December Evelyn Waugh and Graham Greene met at White's for dinner and it was perhaps Waugh's gesture of pity which led to Connolly's last-minute inclusion. A week later Waugh complained to Greene: 'I can't pretend to any sympathy with [Cyril] in his present troubles and I find it indecent in him to proclaim them so widely. But I am a prig. He said you comforted and strengthened him greatly.'[22] 'All London gossip circles round the Connollys' affairs,'[23] Frances Partridge noted later in December, but if wearied spectators hoped that Barbara's holiday with the Davises would resolve matters in her husband's favour they were disappointed. She continued to write to him from Spain but her messages were contradictory. At one moment she was tentative and apologetic: 'I don't want to make you more unhappy, but the decision to give up W. entirely by going back to you I find impossible to make.'[24] At another it was resigned: 'A quiet life makes me brood . . . I don't want to be married to anyone but you, but if you want a divorce I will send the evidence.'[25] Bill and Annie made their feelings quite clear, but to no avail: Weidenfeld arrived in Madrid shortly before Christmas and Barbara flew to the capital to join him. The Davises never had her to La Consula again.

No sooner had she left than Connolly arrived and the news from Spain soon returned to London to be recorded once again in Frances Partridge's diaries:

[Cyril] clamours for female company, but abuses his old friends like Janetta and Joan Raynor. He got on splendidly with Gerald [Brenan] one evening, but after the next declared that he was a fearful bore . . . [Cyril] had been making up to the pretty and amusing wife of Annie Davis' brother Tom Bakewell at a nightclub in Torremolinos, so much that Tom B. began to grumble. 'Well, hang it all, Tom,' said Cyril, 'I haven't had a woman for two months. You really can't complain of my just dancing with Carol.' Next morning Tom . . . drove up to the Davis' house and dashed upstairs calling 'Cyril! Cyril!' 'Oh, hullo, Tom, come in.' Tom had been to Malaga and found a nice tart for Cyril, and booked a date for him there and then.[26]

Early in 1956 Barbara returned to England and settled into Weiden-feld's house in Chester Square, and the latter declared his position: 'I *do not* want you to go back to Cyril and I am not afraid of the divorce scandal. I signed my papers as "Co-Respondent" today and whatever happens will happen.'[27] He was a model of decisiveness; but rather than heeding his example the Connollys continued to unite and separate, decide then reconsider, and having missed each other in Spain they now agreed to meet in Tangier, where Paul and Jane Bowles befriended the notorious couple. Soon, however, Connolly returned to the sanctuary of La Consula, leaving his wife in North Africa, and when they finally agreed to meet again at Algericas at the beginning of March he had come to a decision: he was tired of being 'the Comic Cuckold' and had instigated divorce proceedings. He returned to England and to Oak Cottage and Barbara followed him. The situation now seemed to be that although Barbara had decided she no longer wanted to marry Weidenfeld her husband was still continuing with divorce, guided by alternating convictions that as an artist he had never been intended for marriage and that as an erring human he needed a fresh start and should remarry his wife in a church. He was awarded a decree absolute on 9 May and was immediately consumed with remorse. He would pay Barbara £20 a month until her marriage, after which time he would assume the matter of her subsistence to be out of his hands and would discontinue payment. In the meantime, unless she was going to marry Weidenfeld, he argued against her accepting the job of reader at his publishing house and thus incurring further gossip and head-shaking.

A week before the decree, on 3 May, Peter Watson was found dead in his bath. He was only forty-eight and in some quarters there was immediate and lurid speculation of foul play. After all, Norman Fowler

was in the flat at the time and, as he admitted at the inquest, he and
Watson had had a bad quarrel which ended with the final slamming of
the bathroom door. Furthermore, the vast bulk of the older man's
estate – a large amount of money and works of art by Giacometti,
Henry Moore, Rodin, Braque, Juan Gris and an early Poussin – now
devolved on the American. With Fowler's own death in 1971 the
whispered suspicions about what had really happened that day in
Watson's final home at 53 Rutland Gate – probably begun by Cecil
Beaton, still half in love with the deceased and jealous of all his lovers –
became finally unprovable and irrelevant. It is worth remembering,
however, that Watson had almost died just after the war from jaundice
and acute anaemia and that his illnesses had left him permanently
weakened and his heart vulnerable to the dual onslaughts of fierce
argument followed by immersion in hot water. The coroner recorded a
verdict of accidental death and friends and associates in the art world
attended a grim cremation at Golders Green. Beaton was naturally of
their number, his sharp eye never forsaking him: 'Among the congregation, with its trustees, lawyers and family business associates, it was
difficult to identify Peter's friends. . . . I noticed that Cyril Connolly was
weeping and I loved him for that.'[28] The will revealed that besides the
principal bequest to Fowler, Watson had left £2000 to Sonia and
£1000 to Connolly. Waugh, encountering his friend in White's later
in the year, remarked that since his inheritance, '[Cyril] spends his
time talking to his stockbroker.'[29]

   In the summer Lys married an American called Sigmund Koch and
began her new life as the wife of an academic and psychologist which
would take her to the campuses of Duke and Boston Universities.
Connolly heard the news but was still preoccupied with Barbara and
when Edmund Wilson encountered him again in the first week of
August, '[Cyril] pounced upon me as a wonderful fresh listener. Sonia
Orwell said that she had gone abroad to get away from it; then as soon
as she had got back to England, Cyril had called her up, and she had felt
like leaving again.'[30] With all good intentions, everybody was bored to
death of the whole affair. Later in August Connolly invited himself to
Switzerland to join Stephen Spender and his wife who were in Gstaad
staying with friends. When he had first suggested the idea Spender had
been unenthusiastic: Connolly would not be put off, however, and
promised that all he wanted to do was work and relax among friends.
At first he was as good as his word but then Spender noticed that 'his

boredom began to reassert itself' and with it came old longings for Baby. A telegram arrived from Barbara to say that she was to marry Weidenfeld on 26 August and shortly afterwards she unleashed further turmoil with the remarkable suggestion that she should join the party in Gstaad. Her threat galvanized the Spenders and their friends who 'all became involved in discussing where Cyril should go to console himself'.[31] Finally he invited himself to stay with Auden at his summer home on Ischia, only to learn that the Weidenfelds had decided to spend their honeymoon on the same small island.

On 13 September, three days after marking his fifty-third birthday by lunching with Barbara in Naples, Connolly drafted an extraordinary message to a man he had never met. It was a communication prompted by spleen and self-pity which was as abject as it was foolish and he could later be thankful that it was intercepted before being despatched by the return of common sense and dignity. The letter to dispossessed Farouk petitioned for an audience in which he hoped to win a word of royal sympathy for his loneliness in exchange for telling the former king all he knew about the government's attitude towards the imminent Suez Crisis. Had the monarch heard his revelations he would have been disappointed: although Connolly supported Anthony Eden's combative position towards President Nasser he was without access to secrets and seems to have based his loyalty on the fact that he occasionally dined at Downing Street. In the meantime he and Farouk were both exiles from Baby's affections and had a common interest in her affairs. Connolly could not explain her regard for Weidenfeld, whom in angry distraction he described to the king as 'one of the nastiest Jews I have ever met', and as for Barbara, 'there was always something aggressive, cruel, untameable in her which I could not control.'[32]

VIII
SENTIMENTS OF
TRANSIENCE

CHAPTER TWENTY-EIGHT

IN MARCH 1956 *Encounter* published 'Eyes, look your last', the opening instalment of *Shade Those Laurels*. Not for the first time fictional inspiration, beset by doubts of perfection, had quickly faded, taking with it any fervour for the completion of the project, and the fragment had languished while Connolly awaited the return of enthusiasm and of the domestic tranquillity he considered indispensable to creativity. The months passed, the muse continued her truancy, and finally, aware that Stephen Spender was eager for more of his work, he persuaded him to include the opening of the story in *Encounter*, claiming that its appearance, as an excerpt from 'a work in progress', would stimulate him to resolve the *dénouement*. It never did, although he wrote rough versions of the next two parts before abandoning the endeavour altogether. Characteristically he later suggested to Spender that he was partly responsible for the final neglect of the work: pre-emptive publication, previously a spur to artistry, was now destructive, somehow akin to the exposure of the vivid film of ideas; but the editor–poet knew the author too well to be unsettled by his recriminating excuses.

'Eyes, look your last' was an ambitious overture which flirted simultaneously with several familiar literary settings and conventions, presenting a young *ingénu* torn by infatuations for two disparate women, a literary circle which he encounters and which is divided into producers and consumers and riven with malicious envies, and an idyllic country house defiled by homicide. The young innocent, Stephen Kemble, took his surname and his critical profession from his creator, but for all that he could have come straight from an early and abandoned novel by Aldous Huxley, whilst the banquet which is the strongest part of the instalment evokes the long and garrulous dinners characteristic of the comedies of ideas of Thomas Love Peacock. The fragment ends with the mysterious death of Sir Mortimer Gussage, the great novelist and hopeful perfectionist in whose house the action occurs; rough drafts of the ensuing plot reveal that he was really a fraud, his novels the work of the sinister committee of friends who had attended the banquet. *Shade Those Laurels* was only ever intended as a *jeu d'esprit* and never aimed to say anything profound about the disparity between the public reputations of the great and the reality of their private selves, still less about the succession of literary reputations, the theme of Dryden's laudation of the young Congreve from which Connolly had taken his title. Nor was it even intended to inspire its readers with the nervous curiosity which most crime writers hope to induce. In short, it aimed to do no more than provide brief and sophisticated entertainment but, despite the incidental poetry of some of its lines and the intermittent play of its dialogue, it lacked the confidence, sparkle and curious life which had characterized Connolly's brilliant parodies and literary interludes of the Thirties; its *ingénu* was a dull prefect carelessly sketched and Sir Mortimer Gussage himself a ponderous mouthpiece for Connolly's perfectionist cravings. Only once does he speak arrestingly and then posthumously and from the pages of his last unpublished manuscript:

> The middle-aged are like a roomful of clocks ticking briskly away, striking in uncommunicating union, yet clocks with a memory, clocks that falter before they chime, and which have a way of stopping when we are not looking ... Each moment of human life, however frivolous and inconsequent, becomes tragic when related to any other. Tragedy is the human dimension, it is what is present in a lock of hair and absent from a fossil or the bark of a tree.[1]

Connolly had not attempted self-portraiture – Mortimer, serene and affluent in success, is less interesting and less attractive than his maker – but his melancholy appraisal partially reflected his author's mood in the months after his divorce. England above all he was inclined to avoid – Mediterranean waters at least might console – and he went to stay with Joan Rayner, Patrick Leigh Fermor and Maurice Bowra on Hydra before returning to La Consula in September. As he explained to Jack Lambert, he dreaded returning to London, 'as I have nowhere to live – my life seems quite pointless there whereas in Malaga I am part of a home'.[2] His old girlfriend Peggy Strachey was also staying with Bill and Annie and was struck by the intensity of her former lover's sadness. At least he could escape the big house when he chose and find comfort and sympathy nearby with Gerald Brenan. Meanwhile Kenneth and Elaine Tynan were also spending their first holiday at La Consula and discovered that the older critic, a master of ceremonies who had equipped himself with an extraordinary imitation leopard skin bathing costume, fluctuated in tolerance and good humour. In general, the writers got on well: Tynan, who had been quoting favourite passages from *The Unquiet Grave* since he had first read the book in the sixth form, referred to Connolly as 'The Supreme Commander' and was exempted by age from the competitiveness most contemporaries provoked. Connolly himself admired the younger man's writing and envied the social life which whirled around him and his prosperous young American wife. Nevertheless, as he had once warned Barbara, critical fellowship did not make them kindred spirits: 'You can divide people into ruminative or predatory types. We are ruminants. Tynan is predatory. He has the mentality of the journalist, always on the go.'[3]

Not long after returning to England Connolly was interviewed on 24 October by Charles Wilmot, Margaret Lane and Stephen Black for the BBC Home Service's '*Frankly Speaking*'. He revealed that he considered himself too old to return to editing: 'You can't keep this little hotel for these transient people to come every week, and listen to all their complaints, and cope with them . . . you want privacy.' He endorsed the need for religion, 'because there is something inherently self-destructive about the human heart' but disliked the Church of England. His criticism had changed: 'As I grew older I realized that hurting people through criticism was a form of failure . . . One hurt them for things one hadn't done oneself.' He was not afraid to declare the child's universal fear: 'I'm happy alone from when I wake up [but] I couldn't bear to be alone after the sun goes down.'[4] Country solitude was out of the question – and so was forgetting Baby, now living with her new husband in Chester Square. He began to look for a small flat, even a room, in London, in the meantime putting some of his books in storage and beginning negotiations to sell his treasured Balthus, *The Cherry Trees*, to a Mrs Louise Smith, a Friend of the Museum of Modern Art in New York. She was prepared to pay $1200, a sum Connolly proposed to divide with the artist, and intended eventually to donate the painting to the museum.

Connolly took a room in Chesham Place and was thus conveniently placed to haunt Belgravia generally and Chester Square in particular. He telephoned Barbara insistently and took to waiting for her in a taxi

near her new front door. Not least because her own marriage had
already begun to decline, she found his reproaches, so familiar yet so
potent, irresistible and soon, while his former publisher was in America
on business, Connolly paid a tentative visit to Oak Cottage to remove
some of his books. A second visit lasted several days but later, while
admitting his presence under his former wife's roof, he would deny
adultery. Relations between the Weidenfelds disintegrated still further
and by the early weeks of 1957 they were sleeping separately – according to Barbara's diary – and arguing when together. If her present
husband annoyed her his predecessor bewildered and distracted her: 'If
I get out of touch with Cyril, even for a week, I become miserable. C.
admits that he didn't imagine this situation, thought that either I would
have returned to him by now, or that he would have found someone
else, or have become swept into a more amusing social life.'⁵ His
reasoning had been romantic: it is the prerogative of youth to stumble
carelessly across new lovers or exciting acquaintance but middle age
must fight for its fresh faces or else resign itself to the repetitions of long
friendship. He sought consolation in these long friendships at La Consula at the end of February and when Frances Partridge arrived a few
days after him she found her fellow-guest in reasonable spirits.
Presently, however, his mood declined: 'Cyril retired to a far corner of
the room, flung himself back in a chair with his face parallel to the
ceiling and his eyes closed, and remained thus for the rest of the
evening. (Janetta christened this his "music position".) She said afterwards that his excuse for this ostentatiously rude behaviour was that he
was "desperately miserable".'⁶

His loneliness sometimes projected him into strange company on his
return to England. In May, accompanying Elaine Tynan, he found
himself at dinner with the actors Jill Bennett and Kenneth Williams and
the writer Peter Wildeblood, who had earned a certain amount of
notoriety when his book *Against the Law* described his involvement in
the homosexual scandal surrounding Lord Montagu. Kenneth Williams
considered the evening 'disastrous'⁷ but for Connolly it was preferable
to solitude. As for Tynan's wife, although he found her pretty he was
inclined to dismiss her literary ambitions and suspected that she would
prove unable to develop character. He was public in his scepticism and
when asked whether she would produce anything of worth replied,
'Oh, I shouldn't think so, just another wife trying to prove she exists.'⁸
The following year she was to prove him wrong when her first novel,

The Dud Avocado, became a best-seller; six years later she would unleash a still greater surprise. On 19 July he attended the Foyle's luncheon at The Dorchester in honour of Evelyn Waugh's own account of middle-aged collapse, *The Ordeal of Gilbert Pinfold*, and in August he left once more for Spain.

By the end of the year Weidenfeld and his wife were on the verge of divorce. She had moved into a flat at 3 Lyall Street, again near present and former husbands, and detectives had been sent to Oak Cottage to find witnesses prepared to give evidence of adultery in forthcoming proceedings; Weidenfeld proposed to cite Connolly as a co-respondent. For her part, although Barbara had continued to see her former husband and although she remained extremely fond of him, she had come to the conclusion that they would never live together again.

Connolly spent Christmas with the D'Avigdor Goldsmids at Somerhill and despatched his reviews to London as usual. At least wherever he was staying in England it was always easy to ensure that tardy copy reached the Gray's Inn Road ahead of deadlines but his regular holidays abroad often posed greater challenges of delivery. The *Sunday Times* was happy to indulge a contributor of Connolly's stature and he would frequently put articles on the last possible flight to London, would even write his column in the back of a car going to the airport, although nothing annoyed him more than being incompetently edited or carelessly set up for printing. An undated letter following unagreed alterations in one review gave Leonard Russell an idea of how seriously he took his prose and his standing in his readers' eyes: 'One loses both the confidence essential to a contributor and the sentiment of self-respect if arbitrary liberties are taken with one's text and an epigram intended to provoke discussion is watered down to a cliché.'[9] Early in 1958, however, he had occasion to send a more serious letter to the newspaper's arts department. On 21 January the *Daily Mail* published a story embellished with three photographs – of Connolly and Weidenfeld, who looked like irritable felons, and Barbara, who now resembled a tanned siren:

> Yesterday Mr Weidenfeld was granted a decree of judicial separation on the grounds of [his wife's] misconduct with her first husband, 55 year-old Mr Connolly ... Mr Weidenfeld was awarded the costs of the case ... Last night neither Mr Connolly nor Miss Skelton would speak of their plans.[10]

Such remarks were in themselves anodyne but the newspaper also detailed claims made by the caretaker of Barbara's building that Connolly had often stayed there. Although his allegations were vehemently denied and later disproved they remained potentially damaging as well as irritating; only four years previously, when the historian Hugh Trevor-Roper had been cited as a co-respondent, the *Sunday Times* had informed him that he was no longer qualified to write a recently proposed article about ethics and had given the job to Raymond Mortimer. There was no reason to suppose that Connolly could hope for more indulgent treatment and trusting at once to Lambert's sympathy and discretion he gave him the essentials of the divorce settlement: even though there had been no evidence of adultery between himself and Barbara at Oak Cottage they had both decided to follow legal advice and to avoid publicity and expense by accepting Weidenfeld's offer that he would pay his wife £400 down and a further £5 a week for seven years if she would withdraw her defence. The article in the *Daily Mail* was grossly inaccurate: he had never stayed at Lyall Street, he was unknown to its caretaker, who denied making any statements to newspapers, and he himself had spoken to no reporters. It was journalism of the most irresponsible variety and he proposed to take the matter to the Press Council forthwith. If he did so, no adjudication was made, but even his solicitor, Craig Macfarlane, implied that the affair almost invited distortion when he warned in July that 'the real danger of the situation is that this whole business . . . has the potentialities of being made to seem rather ridiculous.'[11] Happily the publicity died down and no awkward decisions had to be made about whether the merits of Connolly's writing outweighed any embarrassment to Lord Kemsley. Indeed stress and unhappiness seemed to provoke him to particular eloquence and it was reassuring later in the year to receive a note of congratulation from Harold Hobson, the newspaper's drama critic: 'You have lately been writing on top of your form for the *Sunday Times*. The statement that this was so was warmly applauded at our Editorial Conference this morning with Lord Kemsley in the Chair.'[12] In July he wrote a fine appraisal of Harold Nicolson's biography of Sainte-Beuve, and dwelt lingeringly on the matter of Sainte-Beuve's affair with the wife of his friend Victor Hugo. A few months later, when reviewing Nancy Mitford's *Voltaire in Love*, he was at his most memorable and revealing when he diverged from the details of the text to generalize:

With us monogamy, fidelity and honesty are the watchwords, we attempt to be faithful to one person, and when we fail we tell them, or they tell us, and we try again with somebody else. But among the life-lovers dignity is more important than sincerity and pleasure than either. Everyone is entitled to as much love as he or she requires or can assimilate; accretions of new lovers, whole collections are formed round the man or woman most capable of maintaining them. A beautiful and clever woman retains her husband and perhaps three lovers (who each represent a decade of her life) in grateful bondage.[13]

Connolly himself was to prove that a plump and clever man could do no less.

Barbara, meanwhile, though beset by Weidenfeld's divorce proceedings, could still look laconically at the amorous carousel: 'A Co-Respondent hunt still being on, only the most intrepid gentlemen dared to be seen in my company.'[14] Alan Ross, who was later to publish some of her writing when he assumed editorship of the *London Magazine* in 1961, was prepared to prove his intrepidity, but neither he nor Barbara reckoned with the jealous fury Connolly would betray when he learned of their affair. Michael Wishart incurred similar displeasure. In 1950 he had married Anne Dunn and noted at the time that Connolly 'seemed hostile to me and envious and possessive towards Anne'.[15] Now, separated from his wife, he invited Barbara to stay with him at Ramatuelle near St Tropez. Her former husband had no doubts as to the nature of her newest friendship and wrote accusing her of 'shiftiness and deception'.[16] When she and Wishart progressed to Spain Connolly joined them, although as the painter discovered he was not always a relaxing presence: 'His attitude towards her was still very possessive.' The critic's spirits lifted but he and Barbara continued to goad each other, with Wishart uncomfortably suspicious that Barbara could not be trusted to be loyal or discreet: '[She] enhanced and sustained [Cyril's] good mood by complaining about me, while I paid the bills. Her ingratitude was balm compared with Cyril's frosty hostility when she suddenly and without provocation straightened my tie or kissed my mouth.' Trust and affection were at last established, however, and they all three set out to explore Segovia, Madrid and Seville. With characteristic nonchalance Barbara turned the details of her affair with the painter into another novel, *Count On Me*, but Wishart himself was content merely to reflect upon the paradoxes of his other travelling companion: 'His desperate need to be loved was very feminine. Like

many people who dislike their appearance, he was extremely vain . . .
[His] not at all effeminate femininity accounted for the lasting friendships he enjoyed with girls.'[17]

His conclusion – both neat and perceptive – was that his friend
wanted 'cool girls in a warm climate', but although the assessment
was theoretically true it overlooked a practical consideration: Connolly was getting older and although he remained both escapist and
itinerant at heart he also needed some measure of domestic security
which would take into account the fact that his work and his social
life were largely based in England. Besides, there comes a time when it
is neither practical nor seemly to pack lighter clothes, catch the first
ferry and recommence the frantic chase each time the traitor Eros
beckons. At fifty-five he had reached such a brink: intrigue could
continue unabated but soon the time would come when romantic
excursions would have to be more realistically paced. He had begun
preparations. It was widely known amongst his circle that with the
collapse of his second marriage he had compiled a shifting list of
potential brides who might banish the evening solitude, offer him
sympathy and support and perhaps even provide him with a belated
family. He made lists almost compulsively all his life; some were for
public consumption, some were emphatically private, and of the latter
category the catalogue of future wives was the most famous, theoretically shrouded in the extravagant secrecy so dear to him, in fact the
stuff of gossip. Caroline Blackwood had been on the list for some time
but was unmoved by the distinction, since his catalogues struck her as
being 'totally unrealistic'.[18] Given that her marriage to Lucian Freud
had done nothing to diminish Connolly's obsession, it was inevitable
when that partnership collapsed in 1957 that his attentions would
redouble and soon the letters to her began: 'We are the weather in
each other's hearts. I helped Barbara to marry Weidenfeld so as to free
myself for you. This was a miscalculation apparently – but I believe
the real miscalculation to have been yours in disguising the tie
between us . . . you know you really want to settle down and have a
child as much as I do.'[19] She was unconvinced but in any case he had
alternative ambitions: Magouche Fielding was a long-standing interest
he had first befriended in New York in 1947. She now lived in
London and was the next to hear his refrain – 'I must get married, I
must get married.' When she asked what sort of consort he had in
mind and he replied, 'Someone not English and with children', she

recognized the familiarity of the description and felt briefly uncomfortable, since in her eyes his manifold charms fell far short of physical attractiveness.[20] He would continue to dream: in the meantime Janetta, again single, was another possibility, and so was Anne, and even Barbara, aside from the quest but neither oblivious nor indifferent to its outcome, had opinions: 'What he really needs is someone young and entirely new.'[21]

He also needed somewhere to live. Oak Cottage had been put on the market and he could hardly continue indefinitely in makeshift London accommodation, yet the capital, increasingly expensive for the impoverished with lofty ideas, promised no permanent solutions: where, after all, would he be able to find a cheap London house which duplicated the grandeur of Sussex Place and offered the gardening opportunities of rural Kent? Happily, salvation was at hand. Through a vague friendship with Viscount Gage he was offered the tenancy of Bushey Lodge, a farmhouse built on the Gage Estate at Firle in Sussex in about 1800. Although it would need redecoration the property was structurally sound and would be cheap to rent: besides, its garden was pretty, the surrounding countryside was unspoilt and Firle Place itself was auspiciously close. Even though his patrician landlord, soon christened 'The Intelligence Gauge', would not play a prominent part in Connolly's Sussex life there was no question of rural isolation on the edge of the Downs. Opera and society were nearby at Glyndebourne, London was commutable and the Continent, just beyond the sea and the provincial Sybaris of Brighton, seemed psychologically close. Furthermore several writers, including Alan Ross, Cuthbert Worsley, Francis King and Robin Maugham, all lived in the locality at various times. It seemed a perfect solution: the lease was agreed, the rent fixed at £200 per annum, and Connolly installed as the new tenant in the summer of 1958.

Barbara, approached for advice about redecoration, ordained a bright orange in the dining room, while Magouche, enlisted to help with accessories, escorted Connolly on numerous expeditions round the West End. On one occasion she accompanied him to a rendezvous with Sonia at the Ritz and over tea the latter revealed that she was engaged to Michael Pitt-Rivers, who four years earlier had been sentenced to eighteen months' imprisonment after the notorious trial which had followed his involvement with two members of the RAF. Connolly appeared to take her announcement equably, and Magouche noted the affection and sweetness which lay between the two friends. Afterwards, however, brooding in Berkeley Street on another desertion, his mood darkened to melodramatic self-pity and he remarked: 'You walk fast. I walk slowly because I'm walking to my death.'[22] A few days later he had recovered himself sufficiently to entrust Magouche with the buying of sheets – strictly white linen – while he went to Spain. Soon after settling into his new house he sent a letter to Annie Davis thanking her for the holiday and cataloguing his new anxieties. As ever money was scarce, but although he was still short of furniture, country mobility was more important and he had decided that it was well worth spending £150 to acquire Baby's Sunbeam Talbot, always known as 'the little bus'. Not only the furniture was limited: at the moment he had only two charwomen, who came in the morning and occasionally stayed to make his lunch, and the services of the local signalman, who doubled as a gardener, boiler manager and general outdoor factotum. Otherwise, 'nearly all meals except breakfast and all the washing up must be cooked by Deirdre or Barbara or whoever is staying.'[23]

Deirdre Craven was another veteran of Connolly's list. When he first met her she had been staying in London, along with her stepcousin Venetia Murray, with Alan and Jennifer Ross. Besides being blonde, pretty and exceptionally thin, she also satisfied Barbara's prescription of youth and novelty – a winning combination by no means overlooked by Ross himself – and Connolly's interest was quickened, undaunted by later discoveries that she was less untrammelled and independent than first appeared. In 1951, aged nineteen, she had married a prosperous West Country farmer named Jonathan Craven, but the subsequent arrival of two children, Sarah and Simon, had done nothing to stem early disillusion and she instigated a provisional separation. To Connolly such matrimonial complications were trifling – insignificant beside the more elaborate love lives of most of his circle – and he would happily overlook them, just as he would overlook the deficiencies of education which Deirdre shared with most women of her generation and background. After all, a potential acolyte was more attractive than a proven bluestocking and he could himself teach her all she needed to know, conveniently superseding Alan Ross, in any case his own protégé, as both mentor and lover.

Inconveniently, unlike most of the candidates on the brides' list, Deirdre was as penniless as Barbara before her. Unlike Barbara, however, she had connections. In 1921 her grandfather, the first Viscount

Craigavon, had become the first Prime Minister of Northern Ireland. Her father, Dennis Craig, besides being a successful businessman, was a renowned equestrian authority whose classic *Horse-Racing: The breeding of thoroughbreds and a short history of the English turf* was published in 1949 and her stepmother, Joy, was the daughter of the Royal Academician Algernon Newton, sister of the actor Robert Newton and sister-in-law of the brilliant academic and lawyer, Sylvester Gates. Craig was her fourth husband but Joy remained on largely affectionate terms with his predecessors and their families, thus conferring on Deirdre a tenuous but affectionate relationship with numerous ex-step-kin. Craig himself was a popular and charming man and his circle of friendship, when combined with his wife's extended and vicarious clan, gave the couple a vast acquaintance which regularly congregated at the cottage they took on the Longleat Estate at Priston near Bath. When Connolly began to attend their parties he could expect to encounter the writer Simon Raven, Anthony and Violet Powell, Lord and Lady Bath, the future broadcaster Richard Kershaw and the inventor Jeremy Fry and could perhaps begin to understand why Deirdre, a daughter of higher Bohemia, had felt at a loss among the pastures of Somerset.

Connolly himself fitted into this world easily, indeed was the type of husband for which Deirdre's upbringing had implicitly prepared her. Soon they were having an affair and soon Barbara observed that he had 'fallen in love'. At his behest Janetta accompanied him to a party to vet the new girlfriend and found her both affectionate and pretty. Such impressions were encouraging but the affair was still by no means a matter to be publicly discussed, although when Robin Campbell's new fiancée Susan met the critic in 1958 she quickly learned the identity of the girlfriend, who was theoretically known as 'Mrs X'. As the affair progressed the idea began to take shape that Deirdre should somehow extricate herself from her marriage, although as the deserting party she would not instigate divorce proceedings from a position of strength. At first it seemed as though Craven might simplify matters by allowing her to divorce him; but he reconsidered and it became clear not only that the severance would be difficult but also that it might engender publicity; and the last thing Connolly wanted, so soon after named involvement in the Weidenfelds' divorce, was the further stain of scandal. He was not alone in his care for reputations: Alan Ross, who had been married throughout his involvement with Deirdre, refused to accept dictation about the role he should play in any forthcoming trial and an angry exchange of letters followed. Connolly denounced the affair with Barbara as a betrayal of friendship and told Ross that it would be cruel and disloyal of him to defend his name, thus courting publicity and damaging Deirdre's chances of financial settlement, in a case which was going to be heard as discreetly as possible in Leeds. Ross countered. How could he have betrayed any relationship with Barbara when she was married to another man? His only folly had been in overlooking the ambivalences of Connolly's relations with Baby. As for Deirdre, 'I must be allowed to feel that I'm not being very fairly or honestly treated in this matter, that in some way at least you are responsible for [Deirdre's] (what seems to me) v. irresponsible behaviour, and that if people want divorces they should go about it more tidily.'[24]

In the event Ross was named as the co-respondent and by the time the divorce was made absolute on 23 July 1959 Deirdre knew not only that she had lost the case but that she was pregnant. At the beginning of 1960 Cyril Connolly would finally become a father: the famous adage from *Enemies of Promise* – 'There is no more sombre enemy of good art than the pram in the hall' – would soon be put to the test. Maud meanwhile sent her sympathy about the verdict of the divorce, convinced that if her prospective daughter-in-law had been old and ugly matters would have resolved themselves differently. With marriage imminent she also asked him to bear in mind the fact that in the event of her sudden death South African financial restrictions would allow him to remove no more than £5000 of her capital from the country; the balance would be immovable, though he would still be able to claim the interest. A date was set for the wedding, the news spread, and even David Astor, with whom Connolly was tentatively reconciled during the summer, had heard of the development and expressed his happy surprise, to which his long-lost friend assented: 'It's a surprising thing, but Deirdre's the sort of girl who gets ideas in her head and they can't be dislodged, the sort who sees Hitler's sofa at a sale and decides she's got to have it.'[25] He was preoccupied enough and continued reviewing and broadcasting – appearing on 10 August on the television programme *Tonight* to discuss 'Writers of Diaries' and again ten days later to address 'The Growing Cult of the Sun' – as preparations began for his third wedding.

CHAPTER TWENTY-NINE

'WE VIRGOS FIND ourselves compelled to make alliances with others,' Sonia had written when explaining her decision to marry Pitt-Rivers, and her old friend may have contemplated her wisdom as he went to the registry office at Mere in Wiltshire on 26 August, with Stephen Spender as a witness, to meet his twenty-seven-year-old bride.[1] As a student of life's coincidences he may also have contemplated the fact that now, like his grandfather Connolly before him, he was older, at fifty-six, than his fifty-three-year-old father-in-law. Barbara found herself 'shocked and demoralized' by the marriage.[2] His mother, by contrast, was delighted, although she decided that severe arthritis exempted her from attending the ceremony. In the meantime, as she wrote in December, she was going to send Deirdre some pearls. Perhaps they would arrive in time for the christening, since on 14 January 1960 Cressida Louisa Vernon Connolly was born in a London nursing home. She had arrived prematurely and as her father told Barbara on the telephone that night she should by rights have been born an Aquarius. He had never before seen a newly-born baby and had worried that he might find the sight repellent but Barbara noted the excitement his 'breathless' voice betrayed and when she asked for details his description, if not conventionally rhapsodic, was enthusiastic. The baby was 'fetching' and 'like some delicious animal in Harrods pet shop. It made a kind of squeak, has red hair and its eyes are closed.'[3] Perhaps smitten by regret, guilt or nostalgia, perhaps eager to mark her imminent departure for New York, he had presented Barbara with a scarf bought in Turnbull and Asser and when he went to visit her on the day before her departure, she wished him luck with his new marriage. He was confident: 'Oh yes, The baby will cement it.'[4]

The Connollys moved back into Bushey Lodge and Deirdre, between pondering the future custody of Sarah and Simon, attending to Cressida and devoting herself to her new husband, himself half father-figure and half-baby, set about making the house an agreeable home and popular weekend resort for their friends. The bibliophile Anthony Hobson, who married her stepsister Tanya, became a regular guest at the house and retained strong impressions of its casual yet not unsophisticated charm:

> Bushey Lodge was a delightful house, strongly marked by its tenant's personality.

He remembers a crimson sitting-room, a cornflower-blue room and a terracotta dining-room with a brick floor. There were paintings by Vanessa Bell and Lucian Freud, Sèvres china and Portuguese rococo silver, and books everywhere:

> Unlike the cottage in Kent, where books had not been greatly in evidence, they invaded every room in the house at Bushey ... They were shelved roughly by subject. When Cyril showed me my bedroom he explained, 'You've got travel, some cookery and a little sex.'[5]

Deirdre's cooking was famously accomplished but Hobson found other enchantments besides and particularly cherished memories of the summer mornings when Clive Bell and Duncan Grant, also amongst Lord Gage's accomplished tenantry, would arrive from nearby Charleston to drink Böhle in the garden with other guests or neighbours such as the Christies of Glyndebourne. John Craxton, another regular guest, was touched to see how much Duncan Grant and his host adored each other. He found the walled garden particularly delightful and often caught morning glimpses of Connolly inspecting its fruit and flowers in his dressing-gown and looking 'like a Roman poet in exile'.[6] Robert Kee was soon invited to bring down his new wife Cynthia, who had already noted how Connolly's moods of smiling or sulking set the trend of the table and suspected that it would be impossible for anyone who had never met him to fully understand 'the strength of his disapprobation'. In the country, however, she found a mellower figure who playfully asked her if she could name the gourmand's days of the week? 'Munchday, Chewsday, Say-When-s Day, Thirstday, Fried-day, Batterday, Bunday.' Cynthia's sense of the bizarre aspect of their domesticity reached its height one Sunday morning when she was in the garden: while the exceptionally thin Deirdre organized lunch and Cressida lay in a pram under a tree apparently ignored by mother, father and nanny, she noticed her very plump host standing at a bedroom window contemplating the view and apparently unaware that his only item of clothing, a dressing-gown, had fallen open, betraying his girth – and more – to any incurious onlooker.[7] In the confident and liberal enclaves of Glyndebourne and Charleston such reports would not have aroused comment but elsewhere Connolly was viewed uncertainly and his fame was ambivalent. The journalist James Fox, later a colleague on the *Sunday Times*, knew enough, even at fifteen, to hold him in some awe: '[His] reputation in the neighbourhood as an intellectual isolated among the gentry, who labelled him "distinguished and erudite" was also that of a difficult and unreliable guest.'[8]

If David Astor had been happy to break the silence of seventeen-odd years with a writer and journalist he greatly admired, Connolly had his own reasons for satisfaction. Despite the easy terms agreed with the Firle Estate he was increasingly bedevilled by financial anxiety: and besides having to provide for his wife and daughter he also had to face the small but extra costs incurred during the intermittent presences of his stepchildren – Simon Craven, now six, arrived to spend a year at Bushey in 1960 – and the nagging thought that he had reached the early autumn of his life without having accumulated any capital; and although his standing at Gray's Inn Road was high there seemed little hope that his salary would leap either soon or often in recognition of that prestige. Now, however, whether presenting a second chance or else a mere coincidence, the strange patterns of life had prompted the reappearance in his career of an editor he knew to be both powerful and magnanimous. Such happy accidents were not to be lightly dismissed and the more he pondered the matter the surer he felt that Astor's generosity would incline him not only to take back his prodigals but to listen attentively to their anxieties, financial or otherwise. There could be no harm in tentative – and discreet – advances and on 21 May he wrote to the *Observer* with vague enquiries about the possibility of renewed partnership. The response was more enthusiastic than he could have hoped. Encouraged by his literary editor Terence Kilmartin, himself a great admirer of the critic, Astor eagerly considered the overture and on 15 June detailed his liberal proposals in a reply. His newspaper already fielded a significant critical artillery which included Arthur Koestler, Kenneth Tynan and Alan Pryce-Jones: 'But you should not get the idea that we would simply treat you as one of a team. On the contrary, in our preliminary discussions here it has been plainly recognized that the way to get the best value from you would be to encourage you to write in your most personal style and to treat you in every way as a unique figure.'

It seemed there would be virtually no restrictions placed on the subjects Connolly wanted to explore. For his part Astor would be happy to give his new writer a month's annual holiday, a salary of £2500 and a contract enshrining his proposals. He would not dissemble; and if his terms were generous he was also happy to admit their motivation: 'The reason why all concerned here are with me in wanting you to join us is that we intend to let the *Sunday Times* go after its million and to concentrate on making this paper better in quality ... You could be a great help to us and we would treat you like a prince.'[9] At last the rancour of 1942 was purged and in a manner not only personally elating but also somehow reassuringly familiar: Astor's frankness and moral fastidiousness were intact and had survived not only the transiencies inherent in journalism but the particular disappointments of 1956, when his opposition to Eden's invasion of Nasser's Egypt had caused thousands of readers to defect to the *Observer*'s patriotic rival. How could Connolly delay, especially when with migration he would be allying himself with the more liberal and progressive institution? Yet scruples interceded. The arts department at the *Sunday Times* was about to pass from Leonard Russell's control to Jack Lambert's: the sudden defection of its principal critic would seem particularly tactless and ill-conceived and when he joined Astor for lunch at the Ritz he gratefully declined his offer. As usual Connolly contrived to introduce a note of elegy and regret: of the two of them, he intimated, Astor alone had remained true to his principles, whereas he had succumbed to accidie and had traded creative freedom for journeyman reviewing because of a trite and unaesthetic need for security. Astor may have suspected an element of dramatic posturing in his friend's self-lacerations but nevertheless appreciated the comic element of the performance: 'There's a side of me that can't resist big houses with large bath towels. A good bath towel can make me do almost anything.'[10]

Three thousand miles away, in the introduction to a new American publication of *Enemies of Promise*, Connolly spoke simultaneously in tones less self-effacing: 'Do not despise the scrappiness of my book. I work best in scraps and, besides, a little of me goes a long way.'[11] Now his survival in the English-speaking world seemed assured, especially when Penguin Books announced that in 1961 the book would be republished in its Modern Classics series. In the meantime, would Connolly give Penguin's lawyers his opinions of *Lady Chatterley's Lover*, as the company was considering releasing an unexpurgated edition and foresaw problems with the obscenity laws? Evelyn Waugh had already declared his position – in support of its censorship – but he and Connolly would continue to diverge over numerous subjects despite their affinities. In September Connolly reviewed Waugh's latest publication, a travel book. Prefacing his review with the assertion that Waugh's every word was of great interest to him, he nevertheless registered a new disappointment:

> When we are young, we travel to see the world, afterwards to make sure it is still there ... I know the obsession by which revisiting places where one has once felt becomes a substitute for feeling, but it does not make for the best kind of travel book ... *A Tourist In Africa* is quite the thinnest piece of book-making which Mr Waugh has undertaken ... the particular pose he affects – of an elderly, infirm and irritable old buffer, quite out of touch with the times – is hardly suited to enthusiasm, a prerequisite of travel writing.[12]

While sales of the travel book languished Waugh's son Auberon's first novel, *The Foxglove Saga*, sold well. Perhaps he was getting old? Perhaps he was losing his touch? The thought was beginning to dog all his generation, now rising sixty (later in the year Bernard Wall, editor of *The Twentieth Century*, stigmatized Connolly, Raymond Mortimer and Harold Nicolson as obsolete and snobbish dilettantes), yet he stoically and politely acknowledged Connolly's review and assured his friend that 'I wasn't the least put out by [it].'[13] Connolly was pleased to receive the reassurance and even took the letter with him when he and Deirdre joined Angus Wilson and Somerset Maugham for lunch at the Flemings' in October. The occasion was largely devoted to shouting reassurances of genius at the deaf, vain and ageing Maugham, but when Mrs Fleming tired of that sport she could always taunt her other guest, and playfully repeated some malicious remark which Waugh had made at Connolly's expense. Nor would she deny her work and wrote triumphantly to Waugh: 'I find it irresistible to bully Cyril, I don't love him like you do.'[14]

While Waugh had been voyaging in other continents Connolly himself, aware of greater financial obligations and always eager to flee the here and now, had also been planning excursions, not least into his own past. Hence the idea of an autobiography, which he had mentioned to David Astor, hence also his scheme to write a book about the Twenties, of all the decades he had experienced the one which most fascinated him. Bearing in mind the first ambition, he had begun to collect old letters; bearing in mind the second, to contact old friends and surviving witnesses, among them Sylvia Beach, who responded enthusiastically to his announcement in January 1961: 'Your book would make a sensation and you can deal with the subject as not another has done or is able to do. I don't think anybody can compete with you as an essayist today: what amusing things you do, and seemingly so easy.'[15] In the meantime he had a new contract with Hamish Hamilton, in which he undertook to produce the text for a handsome picture book about the pavilions and pleasure domes of the French *ancien régime*. Hamilton engaged the complementary services of Jerome Zerbe, an American photographer who had established his reputation in New York, mainly at the Stork Club, where he documented the nocturnal laughter of the rich and famous. But although Connolly would enjoy the research for the book, he could not pretend that the work would resolve any long-term financial difficulties, and even as he saw the last of his pre-war manuscripts, of *The Rock Pool*, fetch £450 at Sotheby's on 29 May he realized with increasing conviction that his library and papers would constitute his most valuable capital. He became more determined to collect his old letters from friends and correspondents – 'Boots is up to something rather fishy . . . Be wary,' Waugh counselled Nancy Mitford[16] – and his colleagues at the *Sunday Times* noticed that whenever he went into the office he stealthily scoured desktops and wastepaper baskets and set aside any fragments of paper which bore his handwriting.

Even as he began to shore fragments against his ruins, other fixtures of his earlier life disappeared or else admitted their age with reminiscence and autobiography. At the beginning of July Ernest Hemingway died while supposedly cleaning his shotgun. Richard Kershaw was staying at Bushey when news of his death was released and remembered how one newspaper after another rang for Connolly's instant obituary and how the critic somehow managed to suggest both pride and a degree of *schadenfreude* each time he went to the receiver and mouthed with renewed portentousness, 'He was a titan.'[17] On 9 July the *Sunday Times* published his appreciation of the novelist and later in the month he appeared in a television discussion of his achievement along with Anthony Powell, Hercules Belville, Simon Raven and Stephen Spender.

On 16 July, reviewing *The Wandering Years*, the first volume of Cecil Beaton's memoirs, he was once again driven to retrospection. Connolly enjoyed the account, although he no doubt felt slight envy of a life lived so much among the beautiful and grand: 'Reading him is like coming ashore on a hot night in some Mediterranean harbour from the tourist class of the local steamer and suddenly seeing a glamorous party off a yacht sitting in a café. It is no consolation to meet one of them afterwards and be told that on that evening no one was speaking and the feuds of a lifetime were boiling over, or even that they all wondered who we were.'[18] An ending of another sort came in the autumn when Evelyn Waugh completed both his military trilogy and his fictional career with *Unconditional Surrender*. Inevitably the novel contained jokes at Connolly's expense; and few of their mutual friends could question the inspiration behind the character of Everard Spruce, editor of a wartime magazine called *Survival*. The barb was not especially subtle and inevitably found its target. Rashly, Connolly telephoned Ann Fleming for reassurance and advice. Could he come for a drink to discuss the matter? A few days later Mrs Fleming dutifully sent her report to Waugh:

> What grieves him most is Everard Spruce . . . [He] regretted that *Horizon* should have been mocked and reminded me of that whole issue of *Horizon* that was dedicated entirely to one of your morbid works; he asked if I did not think your wit has become bilious with the passage of the years, he has re-read *Men At Arms* and *Officers and Gentlemen*, and I look forward immensely to the result of such mental torture.[19]

The critic disappointed her. He had never been too proud to educate himself publicly and now, having re-read the first two volumes of the trilogy and found them vastly better than on first acquaintance, he devoted a large review to the entire work, which he was now sure constituted the finest fiction yet to emerge from the war. Of course he had his reservations: Waugh was only interested in his major characters and subjected his minor figures to an 'essential biliousness' of contemplation; and the novel lacked descriptions of the principal military engagements, from which Waugh himself had been debarred. Yet *Sword of Honour* was 'most impressive' and he urged its publishers to bring out a one-volume edition forthwith.[20] Such panegyric far exceeded not only Waugh's moral deserts but the more regular loyalties of friendship, particularly when other critics – Kingsley Amis, Gore

Vidal, Philip Toynbee – were less sure of the trilogy's merit. Waugh had sent Connolly his usual disclaimers about the malice inherent in his comedy: 'There are of course asses in London, who don't understand the processes of the imagination, whose hobby it is to treat fiction as a gossip column ... what distresses me (if true) is that you should suppose I would publicly caricature a cherished friend.'[21] Nobody was convinced, although not all onlookers had the perspicacity which Maurice Bowra shared with Mrs Fleming: 'I am not surprised that Cyril is wounded by Evelyn's presentation of him ... It is not very like him, but sufficiently like him to be offensive. It is sad that Evelyn has such an urge to torture him. It must be a form of love.'[22] Connolly himself longed above all to believe the novelist's assertions but could no longer conquer his doubts: 'I do not think posterity will ever believe in our friendship any more than someone who looked me up in the index to your biography.'[23]

As Bowra had shown, however, he was not without allies or admirers. Lord Adrian, Master of Trinity College, Cambridge, tried to persuade Connolly to deliver the Clark Lectures on English Literature during the following academic year. The post, which carried a stipend of £150 with travelling expenses, was prestigious and had previously been occupied by C. V. Wedgwood, Neville Coghill and G. Wilson Knight. Unfortunately the critic was ill with bronchitis when the invitation arrived and felt compelled to decline it. With the reappearance of *Enemies of Promise* John Wain took the opportunity to assess his achievement in *Encounter* and to answer the nagging question put to him by Edmund Wilson when he had first met the American in 1957: 'Why are so many people in England down on Cyril Connolly?' Wain was astute enough to see that the detractors Wilson had encountered were all writers themselves rather than the general public, which held Connolly in such esteem 'that he must be reckoned our most successful literary columnist'.[24]

At the end of 1961 the *Sunday Times* invited its most prominent writers to contribute to an occasional series, 'The Seven Deadly Sins': Cyril Connolly was to consider 'Covetousness'; Edith Sitwell, 'Pride'; Patrick Leigh Fermor, 'Gluttony'; Evelyn Waugh, 'Sloth'; Angus Wilson, 'Envy'; W. H. Auden, 'Wrath'; and Christopher Sykes, 'Lust'. The idea of rapaciousness amused Connolly – sloth would have been too obvious – and he turned in a virtuoso miniature of self-caricature. The newspaper's recently installed editor, Denis Hamilton, was delighted and readily assured his critic that his fictional interlude would appear without cuts. 'The Downfall of Jonathan Edax' – published on 24 December – is the story of a married man, bored by his wife and the trappings of domesticity and interested only in material possessions. His hungry eye falls without discrimination on silver, porcelain or paintings but his special interest lies with the increase of his collection of modern autographed pamphlets. Yet although he is intensely acquisitive Edax is also avaricious and collects through lies, theft, even adultery, rather than honest commerce.

The story was not about Connolly but it contained enough self-mocking parallels to amuse a knowing audience: he too kept his most precious slim volumes and little magazines in a bookcase called 'The Controls'; he too had a streak of irritable misogyny; he too had a dangerous reputation when it came to the rare first editions of his friends. Francis King remembered that when Connolly came for a drink he revealed that he was without a first edition of King's novel *To the Dark Tower* but the novelist had only one copy and he intended to keep it. Presently his guest asked for more ice. King fetched it, drinks were finished; and only when the critic had left did King notice the gap in his bookshelf. Stephen Spender was another victim. Connolly had lunch with Auden and persuaded the poet to prevail upon Spender to give him his one remaining copy of the first volume of Auden's poems, which he himself had printed in 1928. The book had long since become unobtainable but Spender yielded to persuasion when Auden promised to replace the book with the copy he would eventually inherit from his father. He later forgot his assurance.

A few years previously Connolly had accompanied Robert Kee to stay at Lismore Castle, the Duke of Devonshire's home in Ireland, and while there had declared an ambition to buy a property locally. Unfortunately he had annoyed the Duchess, who found him arrogant and unattractive and particularly resented his inability to come to the dinner table on time. By 1962, however, his sins had been forgotten and the year began with another invitation to stay with the Devonshires, this time at Chatsworth on 14 and 15 January. Soon afterwards Connolly received an advance of $2000 from Macmillan in America for a book provisionally entitled *Where Breath Must Breathe*. (Seven years later the company would sue for the return of the money, having had neither sight nor sound of the project.) In February he was asked by the BBC to contribute to the Home Service's *World of Books* and four months later a further invitation followed to participate in a programme to be made about Augustus John, who had died the previous year. In March he saw the past again made famous with the publication of Christopher Isherwood's *Down There on a Visit*, another example of the novelist's autobiographical fiction which contained portraits of Jean ('Ruthie'), Denham Fouts ('Paul') and Tony Bower ('Ronny'). The deceptive simplicity of the novelist's narrative style and his strong sympathy for outsiders and eccentrics had always engaged Connolly's respect and he confided to his readers that 'at any moment one hopes to come on a flattering description of oneself' during the course of one of his novels.[25] He enjoyed this latest excursion and his happy recommendation led to a letter of thanks from Isherwood: 'There is so much of the tone of friendship in your review; I felt that you not only sincerely liked the book but were *glad* you liked it.'[26] *Down There on a Visit* coincided with another publication from California – Aldous Huxley's fictional swansong *Island*, the manuscript of which the author had managed to rescue from the conflagration which destroyed his Hollywood home. Perhaps Connolly erred on the side of generosity when he claimed that Huxley had animated his book with 'real people' but he was nevertheless right to stress that its moral and philosophical pretensions lifted it far beyond the realm of commonplace writing.[27]

As the spring progressed he finished the text of his book, which was to be called *Les Pavillons*, and which would guide its readers around thirty-nine generously illustrated and elegantly described French *bagatelles*. The introduction, too, was now complete:

> The French eighteenth century is a period which we can literally live ourselves into ... It is a civilization which contains everything we can desire except great literature. The seventeenth century and the nineteenth make up for that, but the one is too formal and remote, the other too chaotic and industrialized to challenge our desirable haven.[28]

The book was scheduled (and priced, at 73s 6d) for Christmas publication. Meanwhile in April Frances Partridge invited Connolly for drinks. At first, discovering that he was to share her company with other guests, he was irritable and behaved like 'a crossish baby'. She would not surrender to his moodiness, however: 'I led him to my bookcase and shamelessly offered him baits to ingratiate him. He was soon on the floor, happy, with his fat legs splayed out and hair flying wildly; then his own jokes and embroidered fantasies brought twinkling geniality and he was busy signing my copy of *The Unquiet Grave*.'[29] By the time she saw him again in the summer she knew she not only respected his imagination and intelligence but also rather liked him. They discussed his distant love for Racy Fisher and he admitted that 'he had been until then exclusively homosexual and this was a shattering and new experience.'[30]

CHAPTER THIRTY

AT THE END of July, Connolly went to the Continent to retrace the steps of the Grand Tour for the benefit of two articles for the *Sunday Times*. Owing to a fear of flying, sailing, even train tunnels, Deirdre was an inexperienced traveller and had never before been to Italy but her husband coaxed her into accompanying him: she could take the photographs which would illustrate the articles and in order to retain as much as possible of the Grand Tour's original flavour they would in any case avoid flying and restrict themselves to a sedater progress by train. They booked seats on the Golden Arrow and a cabin for the Channel crossing; in Paris they caught the connecting train at the Gare de Lyon and later glimpsed the misty Lombard plain from the windows of their *wagon-lit*. In Florence they had dinner with Harold Acton, inspected churches, sat in cafés, visited the Pitti Palace and marvelled at the Botticelli room in the Uffizi: 'There is something in the breaking water, the whorl of pale wavelets under Venus' whorled shell, or in the pose of the youth examining a fruit with outstretched arm, which confers a benediction on man's search for knowledge and eases the weariness of living.'[1] I Tatti, transformed since Connolly's last visit from Berenson's home to an immaculate shrine, was now a stately but depressing reminder that even longevity is somehow illusory, its monuments no less so. For those who love grandeur and glamour Rome will always delight more than Florence; and having reserved his ecstasies in the city of the Medici he succumbed with a sigh to the Piazza Navona, the Campidoglio, the Capitoline museum, the Pincio Gardens, the Pantheon and the frescoes from the Empress Livia's villa. With Deirdre he explored beyond the city to the Villa d'Este, Tivoli, Palestrina, Hadrian's Villa, the Villa Lante and the Mannerist monster gardens of Bomarzo before continuing to Naples and then catching the night-boat to Sicily. Palermo was much changed since his last visit: the post-war world had intruded although in the hotel they had chosen it did so in elegant form, since Luchino Visconti and Burt Lancaster were also staying there for the filming of *The Leopard*. Leaving the film team to its re-creation of the past, the Connollys continued to explore its relics: the Villa Palagonia, Bagheria, Segesta, Erice, Syracuse and lastly Noto, 'one of the most southerly towns in Europe with its baroque palaces and blue–green araucarias, the lightly swaying Norfolk island pines which guarantee a mild winter'.

At home once more Connolly learned that the Flemings had bought Augustus John's portrait of him for £300. He himself was in no position for extravagance, although at least Ran Antrim agreed at the end of August to increase his guarantee of Connolly's overdraft to £350, including in his endorsement a present of £100 'which comes from my heart'.[2] In September Warren Roberts of the Humanities Research Center at the University of Austin, Texas, intimated once more that his organization would be prepared to pay well for Connolly's collection of books and papers. Connolly despatched a cautious letter of rejection, explaining that it would be tactless to sell the correspondence of friends such as Betjeman, Auden and Waugh while they were still alive and that he wanted his collection to remain intact, 'as an example of a typical library of one of the last men-of-letters in an age of transition'. Nevertheless he was careful not to appear off-putting: he would retain contact with the Center and content himself for the time being with intimations of future interest: 'I think whether or not I survive as a writer I have some importance as a bridge-passage, via *Horizon*, between the old easy-going literary Establishment of the 1920s, the grimmer 30s and the wartime generations.'[3]

In October Noël Annan, Provost of King's College, tried unsuccessfully to tempt Connolly to Cambridge to attend the Founder's Day banquet; nothing daunted, he threatened to lure the critic and his wife to King's on another weekend in the near future. In December *Les Pavillons* appeared to bromide enthusiasm from Raymond Mortimer in the *Sunday Times* and similar effusions from other reviewers. Connolly sent a copy of the book to his mother in South Africa and told her that the newspaper was to pay him an extra £250 per annum with a further £500 for occasional journalism in 1963. She wrote back enthusiastically on 8 December, hopeful that now at least he would be able to afford 'a proper servant that would save Deirdre'. As for the book: 'I always felt you were someone who had lived before and had to come back.'[4] Early in the New Year the publisher John Calder, having acquired the

rights to Henry Miller's *Tropic of Cancer*, asked the critic if he would
be prepared to counteract potential difficulties with obscenity by tes-
tifying that publication would be in the public interest. Later Calder
would approach him again for support for William Burroughs' *Naked
Lunch*. In the meantime he continued with current projects: a translation of Jarry's *Ubu Cocu* for the theatre director Peter Brook and a
pastiche of Ian Fleming's heady and irresistible fiction which had no
doubt been inspired by the recent premiere of *Dr No* at the London
Pavilion. The translation was finished in February and at first reading
Brook was enthusiastic, assuring his partner, 'You have succeeded in
the absolutely impossible task of inventing an English form of Jarry-
ese.'[5] Later, second thoughts would assail him, and Connolly's version,
which now had 'a literary but not a theatrical energy', lay unper-
formed.[6] 'Bond Strikes Camp' was published in the *London Magazine*
in April and took as its implicit theme what Gavin Ewart, extolling the
pastiche in the same publication later in the year, described as 'James
Bond's concealed queerness'. It captured the tone of its original with
deft and inventive fidelity, despite putting Fleming's hero in a cocktail
dress and having him surrounded by sexual rather than political
turncoats.

Unashamedly flippant though the *capriccio* was, it nevertheless
caught a reflection of contemporary significance, a significance which
Fleming and numerous other writers of espionage fiction so successfully
exploited throughout the Cold War as rumour and counter-rumour,
agent and double agent mysteriously penetrated the two-year-old Berlin
Wall. (Only in January Kim Philby had vanished in Beirut, to reappear
in July in the pages of *Tass* as a fully fledged Soviet citizen.) When
Connolly's joke was published Fleming was wise enough to take it as a
compliment, despatching assurances that his friend's 'minken lashes
tingle more exquisitely than the spoonfuls of tiptree little scarlet'.[7]
Christopher Isherwood, a loyal admirer of Fleming's fiction, wrote
appreciatively from California: 'I think Bond had this coming to him. I
have several times resented his attitude to the Minority to which I have
the honour to belong. And how exquisitely you do it.'[8]

As Connolly neared his sixtieth birthday on 10 September plans
began for celebration. Elizabeth Glenconner volunteered to give a dinner and a party afterwards and invitations were despatched. T. S. Eliot
and his wife were unable to attend as the poet was unwell. Maurice
Bowra also sent his regrets and was eager to convey advice as well as

commemorative gifts: 'It is no fun being sixty ... Don't give up sex whatever you do. Once you knock off, you are done.'[9] Evelyn Waugh could not agree, at least with the first claim, and approaching the same anniversary himself he not only promised the new sexagenarian tributes of wine but sent interim reassurances: 'The fifties are a disagreeable decade. Life begins at sixty.'[10] A few weeks later, however, when Connolly wrote to thank Bowra for his birthday present, which he said he would spend on acquiring the rare 1913 edition of Yeats's *Poems Written in Discouragement*, he had already begun to question Waugh's consolation: 'One is like a sandcastle whose flags and battlements are collapsing one by one, faster and faster – teeth, hair, eyesight, memory, penis – all n[o] b[loody] g[ood].' Disillusion notwithstanding, he contemplated a new literary venture: the collection and publication of his early correspondence, mostly with Noël Blakiston but with fragments of his exchanges with Longden, Balfour and Rachel MacCarthy included for good measure. He had already begun preliminary assortment but as usual had not revisited the past with impunity: the fading documents had had the effect 'of making me desperately in love with them all again'.[11]

The Rock Pool now joined *Enemies of Promise* as a Penguin Modern Classic and its reissue spurred Simon Raven to encomium in the *London Magazine*, where he praised the novel's 'Petronian' quality, which lay in its 'air of burlesque, of succinctness, contrasted with wilful inconsequence, which informs what remains of the *Satyricon*'.[12] Gavin Ewart, who had admired the critic for many years, sent an unsolicited essay, once again to the *London Magazine*, which Alan Ross published intact. Ewart assessed the extent of the critical attention Connolly had so far received in a career spanning almost forty years and having taken into account the sketches written by Quennell, Wain and Raven and such reviews of his rare books as there had been, he detected 'almost a conspiracy of silence'. His own essay was complimentary without being sycophantic, the product of an admirer who at the same time was not a member of Connolly's club of friends and allied reviewers. He gently chastised him for breaking his rule that writers should 'be read and not heard' by appearing on television and pointed out that the famous aphorism about the thin man within the fat echoed something Orwell had said in *Coming Up For Air*. He found *The Rock Pool* and *Enemies of Promise* to be fine, if flawed, works; *The Unquiet Grave* he took to be a masterpiece; 'Where Engels Fears to Tread' left him unashamed: 'It is a complete (literary) justification of the life of Brian Howard that he inspired this ... He was to Mr Connolly what Edward King was to Milton.'[13]

Shortly afterwards Alan Ross gave a party at the offices of the *London Magazine* in order to introduce Ewart to the writer he revered. Not knowing what to expect, the poet went along and found a small group dominated by Connolly, whom he sensed Ross idolized as the embodiment of *la vie littéraire*. Ewart himself found the guest of honour urbane but as their conversation developed he detected a current of tension beneath the imperturbability, a sense 'of steel within the velvet glove'. At once calling him 'Gavin', Connolly referred to Ewart's implied charge of plagiarism and announced that it was the first time such an accusation had been levelled at him. The fact that he cared about the matter seemed an admission of insecurity; and in his airy gambit, 'You're in advertising, aren't you?', the poet thought he heard a subtler charge – that he belonged to a profession of philistines and reprobates and therefore had to be excused his trespasses of taste and inaccuracy.[14] A tribute of another sort was unleashed by Elaine Tynan, whose new novel, *The Old Man and Me*, was now in preparation. Its plot charted the love affair between a young American *ingénue* and an older writer with certain affinities to Connolly, and when Kenneth Tynan read the story he was sufficiently disquieted to waylay Stephen Spender with an unanswerable question: 'Is Cyril an honourable man?'[15]

The biggest event of Connolly's sixtieth birthday celebrations, however, was the publication by Hamish Hamilton of *Previous Convictions*, a new selection of writings drawn principally from the *Sunday Times* but with additional material representing his intermittent presence in *L'Œil*, the *London Magazine*, *Encounter*, the *Times Literary Supplement*, the *New Statesman* and the *New Yorker*. Connolly's initial hope had been to call the selection 'Cast a Cold Eye', a proposal abandoned with the discovery that the title had already been spoken for by Mary McCarthy, but even with a second name chosen, the selection of material provided lengthy agonies of doubt and indecision. As early as April a memorandum circulated the offices of Hamish Hamilton which indicated a prevailing acceptance that particular strategies were required to bring any book of Connolly's to birth: 'I believe that the best way to get [his] script out of him is not to go on chivvying him but to suggest terms, with a large part of the advance (say two-thirds) payable on delivery. We paid him £350 [for *Les Pavillons*] – or, rather, he calmly filled in this amount himself after a talk with Mrs Carlton Cole.'[16] Whatever the terms eventually agreed, Connolly decided that the new book should represent his enthusiasms for art, travel and nature, as well as his constant revisions of his favourite writers and his flair for comic sketches and parodies. His introduction was the customary self-portrait of exquisite disingenuousness: reviews were ephemeral and his last two collections were therefore out of print; besides, a critic is both a failed writer and himself the prey of other critics when he releases any sort of book. *Qui s'accuse s'excuse.* Yet he stressed the virtue of his prose, beyond which, he said, he believed there lay no contentment, and the rewards of reviewing, which had 'prevented *rigor mentis* setting in'.

Immediately after his birthday he went to stay with Anne at the Domaine de St-Estève, her house near Lambesc in the Bouches du Rhône, and Hamish Hamilton, eager for Christmas publication, had to send the forthcoming book's proofs after him. In November, pending publication, he was invited to help mark the fortieth anniversary of the foundation of the Oxford University Railway Club by joining a special excursion from London to Brighton which would involve as many old members, with guests, as could be mustered: the final party included Connolly himself, Evelyn and Auberon Waugh, the founder, John Sutro, Harold Acton, John Sparrow, Lord Antrim, Lord Bath, Roy Harrod and Lord Boothby. Relations with Waugh were easy once again: the novelist had been invited by the BBC to record a discussion of his fiction with the critic of his choice and had nominated Connolly, who accepted. In the event, perhaps suspecting that an unhealthy degree of sympathy would exist between novelist and interlocutor, the Corporation appointed another interviewer. Waugh was benign and told his friend: 'You are in the happy position of having been solicited for a disagreeable service, of having graciously accepted and of now being clear of the nuisance. It was a noble act to have exposed yourself to shame in the first place.'[17] Connolly did not share Waugh's aversion to the devices of broadcasting: on 9 November he reappraised Dylan Thomas for the Third Programme and on 29 November, in concert with the philosopher Maurice Cranston, he discussed Aldous Huxley, who had died a week previously.

He had originally considered dedicating *Previous Convictions* to Bill and Annie Davis but friends were intrigued to note when the book appeared that it was formally inscribed to Barbara rather than Deirdre, a remembrance – Ann Fleming was happy to relay to Waugh – which upset Deirdre sufficiently to dissuade her from accompanying her husband to Hamilton's publication dinner. Noël Annan gave the book a generous reception in the *Sunday Times* but a number of other reviews, especially those written by younger critics, tended to be disparaging and eager to deprecate what they saw as a dragonfly flirtation with subjects meriting sterner disquisition. In the *Evening Standard*, while saluting the critic 'with affection, admiration and respect', Malcolm Muggeridge introduced a tarter note: 'A different Connolly with a different girth and different angsts (his word) and a larger, steadier income would not necessarily have been more productive. His lost masterpieces give a piquancy to his criticism, as childless women make the best baby-sitters and impotent men the most assiduous lovers.'[18] Muggeridge could never resist the temptation to be scathing about Connolly, the result no doubt of some temperamental incompatibility which kept them apart. Elizabeth Bowen sent immediate praise: 'Best of all . . . I like the concreteness. The never being academic or abstract. The almost throw-away lines which all the same lodge in one's being as bits of wisdom. And the actuality, the convergence of mood, of scene (whether scenic or psychological).'[19] Friends are no doubt there to flatter; but nobody could claim that Connolly's were merely obtuse sycophants. Maurice Bowra had also enjoyed the book: 'You have the very rare gift of treating a subject seriously from your own original point of view . . . [you] are always an artist, choosing the right words, putting them into new patterns, and producing something which nobody else can do.'[20]

The recipient was touched and wrote a letter of thanks – with gossip – just after Christmas: he had recently enjoyed seeing Edith Sitwell and he and Deirdre had just met a young Jesuit named Peter Levi whom they had both liked. There was the possibility of a trip to Mexico in 1964 for the newspaper, although 'I rather dread going – one has to examine all one's actions for latent death-wish, don't you find?'[21] As for the hostile reviews of his book, he put them down to envy of the *Sunday Times*, an explanation he also shared with Eddy Sackville-West. He felt now that he would have to 'fight' for the rest of his life, 'just when one was hoping for a respite to enjoy it'.[22] There was enjoyment at least in January 1964 when he and Deirdre stayed at Mouton as guests of Philippe and Pauline de Rothschild. Cecil Beaton was also of the party and found his fellow-guests benign and happy:

Cyril has a reputation for being a glutton. But this is not fair ... He is too much of an artist to gorge himself and there is something very appealing and touching about his restraint ... Completely unsnobbish, he brought out a present for Philippe. From a crumpled brown paper-bag he produced some Cox's Orange Pippins. He shook them against his ear to hear if they rattled. 'Yes, they're ripe. Try this one. There's a very good fruit shop at Victoria Station.'[23]

Back in England, however, he suggested renewed disquiet during an interview with T. G. Rosenthal for a recording to be broadcast on 21 January by the Third Programme. Rosenthal enquired after the remainder of *Shade Those Laurels* – published in West Germany in April as *Besuch Beim Olympier* – only to learn that its author had become depressed 'by the people who went for me' when the first instalment was published. He portrayed himself as a veteran survivor of calumny and unpopularity: 'I have to switch into a kind of masochistic gear for unpleasant situations then I force myself forward like someone going to the guillotine through a crowd of people pelting them with rotten eggs.' It appeared that one of the reasons for his professional unpopularity lay with the fact that he defied categorization as a writer: '[There is] this feeling common to rather bogus creative people that there are these little insects – beetles – called critics who pursue these marvellous butterflies called creators, but everybody's a bit of both ... I'm getting less of a critic I hope and I would like to be more of an entertainer.'[24] Sympathetic listeners may have felt that he was taking literary sectarianism too seriously but although he was unsettled by the thought that his literary values seemed increasingly to be questioned by younger generations of critics and writers he had other private worries besides, not least the health of his mother. She had become much frailer over the last couple of years but when her watchful neighbours warned him just before Christmas 1963 that she now had serious multiple complaints – high blood pressure, angina, kidney deterioration and a stomach ulcer – it became clear that terminal decline had begun. He would have to travel to see her and soon, since further bulletins revealed that she could no longer eat without discomfort or sleep without morphia. He braced himself for the expense before suddenly realizing the obvious solution: he would pay for the trip by writing about South Africa and casting one appreciative eye on its flora and fauna while watching warily with the other for new political developments. Mexico would have to wait.
Early in February 1964 he flew to Johannesburg in the first leg of a

tour that would take him on to Cape Town and then east along the coast to George, where his mother had lived, in Caledon Street, since the death of Christopher Brooke sixteen years before. He found her better than neighbours' reports had led him to expect and sent a postcard to Jack Lambert giving a calmer report of her condition and saying that he hoped to return to London on 29 February. In the meantime the northern metropolis and all its associations had become a distant dream: 'A slight yellowing in the plane trees reminds me of your English autumn and the days when I used to read and write books.'[25] The sense of remoteness was not merely a consequence of the mental distortions induced by air travel: the policy of racial *apartheid* which South Africa had adopted in 1949 had led to the country's withdrawal not only from the United Nations but also, in 1961, from the British Commonwealth, and neither riots nor the later assassination of Prime Minister Verwoerd, architect of the segregation, would deflect the country from its notorious course. For the time being, however, the new republic seemed both stable and prosperous; and although the tourist soon discovered that everyone was obsessed with politics he also quickly began to feel uneasy about the preconceptions he had imbibed in England: 'The visitor who arrives full of righteous indignation is deafened by the clatter of bulldozers and falling masonry as more and more skyscrapers go up. Everything breathes expansion and prosperity, encouraged by restriction on the export of capital and the urge to be independent of any future boycott.'[26] South Africa's politics were to become a cause like Civil War Spain's, where not even distance from the turmoil could induce equivocation in the onlookers. Yet the middle-aged man who had come to say goodbye to his mother cared less about fashionable convictions than the *salon* Marxist who had sent his despatches from Barcelona almost thirty years before. Now he apprehended ambivalence and seemed almost to appreciate it in others: the political division reminded him of the predicament of the Anglo-Irish minority in Ireland and something in Verwoerd's position suggested the pragmatic appeal of Eamon De Valera – because the British South Africans accepted Verwoerd 'the same way as the Ascendancy made the best of De Valera, partly out of expediency, partly out of patriotism'.

As his stay progressed Connolly became increasingly appreciative of the country's climate, vegetation, wildlife and light, which he found especially enchanting: 'It replaces architecture and produces greens and blues and far horizons so bright and luminous as to seem incredible, that liberate the well-being of remembered summers.'[27] Cape Town had restaurants full of seafood, a wildlife sanctuary on the peninsula at the Cape of Good Hope and eighteenth-century Dutch houses clinging to the approaches of the Table Mountain. In George, by contrast, he found a Surrey in the sun where a large fellowship of English expatriates devoted itself to a leisurely calendar of bowls, bridge, sailing, amateur theatricals and golf tournaments. His mother, who had lived a solitary life for many years, was now too frail to join in such activities and he would also avoid them, investigating instead the Knysa elephants, said to be the largest in the world, and the Kruger Park. Nothing in Europe could rival these prodigies yet there was something reminiscent of Scotland in the terrain which surrounded his mother's adopted town and he soon learned that for all the easy contentment of the life homesickness was widespread, especially in April with the falling of the leaves.

'The Flawed Diamond' appeared in the *Sunday Times* in April and although the report he gave his readers was far from dogmatic or hostile, it led to the banning in South Africa of *The Rock Pool*, which had been in print in the country since 1937. However, if Connolly failed to dwell on the complications of South African life, it was not for want of meeting the embattled. In Cape Town he had stayed with Raymond Hoffenberg, who taught at the Medical School of Cape Town University, and through his host he had met a young man named Jonty Driver, who was President of the National Union of South African Students. He could often take a sympathetic interest in the young and their aspirations and so it was with Driver, a brave and hopeful poet whose precocious political activities had already attracted police attention. He remembered seeing the Englishman padding around the Hoffenbergs' house in pyjamas, with the top button done up and a great pink stomach protruding below, yet soon learned that he was not merely an indifferent passing reporter. Connolly wanted to know about his poetry and promised to try to find a publisher for it when he returned to London. He was as good as his word and showed the work to Alan Ross, who included one of the lyrics in the *London Magazine* later in the year, by which time its young author was languishing in solitary confinement. In September 1964, on his release from prison, Driver came to England to continue his studies at Oxford and his friendship with Connolly prospered. The older man treated his young friend with 'avuncular' affection and continued to maintain an interest in his literary ambitions. After reading some of Driver's short stories he insisted that one of them read like the opening chapter of a larger fiction; and the expanded work was later published as Driver's first novel, *Elegy for a Revolutionary*.[28] Meanwhile, the excursion to South Africa had been made just in time: Connolly's mother died in July in the care of neighbours who assured her son that they would supervise funeral arrangements. He had already said his farewells and Maurice Bowra's words of sympathy on 14 July were no more than just:

> I am afraid that your mother's death must have come as rather a shock, but you hid it wonderfully. You have nothing to blame yourself for. Of course in your youth you neglected to write as often as you should, but you made more than ample amends by visiting her instead of going to Mexico. She must have felt in her last months that all was well between you and her.[29]

CHAPTER THIRTY-ONE

BOWRA'S SYMPATHIES were well judged but soon he and Connolly had other need for mutual comfort. On 12 and 19 July the *Sunday Times* published two excerpts from Evelyn Waugh's forthcoming autobiography *A Little Learning* and although the book was to cover only the opening twenty-one years of its author's life friends and enemies alike could take only limited comfort from its narrow scope: its sonorous verdicts would still no doubt settle old scores and would be certain to take into account the excesses and indiscretions which had characterized Waugh's Oxford generation and which now lay buried beneath numerous reputations of eminence and distinction. In the event the book caused less embarrassment than originally feared, although if White's and Brooks's sighed with relief they did so prematurely, for Waugh had also kept diaries and many of his contemporaries would live to see them published. The autobiography insisted that Connolly and its author had had divergent undergraduate careers, since the former had proved 'too fastidious for the rough company I kept'. The claim was essentially true, if slightly evasive: Connolly's time at Balliol had indeed been quiet and unambitious, an interlude for the consolidation of romantic friendships rather than the forging of glamorous connections, but Harold Acton read the book with a feeling that the autobiographer knew more about the future critic and his activities than he pretended: 'Perhaps my passion for Tony [Bushell] was given undue notice in proportion to so many that were not alluded to: Cyril's for Bobby Longden, Robert [Byron]'s, Patrick [Balfour]'s, Brian [Howard]'s and Hugh [Lygon]'s promiscuities.'[1] For Waugh to claim that they had not been friends as undergraduates was one thing, to insist that Connolly and Maurice Bowra 'were both acquaintances who became friends after I attracted some attention as a novelist' was provocative and should be judged as part of a prolonged campaign to humiliate Connolly, who had proved to be a better friend than many of the novelist's fellow-revellers at Oxford. Besides, Waugh was in no position to chastise the socially ambitious; and if a lot of his smart friends only got to know him after he attracted 'some attention as a novelist' it is probably true to say that some of them at least indulged behaviour they would never have accepted in an interloper without talent. Once the imputation was out, however, there was nothing for it but impotent complaint and when Bowra and Connolly met they naturally had plenty to discuss, as the former suggested when he wrote to his friend after *A Little Learning* had appeared: 'It was a great joy to see you . . . and to talk with you about Evelyn's excesses. I find that people who have read his book without knowing him find it dull and are not very interested in his account of his contemporaries.'[2]

The Connollys and the Hobsons took a holiday together at Biarritz in August but returned to the melancholy news that after many months of frailty and many years of hard smoking and martinis Ian Fleming had suffered a mortal heart attack. Connolly had reviewed *You Only Live Twice* enthusiastically in March and had been a regular companion of the ageing charmer in the last months of his life, helping to relieve his wife of the burdens of care and causing her ambivalent regard to swing once more in Connolly's favour. In the early weeks of widowhood she wrote to him more tenderly than ever before: 'You did much for him in these last months; he particularly enjoyed your company and lunching at Brighton: I am everlastingly grateful to you and perhaps we could talk of it.'[3] Only a year previously Louis MacNeice had also died prematurely, earning an appraisal from Connolly in the *Sunday Times*, but it was still a little early for the years of regular obituary and memorial service: there was still time to make plans for the future. Efforts to publish the correspondence with Noël Blakiston received a setback at the end of the summer when William Plomer rejected the scheme on behalf of Jonathan Cape, anxious that the letters contained too many projected itineraries and too much Greek and Latin, and that its Oxonian world was impenetrable and oppressive. Nevertheless Connolly did not want for suggestions and invitations: *Esquire* magazine hoped to recruit him; there was talk of his contributing to a memorial volume dedicated to Aldous Huxley; Hamish Hamilton wanted to persuade him to write the text for a book about James Joyce's Paris; a contract was signed with Meredith and Company for a book to be submitted in December 1965, 'Writers and Writing Around the World'; and he began to consider the idea of a summary of those books from

England, France and America which had shaped the Modern Movement in literature.

In January 1965 T. S. Eliot, one of that movement's greatest arbiters, died, and when Connolly wrote a tribute for the *Sunday Times* a few days later he cast his mind back to his own time at Oxford, when he and his contemporaries had struggled to comprehend the American's early lyrics: 'We were like new-born goslings for ever imprinted with the image of an alien and indifferent foster-parent, infatuated with his erudition, his sophistication, yet sapped and ruined by the contagion of his despair.'[4] The two men had never known each other well but only five months prior to his death Eliot had indicated in a letter to the critic that he also recognized a debt to Connolly:

Personally I liked each one [of the *Four Quartets*] better than its predecessor, and Little Gidding best of all. I may be very conceited, but Little Gidding strikes me as one of the best patriotic poems in the language . . . This gives me the opportunity to express my appreciation and gratitude for your appreciation of my work. I was particularly touched by the way in which you referred, in reviewing my Collected Poems, to my last dedicatory poem to my wife. You were the first sympathetic reader and critic to call attention to the unusual fact that I had at last written a poem of love and of happiness! It would seem that some readers were shocked that I should be happy![5]

On 12 January Connolly appraised the poet's achievement once again in the BBC radio programme *Monitor* and on 16 January he was the guest of the Home Service's *In Town Today*. On 12 May, descending gingerly from the Ivory Tower, he made a first recording of *Take It or Leave It*, a literary quiz programme produced for BBC2 by the youthful Melvyn Bragg, and insisted on watching his performance at dinner at Ann Fleming's when the programme was broadcast five days later. Each appearance on the programme earned forty guineas and Connolly did not hesitate to participate again on 19 May, 23 and 30 June and 8 August, simultaneously befriending the young producer and giving him advice and encouragement about his first novels. Meanwhile he and Deirdre spent a weekend with Cecil Beaton at Reddish, the photographer's house in Wiltshire, and during the course of their stay discussion no doubt veered towards the subject of the forthcoming television documentary about a third St Cyprianite, George Orwell, in which Connolly was due to appear. His contribution to *Orwell and His*

Times was filmed near Eastbourne and Eton at the beginning of July but although he was glad of the twenty-guinea fee and the prestige of appearance, he was irritated by Malcolm Muggeridge's interviewing technique. Even as that programme was being assembled plans were afoot within the BBC for another tribute to Orwell, this time to be transmitted in the World Service's series *The Masters*.

Against this prosperous engagement with the microphone life continued at Bushey Lodge in relative tranquillity. As early as 1962, sending Barbara a bulletin of his recent activities and ambitions, Connolly had intimated a degree of turbulence in his marital relations which can hardly have surprised his second wife: 'At the moment D[eirdre] has whisked [Cressida] off to Lewes after announcing that our marriage is finished as I obviously prefer you.' Deirdre no doubt had her reasons: Connolly was never the easiest of husbands; he had not become less temperamental with age nor had his almost constitutional emotional nostalgia abated. Indeed the same letter suggested that it remained a paramount force: 'I really have only loved you and Jean – everybody else seems to have been part of an hallucination.'[6] In 1964, when Ann Fleming had invited the Connollys to stay shortly after her husband's death, she took Deirdre's refusal to attend as being symptomatic of domestic strain and reported Connolly's explanation of his wife's behaviour to the ever-attentive Waugh: 'Apparently their marriage had reached a sexual standstill, and she felt years of washing and cooking had made her too dull and plain for social life.'[7] Janetta remembered witnessing terrible scenes when she stayed at Bushey in the early and middle Sixties and her impression was endorsed by Susan Campbell, although the latter also sensed happiness and a sort of understanding behind the arguments and was convinced that Connolly still enjoyed the domestic stability which life with Barbara had denied him.

As Susan and Deirdre were contemporaries and both busy with young children their joint interests were inevitably domestic and the former's impressions of Cyril Connolly were set against a background of family life rather than literary and intellectual activity. She knew that he endeavoured to compliment Deirdre's cooking by taking great pains with the silver, the linen and the wine and that guests regularly took him delicacies like *foie gras* and caviare. Tributes of a more valuable, less perishable nature often ended up in pawn, sacrificed to their recipient's chronic insolvency, but in affectionate disregard of this sorry likelihood the Campbells decided one weekend to present their host with a Japanese sword guard, a trophy which they never saw again, for all their discreet glances around the house. Susan was surprised one day to hear Deirdre's claim, 'Cyril's planted all those flowers', and amused by the reply to her mildly incredulous question, 'Surely he didn't dig the holes too?' 'Oh no, Mr Rush dug the holes.' Mr Rush was the gardener and often, wielding a large and rusting key, he would say to the children: 'I'm going to use this key to unlock your heart.' Cressida was called 'Doods', the bulldog, 'Bully', and Connolly himself, 'Youey', at least by Deirdre, who, when she was not treating him semi-maternally, saw him as a sort of surrogate father whose approval was to be courted. In the early stages of the marriage she went to some lengths with this ambition and diligently read Plutarch but her efforts were poorly rewarded when he named her 'Birdbrain' which, in this hour of Bardot's fame, was usually contracted to 'BB'. Deirdre, to her credit, seemed not to mind.[8]

In November, following a complementary article in the *Sunday Times*, *100 Key Books of the Modern Movement from England, France and America 1880–1950* was published by André Deutsch and dedicated to Maurice Bowra. As its title suggested, the book marked the critic's attempt to identify the formative works of the greatest literary revolution since Romanticism, a revolution that had begun before his birth and continued with diminishing reverberations for the whole of his life. He chose not to present a continuous narrative but to supply one or two books for each year of his span and provide a glossary which was both pungent and characteristic: 'Try as we would to be objective, any such list (exhibition of compulsive pedantry or debt of gratitude?) is personal as a cardiogram.' He had avoided German or Russian works, since ignorance of both languages would have made him restlessly dependent on translations; and if his summary was cheerfully incomplete it was also defiantly indifferent to popular culture: 'I have assumed that we can all read French in the original.'[9] As usual his critical notes were gossipy and entertaining and as usual they treated writers as a race apart, since although his introduction referred to Debussy and to the major artistic schools which followed Impressionism, he made no attempt to trace cross-pollination between the various creative disciplines. The critical reception was tepid but if reviewers were anxious about the personal and idiosyncratic quality of Connolly's selection they were at least grudgingly impressed by the distinction of his reading. Bowra himself was delighted: 'I . . . find the book most interesting as a kind of autobiography. It gives the books which you absorbed, and I am amazed at the range.'[10]

The catalogue formed part of the broadcast he gave on 18 December for the Home Service's *The World of Books*, for which he was paid a modest twelve guineas. On 22 January 1966, however, he returned to the BBC to be interviewed by Jonathan Miller for BBC2's *Doubts and Certainties* and came away fifty guineas richer. Television paid better; but perhaps the fee also entitled interviewer and audience to greater intimacy. He declared that he was 'steeped' in the work of Freud, and having applied the psychoanalyst's theories to his own condition and to the incompatibility of his parents, sensed that he 'was apt to be nasty to men because they were like my father; nasty to women, having trapped them into loving me, because they were like my mother'.[11]

Confessions of another sort followed on 28 February when Connolly appeared on *Desert Island Discs*, but it took Roy Plomley little interrogation to establish that his interviewee, who admitted to clumsy hands and a fear of loneliness, would make a reluctant Robinson Crusoe. He considered his chosen music – a Hungarian gypsy song; a Spanish song performed by Nina de los Peines; the opening of Scarlatti's Sonata in C major; an excerpt from the third act of Debussy's *Pelleas and Mélisande*; a scene from the second act of *The Marriage of Figaro*; the opening of the second movement of Beethoven's Quartet number 15 in A minor; a song from Stravinsky's *The Rake's Progress*; and De Monte's *Agnus Dei* – to be representative of a romantic taste and one which sought satisfaction in harmonies as remote as possible from both the written word and the realities of everyday life. He assured Plomley that island solitude would bring him 'fearful remorse over the past and how I'd treated people'. For compensation and distraction he nominated White's (without its members) and *A La Recherche du Temps Perdu*.[12]

In March the *Sunday Times* sent him on an assignment to Jamaica, a British possession when he had taught there forty years before but now independent since 1962. In his account, which appeared in the newspaper at the end of the month, he revealed that although he had flown everywhere for the last thirty years he was still sufficiently superstitious to clutch an improving book during take-off. His precaution seemed to have betrayed him when on arrival he discovered that his luggage had been lost – though only temporarily – in transit. Kingston seemed to lack good hotels but happily, able to stay with Charles D'Costa in a house which reminded him of Sunningdale, he had no need of a White's magically spirited from St James's. His former pupil had retained fond memories of his tutor and kept in distant touch through mutual acquaintances like Evelyn Waugh and Noël Coward, another Jamaican resident, and promptly gave a celebratory lunch which included his son David: 'I remember a rather weary, bored, but pleasant visitor who perked up when we discussed books. He was very pleased when I confessed to having committed a college thesis on Waugh six years earlier. "He'll have *hated* that," he said, with great satisfaction.'[13]

Coward was absent from Jamaica, so there was no possibility of regaling readers with accounts of life at Blue Harbour, the house the entertainer had built in 1948. Ian Fleming had been the real pioneer, however: he had introduced Coward to the island and it was his ghost, and the strange unreality of his reputation, which continued now to haunt the critic: 'It is strange to watch someone one has known for thirty years changing before one's eyes into a myth. What an ironical destiny for a man who was so much more remarkable than his books.'[14]

That myth assumed greater depth later in the year with the publication of a first biography, John Pearson's *The Life of Ian Fleming*, but although he praised the account in the *Sunday Times* Connolly was struck once again by the mysteries of friendship, by the fact that someone he had known for over thirty years had revealed no more of himself than the iceberg. Nevertheless, if it created as many mysteries as it solved, Pearson's book did bring home to him the numerous parallels between the careers of Fleming and Ernest Hemingway: both had intermittently dramatic war careers; both loved sports; both had fractious relations with women and chafed against maternal dominance; both died prematurely; and both yearned romantically for the life of action while at the same time being too sensitive and imaginative to accept its terse and unequivocal canons. So great were the similarities, indeed, that 'I began to imagine a composite character, Ernest Flemingway, author of a macabre thriller, "The Scum Also Rises".'[15]

A month after Connolly's Jamaican expedition Jonty Driver invited himself to stay at Bushey. The critic treated the young émigré with great affection and, with Deirdre, more or less encouraged him to think of Bushey as a regular weekend retreat; Driver encountered preoccupied indifference only once when he telephoned – when Connolly was engrossed in the BBC's *Forsyte Saga* and could not be disturbed. All was well, however, for the Easter weekend and Driver set out for Sussex in pleasurable anticipation of the familiar and easy recreations in store. As usual he would be told to leave his shoes to be polished by the gardener and as usual the food would be delicious. As usual nothing whatever would happen before lunch and post-prandial diversion was unlikely to entail anything more strenuous than a session with the newspapers (unless he was once again offered the key to the case of erotica). As usual – his own solution to the sedentary pattern – he would go for long solitary walks, a trifle shocked by Connolly's assertion that he never took any exercise beyond travelling to London for a massage. Routine was suddenly broken, however, with a telephone call late on Easter Day, 10 April: Evelyn Waugh had died that morning and newspapers needed tributes and obituaries. Although at last he could have spoken with impunity, Connolly declined the request and Driver was intrigued to notice how his mood suddenly declined to frigid prickliness, as though in anticipation of a further assault.

His suspicions proved to be well-founded. In the meantime he left wife and daughter behind and travelled in October to Tunis and Tripoli, returning via Madrid and Paris. In his absence the kitchen at Bushey was to be redecorated and Deirdre sent details of the upheavals to Susan: 'We have to move out, so it's 4 days at the GRAND hotel, & 2 weekends away, & Bully dog to the kennels.' The work was necessary but costly and she apologized: 'No Christmas presents from me this year, as totally numbed by poverty!'[16] Connolly had continued to file his reviews while away and returned on 22 October to the news that the Third Programme hoped to recruit him to a panel discussion about the cult of the spy in literature which was provisionally to be called 'The Bond Dishonoured', and to the imminent appearance of Maurice Bowra's memoirs. The don's account flirted with blandness, as Connolly later suggested when he declared that it was 'too well-mannered though if we know how to look for it, the truth is there'.[17] He had reviewed many books of Bowra's before but for some reason decided not to assess *Memories* and the task fell instead to Peter Levi, whom the Connollys had met a few years previously and who became a regular reviewer for the *Sunday Times* in the late Sixties. He liked *Memories* and admired Bowra but Connolly impressed him much more, not least because, as he later revealed, 'I had left school at seventeen to become a Jesuit and a lot of the fizz in my temperament had therefore been bottled up for eight years. I lavished on Cyril as a writer those affections and loyalties that no doubt ought to have been devoted to duller authors and weightier matters.'[18] In 1964 he had become a priest and in 1965, besides beginning his career as a tutor and lecturer in classics at Campion Hall, Oxford, he joined the British School of Archaeology at Athens. He translated Yevtushenko and later Pausanias, wrote poetry of his own and kept a close and loyal watch over Connolly's literary endeavours. In 1963, on the eve of priesthood, he had assured the critic that his reviews were 'one of the things that reconcile me to Sundays'.[19] Despite his accomplishments he maintained a personal sense of bashfulness, at one stage admitting to the older man: 'I can never get my mouth round what I want to say, and speak wildly in the hope it may be right ... I thought, I think, and always do think I am fundamentally absurd.'[20] Connolly wavered. In December 1966, reviewing Levi's fourth volume of poems, *Fresh Water, Sea Water*, he commended his appreciation of nature, his love of the Mediterranean, his virtues of heart and intellect. All seemed set for true poetic strength and now only maturity of touch was lacking: 'I look on his poems like an old rake watching a finishing school trip by his window. They are not quite ready for me.'[21]

In 1958, when forensic evidence established that he was unfit to stand trial for his treasonable wartime broadcasts from Italy, Ezra Pound was released from the Washington hospital for the insane where he had been interned for thirteen years. During his incarceration his *Pisan Cantos* had been acclaimed and when he returned to Italy in freedom Connolly at once attempted to secure an interview for *Encounter*, only to be told that the poet was too frail to receive his admirers. The overture had been noted, however, and when in 1966 Faber and Faber planned a new anthology of his poetry Olga Rudge, the ageing poet's companion, indicated that Pound would only co-operate with such a scheme on one condition: 'There is *one person* Ezra Pound would trust to select shorter poems and translations and that is Cyril Connolly. Would he?'[22] Naturally he would give the idea serious consideration but whatever happened, the poet was now bound to meet him and later in the year Connolly visited him at his last home outside Rapallo. The encounter was happy but although his host mimicked James Joyce on the possibilities of a Nobel Prize for *Ulysses*, he otherwise contrived to suggest approval and benevolence without resorting to many words:

In the twelve hours I spent with him I do not suppose he uttered more
than twelve words ... When we met he held my hand for a long time
and fixed me with this penetrating gaze while I felt layers of ugliness
and insincerity peeling off me like an onion revealing ever deeper layers
of insincerity and ugliness within. In another moment I felt sure the
ultimate 'nada' would be reached and the onion dissolve on the floor
... Mr Pound spoke and said what sounded like 'There's the artist.' I
looked behind to see whom he meant but we were still alone.[23]

Despite this salute, the projected anthology was never realized but at
least Connolly had met an elusive idol and after the poet's death and
shortly before his own he would be approached to join W. H. Auden
and Stephen Spender for an evening in Pound's honour at the Mer-
maid Theatre. Meanwhile in April 1967 the Humanities Research
Center at the University of Texas announced plans to hold an exhibition based on Connolly's *100 Key Books*. Not least because of its oil
revenues the Center had been able to amass an unrivalled collection of
English and French twentieth-century first editions and authors'
papers (indeed negotiations would soon begin to acquire the manuscripts and entire library – books, furniture, bookcases – of Evelyn
Waugh) and the happy discovery that the majority of the authors
included in Connolly's anthology were represented in its archives at
once suggested the scheme of a celebratory display. Waugh himself
was undergoing posthumous appraisal and on 8 June the critic joined
Christopher Sykes, Raymond Mortimer and Goronwy Rees to discuss
'Evelyn Waugh – The Writer' for the Third Programme. Later in the
summer *The Listener* published a larger collection of 'Reminiscences
of Evelyn Waugh, by his friends', and Connolly's memories appeared
alongside those of John Sutro, Christopher Hollis, Harold Acton,
Derek Verschoyle, John Betjeman, Nancy Mitford, Randolph
Churchill, Diana Mosley and Diana Cooper. He recorded a further
five lucrative appearances on 'Take It or Leave It', now produced by
Julian Jebb, and feeling unusually prosperous went to see Barbara at
her new home at Grimaud in the south of France. The money was
useful: she was alone and so was he (Deirdre, claiming her predecessor
to be a witch, would neither see Baby nor allow Cressida to do so in
case she was given the evil eye), so he decided to stay in a hotel in
order to avoid complications. In August he went to Sardinia with
Maurice Bowra to prepare an article for the *Sunday Times* but whatever the attractions of the island for his readers Connolly found other

distractions, as his hostess for the occasion, Ann Fleming, related to the Duchess of Devonshire:

> Cyril made fearfully restless by vicinity of Snowdons, saying not to meet them was like being in Garden of Eden without seeing God! Local tycoon then called and invited me to dine with 'Margaret and Tony'. Cyril distraught! I corner tycoon and explain situation who invites all three of us. Dinner wholly successful ... Social scene grows tense on Highness's departure, she tells tycoon she has no plans for the morrow, he is filled with despair, for the poor brute is lunching with me. I ask all to lunch, Cyril beams. Next morning Cyril rises at 11.30 and asks what I have ordered special for lunch ... and says did I notice what the Princess drank last night, I say no, he says it was white wine and martinis and may he go to the hotel for the right stuff. I say yes, and have to pay enormous bill.

A later scene she treasured was of 'Princess and Cyril in pool, Cyril looking like blissful hippo!'[24]

Sunday Times business had already taken him abroad again before his article on Sardinia was published in December; but he felt no reluctance about escaping the November mists to research a travel article on Kenya and Uganda. 'An Aesthete in Africa', which was published in January 1968, was little preoccupied with the daily realities of the fledgling republics of Kenyatta and Obote and found more glory in the abiding life of the bush than in the changing vanities of human affairs:

> Driving over the soda mud flats of Lake Nakuru to the rose blur of flamingo from which comes a continuous drowsy croaking, one is happy to be in a Park again. The flamingo are grouped like Monet's water-lilies; in a pastel continuum the pelicans and spoonbills more mobile; the pelican swim in a flotilla and all plunge their bills into the water simultaneously – by what signal? The spoonbills rake from side to side as though scything ... If I have written so much about wild life it is because the animals and the parks are like museums and churches to the traveller in Italy: a day without them is a day wasted, and the further one gets from their innocent world of co-operation and wonder the more ordinary life becomes a dull matter of politics, greed and business like everywhere else.[25]

Yet even amidst these ecstasies he was conscious of an intriguing shadow which darkened the indifferent paradise: the unexplained mur-

der, twenty-six years previously, of the Earl of Erroll, potential leader
of Kenya's entire expatriate community and unchallenged hero of the
notorious 'Happy Valley' hedonists who in the Thirties had made the
White Highlands and the Wanjohi River bywords on both sides of the
Atlantic for almost all the adult vices. In London the scandal of
Erroll's death, unwelcome in 1941, had long since faded to insig-
nificance but Connolly found that Kenya's white settlers were still
seething with explanations, even reminders, of his decease. He knew
and briefly stayed with Jack and Doria Block, who owned Kenya's
best hotels and whose house was situated near to the Muthaiga
Country Club, formerly Happy Valley's lawless sanctum. The Blocks
introduced him to Lazarus Kaplan, at one time solicitor to Sir Jock
Delves Broughton, the chief suspect in the investigations who was
eventually tried and acquitted of Erroll's murder, and to Prince Win-
dishgraetz, another repository of local gossip and folklore. Connolly
left Africa with curiosity intensified and the mystery would continue
to ferment in his mind for months more, surfacing again when he
visited Tanzania for the *Sunday Times* in May 1968 and finally
assuming official investigative shape the following year.

Meanwhile on his way back from Kenya he once again stayed in
Provence with Barbara, now intermittently living with Bernard Frank, a
French writer and close friend of Françoise Sagan. Back at home
Connolly had his own domestic quandaries. Lord Gage had found more
pressing use for Bushey Lodge and there was no alternative accommodation available on his estate: once again the critic would have to move and
once again the financial insecurity which underlay his nomadic condition
would have to be faced. Only the previous year, in an article entitled
'Confessions of a House-hunter', he had confided proprietorial ambitions to his readers: 'All my life I have wanted passionately to own a
house.'[26] Veterans of weekends at Bushey knew well that one of the
favourite recreations entailed going to inspect local houses of varying
degrees of grandeur with a fanciful view to purchase. However, now that
acquisition had become an urgent need the financial implications seemed
all the more daunting. The capital Connolly had been able to remove
from South Africa following his mother's death would at once be locked
away and his income from the newspaper would be inadequate to the
incidental expenses which owning and running a house would entail. He
must apply to the *Sunday Times* for more money and on 19 March
Leonard Russell offered to intercede on his behalf with the editor:

I talked to Denis Hamilton last night . . . I expected him to look gloomy about the budget and the gold rush . . . he said you were of great value to the paper, and that he hoped you would remain our star reviewer for years to come. Naturally I did not fail to emphasize that you had burnt your boats and my final impression was that you would be hearing from him pretty soon.[27]

CHAPTER THIRTY-TWO

WHATEVER HAMILTON'S REPLY, he was in no position to promise substantial increases: the small but perfect country house receded once more into impossibility and moving back to London was out of the question. John Craxton, familiar with the house-hunting excursions from Bushey, suggested that the search for a new house should realistically begin in the southern coastal towns but there was some surprise among friends when Connolly finally announced that he would move to 48 St John's Road, Eastbourne. 'Are you and Deirdre happy about it? I am sure happy is not the right word, was it expediency for Cressida's education? or did you find a homestead that appealed?' wondered Ann Fleming dubiously.[1] Yet in 'Confessions of a House-hunter' he had already admitted to an interest in Victorian domestic architecture: 'There is some part of me that yearns for ... houses of around 1900, with stained glass lilies on the landing, glossy overmantels and coved ceilings, shallow stairs haunted by vanished parlour-maids.' 48 St John's Road was a solid yellow-brick villa with a modest conservatory and flint-walled gardens to front and rear which had been built around 1900 directly above the Eastbourne seafront and which exactly fitted Connolly's description. It was a dignified and practical house with a contemporary value of about £4500; its upper windows searched for France along the grey horizon or else looked out towards the Downs, and only its aura of prosperity and unblinking respectability seemed incongruous to the friends and to the reputation of a man who had once savaged the Edwardian novelists. Perhaps the move to Eastbourne was a step in the direction of retirement but not everybody shared Ann Fleming's bewilderment. Indeed John Betjeman thought the scheme admirable:

If one wants quiet and fresh air and country near, your house in East-bourne with its sloping garden down to trees at the back, cliffs and a chapel of ease on the other side of the road, those wide, comfortable, well-built late Victorian rooms housing your books, are much better than pigging it in the country down rutty, muddy lanes and miles from a letter-box, a shop and schools for the children. Eastbourne is the right place for a man of letters.[2]

In Eastbourne Connolly had a proper library where he could store the reference books essential for his critical writings as well as the treasured components of his book collection and where he could retreat to contemplate future acquisitions. In fact by the time the library was installed it had passed its apogee: only the year before moving he had made several important investments – two books and a letter from the sale of a Cocteau collection, a presentation copy of the first edition of *Swann*, *Les Plaisirs et Les Jours*, again by Proust, signed editions of Elizabeth Bowen's *The Last September* and Hart Crane's *White Buildings*, not to mention rare volumes of Eliot, Valéry, Pound and Marianne Moore – but once he had settled at Eastbourne, chronic insolvency forced him to painful parting with several books, including very rare editions of *Nine Experiments*, Stephen Spender's first volume of poems, and *Pre-Raphaelite Brotherhood*, Evelyn Waugh's privately issued first book.

In 1968 John Whitley joined the *Sunday Times* as a factotum in the literary and arts department and it was one of his weekly responsibilities to sub-edit Connolly's copy, which usually arrived at tea-time on Tuesday, having made its journey by Red Star and courier from Waterloo – an exceptional arrangement which reflected the esteem in which its author was held. The appraisal would be written on different notepaper each week: the great London hotels, White's, the Paris Ritz and other prestigious resorts had all contributed unwittingly to Connolly's stationery reserves and it was quickly understood that any cooling in relations between author and editorial department would lead to the use of paper of more humble origin. The copy was invariably in manuscript – Connolly either could not or would not type – with arbitrary punctuation and blanks awaiting the elusive *mot juste*; after a secretary had deciphered and typed the article it went to Whitley for his refinements. Connolly was supposed to write about 1200 words, but despite an instinctive concision he regularly exceeded his limit; nevertheless by Wednesday morning the article would be set in galleys and at about four o'clock the office would await the critic's appearance. James

Fox, Connolly's young friend from Sussex, was now a feature writer on the newspaper's colour magazine, which had been established in 1962, and occasionally he glimpsed the star reviewer's arrival: 'His unathletic frame was usually clothed in the smartest Savile Row suit of charcoal grey and he would be wearing a black homburg on his head. The dandy of the early 1920s had turned into some merchant banker of the 1960s, although the disguise was not perfect.'³

His arrival in the office was an event and Connolly played his role with knowing art. He would exercise his privilege of rewriting his article on the galleys, but his revisions were often so extensive as to constitute a second creative process. Whitley would look on, keenly aware of hierarchies and aware also that the politest requests for cuts were dangerous; all attempts to make Connolly count his words proved hopeless. It was scarcely surprising that the new recruit at Gray's Inn Road initially found the famous reviewer intimidating but later they became good business friends and Connolly often took his sub-editor for lunch at White's or dinner at Boulestin (with Barbara, whom Whitley found 'terrifying', an occasional presence). Connolly struck the younger man as being 'exceptionally difficult to embarrass', his principal interest was gossip and beyond curiosity about books and films he never betrayed the slightest interest in any of the other arts. Connolly's appearance at the newspaper usually coincided with Raymond Mortimer's and Whitley was intrigued to notice that although the two critics would treat each other with the greatest affection they nevertheless seemed slightly wary of each other, as though anxiously covetous of the same book for next week's column, and would often fence or compete for the last word or 'pace round each other like stags'.⁴

In April Connolly was interviewed for the BBC by Richard Kershaw and paid the generous sum of 100 guineas. He toyed with the idea of reworking and expanding the 'Alpdodger' journal which he had kept many years previously and promised to help Marie-Jaqueline Lancaster, a journalist engaged in writing a biography of Brian Howard, who had died in 1958. The book was to be more an anthology of reminiscence than a conventional biographical narrative and its compiler originally hoped that Connolly would write an introduction to the book and review it when it appeared. He declined to do either, however, insisting that he had never forgiven Howard for opening his letter to Jean during the war; and while he was happy to contribute a memoir – 'Brummell at Calais' – about the holiday he and Jean had taken with

Howard in Greece and Portugal he had sharp reservations about the book's projected title, *Portrait of a Failure*: 'Failure? But Brian wasn't a failure, he didn't compromise, he did what he wanted to do. I'm the failure.'[5] Some thought such disclaimers a sham and were hotly contemptuous of nice degrees of failure, whether of will, conviction or action, and Jerome Zerbe was certainly not the first to court bitter disappointment by assuming that contractual obligation could outweigh Connolly's vulnerability to boredom or his apprehensions of futility or failure. The photographer wrote to the critic on 6 December, having heard that the long-planned sequel to *Les Pavillons* was now annulled, despite his own labours, because the publishers had cancelled contracts on learning that Connolly had done no work at all:

> My lawyer tells me that my only redress will be to sue you for $25,000 for breach of contract. I can't tell you how painful this is to me. After all, I did travel to 13 countries to get the material on the houses I'd chosen ... Of course you will have to return the $1500 advance, they have allowed me out of that, knowing my large expenses. Why, oh why, didn't you do your share?[6]

No documentation survives to tell Connolly's side of the story but it is a safe assumption that the solution to Zerbe's innocent question, a solution as maddening as it was unanswerable, was that he had simply lost interest.

Many of Connolly's admirers were by now men of influence and power and 1969 dawned with a touching confession from Lord Boothby: 'I have tried to make you a knight, along with Charlie Chaplin and Noël Coward. No go!'[7] Perhaps, like Desmond MacCarthy and Edmund Gosse before him, he would indeed be elevated; in the meantime a final obsession awaited satisfaction – the mysterious death of the Earl of Erroll. In May Connolly discussed the matter with James Fox, who had worked on the Nairobi *Daily Nation* shortly after Kenyan independence. He needed no introduction to that country's most lurid scandal and assured the critic that Francis Wyndham, a senior editor at the *Sunday Times* magazine, was eager for any offerings from his pen. Rumours of the preoccupation simultaneously reached Godfrey Smith, who had longed to commission additional journalism from Connolly since assuming the editorship of the magazine in 1965 (and had come close to persuading him to write an account of V. S. Naipaul in 1967).

He at once saw exciting possibilities in Connolly's new ambition and with ample funds at his disposal decided to commission an article and to appoint Fox as his assistant sleuth. Research would begin in June and soon overshadowed the other events of 1969 – trips to Paris and to Venice, where Ezra Pound gave him an eighteenth-century *Virgil* for his sixty-sixth birthday; an appearance on a television programme devoted to Ian Fleming; final and undramatic reconciliation with George Weidenfeld: after fourteen years they were friends again yet did not sit down to reminisce, 'like two old generals discussing a campaign'.[8]

The mystery of Erroll's death had many of the aspects of exemplary detective fiction and it was no coincidence that Somerset Maugham had at one stage considered adapting it for his own literary ends. Self-indulgence characterized the heyday of Happy Valley, and English visitors who escaped the apprehensive London of the late Thirties for the drinking, hunting, horse-racing, drug-taking, gambling, adultery and licensed hedonism of the White Highlands were amazed at the pleasures they saw. However, although the combination of decaying aristocratic fortunes and concerted depravity is absorbing, it is still insufficient to propel any thriller and it took the arrival in November 1940 of two catalysts to destruction to lend Happy Valley its lasting notoriety. Sir Jock Delves Broughton was fifty-seven when he travelled to Africa with a reputation as an irascible, cold, remote and charmless individual whose relations with other men were generally uncomfortable yet whose close friendships with women tended to be strangely asexual. Diana Caldwell, though the same age as Broughton's children, was already a divorcee when the unloved baronet fell for her but it was for her appearance and manner rather than her brief and ill-advised marriage that she was known to the gossips of nightclubs and hunting weekends. Women mostly disliked her and struggled to overlook her cold and stylish face, never smiling but always caught at the right occasion, as it stared from the pages of the *Tatler* and the *Sketch*; men by contrast thought her glamorous and adventurous and applauded her verve on horseback and her style as an aviatrix. Whatever her reasons for marrying Delves Broughton in November 1940 romance was not high among them: shortly before the marriage he had made a contract in which he promised not to obstruct matters if she fell in love with another man but to allow her a divorce and to provide her with an income of £5000 per annum for seven years after the severance. Nobody in the dissolute White Highlands was greatly surprised when

Diana began an affair with Josslyn Hay, Earl of Erroll and leader of the expatriate Kenyan community, whose prominence was as much understood as vested in any proconsular rank. It was true that he had once been a member of the British Union of Fascists and that he had recently been appointed military secretary in Kenya, but his ruling instincts were atavistic and a complement to the glamour of his legend. There was a confident swagger in his manner which chronic insolvency had done nothing to inhibit: after all, he was still the twenty-second incumbent of the earldom, the Hereditary High Constable of Scotland and after royalty the first subject of that kingdom. He had maltreated his two wives and had cuckolded numerous men but because he was handsome and charming and popular with both sexes, the life of the party to Broughton's lonely misfit, Nairobi seemed not to mind. Suddenly, however, his luck ran out and on 24 January 1941, less than three months after the Broughtons' arrival in Kenya, he was found on the floor of his Buick with a bullet in the head.

As in any good murder story suspects proliferated, but doubt fell most heavily on Broughton, whose trial caused a sensation. His counsel, a brilliant but theatrical barrister named Morris, fully justified his exorbitant fee of £5000, and Diana wore a different outfit for every day of the trial, making her first appearance in widow's black and diamonds. By the time that Fox and Connolly began their researches all the protagonists bar one were dead: Broughton had committed suicide in a Liverpool hotel in 1942; Gwladys Delamere, Mayor of Nairobi and another suspect because of her infatuation with Erroll, died in 1943; June Carberry, Diana's closest friend, was dying in Johannesburg of drink and drugs. Diana alone was still alive and had emerged, following marriage to Gilbert Colvile and Tom Delamere, both prominent Kenyan landowners, as one of the richest and most prestigious figures in her adopted country. By chance Connolly encountered her at dinner at Lady Hoare's in South Kensington in July 1969: fellow-guests included her husband Tom Delamere and the diplomat Walter Bell and his wife Tanya. Bell had served with Donald Maclean in the British embassy in Washington; inevitably, however, Connolly had eyes only for Diana Delamere. An interview was out of the question since it was known that she would in no circumstances discuss the past and he could only listen, intrigued to learn that she had bought a painting by Michonze, and note simultaneously her diamond brooch and opulent five-strand pearl necklace. Delamere called her 'Buzzy' and they were clearly on good terms, although it transpired that he affectionately faulted her lack of ear lobes: when she noticed that Connolly had none either she pointed out the fact triumphantly to Delamere. They were both friendly, dropping their vigilant fellow-guest at Victoria Station after dinner; and as he studied the immaculate survivor beside him Connolly well understood the strength of her appeal. There was something about her which suggested Wallis Simpson; and like the Duchess, Diana Delamere also reconciled faint vulgarity with worldliness. She was 'the kind of woman one associates with Cannes, Scotland, Ascot, St Moritz as they used to be but not with giving house parties or any particular purpose except pleasure – not at all bohemian'.[9] She for one would never have regretted that *Horizon* was unobtainable in the Kenya of the Forties but it was that very sense of distance and indifference which made her as fascinating to Connolly as it had to other men, and five months after the dinner, when he wrote his share of the article, her vanished loveliness had blossomed in his imagination.

For now the two detectives were obliged to content themselves with meeting the numerous secondary players in the drama, many of whom had settled, after Kenyan independence, in the retirement colonies of the Sussex coast. During the course of the fifty or more interviews which Connolly and Fox conducted, the result of obscure leads and improbable alibis, the latter was impressed by his partner's diligence, his 'startling powers of recall', his relentlessness as a 'close interrogator', the very professionalism with which he conducted lunch-time interviews: 'The eating never affected Connolly's attention, nor could it affect mine: he forbade the use of tape recorders or even note books at every one of our interviews, relying on total recall and the writing up of our notes together as soon after the event as we could manage it.'[10]

'Christmas at Karen' appeared on 21 December and extended to 6000 words, of which just 4000 came from Connolly's pen, although as Fox revealed, 'they were distilled from a monumental store of notes and documents ... He wrote towards the deadline at great speed, in longhand, with hardly a correction on his one and only draft.'[11] Fox noted that his partner approached the mystery 'like a novelist, believing in a solution through the study of character' and that there was 'a hint of passion and even a voyeuristic streak in his quest'. Connolly may have been excited by the blonde aloofness of Diana, but there was a particular understanding in his portrayal of men like the ageing and disappointed baronet: 'They find themselves in a prison of the *déjà vu*, surrounded by good advice and grey hair; within the spirit is as youthful as ever, protesting "Can this be all?"[12] Some imagine that a younger woman is the cure for such distemper but there was no mistaking the eloquence of Connolly's denials:

> A great love, if extramarital, eats away at family, friends, position, and if it be for someone thirty years younger there are moments of loneliness almost more agonizing than those which it is designed to cure. Couples with a big difference in age cannot share all the same pleasures or even the same jokes; the younger carry a balloon of hope before them, the older trail a heavy kitbag of unpleasant memories.[13]

The detectives' researches had revealed much new evidence and Fox noted that 'our article was well received and judged a success, as much I suspect for its evocation of time and place as its exposition'. Nevertheless there were several powerful voices of complaint. Erroll's brother, Lord Kilmarnock, insisted that the article was in poor taste and that Connolly's assertions of Erroll's schoolboy homosexuality constituted 'a most damaging piece of imaginative reporting calculated to cast an aspersion on [his] character as a schoolboy'.[14] Furthermore he expressed particular annoyance at the inclusion of a photograph taken close to the corpse's bullet-violated brow. Sir Iain Moncreiffe of that Ilk, who had married Erroll's only child, Diana, wrote to the *Sunday Times* to complain that the article was nothing more than 'servants' hall gossip' and that it misleadingly overlooked Erroll's military career. He and his wife also wrote separately to complain to the newspaper's deputy editor, Frank Giles, whose wife was Diana's cousin. There was even talk of libel proceedings, a possibility which upset Connolly enormously, and when he and Godfrey Smith discussed the matter in conference the critic's refrain was plaintive and apologetic: 'I can't tell you how sorry I am about all this.'[15] For his part Smith was sanguine: he knew the *Sunday Times* to be a wealthy institution and was more impressed by the pleading remorse of a man many years his senior. It seemed familiar; and he remembered the passage in *Enemies of Promise* where Connolly had admitted to a chronic fear, instilled in his days as a fag, of the summons from the throne of arbitration. There was no action, but both Lord Kilmarnock and Gwladys Delamere's daughter complained to the Press Council and early in 1970 Connolly was called to defend his position. However, the Council was sympathetic to the argument advanced by the *Sunday Times*, that it was unacceptable to suggest that any infamous crime could only be investigated with the permission of the relations of those involved, and found the article 'responsibly written'. Meanwhile, Connolly's conscience was clear. As he had written to Lord Kilmarnock: 'Surely the press is entitled to disregard the general wish of all families to keep their skeletons in their cupboards.'[16]

CHAPTER THIRTY-THREE

ON 14 APRIL 1970 Deirdre gave birth to a son: her husband had at last perpetuated the fame of his forefathers, and although the baby soon became known as 'Gugg' he was christened Matthew Vernon Connolly. Deirdre wrote to Susan Campbell a few days after her confinement: 'Matthew has all the attributes of the Perfect and Beautiful baby ie – wizened and wrinkled face, puffy shut eyes, long purple fingers and toes, scarlet stick-like legs!! We are so fond of him already. Cyril went Ashen with delayed shock for two days, and hasn't slept a wink ever since. He is so thrilled it's a son.'[1] Such a rare physical phenomenon could not last and within the next four years the infant had developed into the pretty white-blond child who gazes solemnly from the last photographs taken of his old father, as though precociously oppressed by life's disappointments. Contrary to legend, however, the camera does little but lie and far from suggesting to Stephen Spender that his young son seemed marked by melancholy, Connolly gave the impression that he was a contented and vital little boy: 'He's like a non-stop movie of which one can't bear to lose ten minutes.'[2]

Optimistically his name was at once entered on the waiting list for Eton though Connolly knew there was no hope of his following him there unless he too won a scholarship. Even as he was born his father learned from Coutts that his overdraft stood in excess of £9000, by the standards of the time a substantial sum, more than double the stipend he received from the *Sunday Times* for his book reviewing. Immediate action would have to be taken and he reluctantly agreed to sell Lucian Freud's early portrait of Anne Dunn to the sitter herself. Compensation of a sort came with the news that Percy King, a cousin on his mother's side, had left him two miniatures and some French eighteenth-century porcelain but it would have taken far more to redeem the critic's finances. In May Maurice Bowra belatedly saluted Matthew's arrival but wondered if the news had 'appalling financial reverberations'.[3]

Connolly's reply was gloomy: a nurse had been engaged and even though she cost £3 10s a day he felt obliged to retain her for two months to spare Deirdre as much as possible. Eventually she would have to be replaced by an au pair and he already employed two cleaning women and a gardener. He could only hope that the boy would one day follow the example of his great-grandfather and marry an heiress.

Connolly's initial financial calculations had reckoned without the loyalty and generosity he inspired in his friends and Enid Bagnold immediately offered to pay for a maternity nurse for three months. A yet more remarkable overture arrived from Harry D'Avigdor Goldsmid's wife, Rosie: 'I'm afraid I am ignorant of the costs of schooling these days. I know they are prohibitive but less than to keep a horse in training.'[4] In conjunction with Jennifer Ross she proposed to pay the boy's fees and in the end Matthew did indeed follow his father to Eton. No suspicion of financial constraint was allowed to over-shadow the christening, however, which took place in Eastbourne with a party afterwards at St John's Road. Ran Antrim, the Robin Camp-bells and the Robert Kees, having been for a picnic beforehand, arrived in expectation of an intimate and informal celebration and were aston-ished to find a house and garden full of smart people. (Michael Wishart always remembered Connolly's half-serious boast that every degree of the peerage was represented, along with a baronet and a knight.) Orchids were in bloom in the conservatory and the baby's godmother, Diana Cooper, presented her charge with a silver christening cup, and nobody minded that 'Connolly' was incorrectly spelt in the engraved dedication. Her fellow guardians were John Betjeman and the twenty-five-year-old James Fox, the latter deliberately chosen with a view to providing male supervision for the boy's adolescence, which Connolly suspected he might not live to see himself.

Certainly, aside from his son's birth, Connolly found less and less that could stimulate or amuse. He had complained to Bowra of being 'sunk in torpor all the time'[5] and it seemed to count for little that, accompanied by Deirdre and Peter Levi, he was given an enthusiastic reception when he delivered a talk to the Eton College Literary Society, or that the National Trust was eager to lure him to the Farne Islands to write an account of its management, or that the British Council hoped to persuade him to give a series of lectures on English literature in France. He declared that he read less and concentrated less and the weekly column had become 'a chore'. He still undertook occasional commissions, such as the lyrical introduction he completed to Robin Maugham's novel *The Wrong People*, but such exercises were increasingly gestures of favour rather than enthusiasm and their grace and individuality could not alter the fact that every writer needs a motivating zeal. Broadcasting also continued to claim him, and in June, assisted by the actor Robert Hardy, he recorded excerpts from his favourite books for BBC Television's *An Evening with Cyril Connolly*. Between these engagements, however, it was impossible to overlook the slow erosion of enthusiasm: friends and contemporaries were dying; travel was more tiring and vastly more expensive; he was too poor to buy books; his marriage was no less turbulent; and although he was an adoring father, he was also an old one, like his father's father before him. Yet even autumn has its flowers and there was a consolation or rather distraction to his declining years which he did not vouchsafe to Bowra, greatly though he trusted him. Her name was Shelagh Levita and if she was Connolly's last love affair she was also his most secret: Peter Quennell, Joan Leigh Fermor, Barbara and Deirdre were told or found out but beyond these initiates the matter was undiscussed and the majority of Connolly's circle remained unsure where or how he and his Dark Lady, as she was later occasionally known, had met.

The Levitas, the prosperous family of Portuguese émigrés into which Shelagh had married, were slightly better informed and later remarked among themselves that the wedding they had attended in 1963 was a strange affair. It was rumoured, after all, that Arthur Levita had been deeply in love with another woman and that on the very morning of the marriage Shelagh, then aged thirty, had received a letter from Cyril Connolly in which the critic called her his one true love and begged her to marry him. She had no choice but to honour the promises of her engagement but the marriage failed and the Levitas separated, and when Shelagh returned to nurse her husband through terminal illness in 1971 she did so sustained by Connolly's sympathy and tact. Because her flat was situated in Cadogan Gardens behind Sloane Square Connolly became a regular guest at the Wilbraham Hotel, a tranquil and pleasingly neglected establishment nearby. For such an eager schemer, however, the day's truancy involved more than a mere rendezvous; and following his furtive arrival at Waterloo he would always go first to White's in the belief that familiarity with the club's menu would provide him with an alibi in the event of awkward domestic interrogation. There was an almost theatrical note to these subterfuges but they seem to have been deployed with all the conviction of first love, and the Duke of Devonshire later heard that when Connolly returned to Eastbourne on the evening train Shelagh would travel with him and then go back to London in solitude, having disembarked at Hampden Park or Lewes to avoid the coast town gossips.

As far as Connolly was concerned the secrecy was justified at least in part by his public reputation and by the fact that even at this late stage, whatever the more clement morality of the Sixties, it would be foolish to provoke the *Sunday Times* with further extramarital scandal. As for sparing Deirdre's feelings, it was not the least of the situation's comic aspects that she knew yet scarcely seemed to mind, a position indicated by a domestic vignette which Susan witnessed shortly after Connolly's return from Venice, where he had supposedly been alone. One of his suits needed to be cleaned but when Deirdre was emptying its pockets, and two *pedalo* ticket counterfoils rather than one fluttered incriminatingly to the floor, her only comment was '*Two* pedalo tickets, Youey?'[6] Quite simply she seems to have wanted not to know and Michael Wishart was not alone in praising her diplomacy and sensing that '[her] devotion to him was tempered with tact and, when necessary, a tolerance which verged upon apparent detachment'.[7] In any case she had her own preoccupations – not least her friendship with the mysterious Peter Levi, a friendship which, owing to his Jesuit office, was at once entirely confidential and widely yet inconclusively discussed. After all, nobody could be sure as to the exact nature of their relationship; and who could say precisely what Connolly thought? Of course he was malicious behind Levi's back but old friends had heard all the complaints before and knowing his gusto for the dramas of jealousy listened with reservations; even the most partisan, if aware of his involvement with Shelagh, found it hard to overlook the rights of marital equality. It was obvious that he liked the priest and respected his intellect and although he could complain to Peter Quennell that every morning Deirdre and Levi had long telephone conversations, when his friend asked him how he felt about it, he could only reply: 'I don't know whether to be jealous of him or glad that she isn't talking to me.'[8] As for Levi himself, his friendship with Deirdre was to alter his life profoundly. At their first meeting, 'I recognized the love of my life. We recognized each other ... I thought simply and suddenly, there is the only woman I have met I could love for ever and might, if things had been otherwise, have married.'[9]

Easter 1971 took the Connolly family to Portmeirion: the critic was amused by Clough Williams Ellis's bizarre Italianate town and enjoyed inspecting Snowdonia, the magnolias of Bodnant and the houses which faced one another across the Menai Straits. In April he contributed to David Bailey's documentary *Beaton by Bailey* and in May he flew to Austin for the exhibition based on *100 Key Books* which was about to open at the Humanities Research Center. The visit combined business and pleasure: having been paid $1500 as an honorarium he was able to sell the Texans two manuscript fragments of journalism for a further $1000. Yet commerce was not all and as he had already implied in his introduction to the exhibition's catalogue he could easily be forgiven for taking the entire event as a great compliment: 'I suppose this Exhibition makes me one of the few writers who have seen their dream implemented by reality, who have rubbed the magic lamp and beheld a huge djinn turn the contents of an imaginary bookcase into the living word, the word made flesh.'[10] Insecurities of importance and fame were for the young alone: now he should relax and enjoy the hot climate and savour the Center's flattering and open-handed attentions.

Having installed himself at the Forty Acres Club – named in commemoration of the original limits of the campus – he went in search of John Lehmann, temporarily a member of the Austin Faculty, and through him met Harry H. Ransom, the President of the University, Warren Roberts, Director of the Center, and Mary Hirth, its Librarian. Relations began and continued on a happy footing, with Connolly at once aware that his hosts were more than mere university officials: they had worked in dedicated tandem to build the greatest collection of its kind and beyond the magnolias and ilex trees of the campus the new Harry Ransom Humanities Research Center was rising as a monument to their convictions. Lehmann found his visitor in 'wonderful form' and was disarmed by his 'smile of immense satisfaction'. He was immediately appointed what Connolly later described as 'Virgil for once to my Dante', and soon learned that the visitor thought nothing of imposing exacting tasks on his dragomans.[11] During the course of his introductions around the Faculty his eye had been caught by a young woman who was married to one of its professors and he lost no time in revealing his ambitions to his old friend. Lehmann recalled that she was 'a devoted acolyte and more than that of Cyril ... The intrigue got deeper and deeper and I had to resort to all sorts of devices to bring Cyril and this lady together without her husband knowing.'[12]

Meanwhile Robert Murray Davis, a newly tenured associate professor at the University of Oklahoma, was trying to resolve complexities of another sort. He had come to Austin to catalogue the recently arrived papers of Evelyn Waugh and when he was introduced to Connolly he eagerly engaged his help in trying to solve some of the conundrums of place and identity posed by the hitherto unseen diaries:

> At the time, I thought that he was being extraordinarily obliging; now I suspect that he was even more delighted than I to be privy to information, some of it libellous and most of it discreditable, about people he had actually known ... [He] stopped at the reference to an Audrey who thought she was pregnant but turned out not to be. 'That has to be Audrey Lucas,' he said, and gave further details about her family and fate. Other names he identified with less editorial comment.[13]

There was no mention of him in these few forbidden pages and he and Davis set out together to finish other business elsewhere on the campus. However, as they were walking through the undergraduate library, where the exhibition continued in glass-case displays, Connolly stopped abruptly in front of one of the stands and stared in fascination at Waugh's annotated copy of *The Unquiet Grave* and decided at once that he wanted to read beyond the few graffiti visible in the display case. Soon, with Mary Hirth's intervention, the book was in its author's hands; soon he could read the brutal marginalia; soon Davis saw the consequences of his erring human curiosity. 'I don't remember his exact words when he finished, but he was obviously quite disturbed ... [His] obvious unhappiness put me in the uncomfortable position of trying to console a much older and far more distinguished man.' He tried to point out the difficult circumstances in which Waugh had made his observations and the fact that he had valued the book enough to have it bound but his words were to no avail. Connolly's triumph had been spiked; the unkind genius of his generation cast his long shadow even from the grave to this remote haven: 'For the rest of my stay in Texas I remained obsessed with Evelyn, and on my return flight I attributed every sudden turbulence to him.'[14] The description of the visit which he gave in June intrigued the readers of the *Sunday Times* and prompted reassurances not only from Sacheverell Sitwell but also from Maurice Bowra.

> We all knew that though [Evelyn] was servile enough to our faces he was beastly about us behind our backs ... He found it impossible to be

generous and he was really devoured by envy of almost everything –
money, birth, talent, looks, health, success ... I suppose that there is a
great deal of his unpublished records – the thought makes the blood run
cold.[15]

Bowra was right – there were other records; but he would be dead by
the time the diaries were serialized in 1973 by the *Observer*. To Connolly that event was no more than 'a fart from the grave'[16] and by then,
as he explained in a letter to the editor of the *Daily Mail*, he had 'long
written off my friendship with Evelyn Waugh as an illusion'.[17]

Meanwhile David Bruce and Watson, a small publishing company
based in Gray's Inn Road and sustaining itself since inception on
cookery books, science fiction and first novels, had approached Connolly with the scheme which had entertained Hamish Hamilton and
Cass Canfield in the years after the war, that the critic should write
introductions to a series of classic novels, which could then be reissued
as a selective and distinguished library. The overture was accepted and
a fee agreed but by the end of 1971 events had repeated themselves yet
again and Bruce and Watson, who had seen partnership with the critic
as a golden augury of prosperity which immediately entitled them to
larger offices in Great Russell Street, learned that their prestigious
colleague had done no work at all. His conscience remained nimble,
however, and he proposed an alternative scheme: that Bruce and
Watson should publish a new collection of essays to mark his seventieth
birthday. No fledgling imprint could resist such an offer and ideas of
Connolly's library of classics were hastily forgotten. There was one
proviso: that the publishers should secure the services of what the critic
called 'a thrusting young academic' to make a preliminary selection
which Connolly could then refine and approve. Perhaps Christopher
Ricks might be interested? Connolly was to be disappointed, however:
his publishers were happy to secure some sort of factotum for the
project but had candidates of their own, and the job went instead to a
young man called Andrew Rossabi.

The new apprentice had not accepted the position without misgivings: besides a classical training, St Paul's School and Cambridge had
left him with socialist sympathies and in his integrity he had shied at the
critic's Etonian nostalgia. Yet although as an undergraduate he had
heard F. R. Leavis lecture on Wordsworth and been disinclined to
question the orthodox certainty that Connolly was no more than a

supine belletrist, he had read *Enemies of Promise* with grateful surprise: here was a book which was written without dishonesty or puritan high-mindedness and which indicated great originality and an indifference to prevailing literary evaluations. Rossabi was invited to join Connolly, Bruce, Watson and Robin Maugham for lunch at a restaurant in Pont Street. He was disappointed that the writer seemed smaller and thinner than the figure on the front of the Penguin edition of *Enemies of Promise*, but still found him intimidating and during lunch, when Connolly ignored him entirely, he was too shy to speak and assumed that he had made a bad impression. He was wrong, however, and when the gossip ended and the table began to disperse, the critic wrote a letter of introduction for his young assistant to present to Stella Franks, his secretary at the *Sunday Times*, and research began without further delay for a book provisionally entitled 'The Last of Cyril Connolly'.[18]

The name had a valedictory ring which might have unnerved the suspicious, but Connolly and the surviving members of his generation had suddenly found themselves venerated elders of letters and there was a sense of apogee and inevitably of culmination in the realization. In February 1972, along with L. P. Hartley, he was made a Companion of Literature by the Royal Society of Literature, but Alan Ross, a spectator of the investitures, found the ceremony mismanaged, the presiding authority of R. A. Butler notwithstanding: 'I cannot remember a more farcical occasion. Butler, curiously inept and seeming almost gaga, referred to Connolly as a well-known novelist and had nothing to say about Hartley except that there was a racehorse called The Go-Between which he himself had once successfully backed.'[19]

In March a convivial gathering at Ann Fleming's, which included Peter Quennell, Raymond Mortimer, Christopher Sykes, Caroline Blackwood and her current husband Robert Lowell, failed to divert Connolly, and his hostess noted that he wanted no part of the bibulous exchanges of Baudelaire traded by Quennell and Lowell as midnight chimed. He had renounced alcohol altogether, only to discover that it alone makes parties bearable, but at least travel remained a pleasure and later in March he went to Spain. In April he learned that his name had been put forward for a CBE (Ordinary Commander of the Civil Division) in the Birthday Honours, and simultaneously David Bathurst of Christie's, whom he had met only once at Somerhill, invited him to lunch to discuss an unexpected proposal. They went to Pruniers and Bathurst was fascinated to notice not only that the front rim of his guest's blue homburg was turned up 'like a bookmaker's in a high wind' but also that indecision undid him in the restaurant: 'Since he couldn't make up his mind between oysters mornay and salmon fishcakes, he had both.'[20] The auction house intended to establish a modern book section to rival the parallel office run at Sotheby's by Anthony Hobson and hoped that Connolly might want to run the venture. Payment would be £1000 per annum and 3 per cent of 15 per cent on lots which made less than £500; the association might perhaps begin with a trial sale which would concentrate on quality rather than quantity. On 25 April Connolly formally accepted the offer by letter and promised to begin his reconnaissances during his imminent trip to Paris: he would be calling on Nancy Mitford, and could establish whether she had any first editions she no longer wanted.

The first-born of the Mitfords was dying slowly and in great pain in her adopted city and, for all her courage, fluctuated inevitably between gloom and irritability. The Connollys' visit was not a success: their hostess had opened Château Lafitte without knowing of the critic's new abstention and the plovers' eggs which he had brought in tribute from Hédiard turned out to be uncooked and spilt everywhere. It was clearly not the time to mention Christie's business and the visitors left in mild disgrace. The novelist was still fulminating when she described the visit to Anthony Powell on 13 June: 'The truth is Cyril is not sortable & I shall never ask him here again.'[21] A little later, however, she relented and sent congratulations on his honour, which she too had been awarded: 'I was much pleased to be the Companion of you & Harold A[cton] as well as of the ghostly Empire ... I wish I could go with you & collect it.'[22] The investiture was set for 2 November but before then he would have to acknowledge his letters of congratulation, though perhaps not the succinct message of applause which arrived from Margaret Thatcher, the Secretary of State for Education and Science. The journalist Alastair Forbes was not satisfied, however, and wrote to Connolly promising that he would campaign for another, and greater, honour on his behalf: 'We shall mount a fuller operation with superior generals, for your 70th birthday.'[23] Time would tell.

Bernard Levin delivered himself of a lengthy panegyric in *The Times* – which addressed itself principally to the abiding significance of *Horizon* – and in so doing invoked the old story about Lytton Strachey being asked during the First World War why he was not fighting to preserve civilization and suggested that Connolly, if asked the same question in the following war, could have repeated his just rejoinder: 'Madam, I am the civilization that they are fighting to preserve.' Simultaneously readers were made privy to Connolly's own views of his career subsequent to *Horizon* when he contributed to *The Pearl of Days: An Intimate Memoir of the Sunday Times* produced by Harold Hobson, Philip Knightley and Leonard Russell and published by Hamish Hamilton to mark the newspaper's 150th anniversary. His contribution was one of gratitude and gave assurances that his job did more than keep him learning:

> It forces me to be just (so much harder than being merciful), it keeps me humble, for there is nothing I write that might not be used to light a fire a few hours later ... I love books; I am paid to read them; when people commiserate with me on my weekly grind I thank them but I know that without it the duns would long have been picking my bones.

Even as he wrote the duns were closing in and although his salary for 1972 had been increased to £4250, excluding occasional travel writing and sundry work for the magazine, he was informed by Coutts in October that his overdraft now stood at £16,302. The first weeks of 1973 found him doubly preoccupied and in February, in a review nominally devoted to the first volume of Pevsner's guide to London architecture, he revealed in the *Sunday Times* that recent and frequent funeral attendance had led him to give consideration to the details of his own requiem: his overriding anxiety was strictly practical: 'Who's going to pay?'[24] Life had been sad enough since Bowra's death in 1971 but now Elizabeth Bowen was dying and he dutifully visited her in hospital, taking the new *ADAM* number which was devoted to Proust and Virginia Woolf; she telephoned to thank him for the gift only hours before her death. They had been friends for almost longer than it was possible to remember but private sadness was no more than implicit in the public tribute he wrote for the newspaper: 'She made everyone she met into something more than they usually seemed and every situation became part of a comedy ... she was at heart a romantic, with a keen sense of betrayal, the betrayal of youthful ideals, intellectual promise, worldly ambition.'[25] Mrs Cecil Day-Lewis wrote to congratulate him on his obituary: 'There must be so many who loved Elizabeth, as we did, who have wept today because you so perfectly brought to life for us what she was.'[26] In March Noël Coward died, in June Nancy Mitford, in September W. H. Auden – and for their friends and acquaintances each departure was an affirmation of the intense sadness of old age.

On 4 April Christie's held a sale of the items its new book consultant had managed to procure. The range, a tribute to his dedication as much as to his persuasive charm, was impressive, and bibliophiles could fight over autograph letters from the Woolfs, the original manuscript of *Room at the Top*, a collection of Verlaine first editions consigned by Harry D'Avigdor-Goldsmid and other items surrendered by Tom Driberg, Stephen Spender and Ann Fleming, to say nothing of fifty-two lots from his own collection advertised with the familiar yet enigmatic provenance 'The Property of a Gentleman'. (Meanwhile in New York at Sotheby's dispersal of the Iselin Collection the manuscript of *Enemies of Promise* realized $2200 prior to its final acquisition by Austin's Harry Ransom Humanities Research Center.) In May Miron Grindea, the editor of *ADAM* magazine, announced that he was planning to devote a forth-coming number to memories of *Horizon* and called on Connolly, who seemed to him to symbolize 'the very notion of literature'.[27]

During the course of these honours and farewells work had progressed on 'The Last of Cyril Connolly'. Rossabi had taken *Previous Convictions* as his model and established four categories of subject as the framework for the new book. It had taken him about a month to make his preliminary selection and shortly after completing his task he was invited to Eastbourne to discuss the various choices over lunch. To his relief the critic was in benign mood and declaring himself delighted with his apprentice's work proved to be a genial and enthusiastic host. However, no sooner had Connolly insisted that the selection satisfied than he began to pursue furtive revisions and to toy with the idea of including different articles or ones which he had hoped to fit into *Previous Convictions*. David Bruce and Watson thought too highly of him to try to curtail his indecision and three sets of proofs and huge additional expenses were incurred. Irresolution also infected the choice of title and even the book's cover: 'Penultimatum', 'House of Two Doors', 'The Meeting Rivers' and 'A Carp for Epicurus' were all dismissed before the new book was finally named; and since he so hated the photograph of himself which had appeared on the Penguin edition of *Enemies of Promise* Connolly at first rejected outright the idea of another cover with himself on it and it took a concerted campaign to bring about a change of heart and the final design, with its informal portrait by Beaton superimposed on a classical yet surreal architectural setting suggestive of de Chirico.

The book was scheduled for release at the end of the summer and

feeling that he had earned a holiday Connolly took Shelagh to stay with
Barbara at Grimaud. Barbara's appraisal of the secret girlfriend was
almost generous: She was 'the calm mother that [Cyril] had always
claimed he needed [and] had long, sleek, dark hair, and a certain chic;
she dressed in simple, well-cut, tailored suits. She was someone you
could count on, self-sacrificing and kind. The only thing she lacked,
from my point of view, was a sense of humour.'[28] One incident alone
later assumed ominous significance: 'After swimming in the pool,
[Cyril] had had great difficulty climbing out and complained of a
terrible pain in his chest, blaming it on the absence of steps leading out
of the swimming pool.'[29] The brief anxiety passed, however, and
seemed no reason to alter the elaborate plans now taking shape for his
imminent seventieth birthday. As Hamish Hamilton and André
Deutsch prepared to reissue *The Unquiet Grave* and *Enemies of
Promise*, Connolly was interviewed in the *Guardian* by Simon Blow,
while in the *Sunday Times* he formed the subject of a long appraisal by
Kenneth Clark. He was interviewed by W. Hardcastle for BBC Radio
and told his audience that far from being lazy he could boast an annual
output of between sixty and one hundred thousand words: 'At the age
of seventy I've still got to earn my living.'[30] Finally *The Evening
Colonnade*, his new collection of reviews, was published on 10 September and marked with a party at Brown's Hotel in Mayfair which
Connolly organized and David Bruce and Watson financed.

The most significant celebration, however, was the party held at
London Zoo and organized by Jack Lambert and Frank Giles, whose
friend Solly Zuckerman, Secretary to the Zoological Society of London,
was happy to provide the necessary clearance. The venue was a closely
guarded secret and was chosen to honour Connolly's lifelong dedication to exotic animals and the frequent calls for conservation which
he had made in the newspaper. Connolly himself knew nothing of the
choice of locality but was involved with the invitations and the seating
in numerous semi-flippant memoranda to Lambert. One was headed
with the injunction 'For your eyes only: eat after reading' and contained
fresh suggestions about how to seat an august but not always mutually
admiring throng. He gave Lambert a few hints about the disposition of
some of the more problematic guests: regarding Powell, it was all 'grist
to his mill'; D'Avigdor-Goldsmid thought 'Father Peter a bit of a
renegade'; and Ann Fleming was 'allergic' to Alastair Forbes.[31] As for
the venue, he imagined it to be either 49 Bedford Square or 25 Sussex

Place or even Downing Street but would settle for anywhere apart from the offices of the *Observer*. Writing events up in his diary on 11 September, Cecil Beaton recorded Deirdre's disclosure that her husband now did little apart from read in bed almost all day and that they saw no one. However, he concluded that the regime was beneficial:

> Cyril looked calm, pretty as a celluloid cupid in a bath, with no apparent nervousness, and although he says he has never made a speech, did in fact deliver himself of a spontaneous one. It was a typical piece of Cyril embroidery about his having an unhappy childhood . . . [32]

Lambert received many letters of congratulation and thanks: Anthony Powell thought the claret the finest he had had in weeks; and Diana Cooper decreed it one of the best parties she had ever attended and considered the 'soufflé' of Connolly's speech 'only equalled in taste by the excellence of the zoo food'.[33]

October presented further opportunities for the pleasures of the table when Connolly flew to Spain to research his contribution to 'Cooking For Love', an occasional series being run by the *Sunday Times* magazine in which writers assessed the culinary skills of their favourite amateur cooks. He had chosen to introduce his readers to Andalusian cookery as practised by Janetta, 'a phenomenon of our time it would take too long to describe . . . the pleasantest and most stimulating companion that an artist could hope for, one who would drive you to Angkor at the drop of a map'.[34] Since the early Sixties she had spent most of her time in southern Spain and was now married to a Spanish nobleman and living at Tramores, a farmhouse beside a ruined Moorish tower situated in a valley among the lower slopes of the Ronda mountains. The critic arrived to find that his hostess had extended the feast to include not only her neighbours the Bill Davises but also their friends Joseph and Patricia Losey. The Davises were always delighted to see Connolly, while Losey's enthusiasm for the writer bordered on sycophancy. Barry Lategan, the photographer sent by the *Sunday Times* to record the occasion, was surprised that one of his eminence could prove so fawning and amused by Connolly's attempt to check him: 'Don't flatter me any more – you'll embarrass yourself.'[35] When not praising the critic's achievement, Losey was preoccupied with his latest cinematic ambition, a film of *A La Recherche du Temps Perdu*, and the company tried to gauge the scale and possibilities of the project – in the end never realized – over lunch: *tapas*, a cold white almond and garlic soup, marinated lamb with rice, cumin and coriander and a 'heavenly' cake.

The article remained unpublished until the following summer and by then its author's gusto for food had faded sharply. Indeed after his return from Spain in November, when Christopher and Elizabeth Glenconner gave a dinner in honour of his seventieth birthday in the Pinafore Room at the Savoy, friends were alarmed to notice the ebbing of his health. Connolly was almost too frail to eat; furthermore he had developed cataracts and confided to Stephen Spender that he was scarcely able to distinguish any of the guests. In any case they were familiar: the Leigh Fermors, Beaton and Diana Cooper, with David Pryce-Jones as a token innovation. Pryce-Jones felt as though he were on board the departing *Titanic*, and beyond the walls of the Savoy there were indeed more treacherous waters than the Thames: only that day the stock market had plunged and the government had declared a national emergency. Early in 1974 Spender began to collect impressions for a memorial volume dedicated to W. H. Auden and Connolly's contribution, a fine example of the literary portrait he had long perfected, began with a poignant reminder that latterly dead poet and ailing critic had seen less of each other than they would have liked: 'I used to imagine the old as yarning away together or locked in pregnant silence like Tennyson and Carlyle. But age is not like that: the old are diminishing universes racing further and further apart, piling up space between them, unable to cope with the simplest mechanics of meeting.'[36]

Notionally at least, Connolly was still committed to working on his autobiography and Andrew Rossabi had been provisionally enlisted to lend assistance. The younger man saw him as having a serene, almost inscrutable sagacity which, combined perhaps with his appearance, suggested the Buddha. Yet his wisdom could be briskly practical: when Rossabi mentioned that his wife had left him Connolly told him, 'Find another.'[37] But, as preparation for the autobiography languished, Rossabi knew his colleague was afraid of dying. With his eyesight failing, all literary ambitions were in question and it was decided he should undergo surgery to have his cataracts removed later in the year. Gerald Brenan sent reassurances: he had himself endured the operation and recommended tinted glasses for convalescence. Joan Leigh Fermor wrote anxiously in February suggesting that he should seek out winter sunshine and hotter summers to alleviate bronchial difficulties. Peter Quennell told his friend he should feel free to escape with Shelagh, and assured him that Deirdre would surely agree to such an arrangement. Doctors also plied him with advice which he relayed in turn to Barbara: his condition was stable, his blood pressure normal, he could eat within reason and climb staircases; indeed the only hazards he was to avoid were infection, which would counteract his heart pills, and exposure to cold, particularly after food.

By May his overdraft had climbed to £25,000 and distress of another sort ensued when he quarrelled with Gerald Brenan over the latter's autobiography, which was eventually called *Personal Record*. Brenan had provisionally included a portrait which he considered to be unmistakably encomiastic and which emphasized Connolly's wit, conversational virtuosity and originality. Unfortunately he also indicated that these virtues were offset by laziness and moodiness and compounded his crime by making not entirely flattering remarks about his subject's appearance. Connolly asked for proofs which Brenan confidently sent, only to be appalled by the savagely scored and contradicted manuscript which was eventually returned to him. He hastened to mend fences:

> Your strong changing moods and so forth are things that fascinate people about you and give you a distinction and originality that most writers lack ... I said to myself, 'Cyril is so frank about himself that he will accept what I have said.' ... You have an attitude to life and literature that appeals to me more strongly than that of any writer of our time.[38]

Perhaps Brenan had been undiplomatic or Connolly too sensitive; either way, as though resolving all terrestrial misunderstandings, the critic sent a letter several weeks later indicating that all had been forgiven and forgotten. In May he was in Portugal and sent Lambert a postcard from Lisbon extolling the sunshine, the seafood, the custard apples, the Gulbenkian Collection and the city's surviving Rococo palaces. In June he was presented with the membership and insignia of the American Academy of Arts and Letters and in August, admitted to Moorfields Hospital for the removal of his cataracts, he was the patient of the distinguished ophthalmologist Patrick Trevor-Roper and submitted patiently to an operation which proved entirely successful. No review appeared in the newspaper for two weeks and by the time his column appeared again on 8 September, devoted to Oskar Kokoschka's *My Life*, Connolly had once again taken Shelagh to stay with his ex-wife at Grimaud. Barbara later wrote poignantly of his intention to take his two women friends out for lunch on his birthday, 10 September,

and of how, when she went in search of him, she found him doubled
over in pain and in the throes of cardiac crisis. He was taken to a
hospital in St Tropez and underwent an operation to remove liquid
from around the heart but when Barbara consulted the surgeon as to his
patient's long-term condition she was distressed by his analogy – that
the invalid should be compared to an old car in which all major
components were now in need of replacement.

Barbara rang Deirdre and suggested that she should join her husband
in St Tropez but she declined to do so, not least because of the complications entailed by her stepmother Joy's recent death; in any case the
decision was soon taken to transfer the patient to a more suitable
hospital in Cannes. When the day of departure arrived Connolly
refused to leave St Tropez on a stretcher and insisted on dressing
himself and climbing into the ambulance. Shelagh travelled with him
and resolved to move into a hotel in Cannes for the duration of his
treatment. The second set of doctors proved more optimistic and soon
the patient was thought sufficiently improved to fly home. Pending
admission to the Harley Street Clinic he stayed at the Wilbraham and
even managed to attend a party given by the Society of Literature, but
when Kenneth Clark saw him there he was appalled by his decline and
somewhat tactlessly wrote to tell him so: 'One must never tell people
that they look ill, or it makes them feel even iller, but I had great
difficulty in restraining myself.'[39] In the interim Anne Dunn had heard
about the collapse via Sonia but was at first unable to find the ailing
writer or his wife. She finally traced them to the Wilbraham but when
she telephoned Deirdre's manner failed to suggest any kind of crisis:
'The news is good, there is nothing wrong with him that complete rest
won't cure. Hold on, Cyril's simply thrilled it's you and wants to
speak.'[40] It transpired, however, that the porter had had to be summoned to help Connolly from his bath and when Janetta arrived at the
hotel to try to assess his condition herself she was shocked to find him
shrunken and diminished.

Once in the Harley Street Clinic Connolly remained very weak and
Shelagh reported to Barbara that he found even the journey from
bedroom to bathroom exhausting. He was plagued by breathlessness at
night owing to excess fluid in the chest and twice daily was subjected to
X-rays and cardiograms and tests for high blood pressure. When Anne
visited him two days after his installation she saw him further
debilitated: 'His head fragile and bald, his mouth large on his face,

hands puffy, covered in scabs, relaxed on the sheet.' Having sent freesias, a cactus and a gardenia ahead of her, she arrived to find that Janetta had already deposited a store of custard apples. She had also brought muscat grapes from the Chatsworth hothouses on behalf of the Duke of Devonshire but Connolly had murmured, more in regret than in reproach, 'I wish Andrew would bring the grapes himself.'[41] When Noël Blakiston arrived he found the patient with his eyes firmly shut; on instruction the visitor read aloud Ezra Pound's 'The Tomb of Akr Caar'. John Craxton understood that only women were encouraged in bedside attendance and so stayed away; and Alan Ross's last conversation with his friend took place over the telephone: 'To my question about how he felt he replied, "Liver's lousy." Instead of his putting the receiver down I heard it drop from his hand and lie on the bed, the sounds of the room like the sea in a shell continuing to reverberate.'[42] Connolly was far from lonely, however. Indeed Alastair Forbes later suggested that the traffic of well-wishers was almost overwhelming: 'From far and wide there arrived in London women of very varied ages, character and appearance who had been loved by and who still loved this difficult and demanding but unique *homme à femmes*.'[43]

Yet even in the gentle ministrations of women there were complications – legacy of a lifetime of intrigue – and Barbara noted: 'My visits could not coincide with Deirdre, Sonia, Joan or Janetta's. But Shelagh was always there until my last visit, when C. was alone.'[44] (Equally, Deirdre, who was getting up at six to cook Cressida's lunch, get Matthew to school and then catch the train to London, could not coincide with Shelagh and it fell to Joan to arrange against bedside collision.) When Barbara did visit her former husband was 'pitifully thin' and without any appetite and could only be tempted to drink glucose. He complained that neither John Betjeman nor Ann Fleming had been to visit him and was querulous with inspecting doctors, who seemed not to know whether his decline had been brought about by malfunctions of liver or heart. He was transferred to King's College Hospital, which boasted expertise in the infirmities of the liver, and Shelagh was impressed by its skilled supervision. Nevertheless the new doctors sensed that the liver could never mend without some prior cardiac improvement and soon he was being fed intravenously. Stephen Spender had already begun the composition of a memorial tribute for the *Times Literary Supplement* but when he went to visit his friend, by now back in the Harley Street Clinic, he heard something approaching rebuff in Connolly's words: 'I do not recommend dying. I am dead to this world.'[45] He was certainly remote to the practicalities of dying and it was fortunate that Harry D'Avigdor-Goldsmid was on hand to meet the steep weekly expenses of treatment. Not long after his return, however, the Harley Street Clinic suggested a further move, since the patient was too weak to respond to treatment, and Connolly made his final journey, to the St Vincent's Clinic in Ladbroke Terrace in West London.

Less than twenty-four hours after his arrival, that establishment telephoned Deirdre asking her to organize her husband's removal – there must have been a mistake: St Vincent's did not take terminal cases. She pleaded for time and the patient rallied; Spender rang Eastbourne for a bulletin and was told by Sarah Craven that both heart and liver had improved. Deirdre visited St Vincent's, taking Peter Levi with her, and because anger and imprecation belong to the world of the living they found the dying man absolving and benign, and heedless of the world beyond the clinic's curtains and the raging election campaign in which Edward Heath was predicting 30 per cent inflation and Margaret Thatcher secretly contemplating the Conservative leadership. Cyril Connolly died on 26 November 1974. He was a little over seventy-one years old, the victim, according to his death certificate, of congestive cardiac failure, coronary atherosclerosis and hypertension – that is, heart failure, leading to water retention and breathlessness, and aggravated by a narrowing of the blood vessels possibly causing angina and high blood pressure without any apparent cause. After all, the liver was blameless and he died, as he had lived, by the heart.

The funeral took place on 2 December at Berwick Church near Lewes and those whose minds wandered from the writer and his exequies could contemplate the murals by Duncan Grant and Vanessa Bell, while Grant himself sat at the back of the church with his daughter. Stephen Spender went by train from London with Sonia, Jack Lambert and Noël Blakiston and suggested the nagging sense of anticlimax and unfinished business which often attends the burial of the dead: 'Lesson and psalm all about the resurrection of the body – seemed unsuitable for Cyril ... We all stood round the flower-covered grave in the wet and cold, just a tarpaulin of some kind over the coffin.'[46] Afterwards there was a champagne party at St John's Road. Later still, a tombstone was erected, inscribed with the description of the nymphs' cave from the first Book of the *Aeneid*: *intus aquae dulces vivoque sedilia saxo* – 'Within are fresh waters and seats in the living stone'. On 20 December a memorial service was held at St Mary-Le-Strand punctuated by Psalm 91, 'O come, O come, Emmanuel!' and Michael Berkeley's *Requiem Aeternum*, which had been composed in memory of Connolly. John Betjeman took the lesson from The Wisdom of Solomon; Stephen Spender gave the address; Peter Levi, not entirely uncontroversially, read from *The Unquiet Grave*. Only later was the disquisition on death which Connolly had written to console Jennifer Ross discovered, and by then others of his generation could weigh its beautiful contentions within prospect of their own mortality:

> The opposite of fearing death is to love life, and the painful consideration of non-existence will be found to disappear when life is lived fully and to arise chiefly when apathy and fear of life exist as well. Lovers hardly fear death at all, which is why they can afford closely to contemplate it.[47]

The *Sunday Times* published the last article Connolly wrote for the newspaper as a tribute the Sunday after he died. 'Poetry – My First and Last Love' could well have been written for the occasion, yet all his life Connolly had been acutely aware that evanescence was almost the defining aspect of all beauty, all pleasure, and it was that wisdom which lent his lyrical celebrations their tension:

> Poetry, even the best, holds no brevet of immortality and is no more lasting than man's other creations. As civilizations die they become incomprehensible; every language will one day be a dead language and we ourselves wear out ... and lose our zest for our memories. For this reason the poetry of mortality has the edge on the poetry of love; for the sentiment of transience remains with us longer, together with an abiding love of nature.[48]

On the following page there was an obituary by John Betjeman which was more affectionate reminiscence than incisive appraisal. *The Times* took the critic at his own pre-emptive and self-deprecating word and saw him as an also-ran. Only Philip Toynbee, writing in the *Observer*, produced a tribute which suggested that Connolly turned his apparent deficiencies into virtues which, allied to a strong character, enabled him to dominate the imaginations of so many friends, admirers, acquaintances and detractors:

> He was certainly one of the funniest men I have ever known, in a remarkable way one of the most lovable, and, for all his constant

moaning, one of the most perversely life-enhancing ... It is also true that the closeness of this friendship was a constant source of anxiety, even nervous strain, not only to me but to all those of us who were in the same position as mine; in whom, that is, an element of discipleship had crept unwillingly into the relationship with that most unusual but indubitable maestro.[49]

Meanwhile the dead man's family and friends had other concerns besides the drawing down of blinds. In his will, drawn up on 22 June 1972 and witnessed by Auden and Spender, Connolly had named Deirdre his legatee and executrix, with Coutts – which already held the deeds to St John's Road – and Joan Leigh Fermor nominated as further executors. Beyond the matter of literary copyright, however, the disposition was notional, since over every posthumous directive lay the matter of the debt, which by now stood at £27,000, and against which there were no standing assets apart from Connolly's book collection and his hoard of accumulated papers, saved since before St Cyprian's as though for this very moment. It was an aspect of his genius, however, that he had always been able to charm money out of wealthy friends, and that charm held good from beyond the grave. A Cyril Connolly Fund was established and an appeal circulated, bearing at its head a roll of sponsors – among them Spender, Betjeman, Anthony Powell and Kenneth Clark – which declared its ambitions to discharge the overdraft, secure the ownership of the house to Deirdre and provide a fund to support her and Connolly's children. Not everybody warmed to the petition's brisk tone, reputed to be the work of Sonia Orwell, the Fund's secretary, but in the midst of grave domestic financial crisis money was nevertheless pledged and through the dealings and contacts of Anthony Hobson and Harry D'Avigdor-Goldsmid Connolly's library and papers were eventually sold – not to the Humanities Research Center, then suffering an unusual eclipse of funds – but to the McFarlin Library at the University of Tulsa, Oklahoma, for approximately £30,000.

In 1975 Noël Blakiston published *A Romantic Friendship*, which collected the bulk of the letters between himself and Connolly as schoolboys and undergraduates, and Miron Grindea produced a memorial issue of *ADAM* which was dedicated to Connolly and contained contributions from a wide spectrum of his friends. In 1977 Peter Levi left the Jesuits, married Deirdre and settled down to a literary and academic career of distinction which was belied by the modesty of aspiration revealed by his memoir *The Flutes of Autumn*: 'A piece of blank paper is the only thing in the world I have a serious ambition to control.'[50] As for Connolly himself, he has refused to surrender his hold on the imaginations of those who care for beautiful writing and the civilized delight of the senses or are interested in the literature of our mid-century; and as books continue to appear which chronicle the achievements of his more prolific but less elusive contemporaries, he becomes an ever more inescapable figure in recent cultural history. He was many different things to many different friends and acquaintances but now we are left only with the essential aspect of his marvellous literary legacy, with its prevailing conviction that literature was a jealous god which would countenance no distraction, and its plaintive and misleading regrets for the poetry he never wrote.

NOTES

The Select Bibliography is a list of sources consulted in the writing of this book and gives full bibliographical details of works referred to in the following notes. 'Tulsa' indicates documents now belonging to the McFarlin Library at the University of Tulsa, Oklahoma; 'Huntington' to those at the Huntington Library, Pasadena; 'Berg Collection' to those at the Berg Collection at New York Public Library; and 'Austin' to those at the Harry Ransom Humanities Research Center at the University of Texas. The correspondence between Cyril Connolly and Routledge is now held by Reading University Library and that between Connolly and Hamish Hamilton belongs to Bristol University Library. Arthur Koestler's correspondence is now at Edinburgh University Library while George Orwell's papers are held by the Orwell Archive at University College, London (UCL). Cyril Connolly's letters to Evelyn Waugh belong to the British Library.

Epigraph

1. The critics were discussing their great precursor Sainte-Beuve. The anecdote appears in John Russell, *Reading Russell*, Thames and Hudson, London, 1989.

PART I: AN EDWARDIAN BOYHOOD

Chapter One

1. Quoted by Cyril Connolly in the *Sunday Times*, 3 June 1973.
2. *Enemies of Promise*, p. 158 (Penguin revised edition).
3. Dennis McIntyre, *The Meadow of the Bull: A History of Clontarf*, 1987.
4. In a letter to Cyril Connolly, 14 September 1972 (Tulsa).
5. In a letter to Cyril Connolly [no date], 1947 (Tulsa).
6. *Illustrated London News*, 12 September 1903.

7. George Orwell, 'Why I Write', *Collected Essays, Journalism and Letters, Vol. One.*

8. *Enemies of Promise*, p. 159.

9. Ibid.

10. David Pryce-Jones, *Cyril Connolly: Journal and Memoir*, p. 18.

11. Cyril Connolly in the *Sunday Times*, 10 October 1954.

12. *Enemies of Promise*, p. 162.

13. Ibid., p. 163.

14. Undated letter to the Connollys (Tulsa).

Chapter Two

1. George Orwell, 'Such, Such Were The Joys', *Collected Essays, Journalism and Letters, Vol. Four.*

2. Quoted in Hugo Vickers, *Cecil Beaton*, p. 17.

3. David Ogilvy, *Blood, Brains and Beer: An Autobiography.*

4. Quoted in Michael Shelden, *Orwell*, p. 32.

5. W. H. J. Christie, 'St Cyprian's Days', *Blackwood's Magazine*, May 1971.

6. Connolly Family Record Book (Tulsa).

7. In a letter to Cyril Connolly, 14 December 1938 (Orwell Archive, UCL).

8. *Enemies of Promise*, p. 179.

9. In a letter to Cyril Connolly, 14 December 1938 (Orwell Archive, UCL).

10. Quoted in Bernard Crick, *George Orwell*, p. 42.

11. Quoted in Hugo Vickers, *Cecil Beaton*, p. 17.

12. Cecil Beaton, *The Wandering Years*, p. 29.

13. Gavin Maxwell, *The House of Elrig*, Longman, London 1965.

14. Orwell's comments and the poems are preserved in the Orwell Archive, UCL.

15. *St Cyprian's Chronicle*, Christmas 1916.

16. David Pryce-Jones, *Cyril Connolly: Journal and Memoir*, p. 33.

PART II: GRATEFUL SCIENCE

Chapter Three

1. Lord Gladwyn, *The Memoirs of Lord Gladwyn*, p. 10.

2. Dadie Rylands in conversation with the author, 19 March 1992.

3. *Enemies of Promise*, p. 198.

4. David Pryce-Jones, *Cyril Connolly: Journal and Memoir*, p. 35.

5. School report, Michaelmas term 1918 (Tulsa).

6. *Enemies of Promise*, p. 183.
7. Ibid., p. 187.
8. Ibid., p. 196.
9. School report, Michaelmas term 1919 (Tulsa).
10. In a letter to the Connollys, 6 April 1920 (Tulsa).
11. *Enemies of Promise*, p. 204.
12. George Orwell, 'Inside The Whale', *Collected Essays*, p. 132.
13. Cyril Connolly, in BBC TV's 'George Orwell', November 1965.
14. Steven Runciman in conversation with the author, 12 March 1992.
15. Cyril Connolly in the *Sunday Times*, 16 March 1958.
16. Dadie Rylands in conversation with the author, 19 March 1992.
17. David Pryce-Jones, *Cyril Connolly: Journal and Memoir*, p. 38.
18. Quoted in Bernard Crick, *George Orwell*, p. 54.

Chapter Four

1. Anthony Powell, *To Keep the Ball Rolling*, p. 57.
2. John Lehmann, *The Whispering Gallery*, p. 97.
3. Orwell's note is contained in an undated letter from Cyril Connolly to Terence Beddard (Tulsa).
4. In a letter to Noël Blakiston written 4 January 1927 and reproduced in *A Romantic Friendship*, p. 207.
5. *Enemies of Promise*, p. 250.
6. Quoted in Bernard Crick, *George Orwell*, p. 50.
7. From a diary kept by William Le Fanu (Tulsa).
8. *Enemies of Promise*, p. 228.
9. Ibid., p. 235.
10. Cyril Connolly in the *Sunday Times*, 12 May 1957.
11. In a letter to Cyril Connolly, 8 June 1922 (Tulsa).
12. *Enemies of Promise*, p. 252.
13. Ibid., p. 270.
14. Anthony Powell, *To Keep the Ball Rolling*, p. 58.
15. Harold Acton, *Memoirs of an Aesthete*, p. 97.
16. *Times Literary Supplement*, 20 April 1922.
17. *Enemies of Promise*, p. 265.
18. Undated letter to Noël Blakiston (Tulsa).
19. Undated letter to Cyril Connolly (Tulsa).
20. Cyril Connolly in the *Sunday Times*, 13 February 1972.

Chapter Five

1. Peter Quennell, *The Marble Foot*, p. 122.
2. David Pryce-Jones, *Cyril Connolly: Journal and Memoir*, p. 58.
3. In an undated letter to William Le Fanu (Tulsa).
4. David Pryce-Jones, *Cyril Connolly: Journal and Memoir*, p. 64.
5. From a notebook of Cyril Connolly's (Austin).
6. Kenneth Clark, *Another Part of the Wood*, p. 95.
7. *ADAM*, 1974–5, p. 27.
8. 'Going Down Well', *Harper's and Queen*, June 1973.
9. Cyril Connolly in an interview with W. Hardcastle, BBC Radio, August 1973.
10. 'Going Down Well', *Harper's and Queen*, June 1973.
11. Dadie Rylands in conversation with the author, 19 March 1992.
12. Noël Annan, *Our Age*, p. 129.
13. Cyril Connolly in the *Sunday Times*, 10 August 1952.
14. Maurice Bowra, *Memories*, p. 158.
15. Anthony Powell, *To Keep the Ball Rolling*, p. 100.
16. In a letter to William Le Fanu, February 1924 (Tulsa).
17. In an undated letter to Patrick Balfour (Tulsa).
18. In a letter to Robert Longden, 23 July 1923 (Tulsa).
19. Cyril Connolly, 'The Twenties', *The Evening Colonnade*.
20. In a letter to Cyril Connolly, 9 March 1923 (Tulsa).
21. In a letter to Noël Blakiston, 21 April 1927, *A Romantic Friendship*, p. 295.
22. Peter Quennell, *The Marble Foot*, p. 118.
23. In a letter to Noël Blakiston, December 1924, *A Romantic Friendship*, p. 32.
24. David Pryce-Jones, *Cyril Connolly: Journal and Memoir*, p. 70.
25. In a letter to Robert Longden, 26 December 1923 (Tulsa).
26. Cyril Connolly, 'When Frontiers Fell Like Ninepins', *The Evening Colonnade*.
27. Ibid.
28. Ibid.
29. David Pryce-Jones, *Cyril Connolly: Journal and Memoir*, p. 61.
30. Quoted in John Pearson, *Façades*, p. 189.
31. In an undated letter to Patrick Balfour (Huntington Library, Pasadena).
32. Cyril Connolly in the *Sunday Times*, 13 July 1958.
33. In a letter to Cyril Connolly, 3 August [1925] (Tulsa).
34. A testimonial dated 8 October 1925 (Tulsa).

35. In a letter to Cyril Connolly, 16 November 1925 (Tulsa).
36. From a notebook of Cyril Connolly's (Tulsa).

PART III: MANDARINS ON THE THAMES AT CHELSEA

Chapter Six

1. In an undated letter to Noël Blakiston [January 1926], *A Romantic Friendship*, p. 110.
2. David D'Costa in a letter to the author, 16 September 1992.
3. In an undated letter to Noël Blakiston [January 1926], *A Romantic Friendship*, p. 115.
4. Ibid.
5. Cyril Connolly in the *New Statesman*, 25 August 1928.
6. From a notebook of Cyril Connolly's (Tulsa).
7. In an undated letter to Noël Blakiston [March or April 1926], *A Romantic Friendship*, p. 118.
8. The letters to Robert Longden and Dorothy Brandon are quoted in David Pryce-Jones, *Cyril Connolly: Journal and Memoir*, pp. 84 and 83 respectively.
9. In a letter to Noël Blakiston, 26 July 1926, *A Romantic Friendship*, p. 154.
10. In an undated letter to Cyril Connolly (Tulsa).
11. Robert Gathorne-Hardy, *Recollections of Logan Pearsall Smith*, p. 10.
12. Quoted in Barbara Strachey, *Remarkable Relations*, p. 163.
13. The remarks by Beatrice Webb and Pearsall Smith are quoted in John Russell, *A Portrait of Logan Pearsall Smith*, pp. 7 and 108.
14. *The Diary of Virginia Woolf, Vol. IV, 1931–1935.*
15. Kenneth Clark, *Another Part of the Wood*, p. 145.
16. In a letter to Cyril Connolly, 1 August 1926 (Tulsa).
17. In a letter to Noël Blakiston, July 1926, *A Romantic Friendship*, p. 149.
18. Cecil Beaton, *The Wandering Years*, p. 145.
19. In a letter to Cyril Connolly, 21 November 1926 (Tulsa).
20. In a letter to Cyril Connolly, 24 April 1927 (Tulsa).
21. Quoted in Michael Holroyd, *Lytton Strachey*, p. 228.
22. From a notebook of Cyril Connolly's (Tulsa).
23. Cyril Connolly in the *Sunday Times*, 25 January 1959.
24. In an undated letter to Patrick Balfour (Huntington Library, Pasadena).
25. Cyril Connolly in the *Sunday Times*, 19 March 1967.

26. Quoted in *Lady Ottoline's Album*, ed. Carolyn G. Heilbrun and introduced by Lord David Cecil, Knopf, New York, 1976, p. 102.
27. Quoted in Hugh and Mirabel Cecil, *Clever Hearts*, p. 188.
28. In a letter to Noël Blakiston, 25 December 1926, *A Romantic Friendship*, p. 201.
29. In an undated letter to Denis Dannreuther (Tulsa).
30. In a letter to Noël Blakiston, November 1926, *A Romantic Friendship*, p. 195.
31. In a letter to Noël Blakiston, 25 January 1927, *A Romantic Friendship*, p. 225.
32. Frances Partridge in conversation with the author, 28 November 1991.
33. In an undated letter to Cyril Connolly (Tulsa).

Chapter Seven

1. In a letter to Noël Blakiston, 7 March 1927, *A Romantic Friendship*, p. 281.
2. Quoted in Harold Hobson, Philip Knightley and Leonard Russell, *The Pearl of Days*, p. 182.
3. Cyril Connolly, 'Distress of Plenty', *The Condemned Playground*.
4. Cyril Connolly in the *Sunday Times*, 20 August 1972.
5. David Pryce-Jones, *Cyril Connolly: Journal and Memoir*, p. 149.
6. Both Molly MacCarthy's remarks are quoted in Hugh and Mirabel Cecil, *Clever Hearts*, p. 230.
7. Cyril Connolly in the *Sunday Times*, 21 April 1963.
8. In a letter to Patrick Balfour, May 1927 (Huntington Library, Pasadena).
9. Cyril Connolly in the *New Statesman*, 3 September 1927.
10. Cyril Connolly in the *New Statesman*, 17 September 1927.
11. Cyril Connolly in the *New Statesman*, 7 January 1928.
12. Cyril Connolly in the *New Statesman*, 25 August 1928.
13. Cyril Connolly in the *New Statesman*, 19 January 1929.
14. In a letter to Cyril Connolly, 2 January 1927 (Tulsa).
15. In a letter to Cyril Connolly, August 1928 (Tulsa).
16. Cyril Connolly in the *New Statesman*, 18 August 1928.
17. In an undated letter to Patrick Balfour (Huntington Library, Pasadena).
18. In an undated letter to Cyril Connolly [July 1927] (Huntington Library, Pasadena).
19. His description of Chelsea occurs in his introduction to *The Condemned Playground*.
20. In an undated letter to Cyril Connolly [June/July 1927] (Huntington Library, Pasadena).

21. Ibid.
22. Giana Blakiston in conversation with the author, 22 November 1991.
23. 'From John Betjeman to Cyril Connolly', the *London Magazine*, August/ September 1973.
24. From a notebook of Cyril Connolly's (Austin).
25. Cyril Connolly in the *Sunday Times*, 11 August 1968.
26. Cyril Connolly in the *Sunday Times*, 26 June 1966.
27. David Pryce-Jones, *Cyril Connolly: Journal and Memoir*, p. 131.
28. Cyril Connolly, 'One of My Londons', *Previous Convictions*.
29. Quoted in Marie-Jaqueline Lancaster, *Brian Howard: Portrait of a Failure*, p. 253.
30. Quoted in Anthony Powell, *To Keep the Ball Rolling*, p. 64.
31. In a letter to Cyril Connolly, 26 January 1928 (Tulsa).
32. In a letter to Cyril Connolly, 27 November [no year] (Tulsa).
33. In an undated letter to Patrick Balfour (Huntington Library, Pasadena).
34. David Pryce-Jones, *Cyril Connolly: Journal and Memoir*, p. 163.
35. Ibid, p. 143.
36. Quoted in Lord Gladwyn, *The Memoirs of Lord Gladwyn*, p. 35.
37. David Pryce-Jones, *Cyril Connolly: Journal and Memoir*, p. 146.
38. Cyril Connolly in the *New Statesman*, 3 November 1928.
39. In an interview with Naim Attallah, *Singular Encounters*, p. 7.
40. Cyril Connolly in an interview with the BBC, reprinted in the *Listener*, 24 August 1967.

Chapter Eight

1. David Pryce-Jones, *Cyril Connolly: Journal and Memoir*, p. 147.
2. Raymond Mortimer, 'Survivor of a Vanishing Species', the *London Magazine*, August/September 1973.
3. In an undated letter to Cyril Connolly (Tulsa).
4. George Beaton (Gerald Brenan), *Jack Robinson: A Picaresque Novel*, Chatto and Windus, London, 1933, p. 207.
5. In a letter to Cyril Connolly, 17 August 1928 (Tulsa).
6. In an undated letter to Cyril Connolly (Tulsa).
7. David Pryce-Jones, *Cyril Connolly: Journal and Memoir*, p. 196.
8. Ibid., p. 200.
9. Ibid., p. 201.
10. Cyril Connolly, *The Unquiet Grave*, p. 118 (Hamish Hamilton revised edition).
11. In a letter to Cyril Connolly, 28 March 1929 (Tulsa).

12. Cyril Connolly, 'Memories of André Gide'. Corrected proof copy, *ADAM*, *ADAM* Archive, King's College, London.
13. David Pryce-Jones, *Cyril Connolly: Journal and Memoir*, p. 120.
14. Ibid., p. 208.
15. In a letter to Cyril Connolly, 4 July 1929 (Tulsa).
16. David Pryce-Jones, *Cyril Connolly: Journal and Memoir*, p. 222.
17. In an undated letter from Cyril Connolly (Tulsa).
18. 'Ninety Years of Novel-Reviewing', *The Condemned Playground*, p. 90 (Hogarth Press edition, 1985).
19. Quoted by Cyril Connolly in the *Sunday Times*, 28 October 1973.
20. In a letter to Cyril Connolly, 11 July 1929 (Tulsa).
21. David Pryce-Jones, *Cyril Connolly: Journal and Memoir*, p. 214.
22. Sybille Bedford, from 'Memories of Cyril Connolly: A Recorded Discussion at the P.E.N. Club', 13 June 1984 (National Sound Archive).
23. In a letter to Cyril Connolly, 11 June 1929 (Tulsa).
24. In a letter to Cyril Connolly, 11 July 1929 (Tulsa).
25. Cyril Connolly, *The Unquiet Grave*, p. 109.
26. David Pryce-Jones, *Cyril Connolly: Journal and Memoir*, p. 122.
27. In an undated letter from Robert Longden (Tulsa).
28. In a letter from Logan Pearsall Smith, 25 October 1929 (Tulsa).
29. Giana Blakiston in conversation with the author, 22 November 1991.
30. In a letter to Noël Blakiston, November 1929, *A Romantic Friendship*, p. 327.
31. In a letter to Jean, 19 October [1929] (Tulsa).
32. In a letter to Cyril Connolly, 7 June 1929 (Tulsa).
33. In a postcard to Cyril Connolly, 25 October [1930] (Tulsa).
34. In a letter to Noël Blakiston, 2 April 1930, *A Romantic Friendship*, p. 337.

PART IV: CONDEMNED PLAYGROUNDS

Chapter Nine

1. David Pryce-Jones, *Cyril Connolly: Journal and Memoir*, p. 275.
2. Sybille Bedford, *Aldous Huxley*, vol. I, p. 262.
3. Cyril Connolly discussing the career of Aldous Huxley on BBC Radio, 17 August 1964 (National Sound Archive).
4. Cyril Connolly in the *Sunday Times*, 2 April 1972.
5. 'Memories of Cyril Connolly: A Recorded Discussion at the P.E.N. Club', 13 June 1984 (National Sound Archive).

6. David Pryce-Jones, *Cyril Connolly: Journal and Memoir*, p. 241.
7. In a letter to Cyril Connolly, 16 September 1930 (Tulsa).
8. In an undated letter to Cyril Connolly (Tulsa).
9. David Pryce-Jones, *Cyril Connolly: Journal and Memoir*, p. 239.
10. Cyril Connolly, *The Unquiet Grave*, p. 110.
11. Evelyn Waugh, *Diaries*, p. 55.
12. David Pryce-Jones, *Cyril Connolly: Journal and Memoir*, p. 242.
13. Anthony Powell, *To Keep the Ball Rolling*, p. 144.
14. Giana Blakiston in conversation with the author, 22 November 1991.
15. Mary Lutyens in conversation with the author, 29 January 1992.
16. David Pryce-Jones, *Cyril Connolly: Journal and Memoir*, p. 247.
17. Quoted in Stephen Spender, *Journals*, p. 390.
18. Quoted in Christopher Sykes, *Evelyn Waugh*, p. 120.
19. Alan Pryce-Jones, *The Bonus of Laughter*, p. 84.
20. Peter Quennell, *The Marble Foot*, p. 220.
21. Cyril Connolly, *The Unquiet Grave*, p. 3.
22. David Pryce-Jones, *Cyril Connolly: Journal and Memoir*, p. 278.
23. In a letter to Cyril Connolly, 17 June 1933 (Tulsa).
24. In an undated letter to Cyril Connolly (Tulsa).
25. Giana Blakiston in conversation with the author, 22 November 1991.

Chapter Ten

1. Cyril Connolly, 'Spring Revolution', *The Condemned Playground*.
2. In a letter to Cyril Connolly, 17 June 1933 (Tulsa).
3. In a letter to Enid Bagnold, 8 September 1933 (Tulsa).
4. 'Te Palinure Petens', *ADAM*, 1974–5, p. 44.
5. David Gascoyne, from 'Memories of Cyril Connolly: A Recorded Discussion at the P.E.N. Club', 13 June 1984 (National Sound Archive).
6. David Pryce-Jones, *Cyril Connolly: Journal and Memoir*, p. 244.
7. Ibid., p. 242.
8. Christopher Sykes, *Evelyn Waugh*, p. 138.
9. In a letter to Vanessa Bell, 4 May 1934, *The Letters of Virginia Woolf*, vol. V, p. 299.
10. Peter Quennell in the introduction to *The Rock Pool* (OUP, 1981).
11. David Pryce-Jones, *Cyril Connolly: Journal and Memoir*, p. 269.
12. Cyril Connolly in the *New Statesman*, 16 February 1935.
13. Cyril Connolly in the *New Statesman*, 13 April 1935.
14. Cyril Connolly in the *New Statesman*, 4 May 1935.
15. In a letter to Cyril Connolly, 9 May 1935 (Tulsa).

16. In a letter to Cyril Connolly, 29 May 1935 (Tulsa).
17. Cyril Connolly in the *New Statesman*, 6 July 1935.
18. Quoted in Michael Shelden, *Orwell*, p. 233.
19. Anthony Powell, *To Keep the Ball Rolling*, p. 66.
20. Malcolm Muggeridge, *Like It Was*, p. 330.
21. Cyril Connolly in the *New Statesman*, 27 April 1935.
22. Cyril Connolly in the *New Statesman*, 1 June 1935.
23. Cyril Connolly in the *New Statesman*, 8 June 1935.
24. Cyril Connolly in the *Daily Telegraph*, 17 December 1935.
25. Cyril Connolly in the *New Statesman*, 15 February 1936.
26. Cyril Connolly in the *New Statesman*, 29 February 1936.
27. In a letter to Lawrence Durrell, October 1935, *The Durrell–Miller Letters, 1935–1980*, ed. Ian S. MacNiven.
28. Cyril Connolly, 'The Novel-Addict's Cupboard', *The Condemned Playground*.

Chapter Eleven

1. David Pryce-Jones, *Cyril Connolly: Journal and Memoir*, p. 267.
2. From Cyril Connolly's introduction to *The Rock Pool*.
3. In an undated letter to Sylvia Beach (Rare Books and Manuscripts, Princeton University Library).
4. Cyril Connolly, 'Postscript 1946', *The Rock Pool*.
5. Quoted in David Pryce-Jones, *Cyril Connolly: Journal and Memoir*, p. 267.
6. Quoted in 'Advance and be Recognized', an unpublished essay by Robin McDouall (courtesy of Auberon Waugh).
7. Ibid.
8. In a letter to Maud Connolly, 7 December 1935 (Tulsa).
9. Ibid.
10. David Pryce-Jones, *Cyril Connolly: Journal and Memoir*, p. 271.
11. Anthony Powell, *To Keep the Ball Rolling*, p. 232.
12. Quoted in Paul Ferris, *Dylan Thomas*, p. 131.
13. Cyril Connolly in the *New Statesman*, 8 February 1936.
14. Cyril Connolly in the *New Statesman*, 25 April 1936.
15. In an undated letter to George Orwell (Tulsa).
16. George Orwell in *New English Weekly*, 23 July 1936.
17. Desmond MacCarthy in the *Sunday Times*, 23 August 1936.
18. In a letter to Cyril Connolly, 21 March 1938 (Tulsa).
19. In a letter to Cyril Connolly, 3 June 1936 (Tulsa).

20. Reproduced in Cyril Connolly, 'A. E. Housman: A Controversy', *The Condemned Playground*.

21. Noël Annan, *Our Age*, p. 149.

22. In a letter to Princess Bibesco belonging to Eton College and quoted in the exhibition catalogue 'The Last Two Hundred Years', Eton, 1984.

23. Quoted in Marie-Jaqueline Lancaster, *Brian Howard: Portrait of a Failure*, p. 197.

24. Cyril Connolly in an interview with T. G. Rosenthal on BBC Radio's Third Programme, broadcast 21 January 1964 (National Sound Archive).

25. In a letter to Cyril Connolly, 28 October 1937 (Tulsa).

26. Quoted in Marie-Jaqueline Lancaster, *Brian Howard: Portrait of a Failure*, p. 198.

27. Quoted in ibid., p. 199.

28. *Enemies of Promise*, p. 119.

Chapter Twelve

1. Henry d'Avigdor-Goldsmid, 'Du Côté de chez Connolly', *ADAM*, 1974–5, p. 34.

2. Peggy Strachey in a letter to the author, 3 April 1992.

3. In an undated letter to Peggy Strachey (private collection).

4. Peggy Strachey in a letter to the author, 3 April 1992.

5. From a notebook of Cyril Connolly's (Austin).

6. Cyril Connolly in the *New Statesman*, 5 June 1937.

7. Cyril Connolly, 'Barcelona', *The Condemned Playground*.

8. Ibid.

9. Cyril Connolly, 'Some Memories', *W. H. Auden: A Tribute*.

10. In an undated letter to Peggy Strachey (private collection).

11. Cyril Connolly in the *New Statesman*, 16 January 1937.

12. Cyril Connolly, 'Louis MacNeice: A Radio Portrait', typescript proof, 7 September 1966 (Berg Collection).

13. In a letter to Virginia Woolf, 2 April [1937] (Berg Collection).

14. In a letter to Cyril Connolly, 16 June 1937 (Tulsa).

15. In a letter to Cyril Connolly, 8 June 1937 (Orwell Archive, UCL).

16. In a letter to Cyril Connolly, 12 October 1937 (Orwell Archive, UCL).

17. Cyril Connolly, 'The Fate of an Elizabethan', *The Condemned Playground*.

18. Cyril Connolly in the *New Statesman*, 6 March 1937.

19. For a fuller account see Cyril Connolly in the *Sunday Times*, 18 June 1967.

20. Cyril Connolly, 'Some Memories', *W. H. Auden: A Tribute*.

21. David Pryce-Jones, *Cyril Connolly: Journal and Memoir*, p. 283.

22. Peggy Strachey in a letter to the author, 3 April 1992.
23. Quoted in Victoria Glendinning, *Elizabeth Bowen*, p. 121.
24. In a letter to the Connollys, 19 August 1937 (Tulsa).

Chapter Thirteen
1. In a letter to Cyril Connolly, 1 October 1937 (Reading).
2. Quoted in Michael Shelden, *Orwell*, p. 306.
3. Cyril Connolly to the BBC, BBC LP 3441 (National Sound Archive).
4. In a letter to Routledge, 13 October 1937 (Reading).
5. In a letter to Cyril Connolly, 15 October 1937 (Reading).
6. From a notebook of Cyril Connolly's (Austin).
7. In a letter to Cyril Connolly, 15 December 1937 (Reading).
8. At her request, Diana is referred to in this book by her first name only.
9. Diana in conversation with the author, 20 March 1993.
10. In a letter to Cyril Connolly, 28 January 1938 (Tulsa).
11. In a postcard to Cyril Connolly, 4 February 1938 (Tulsa).
12. In a letter to Cyril Connolly, 14 March 1938 (Orwell Archive, UCL).
13. In a letter to Routledge, 12 June 1938 (Reading).
14. In a letter to Cyril Connolly, 8 July 1938 (Orwell Archive, UCL).
15. Peggy Strachey in a letter to the author, 3 April 1992.
16. In a letter to Cyril Connolly, 12 August 1938 (Reading).
17. In an undated letter to Jean Connolly (Tulsa).
18. Desmond MacCarthy in the *Sunday Times*, 6 November 1938.
19. Harold Nicolson in the *Daily Telegraph*, 11 November 1938.
20. James Agate in the *Daily Express*, 17 November 1938.
21. Ralph Wright in the *Daily Worker*, 23 November 1938.
22. *Punch*, 30 November 1938.
23. Q. D. Leavis, 'The Background of Twentieth-century Letters', *Scrutiny*, June 1939.
24. Evelyn Waugh in the *Tablet*, 3 December 1938.
25. In a letter to Cyril Connolly, 15 November 1938 (Tulsa).
26. In a letter to Cyril Connolly, 17 February 1941 (Tulsa).
27. In a letter to Cyril Connolly, 10 September 1944 (Tulsa).
28. In a letter to Cyril Connolly, 10 November 1938 (Tulsa).
29. 22 November 1938, from *A Moment's Liberty*, ed. Anne Olivier Bell.
30. Compton Mackenzie, *My Life and Times, Octave Eight*.
31. In a letter to Cyril Connolly, 29 October 1938 (Tulsa).
32. In a letter to Cyril Connolly, 8 December 1938 (Tulsa).
33. In a letter to Cyril Connolly, 14 December 1938 (Orwell Archive, UCL).

34. Valentine Cunningham, *British Writers of the Thirties*, p. 132.
35. In a letter to Cyril Connolly, 9 December 1938 (Reading).
36. 'Memories of Cyril Connolly: A Recorded Discussion at the P.E.N. Club', 13 June 1984.
37. In a letter to Routledge, 17 May 1939 (Reading).
38. In a letter to Routledge, 11 April 1939 (Reading).
39. In a letter to Cyril Connolly, 15 May 1939 (Tulsa).
40. *The Unquiet Grave*, p. 83.
41. In a letter to Jean Connolly, 10 July 1939 (Tulsa).
42. In a letter to Cyril Connolly, 15 July 1939 (Tulsa).
43. In a letter to Jean Connolly, 18 July 1939 (Tulsa).
44. Cyril Connolly in the *New Statesman*, 15 July 1939.
45. Cyril Connolly in the *New Statesman*, 12 August 1939.
46. Cyril Connolly in the *New Statesman*, 22 July 1939.
47. Cyril Connolly in the *New Statesman*, 12 August 1939.

PART V: THE IVORY SHELTER

Chapter Fourteen

1. In a letter to Cyril Connolly, 17 August [1939] (Tulsa).
2. In an undated letter to Jean Connolly (Tulsa).
3. Alan Pryce-Jones, *The Bonus of Laughter*, p. 28.
4. Cecil Beaton, *The Wandering Years*, p. 270.
5. Quoted in Hugo Vickers, *Cecil Beaton*, p. 148.
6. Quoted in Marie-Jaqueline Lancaster, *Brian Howard: Portrait of a Failure*, p. 450.
7. Evelyn Waugh, *Diaries*, p. 451.
8. John Lehmann, *I Am My Brother*, p. 42.
9. Stephen Spender, *Journals*, p. 41.
10. Cyril Connolly, 'Little Magazines', *The Evening Colonnade*, p. 425,
11. Tony Witherby in conversation with the author, 9 January 1992.
12. Quoted in Robert Hewison, *Under Siege*, p. 23.
13. George Orwell, 'Inside The Whale', *Collected Essays*, p. 157.
14. In a letter to Cyril Connolly, 1 November 1939 (Tulsa).
15. In a letter to Cyril Connolly, 19 October 1939 (Tulsa).
16. Cyril Connolly in the *New Statesman*, 7 October 1939.
17. Stephen Spender, *The Thirties and After*, p. 87.
18. In a letter to Maud Connolly, 14 October 1939 (Tulsa).

19. In a letter to Cyril Connolly, 8 November 1939 (Tulsa).
20. The *New Statesman*, 16 December 1939.
21. 'William Hickey', the *Daily Express*, 22 December 1939.
22. Quoted in Michael Shelden, *Cyril Connolly*, p. 41.
23. Stephen Spender, *World Within World*, p. 293.
24. 'Comment', *Horizon*, January 1940.

Chapter Fifteen

1. 'The Ant-Lion', *Horizon*, January 1940.
2. In a letter to Cyril Connolly, 3 March [1940] (Tulsa).
3. Quoted in Humphrey Carpenter, *W. H. Auden*, p. 291.
4. In an undated, unaddressed letter from Peter Watson (Tulsa).
5. Quoted in Bernard Crick, *George Orwell*, p. 171.
6. Cyril Connolly in the *Sunday Times*, 11 March 1956.
7. 'Comment', *Horizon*, December 1942.
8. Julian Maclaren-Ross, *Memoirs of the Forties*, p. 62.
9. Ibid., p. 75.
10. Stephen Spender, *World Within World*, p. 295.
11. Stephen Spender, *The Thirties and After*, p. 87.
12. Stephen Spender, *World Within World*, p. 292.
13. Diana in conversation with the author, 20 March 1993.
14. In a letter to Cyril Connolly, 15 January 1940 (Tulsa).
15. Diana in conversation with the author, 20 March 1993.
16. In a letter to Cyril Connolly, 29 February 1940 (Tulsa).
17. In a letter to Cyril Connolly, 26 March 1940 (Tulsa).
18. In an undated letter to Jean Connolly (Tulsa).
19. In a letter to Cyril Connolly, 10 June 1940 (Tulsa).
20. In a letter to Cyril Connolly, 14 June 1940 (Tulsa).
21. 'My long dark lovely thinking one' (Tulsa).

Chapter Sixteen

1. *Collected Essays, Journalism and Letters of George Orwell*, Vol. Two, p. 400, 20 June 1940.
2. 'Comment', *Horizon*, May 1940.
3. 'Comment', *Horizon*, July 1940.
4. In a letter to Cyril Connolly, 6 July 1940 (Tulsa).
5. *Collected Essays, Journalism and Letters of George Orwell*, Vol. Two, p. 400, 8 April 1941.
6. Cyril Connolly in the *New Statesman*, 30 November 1940.

7. In a letter to Cyril Connolly as editor of *Horizon*, 17 December 1940 (original copy, Berg Collection).

8. Diana in conversation with the author, 20 March 1993.

9. Quoted by Stephen Spender in the *Sunday Times*, 19 February 1989.

10. Quoted in Michael Shelden, 'Broken Reel: Lys Lubbock and Cyril Connolly', *London Magazine*, June/July 1993.

11. Liza Mann in conversation with the author, 28 June 1992.

12. Barbara Skelton, *Tears Before Bedtime*, p. 40.

13. Cyril Connolly in the *New Statesman*, 18 January 1941.

14. John Lehmann, *I Am My Brother*, p. 105.

15. Clement Greenberg in conversation with the author, 28 October 1991.

16. Quoted in John Pikoulis, *Alun Lewis*, p. 126.

17. In a letter to Cyril Connolly, 17 February 1941 (Tulsa).

18. In a letter to Cyril Connolly, 27 February 1941 (Tulsa).

19. John Lehmann, *I Am My Brother*, p. 188.

Chapter Seventeen

1. In a letter to Cyril Connolly, 9 February 1941 (Koestler Archive, Edinburgh University Library).

2. 'Koestler at Sixty Talks to Cyril Connolly', the *Sunday Times*, 19 September 1965.

3. Cyril Connolly in the *Sunday Times*, 26 October 1952.

4. Cyril Connolly, 'Sotheby's as an Education', *Sotheby's 217th Season*, Sotheby, London, 1960.

5. For a fuller account see Cyril Connolly in the *Sunday Times*, 29 March 1964.

6. 'Comment', *Horizon*, January 1942.

7. Quoted in Michael Shelden, *Cyril Connolly*, p. 86.

8. In a letter to Cyril Connolly, 21 July 1941 (Tulsa).

9. Stephen Spender, *Journals*, p. 433.

10. Liza Mann in conversation with the author, 28 June 1992.

11. Quoted in Michael Shelden, *Orwell*, p. 448.

12. Woodrow Wyatt, *Confessions of an Optimist*, p. 88.

13. Quoted in Michael Shelden, *Cyril Connolly*, p. 82.

14. 'Comment', *Horizon*, February 1943.

15. Cyril Connolly in the *Sunday Times*, 15 March 1953.

Chapter Eighteen

1. David Astor in conversation with the author, 17 January 1992. Regarding

Connolly's mimicry of Koestler, Tosco Fyvel was a journalist and General Wavell was the hero of the Libyan campaign.

2. David Astor in conversation with the author, 17 January 1992.
3. Peter Quennell, *The Wanton Chase*, p. 21.
4. In an undated note to Cyril Connolly (Tulsa).
5. Woodrow Wyatt, *Confessions of an Optimist*, p. 88.
6. In a letter to Cyril Connolly, 23 April 1942 (Tulsa).
7. In a letter to Cyril Connolly, 1 July 1942 (Tulsa).
8. In a letter to Cyril Connolly, September 1942 (Orwell Archive, UCL).
9. Quoted in Michael Shelden, *Cyril Connolly*, p. 104.
10. In an undated letter to Cyril Connolly (Orwell Archive, UCL).
11. In an undated letter to Cyril Connolly (Tulsa).
12. In a letter to Cyril Connolly, 20 August 1943 (Tulsa).
13. David Astor in conversation with the author, 17 January 1992.
14. Cyril Connolly in the *Observer*, 5 September 1943.
15. Cyril Connolly, 'Literature in the Nineteen-Thirties', BBC Radio, broadcast 31 March 1942.
16. Stephen Spender, *The Thirties and After*, p. 87.
17. In a letter to Cyril Connolly, 16 March 1942 (Tulsa).
18. Tom Pain in conversation with the author, 15 January 1992.
19. In an undated letter to Cyril Connolly (Tulsa).
20. Cyril Connolly, *The Unquiet Grave*, introduction to the second revised edition, Hamish Hamilton, London, 1951.
21. In a letter to Cyril Connolly, 19 October 1942 (Tulsa).
22. Peter Quennell in conversation with the author, 20 November 1991.
23. In a letter to Cyril Connolly, 25 March 1943 (Tulsa).
24. In a letter to Routledge, 1 January 1943 (Reading).
25. In an undated letter to Routledge (Reading).
26. Cyril Connolly, 'French and English Cultural Relations', *The Condemned Playground*.
27. Arthur Koestler in *Tribune*, 26 November 1943.

Chapter Nineteen

1. Evelyn Waugh, *Letters*, p. 169.
2. Cyril Connolly, *The Unquiet Grave*, pp. 85–6.
3. Quoted in Kenneth S. Lynn, *Hemingway*, p. 510.
4. In a letter to Cyril Connolly, 15 March 1948 (Tulsa).
5. *The Diaries and Letters of Harold Nicolson, 1930–39*, p. 388.
6. Cyril Connolly, *The Unquiet Grave*, p. 137.

7. Ibid., p. 1.
8. Ibid., p. 24.
9. Ibid., p. 60.
10. Ibid., p. 70.
11. Ibid., p. 124.
12. Quoted in James King, *The Last Modern*, p. 220.
13. Gavin Ewart, 'Cyril Connolly', the *London Magazine*, December 1963.
14. In a letter to Cyril Connolly, 2 October 1951 (Tulsa).
15. In a letter to Cyril Connolly, 6 January 1945 (Tulsa).
16. In a letter to Cyril Connolly, 11 January 1946 (Tulsa).
17. In a letter to Cyril Connolly, 10 December 1945 (Tulsa).
18. Edmund Wilson in the *New Yorker*, 27 October 1945.
19. Elizabeth Bowen in the *Tatler*, 3 January 1945.
20. Raymond Mortimer in the *New Statesman*, 30 December 1944.
21. George Orwell in the *Observer*, 14 January 1945.
22. Quoted in Alan Bell, 'Waugh Drops The Pilot', the *Spectator*, 7 March 1987.

Chapter Twenty

1. In a letter to Cyril Connolly, 22 October 1944 (King's College, Cambridge).
2. Quoted in Michael Shelden, *Cyril Connolly*, p. 122.
3. *Mr Wu and Mrs Stitch*, ed. Artemis Cooper, p. 81.
4. 'Comment', *Horizon*, May 1945.
5. 'Comment', *Horizon*, November 1945.
6. 'Comment', *Horizon*, May 1945.
7. The replies by Sitwell, Greene, Bell and Lehmann are all housed at the Harry Ransom Humanities Research Center.
8. Evelyn Waugh, *Diaries*, p. 627.
9. Quoted in Victoria Glendinning, *Elizabeth Bowen*, p. 158.
10. Quoted in ibid., p. 173.
11. Evelyn Waugh, *Diaries*, p. 625.
12. Edmund Wilson in the *New Yorker*, 27 October 1945.
13. Quoted in Selina Hastings, *Nancy Mitford*, p. 158.
14. Quoted in Martin Stannard, *Evelyn Waugh*, vol. II, p. 172.
15. Quoted in ibid., vol. I, p. 499.
16. In a letter to Cyril Connolly, 2 April 1945 (Tulsa).
17. Frances Partridge, *Everything to Lose*, p. 19.
18. Ibid., p. 28.
19. John Craxton in conversation with the author, 7 January 1993.

PART VI: HIGHBROWS AND LOWBROWS

Chapter Twenty-one
1. 'Comment', *Horizon*, June 1945.
2. Quoted in Marie-Jaqueline Lancaster, *Brian Howard: Portrait of a Failure*, p. 473.
3. Evelyn Waugh, *Diaries*, p. 655.
4. Quoted in Martin Stannard, *Evelyn Waugh*, vol. II, p. 172.
5. Quoted in Michael Shelden, *Cyril Connolly*, p. 133.
6. 'Comment', *Horizon*, September 1945.
7. 'Comment', *Horizon*, February 1946.
8. Quoted in Michael Shelden, *Cyril Connolly*, p. 144.
9. In a letter to Cyril Connolly, 5 October [1945] (Tulsa).
10. Quoted in Marie-Jaqueline Lancaster, *Brian Howard: Portrait of a Failure*, p. 490.
11. In an undated letter to John Piper (Myfanwy Piper).
12. Cyril Connolly, 'Introduction', *The Condemned Playground*.
13. In a letter to Cyril Connolly, 28 December 1945 (Tulsa).
14. Julian Symons in a letter to the author, 29 February 1992.
15. In a letter to Cyril Connolly, 16 November 1945 (Tulsa).
16. Jacqueline Hélion in a letter to the author, 27 March 1992.
17. In a letter to Cyril Connolly, 7 April 1947 (Tulsa).
18. Cyril Connolly in the *Sunday Times*, 18 March 1956.
19. In a letter to Arthur Koestler, 10 February 1946 (Koestler Archive, Edinburgh University Library).
20. In a letter to Cyril Connolly, 27 May 1946. (Hamish Hamilton Archive, Bristol University Library).
21. Quoted in Michael Shelden, *Cyril Connolly*, p. 151.
22. In a letter to Cyril Connolly, 13 March 1946 (Tulsa).
23. In a letter to Cyril Connolly, 9 January 1950 (Tulsa).
24. Responses to the questionnaire 'The Cost of Letters' appeared in *Horizon*, September 1946.
25. *Mr Wu and Mrs Stitch*, ed. Artemis Cooper, p. 92.

Chapter Twenty-two
1. John Craxton in conversation with the author, 7 January 1993.
2. Jacques Barzun in *Atlantic Monthly*, April 1946.
3. 'Introduction', *Horizon*, October 1947.
4. In a letter to Cyril Connolly, 20 December [1947] (Tulsa).

5. 'Introduction', *Horizon*, October 1947.
6. Quoted in Michael Shelden, *Cyril Connolly*, p. 171.
7. Quoted in ibid., p. 164.
8. 'State of Art', the *New Yorker*, 14 December 1947.
9. Quoted in Michael Shelden, *Cyril Connolly*, p. 170.
10. Clement Greenberg in conversation with the author, 28 October 1991.
11. 'Introduction', *Horizon*, October 1947.
12. In a letter to Cyril Connolly, 5 November 1946, *The Letters of Aldous Huxley*, ed. Grover Smith, p. 555.
13. 'A Potter', *Pottery, or Home Made Potted Foods, Meat and Fish Pastes, Savoury Butters and Others*, The Wine and Food Society, 1946.
14. In a letter to Maud Connolly, April 1947 (Tulsa).
15. In a letter to Cyril Connolly, 6 March 1947 (Tulsa).
16. 'Comment', *Horizon*, April 1947.
17. Cyril Connolly, 'Some Memories', *W. H. Auden: A Tribute*, p. 73.
18. Evelyn Waugh, *Diaries*, p. 681.
19. Quoted in Martin Stannard, *Evelyn Waugh: No Abiding City*, p. 199.
20. Ian Mackay, 'Diary', the *News Chronicle*, 26 September 1947.
21. Edmund Wilson, *The Fifties*, p. 107.
22. In a letter to Cyril Connolly, 20 December [1947] (Tulsa).
23. In a letter to Cyril Connolly, 26 December 1947 (Tulsa).
24. Evelyn Waugh, *Letters*, p. 259.
25. Quoted in Martin Stannard, *Evelyn Waugh: No Abiding City*, p. 205.
26. In a letter to Evelyn Waugh, 2 September 1947 (British Library).
27. Evelyn Waugh, *Letters*, p. 262.
28. In a letter to Evelyn Waugh, 1 January 1948 (British Library).
29. In a letter to Evelyn Waugh, 2 February 1948 (British Library).
30. In a letter to Cyril Connolly, 8 February 1948 (Tulsa).
31. In an undated letter to Cyril Connolly (Tulsa).
32. Evelyn Waugh, *Diaries*, p. 694.
33. Evelyn Waugh, *Letters*, p. 270.
34. In a letter to Evelyn Waugh, 1 March 1948 (British Library).
35. In a letter to Evelyn Waugh, 8 September 1948 (courtesy of Auberon Waugh).

Chapter Twenty-three

1. Years later Connolly was intrigued to discover that books of a different sort had preoccupied the apartment: 53 Bedford Square had once been the home of H. S. Ashbee, a successful businessman who had formed an important collection of Cervantic literature as well as the largest pornography library

in Europe. He had adopted the pseudonym 'Pisanus Fraxi', an anagram of 'Fraxinus Apis', 'Ash-bee', and Connolly treasured the rumour that he had left his Cervantic papers to the British Museum on condition that it also accepted his pornographic collection. (For a fuller account, see Cyril Connolly in the *Sunday Times*, 22 January 1967.) As for the chandelier, it went into storage with all the other office furnishings when *Horizon* ceased publication. Eventually, after Watson's death, these objects slowly found their way back into circulation and in the early Seventies John Craxton found Giacometti's chandelier in a shop in Marylebone High Street. Dismantled, stripped of its bronze patina and encumbered with glass globes for the lights, it was still instantly recognizable and he struggled to raise £250 to buy it.

2. 'Comment', *Horizon*, April 1948.
3. Oxford University Writers' Club, society minutes (the Bodleian Library).
4. Quoted in Michael Shelden, *Cyril Connolly*, p. 173.
5. In a letter to Cyril Connolly, 6 September 1973 (Tulsa).
6. Joan Wyndham, *Anything Once*, p. 4
7. Quoted in Michael Shelden, *Cyril Connolly*, p. 192
8. Alan Ross, *Coastwise Lights*, p. 94
9. Quoted in Michael Shelden, *Cyril Connolly*, p. 206.
10. Janetta Parladé in conversation with the author, 10 January 1992.
11. Anne Dunn-Moynihan in conversation with the author, 26 November 1992.
12. In a letter to Hamish Hamilton, 21 April 1948 (Bristol University Library).
13. Quoted in Michael Shelden, *Cyril Connolly*, p. 198.
14. In a letter to Maud Connolly, 11 January 1949 (Tulsa).
15. Ibid.
16. In a letter to Cyril Connolly, 25 May [1948] (Tulsa).
17. *Time*, 29 November 1948.
18. *The Bugle*, vol. 41, no. 1.
19. In a letter to Cyril Connolly, 20 April 1949 (Tulsa).
20. Quoted in Michael Shelden, *Cyril Connolly*, p. 216.
21. Evelyn Waugh, *Letters*, p. 311.
22. In an undated letter to Evelyn Waugh (courtesy of Auberon Waugh).
23. John Lehmann, *The Ample Proposition*, p. 120.
24. In an undated letter to Evelyn Waugh (courtesy of Auberon Waugh).
25. In a letter to Cyril Connolly, 15 November 1949 (Tulsa).
26. In a letter to Cyril Connolly, 4 December 1949 (Tulsa).
27. Cyril Connolly, 'Introduction', *Ideas and Places*.

PART VII: 'DEAR, DAMN'D, DISTRACTING TOWN, FAREWELL!'

Chapter Twenty-four

1. Barbara Skelton, *Tears Before Bedtime*, p. 4.
2. Ibid., p. 65.
3. Michael Wishart, *High Diver*, p. 150.
4. Edmund Wilson, *The Fifties*, p. 373.
5. Barbara Skelton, *Tears Before Bedtime*, p. 40.
6. Evelyn Waugh, *Letters*, p. 320.
7. Barbara Skelton, *Tears Before Bedtime*, p. 83.
8. Ibid.
9. John Lehmann, *The Ample Proposition*, p. 110.
10. Naim Attallah, *Of a Certain Age*, p. 283.
11. Janetta Parladé in conversation with the author, 31 March 1992.
12. Barbara Skelton, *Tears Before Bedtime*, p. 86.
13. Quoted in Sybille Bedford, *Aldous Huxley*, vol. II, p. 113.
14. Barbara Skelton, *Tears Before Bedtime*, p. 84.
15. Ibid., p. 88.
16. Ibid., p. 91.
17. *Mr Wu and Mrs Stitch*, ed. Artemis Cooper, p. 113.
18. Barbara Skelton, *Tears Before Bedtime*, p. 96.
19. In a letter to Hamish Hamilton, 24 November 1950 (Bristol University Library).
20. John Lehmann, *The Ample Proposition*, p. 120.
21. Barbara Skelton, *Tears Before Bedtime*, p. 103.
22. Frances Partridge, *Everything to Lose*, p. 136.
23. Barbara Skelton, *Weep No More*, p. 146.
24. Quoted in Michael Shelden, *Cyril Connolly*, p. 99.
25. Evelyn Waugh, *Letters*, p. 346.
26. Ibid., p. 348.
27. Cyril Connolly in the *Sunday Times*, 8 April 1951.
28. Barbara Skelton, *Tears Before Bedtime*, p. 99.
29. Ibid., p. 105.
30. Ibid., p. 113.
31. Stephen Spender, *Journals*, p. 108.
32. Evelyn Waugh, *Letters*, p. 353.
33. In a letter to Cyril Connolly, 12 July 1952 (Tulsa).
34. In a letter to Cyril Connolly, 21 September 1952 (Tulsa).

35. Cyril Connolly, 'Evelyn Waugh', unpublished typescript (Austin).

Chapter Twenty-five
1. Barbara Skelton, *Tears Before Bedtime*, p. 115.
2. Ibid., p. 124.
3. In a letter to Cyril Connolly, 10 April 1952 (the Bodleian Library).
4. In a letter to Cyril Connolly, 17 April 1952 (the Bodleian Library).
5. Harold Hobson, Philip Knightley and Leonard Russell, *The Pearl of Days*, p. 323.
6. Quoted in Martin Green, *Children of the Sun*, p. 433.
7. Cyril Connolly, *The Missing Diplomats*, p. 32.
8. Ibid., p. 17.
9. Barbara Skelton, *Tears Before Bedtime*, p. 108.
10. Ibid., p. 135.
11. Cyril Connolly, *The Missing Diplomats*, p. 13.
12. Ibid., p. 16.
13. Barbara Skelton, *Tears Before Bedtime*, p. 135.
14. Quoted in Francis Wheen, *Tom Driberg*, p. 308.
15. Cyril Connolly in the *Sunday Times*, 7 September 1952.
16. Evelyn Waugh, *Letters*, p. 382.
17. Quoted in Martin Stannard, *Evelyn Waugh: No Abiding City*, p. 307.
18. Evelyn Waugh, *Letters*, p. 384.
19. Barbara Skelton, *Tears Before Bedtime*, p. 137.
20. Quoted in Jonathan Gathorne-Hardy, *The Interior Castle*, p. 410.
21. Barbara Skelton, *Tears Before Bedtime*, p. 152.
22. Ibid., p. 154.
23. Cyril Connolly in the *Sunday Times*, 31 March 1957.
24. In an undated letter to Cyril Connolly (Tulsa).

Chapter Twenty-six
1. Ann Fleming, *Letters*, p. 127.
2. Maurice Bowra in the *Sunday Times*, 7 June 1953.
3. Philip Toynbee in the *Observer*, 17 May 1953.
4. Philip Toynbee in the *Observer*, 1 December 1974.
5. Barbara Skelton, *Tears Before Bedtime*, p. 159.
6. Ibid., p. 164.
7. Ibid., p. 158.
8. Catherine Lambert in conversation with the author, 31 January 1992.
9. Barbara Skelton, *Tears Before Bedtime*, p. 115.

10. Naim Attallah, *Of a Certain Age*, p. 280.
11. Quoted in Michael Shelden, *Cyril Connolly*, p. 227.
12. George Weidenfeld in conversation with the author, 25 November 1992.
13. Quoted in Barbara Skelton, *Weep No More*, p. 2.
14. David Pryce-Jones, *Cyril Connolly: Journal and Memoir*, p. 10.
15. Anthony Hobson, *Cyril Connolly as a Book Collector*, p. 7.
16. 'Cyril Connolly', *Harper's Bazaar*, March 1954.
17. Cecil Beaton, *Self-Portrait with Friends*, p. 273.
18. Edmund Wilson, *The Fifties*, p. 105.
19. 'Joker in the Pack', the *New Statesman*, 13 March 1954.
20. In a letter to Cyril Connolly, 13 March 1954 (Tulsa).
21. In a letter to Cyril Connolly, 30 March 1954 (Tulsa).
22. Godfrey Smith in conversation with the author, 14 January 1992.

Chapter Twenty-seven

1. In a letter to Cyril Connolly, 8 April 1954 (Tulsa).
2. Evelyn Waugh, *Letters*, p. 423.
3. Caroline Blackwood in conversation with the author, 27 October 1991.
4. Barbara Skelton, *Weep No More*, p. 5.
5. Cyril Connolly in the *Sunday Times*, 25 July 1954.
6. Ann Fleming, *Letters*, p. 144.
7. Barbara Skelton, *Tears Before Bedtime*, pp. 195–7.
8. 'London Calling Asia', BBC Radio, 14 February 1955.
9. Cyril Connolly in the *Sunday Times*, 27 February 1955.
10. Ann Fleming, *Letters*, p. 154.
11. In a letter to Cyril Connolly, 9 May 1955 (Tulsa).
12. Cyril Connolly in the *Sunday Times*, 3 July 1955.
13. Barbara Skelton, *Weep No More*, pp. 7 and 9.
14. Ibid., p. 11.
15. Nicholas Henderson in conversation with the author, 4 March 1992.
16. In a letter to Cyril Connolly, 18 July 1955 (Tulsa).
17. Ann Fleming, *Letters*, p. 160.
18. John Craxton in conversation with the author, 7 January 1993.
19. In a letter to Cyril Connolly, 10 October 1955 (Tulsa).
20. In a letter to Cyril Connolly, 31 October 1955 (Tulsa).
21. Barbara Skelton, *Weep No More*, p. 15.
22. Evelyn Waugh, *Letters*, p. 456.
23. Frances Partridge, *Everything to Lose*, p. 240.
24. Barbara Skelton, *Weep No More*, p. 23.

25. Ibid., p. 26.
26. Frances Partridge, *Everything to Lose*, p. 243.
27. Barbara Skelton, *Weep No More*, p. 28.
28. Cecil Beaton, *The Restless Years*, p. 45.
29. Evelyn Waugh, *Diaries*, p. 770.
30. Edmund Wilson, *The Fifties*, p. 374.
31. Stephen Spender, *Journals*, p. 179.
32. In a letter to King Farouk, 13 September [1956] (Tulsa).

PART VIII: SENTIMENTS OF TRANSIENCE

Chapter Twenty-eight

1. Cyril Connolly (completed by Peter Levi), *Shade Those Laurels*, p. 82.
2. In an undated letter to Jack Lambert (Lambert Collection, the Bodleian Library).
3. Barbara Skelton, *Weep No More*, p. 68.
4. 'Frankly Speaking', BBC Home Service, 9 November 1956.
5. Barbara Skelton, *Weep No More*, p. 55.
6. Frances Partridge, *Everything to Lose*, p. 274.
7. Kenneth Williams, *Diaries*, ed. Russell Davies, HarperCollins, London, 1993, p. 132.
8. Kathleen Tynan, *Kenneth Tynan*, p. 139.
9. In an undated letter to Leonard Russell (Tulsa).
10. The *Daily Mail*, 21 January 1958.
11. In a letter to Cyril Connolly, 14 July 1958 (Tulsa).
12. In a letter to Cyril Connolly, 7 October 1958 (Tulsa).
13. Cyril Connolly in the *Sunday Times*, 27 October 1957.
14. Barbara Skelton, *Weep No More*, p. 66.
15. Michael Wishart, *High Diver*, p. 132.
16. Barbara Skelton, *Weep No More*, p. 69.
17. Michael Wishart, *High Diver*, p. 87.
18. Caroline Blackwood in conversation with the author, 27 October 1991.
19. In an undated letter to Caroline Blackwood (Tulsa).
20. Magouche Fielding in conversation with the author, 16 March 1992.
21. Barbara Skelton, *Weep No More*, p. 55.
22. Magouche Fielding in conversation with the author, 16 March 1992.
23. In an undated letter to Annie Davis (Tulsa).
24. In an undated letter to Cyril Connolly (Tulsa).

25. David Astor in conversation with the author, 17 January 1992.

Chapter Twenty-nine

1. Quoted in Michael Shelden, *Orwell*, p. 534.
2. Barbara Skelton, *Weep No More*, p. 79.
3. Ibid.
4. Ibid.
5. Anthony Hobson, *Cyril Connolly as a Book Collector*, p. 8.
6. John Craxton in conversation with the author, 7 January 1993.
7. Cynthia Kee in conversation with the author, 4 March 1993.
8. James Fox, *White Mischief*, p. 126.
9. In a letter to Cyril Connolly, 15 June 1960 (Tulsa).
10. David Astor in conversation with the author, 17 January 1992.
11. Quoted in Michael Shelden, *Cyril Connolly*, p. 229.
12. Cyril Connolly in the *Sunday Times*, 25 September 1960.
13. In a letter to Cyril Connolly, 28 September 1960 (Tulsa).
14. Ann Fleming, *Letters*, p. 272.
15. In a letter to Cyril Connolly, 9 January 1961 (Tulsa).
16. Evelyn Waugh, *Letters*, p. 596.
17. Richard Kershaw in conversation with the author, 3 August 1993.
18. Cyril Connolly in the *Sunday Times*, 16 July 1961.
19. Ann Fleming, *Letters*, p. 294.
20. Cyril Connolly in the *Sunday Times*, 29 October 1961.
21. Evelyn Waugh, *Letters*, p. 578.
22. Quoted in Ann Fleming, *Letters*, p. 294.
23. Quoted in Martin Stannard, *Evelyn Waugh: No Abiding City*, p. 439.
24. John Wain, 'Lost Horizons?', *Encounter*, January 1961.
25. Cyril Connolly in the *Sunday Times*, 11 March 1962.
26. In a letter to Cyril Connolly, 19 March 1962 (Tulsa).
27. Cyril Connolly in the *Sunday Times*, 1 April 1962.
28. Cyril Connolly, 'Pavane for a Vanished Society', *Les Pavillons*.
29. Frances Partridge, *Hanging On*, p. 106.
30. Ibid., p. 117.

Chapter Thirty

1. Cyril Connolly in the *Sunday Times*, 5 August 1962.
2. In a letter to Cyril Connolly, 30 August 1962 (Tulsa).
3. In an undated letter to Warren Roberts (Tulsa).
4. In a letter to Cyril Connolly, 8 December 1962 (Tulsa).

5. In a letter to Cyril Connolly, 18 February 1963 (Tulsa).
6. Peter Brooke in a letter to the author, 15 December 1992.
7. In a letter to Cyril Connolly, April 1963 (Tulsa).
8. In a letter to Cyril Connolly, 31 May 1963 (Tulsa).
9. In a letter to Cyril Connolly, 12 October 1963 (Tulsa).
10. In a letter to Cyril Connolly, 8 September 1963 (Tulsa).
11. In an undated letter to Maurice Bowra (Wadham College, Oxford).
12. Simon Raven, 'Nymphs and Satyrs and Mr Connolly', the *London Magazine*, August 1963.
13. Gavin Ewart, 'Cyril Connolly', the *London Magazine*, December 1963.
14. Gavin Ewart in conversation with the author, 18 February 1992.
15. 'The ripening of a not-so dud avocado', the *Evening Standard*, 27 August 1993.
16. Hamish Hamilton internal memorandum, 2 April 1963 (Bristol University Library).
17. In a letter to Cyril Connolly, 13 December 1963 (Tulsa).
18. Malcolm Muggeridge in the *Evening Standard*, 14 January 1964.
19. In a letter to Cyril Connolly, 4 January 1964 (Tulsa).
20. In a letter to Cyril Connolly, 21 December 1963 (Tulsa).
21. In a letter to Maurice Bowra, 3 January [1964] (Wadham College, Oxford).
22. In a letter to Eddy Sackville-West, 3 January [1964] (Berg Collection, New York Public Library).
23. Cecil Beaton, *The Parting Years*, p. 5.
24. Interview with T. G. Rosenthal, BBC Radio Third Programme, 21 January 1964 (National Sound Archive).
25. In an undated postcard to Jack Lambert (Lambert Collection, the Bodleian Library).
26. Cyril Connolly in the *Sunday Times*, 19 April 1964.
27. Ibid.
28. Jonty Driver in conversation with the author, 4 June 1992.
29. In a letter to Cyril Connolly, 14 July 1964 (Tulsa).

Chapter Thirty-one
1. Quoted in Martin Stannard, *Evelyn Waugh: No Abiding City*, p. 481.
2. In a letter to Cyril Connolly, 9 October 1964 (Tulsa).
3. In a letter to Cyril Connolly, 23 August [1964] (Tulsa).
4. Cyril Connolly in the *Sunday Times*, 10 January 1965.
5. In a letter to Cyril Connolly, 20 August 1964 (Tulsa).

6. Quoted in Barbara Skelton, *Weep No More*, p. 87.
7. Ann Fleming to Evelyn Waugh, 15 November 1964 (courtesy of Auberon Waugh).
8. Susan Campbell in conversation with the author, 3 March 1992.
9. Cyril Connolly, 'The Modern Movement', *100 Key Books*.
10. In a letter to Cyril Connolly, 28 November 1965 (Tulsa).
11. 'Doubts and Certainties', the *Listener*, 3 November 1966.
12. 'Desert Island Discs', BBC Home Service, 28 February 1966.
13. David D'Costa in a letter to the author, 16 September 1992.
14. Cyril Connolly in the *Sunday Times*, 27 March 1966.
15. Cyril Connolly in the *Sunday Times*, 23 October 1966.
16. In a letter to Susan Campbell, 17 October 1966 (private collection).
17. Cyril Connolly, 'Sir Maurice Bowra', *The Evening Colonnade*, p. 41.
18. Introduction by Peter Levi, *Shade Those Laurels*.
19. In a letter to Cyril Connolly, 17 November 1963 (Tulsa).
20. In an undated letter to Cyril Connolly (Tulsa).
21. Cyril Connolly in the *Sunday Times*, 18 December 1966.
22. In a letter to Faber and Faber, 18 January 1967 (Tulsa).
23. Cyril Connolly in the *Sunday Times*, 17 September 1967.
24. Ann Fleming, *Letters*, p. 385.
25. Cyril Connolly in the *Sunday Times*, 7 January 1968.
26. Cyril Connolly in the *Sunday Times*, 27 August 1967.
27. In a letter to Cyril Connolly, 19 March 1968 (Tulsa).

Chapter Thirty-two

1. In a letter to Cyril Connolly, 3 March [1969] (Tulsa).
2. 'From John Betjeman to Cyril Connolly', the *London Magazine*, August/ September 1973.
3. James Fox, *White Mischief*, p. 126.
4. John Whitley in conversation with the author, 3 February 1992.
5. Marie-Jaqueline Lancaster in conversation with the author, 14 March 1992.
6. In a letter to Cyril Connolly, 3 December 1968 (Hamish Hamilton Archive, Bristol University Library).
7. In a letter to Cyril Connolly, 3 January 1969 (Tulsa).
8. George Weidenfeld in conversation with the author, 25 November 1992.
9. Quoted in James Fox, *White Mischief*, p. 252.
10. Ibid., p. 160.
11. Ibid., p. 129.

12. Quoted in ibid., p. 53.
13. 'Christmas at Karen', the *Sunday Times*, 21 December 1969.
14. Quoted in James Fox, *White Mischief*, p. 136.
15. Godfrey Smith in conversation with the author, 14 January 1992.
16. Quoted in James Fox, *White Mischief*, p. 136.

Chapter Thirty-three

1. In an undated letter to Susan Campbell (private collection).
2. Quoted in Stephen Spender, 'Cyril Connolly', the *Times Literary Supplement*, 6 December 1974.
3. In a letter to Cyril Connolly, 17 May 1970 (Tulsa).
4. In an undated letter to Cyril Connolly (Tulsa).
5. In an undated letter to Maurice Bowra (Wadham College, Oxford).
6. Susan Campbell in conversation with the author, 3 March 1992.
7. Michael Wishart, 'He Died of Living', *ADAM*, 1974–5.
8. Peter Quennell in conversation with the author, 20 November 1991.
9. Peter Levi, *The Hill of Kronos*, p. 114.
10. Cyril Connolly, 'Introduction to the Exhibit', from *Cyril Connolly's 100 Key Books*, Humanities Research Center, Austin, 1971.
11. Cyril Connolly in the *Sunday Times*, 6 June 1971.
12. 'Memories of Cyril Connolly: A Recorded Discussion at the P.E.N. Club', 13 June 1984 (National Sound Archive).
13. Robert Murray Davis, 'Man Overboard: Cyril Connolly in Austin', University of Oklahoma (unpublished).
14. Cyril Connolly in the *Sunday Times*, 6 June 1971.
15. In a letter to Cyril Connolly, 6 June 1971 (Tulsa).
16. Quoted in Hugo Vickers, *Cecil Beaton*, p. 551.
17. In a letter to the editor of the *Daily Mail*, 10 December [no year] (Tulsa).
18. Andrew Rossabi in conversation with the author, 24 June 1992.
19. Alan Ross, *Coastwise Lights*, p. 126.
20. David Bathurst, 'Christie's Book Consultant', *ADAM*, 1974–5.
21. Nancy Mitford, *Letters*, p. 517.
22. Ibid., p. 518.
23. In a letter to Cyril Connolly, 5 May 1972 (Tulsa).
24. Cyril Connolly in the *Sunday Times*, 4 February 1973.
25. Cyril Connolly in the *Sunday Times*, 25 February 1973.
26. In a letter to Cyril Connolly, 25 February 1973 (Tulsa).
27. Miron Grindea, 'Sans Titre', *ADAM*, 1974–5.
28. Barbara Skelton, *Weep No More*, p. 146.

29. Ibid., p. 147.
30. 'An Interview at Seventy', Cyril Connolly to W. Hardcastle, BBC Radio, 31 August 1973 (National Sound Archive).
31. In an undated memorandum to Jack Lambert (Lambert Collection, the Bodleian Library).
32. Cecil Beaton, *Self-Portrait with Friends*, p. 418.
33. In an undated letter to Jack Lambert (Lambert Collection, the Bodleian Library).
34. Cyril Connolly in the *Sunday Times*, 30 June 1974.
35. Barry Lategan in conversation with the author, 5 July 1994.
36. Cyril Connolly, 'Some Memories', *W. H. Auden: A Tribute*, p. 68.
37. Andrew Rossabi in conversation with the author, 24 June 1992.
38. In a letter to Cyril Connolly, 1 May 1974 (Tulsa).
39. In a letter to Cyril Connolly, 2 October 1974 (Tulsa).
40. 'Cyril' by Anne Dunn-Moynihan (courtesy of Anne Dunn-Moynihan).
41. The Duke of Devonshire in conversation with the author, 12 February 1992.
42. Alan Ross, *Coastwise Lights*, p. 192.
43. Alastair Forbes, 'Connolly First and Last', *Times Literary Supplement*, 6 February 1976.
44. Barbara Skelton, *Weep No More*, p. 150.
45. Stephen Spender, 'Cyril Connolly', *Times Literary Supplement*, 6 December 1974.
46. Stephen Spender, *Journals*, p. 281.
47. An undated document to Jennifer Ross (Tulsa).
48. Cyril Connolly in the *Sunday Times*, 1 December 1974.
49. Philip Toynbee in the *Observer*, 1 December 1974.
50. Peter Levi, *The Flutes of Autumn*, p. 154.

SELECT BIBLIOGRAPHY

BOOKS BY CYRIL CONNOLLY

The Rock Pool, the Obelisk Press, Paris, 1936; rev. edn, Hamish Hamilton, London, 1947.

Enemies of Promise, Routledge and Kegan Paul, London, 1938; rev. edn, 1948.

The Unquiet Grave, Horizon, London, 1944; rev. edn, Hamish Hamilton, London, 1945; second rev. edn, Hamish Hamilton, London, 1951.

The Condemned Playground, George Routledge and Sons, London, 1945.

The Missing Diplomats, The Queen Anne Press, London, 1952.

Ideas and Places, Weidenfeld and Nicolson, London, 1953.

The Golden Horizon, Weidenfeld and Nicolson, London, 1953.

Les Pavillons: French Pavilions of the Eighteenth Century, with photographs by Jerome Zerbe, Hamish Hamilton, London, 1962.

Previous Convictions, Hamish Hamilton, London, 1963.

100 Key Books of the Modern Movement from England, France and America 1880–1950, André Deutsch, London, 1965.

The Evening Colonnade, David Bruce and Watson, London, 1973.

A Romantic Friendship: The Letters of Cyril Connolly to Noël Blakiston, Constable, London, 1975.

Shade Those Laurels, completed by Peter Levi, Bellew Publishing, London, 1990.

RELATED WORKS

Ackroyd, Peter. *T. S. Eliot: A Life*, Hamish Hamilton, London, 1984.

Acton, Harold. *Memoirs of an Aesthete*, Methuen, London, 1948.
  More Memoirs of an Aesthete, Methuen, London, 1970.

ADAM International Review: Cyril Connolly Commemorative Number, ADAM/Miron Grindea, London, 1974–5.

Annan, Noël. *Our Age*, Weidenfeld and Nicolson, London, 1990.

Attallah, Naim. *Singular Encounters*, Quartet Books, London, 1990.

 Of a Certain Age, Quartet Books, London, 1992.

W. H. Auden: A Tribute, ed. Stephen Spender, Weidenfeld and Nicolson, London, 1974, 1975.

Bagnold, Enid. *An Autobiography*, William Heinemann, London, 1969.

Baron, Wendy. *Miss Ethel Sands and her Circle*, Peter Owen Ltd, London, 1977.

Beaton, Cecil. *The Wandering Years*, Weidenfeld and Nicolson, London, 1961.

 The Restless Years, Weidenfeld and Nicolson, London, 1976.

 The Parting Years, Weidenfeld and Nicolson, London, 1978.

 Self-Portrait with Friends. The Selected Diaries, 1926–1974, Weidenfeld and Nicolson, London, 1979.

Bedford, Sybille. *Aldous Huxley: A Biography*, Chatto and Windus and William Collins Sons and Co. Ltd, London, 1973 and 1974.

Bowra, Maurice. *Memories*, Weidenfeld and Nicolson, London, 1966.

Carpenter, Humphrey. *W. H. Auden: A Biography*, George Allen and Unwin, London, 1981.

 The Brideshead Generation: Evelyn Waugh and His Friends, Houghton Mifflin, Boston, 1990.

Cecil, Hugh and Mirabel. *Clever Hearts: A Biography of Desmond and Molly MacCarthy*, Victor Gollancz, London, 1990.

Clark, Kenneth. *Another Part of the Wood: A Self-Portrait*, John Murray, London, 1974.

Cooper, Artemis (ed.). *Mr Wu and Mrs Stitch: The Letters of Evelyn Waugh and Diana Cooper*, Hodder and Stoughton, London, 1991.

Crick, Bernard. *George Orwell: A Life*, Secker and Warburg, London, 1980.

Cummings, E. E. *Selected Letters of e. e. cummings*, ed. F. W. Dupee and George Stade, Harcourt Brace, New York, 1969.

Cunningham, Valentine. *British Writers of the Thirties*, Oxford University Press, Oxford, 1988.

David, Hugh. *Stephen Spender: A Portrait With Background*, Heinemann, London, 1992.

De-La-Noy, Michael. *Denton Welch: The Making of a Writer*, Viking, London, 1984.

The Durrell-Miller Letters, 1935–1980, ed. Ian S. MacNiven, Faber and Faber, London, 1988.

Ferris, Paul. *Dylan Thomas*, Hodder and Stoughton, London, 1977.

Finney, Brian. *Christopher Isherwood: A Critical Biography*, Faber and Faber, London, 1979.

Fleming, Ann. *The Letters*, ed. Mark Amory, Collins Harvill, London, 1985.

Fox, James. *White Mischief*, Jonathan Cape, London, 1982.

Fyvel, T. R. *George Orwell: A Personal Memoir*, Weidenfeld and Nicolson, London, 1982.

Gathorne-Hardy, Jonathan. *The Interior Castle: A Life of Gerald Brenan*, Sinclair-Stephenson, London, 1992.

Gathorne-Hardy, Robert. *Recollections of Logan Pearsall Smith*, Constable, London, 1949.

Lord Gladwyn. *The Memoirs of Lord Gladwyn*, Weidenfeld and Nicolson, London, 1972.

Glendinning, Victoria. *Elizabeth Bowen*, Weidenfeld and Nicolson, London, 1977.

Green, Martin. *Children of the Sun: A Narrative of 'Decadence' in England after 1918*, Constable, London, 1977.

Hastings, Selina. *Nancy Mitford*, Hamish Hamilton, London, 1985.

Hewison, Robert. *Under Siege: Literary Life in London 1939–45*, Weidenfeld and Nicolson, London, 1977.

Hobson, Anthony. *Cyril Connolly as a Book Collector*, The Tragara Press, Edinburgh, 1983.

Hobson, Harold, Knightley, Philip, and Russell, Leonard. *The Pearl of Days: An Intimate Memoir of the Sunday Times, 1822–1972*, Hamish Hamilton, London, 1972.

Holroyd, Michael. *Lytton Strachey: The Years of Achievement, 1910–1932*, Heinemann, London, 1968.

Huxley, Aldous. *The Letters*, ed. Grover Smith, Chatto and Windus, London, 1969.

Hyams, Edward. *The New Statesman: The History of the First Fifty Years, 1913–63*, Longmans, London, 1963.

Hynes, Samuel. *The Auden Generation*, The Bodley Head, London, 1976.

Johnson, Paul. *Intellectuals*, Weidenfeld and Nicolson, London, 1988.

Kennedy, Ludovic. *On My Way To The Club*, Collins, London, 1989.

King, James. *The Last Modern: A Life of Herbert Read*, Weidenfeld and Nicolson, London, 1990.

Lancaster, Marie-Jaqueline. *Brian Howard: Portrait of a Failure*, Anthony Blond, London, 1968.

Lees-Milne, James. *Harold Nicolson: A Biography, Vol. Two*, Chatto and Windus, London, 1981.

Lehmann, John. *The Whispering Gallery*, Longmans, Green and Co., London, 1955.

  I Am My Brother, Longmans, London, 1960.

  The Ample Proposition, Eyre and Spottiswood, London, 1966.

Levi, Peter. *The Hill of Kronos*, Arrow Books Ltd, London, 1980.

  The Flutes of Autumn, Harvill Press Ltd, London, 1983.

Lewis, Peter. *George Orwell: The Road To Wigan Pier*, Heinemann, London, 1981.

Lynn, Kenneth S. *Hemingway*, Simon and Schuster, New York, 1987.

Mackenzie, Compton. *My Life and Times, Octave Eight, 1939–46*, Chatto and Windus, London, 1969.

Maclaren-Ross, Julian. *Memoirs of the Forties*, Alan Ross Ltd, London, 1965.

Mitford, Nancy. *The Blessing*, Hamish Hamilton, London, 1951.

  The Letters, ed. Charlotte Mosley, Hodder and Stoughton, London, 1993.

Muggeridge, Malcolm. *Like It Was: A Selection from the Diaries of Malcolm Muggeridge*, Collins, London, 1981.

Nicolson, Harold. *The Diaries and Letters, 1930–1939*, ed. Nigel Nicolson, Collins, London, 1966.

Ogilvy, David. *Blood, Brains and Beer: An Autobiography*, Hamish Hamilton, London, 1978.

Orwell, George. *Collected Essays*, Martin Secker and Warburg Ltd, London, 1961.

  The Collected Essays, Journalism and Letters, ed. Sonia Orwell and Ian Angus, four volumes, Secker and Warburg, London, 1968.

Partridge, Frances, *Everything to Lose: Diaries 1945–1960*, Victor Gollancz, London, 1985.

  Hanging On: Diaries 1960–1963, Collins, London, 1990.

Pearsall Smith, Logan. *All Trivia*, Penguin, London, 1986.

Pearson, John. *The Life of Ian Fleming*, Jonathan Cape, London, 1966.

  Façades: Edith, Osbert and Sacheverell Sitwell, Macmillan, London, 1978.

Perles, Alfred. *My Friend Henry Miller*, Neville Spearman Ltd, London, 1955.

Pikoulis, John. *Alun Lewis: A Life*, Poetry Wales Press, Bridgend, 1984.

Powell, Anthony. *To Keep the Ball Rolling*, Penguin, London, 1983.

Pryce-Jones, Alan. *The Bonus of Laughter*, Hamish Hamilton, London, 1987.

Pryce-Jones, David. *Cyril Connolly: Journal and Memoir*, Collins, London, 1983.

Quennell, Peter. *The Marble Foot: An Autobiography, 1905–1938*, Collins, London, 1976.

  The Wanton Chase: An Autobiography from 1939, Collins, London, 1980.

Ross, Alan. *Coastwise Lights*, Collins Harvill, London, 1988.

Russell, John. *A Portrait of Logan Pearsall Smith*, Dropmore Press, London, 1950.

Sebba, Anne. *Enid Bagnold: A Biography*, Weidenfeld and Nicolson, London, 1986.

Shelden, Michael. *Friends of Promise: Cyril Connolly and the World of Horizon*, Hamish Hamilton, London, 1989.

   Orwell: The Authorized Biography, Heinemann, London, 1991.

Skelton, Barbara. *Tears Before Bedtime*, Hamish Hamilton, London, 1987.

   Weep No More, Hamish Hamilton, London, 1989.

Spender, Stephen. *World Within World*, Faber and Faber, London, 1951.

   The Thirties and After: Poetry, Politics, People (1933–75), Macmillan, London, 1978.

   Journals 1939–1983, Faber and Faber, London, 1985.

Stannard, Martin. *Evelyn Waugh: The Early Years, 1903–1939*, J. M. Dent, London, 1986.

   Evelyn Waugh: No Abiding City, 1939–1966, J. M. Dent, London, 1992.

Strachey, Barbara. *Remarkable Relations: The Story of the Pearsall Smiths*, Victor Gollancz, London, 1980.

Sykes, Christopher. *Evelyn Waugh: A Biography*, Collins, London, 1975.

Thwaite, Ann. *Edmund Gosse: A Literary Landscape*, Secker and Warburg, London, 1984.

Tynan, Kathleen, *The Life of Kenneth Tynan*, Weidenfeld and Nicolson, London, 1987.

   Profiles, Nick Hern Books, London, 1989.

Vickers, Hugo. *Cecil Beaton* , Weidenfeld and Nicolson, London, 1985.

Waugh, Evelyn. *The Diaries*, ed. Michael Davie, Weidenfeld and Nicolson, London, 1976.

   The Letters, ed. Mark Amory, Weidenfeld and Nicolson, London, 1980.

Wheen, Francis. *Tom Driberg: His Life and Indiscretions*, Chatto and Windus, 1990.

Wilson, Edmund. *The Fifties*, ed. Leon Edel, Farrar, Strauss and Giroux, New York, 1983.

Wishart, Michael. *High Diver*, Blond and Briggs, London, 1977.

Woolf, Virginia. *The Diaries, Vol. Four, 1931–1935*, ed. Anne Olivier Bell and Andrew McNeillie, The Hogarth Press, London, 1982.

   A Moment's Liberty: The Shorter Diary of Virginia Woolf, ed. Anne Olivier Bell, The Hogarth Press, London, 1990.

Wyatt, Woodrow. *Confessions of an Optimist*, Collins, London, 1985.

Wyndham, Joan. *Anything Once*, Sinclair-Stevenson, London, 1992.

Ziegler, Philip. *Diana Cooper*, Hamish Hamilton, London, 1981.

ACKNOWLEDGEMENTS

The excerpts from Cyril Connolly's articles from the *New Statesman* appear by permission of *New Statesman and Society*.

The excerpts from the *Sunday Times* articles are reproduced by kind permission of Times Newspapers Limited.

Extracts from the correspondence of W. H. Auden are Copyright by the Estate of W. H. Auden. Extracts from the writings of Cecil Beaton are reproduced by kind permission of the Literary Trustees of the Late Sir Cecil Beaton and Rupert Crew Limited. Extracts from Sir John Betjeman's correspondence are reproduced by kind permission of Candida Lycett Green. Extracts from Elizabeth Bowen's correspondence are reproduced by permission of Curtis Brown, London. Extracts from Sir Maurice Bowra's correspondence are reproduced by kind permission of the Warden, Fellows and Scholars of Wadham College, Oxford, and the Warden and Fellows of All Souls College, Oxford. Extracts from *Another Part of the Wood* by Kenneth Clark are reproduced by kind permission of John Murray (Publishers) Limited. Extracts from the correspondence of Kenneth Clark are Copyright Kenneth Clark reproduced by permission of the Literary Agent for the Estate of the late Lord Clark, Margaret Hanbury, 27 Walcot Square, London SE11 4UB. The extract from T. S. Eliot's letter to Cyril Connolly is reproduced by kind permission of Valerie Eliot. Extracts from Ann Fleming's correspondence are reproduced by kind permission of Mark Amory. Extracts from the correspondence of Christopher Isherwood are reproduced by permission of the Curtis Brown Group Limited. Extracts from the writings of John Lehmann are reproduced by permission of David Higham Associates. Extracts from Nancy Mitford's correspondence are reproduced by kind permission of the Duchess of Devonshire. Extracts from the correspondence of Harold Nicolson are reproduced by kind permission of Nigel Nicolson. Extracts from the writings of George Orwell are reproduced by kind permission of the Estate of the late Sonia Brownell Orwell and Martin Secker and Warburg Limited. Extracts from the writings of Frances Partridge are reproduced by permission of Rogers, Coleridge and White Limited.

Extracts from *The Marble Foot* and *The Wanton Chase* by Peter Quennell are reproduced in the United Kingdom by kind permission of HarperCollins and in the United States by kind permission of the Curtis Brown Group Limited. Extracts from the writings of Evelyn Waugh are reproduced by permission of the Peters Fraser and Dunlop Group Limited. The extract from Angus Wilson's letter to Cyril Connolly is copyright Angus Wilson 1973 reproduced by permission of Curtis Brown Limited, London. Extracts from *The Fifties* by Edmund Wilson are copyright 1986 by Helen Miranda Wilson and are reprinted by permission of Farrar, Straus and Giroux, Limited.

Every effort has been made to trace all copyright holders but if any have been inadvertently overlooked the publishers will be pleased to make the necessary arrangement at the first opportunity.

Beyond my formal acknowledgements I must declare debts to the large number of people who in various ways made the researching of this book a greater pleasure and an easier undertaking: to Sally Brown of the British Library; to Robert Murray Davis of the University of Oklahoma, who visited me amidst Tulsa's alien corn and shared his insights into the intricacies of Evelyn Waugh's friendship with Cyril Connolly; to Jonathan Goodman, who translated the Greek quotations in *A Romantic Friendship*; to Penelope Hatfield, the College Archivist, Eton College; to Cathy Henderson of the Harry Ransom Humanities Research Center at the University of Texas; to Sid Huttner, Lori Curtis and the staff of the Department of Special Collections at the McFarlin Library of the University of Tulsa; to the staff of the Special Collections Department of New York Public Library; to Mitch Owens, who alerted me to the Raymond Mortimer file in the Harvey Firestone Library at the University of Princeton; to Michael Scammell of Cornell University, who advised me about the relations and correspondence of Cyril Connolly and Arthur Koestler; to Auberon Waugh, who kindly gave me access to his own collection of Connolly documents; and to Janetta Parladé, whose help, support and encouragement have done more than anything else to make this book possible.

For further assistance in correspondence and interviews I am obliged to Lord Annan, David Astor, the Countess of Avon, Caroline Blackwood, Georgiana Blakiston, Peter Brook, Susan Campbell, Juanita Carberry, Morris Cargill, Simon Craven, John Craxton, Angela Culme-Seymour, David D'Costa, the Duke and Duchess of Devonshire, Margaret Drabble, Jonty Driver, Glur Dyson-Taylor, Gavin Ewart, Magouche Fielding, James Fox, Frank Giles, Lady d'Avigdor-Goldsmid, the late Clement Greenberg, Miron Grindea, Jonathan Guinness, Yvonne Hamilton, Comtesse Anne-Pierre d'Harcourt,

Ian Irvine, James Knox, Selina Hastings, Jacqueline Hélion, Sir Nicholas Henderson, Lady Anne Hill, Robert Kee, Cynthia Kee, Ludovic Kennedy, Richard Kershaw, Francis King, Lord Kinross, Catherine Lambert, Marie-Jaqueline Lancaster, Barry Lategan, Joan and Patrick Leigh Fermor, Mary Lutyens, Liza Mann, Dennis McIntyre, Ivan Moffat, the Honourable Lady Mosley, Anne Dunn Moynihan, Tom Pain, Frances Partridge, Myfanwy Piper, Dilys Powell, Spider Quennell, the late Sir Peter Quennell, Andrew Rossabi, A. L. Rowse, the Honourable Sir Steven Runciman, the late Vera Russell, Dadie Rylands, George Sims, Christopher Sinclair-Stevenson, Godfrey Smith, Hilary Spurling, Martin Stannard, Barbara Strachey, Peggy Strachey, Julian Symons, Patrick Trevor-Roper, Lord Weidenfeld, John Whitley, Michael Wishart, Antony Witherby, Anne Wollheim and Sebastian Yorke.

INDEX